MODERN NEWSPAPER EDITING
SECOND EDITION

Modern Newspaper Editing

Second Edition

Gene Gilmore
University of Illinois

Robert Root

boyd & fraser publishing company
san francisco

To Virginia

Gene Gilmore and Robert Root

MODERN NEWSPAPER EDITING
SECOND EDITION

Library of Congress Catalog Card Number: 75–40871
International Standard Book Number: 0–87835–054–3

Composition by Text Craft, Inc., Palo Alto, California.
Printed by Publishers Press, Inc., Phoenix, Arizona.
Binding by Roswell Bookbinding, Phoenix, Arizona.

3 4 5 * 9 8

Acknowledgments

Thanks must go to the dozens of people who helped in large and small ways in the preparation of this second edition. Acknowledgement of aid given in the first edition must be cited, too, for much of the heart of that book carries over into the second.

Most of the thanks go to colleagues at the University of Illinois: Glenn G. Hanson, Richard L. Hildwein, Lynn Slovonsky, John H. Schacht, W. William Alfeld, and those superb librarians, Dr. Eleanor Blum and Virginia Guthrie.

My gratitude also goes to Charles W. Puffenbarger of the *Washington Post;* Charles—Gene McDaniel, science writer of the Chicago bureau of the Associated Press; Larry Blasko of the same bureau; Pat Kilian of the Chicago bureau of United Press International; Charles Scott, picture editor of the *Chicago Tribune;* Jack Vernon research director of the *St. Petersburg Times* and *Independent;* John Timberlake, research director of the *Chicago Tribune;* Robert L. M. Ahern, research director of the *Boston Globe;* Phil Greer of the *Courier* in Champaign-Urbana, Illinois; and Gene Smedley, managing editor of the *Bloomington,* Illinois *Pantagraph.*

Special thanks go to Dr. D. Wayne Rowland, former chairman of the journalism school at Drake University; Dr. Jack Haskins of the University of Tennessee; and Edmund C. Arnold of Syracuse University.

I appreciate also information and suggestions from Robert Kerns, assistant professor of photography, Syracuse University; Prof. Roland E. Wolseley, retired chairman of the Magazine Department, Syracuse; Prof. Olin Hinkle, University of Texas; Larry Hale of the *Binghamton* (N. Y.) *Press;* Gerald Bean of the *Rockford* (Ill.) *Register-Republic;* and Vincent S. Jones, executive editor of the Gannett newspapers and past president of the American Society of Newspaper Editors.

The editors of *Editor & Publisher* deserve thanks for the many articles printed about newspaper editing and the new technology, which have been invaluable in the preparation of several chapters; serious professionals should keep up with *E & P* in order to get the most out of these pages. They will also find, as we have, that *Journalism Quarterly* and *Quill* publish articles useful to both the scholar and the professional journalist.

Preface

For nearly a century, few changes came to newspaper printing. The newspaper plant of 1965 closely resembled the plant of 1885. The computer finally slipped into a few composing rooms, and after several years of worry and doubt by publishers, computers swept the country. The impact can hardly be exaggerated. Typesetting that once took hours now takes minutes. Where a hundred people once worked as printers, only twenty remain. The long-range savings in labor costs will amount to millions of dollars. Those savings should help some newspapers survive and, possibly, a few new ones to start. Journalists should receive higher salaries and readers get cheaper newspapers.

The new technology, however, may turn out to be only the second most important development in the late twentieth century. Perhaps changes in public attitudes and the effects on journalists may surpass the new technology in importance. A few years ago "official sources" were quoted at length and "official versions" usually were swallowed whole. Now much of the public and almost all journalists are skeptical to the point of suspicion. This attitude started to grow because of the deceptions practiced by military and political leaders during the Vietnam War. The corruption of the Nixon-Agnew administration helped it bloom. News of secret tyranny practiced by the FBI and CIA, both treated previously as untouchable, brought details of how the highest officials seriously jeopardized the Bill of Rights. If all this corruption has seriously reduced timid and obsequious journalism, then surely the change is greater than the one produced by the new technology.

So in this second edition we emphasize both the monumental change produced by the new technology *and* the shift to more aggressive, comprehensive, and skeptical journalism. At the same time we aim to guide the student copyeditor to learn the fundamentals of accuracy and good writing that are at the heart of editing.

The impact of new technology and its computers is explained to show how technology can save costs and contribute to more responsible editing. Finally, the book includes a chapter on newspaper research with suggestions to the editor on conducting studies as well as on using the findings of professional researchers.

The term "we" is used here with sorrow. The first edition was written by Robert Root and me, but he died at the age of fifty-five before that edition was printed. This second edition is still *our* book, for the planning and much of the writing of that first edition remains in the second. His name deserves to stay on this book.

Gene Gilmore

Foreword

It pleases me that Gene Gilmore is bringing out the second edition of *Modern Newspaper Editing*. For a book of its kind the first edition had marked success. It was received with high praise from reviewers and nearly one hundred journalism schools or departments adopted it.

This new edition pays much attention to the rapid technological changes in newspapers and how the copy-editor must adjust to those changes.

In addition to explaining these recent technological changes, this edition retains the thoughtful discussion of some of the ethical and moral questions which every editor has to face in appraising the news, in deciding what to print, what to feature, and how to display it.

I believe any student of journalism will find this book useful.

Gardner Cowles

Former Editorial Director of LOOK
Former President of the Des Moines Register and Tribune Co.

Contents

MODERN NEWSPAPER EDITING
SECOND EDITION

1 News editing today and tomorrow

When he was President, John F. Kennedy described what an editor should be. In a speech at the University of North Carolina he said the press needed people "educated in the liberal traditions, willing to take the long look, undisturbed by prejudices and slogans of the moment, who attempt to make an honest judgment on difficult events." Such people, he added, "could distinguish the real from the illusory, the long range from the temporary, the significant from the petty."

These stiff requirements will always mean a shortage of ideal editors. If the democratic society is to function properly, however, it must have a sizable number of editors who come close to the ideal. Many of the highly qualified professionals of 1985 and 1990 will be men and women who today are journalism students or beginning journalists.

Because journalism professionals rise rapidly, the responsibilities of executive positions may come early. The city editor on a major newspaper can be a person less than thirty. Sometimes the news editor on a quality, medium-sized paper is barely thirty. Higher administrative positions like managing editor or executive editor often come well before middle age. Increasingly, women are taking some of these key posts. If the journalists are to approach the qualities cited by President Kennedy, they must learn the skills of the reporter and copyeditor rapidly and well. Rarely can a person leap into an executive position without solid preparation as a writer or copyeditor. Nor should anyone wish to make that leap unprepared.

The ideal editor has been a reporter of various worlds: politics, government, social welfare, labor, and business. The reporter has followed such experience with a period of editing—working to improve the copy of others. Then the young journalist may be ready for the moves to city, state, or telegraph editor; news editor; managing editor; and, eventually, editor.

To grow professionally, young news people must learn each job well. They prepare for positions of greater responsibility by combining observation, reading, listening, discussion, writing, and introspection. They look about the newsroom and around their city to see how jobs are done and how they might be done better. They read about what they cannot possibly observe first hand and they seek fresh insights. They open minds by listening to others who report how the job has been done and how it should be done. They sharpen ideas and challenge each other's thoughts in discussions with professionals inside and outside of journalism. They examine themselves to recognize and reduce their shortcomings.

Men and women at every level of journalism usually will find satisfaction in helping to inform hundreds or even thousands of people about vital public affairs. Magazines, books, radio, television, and word-of-mouth contribute, but much of what ordinary citizens know about current problems they have learned through the work of the editors of their newspapers.

Emphasis changing

To meet this responsibility to the reader, editors at all levels must be thorough and painstaking. This is particularly difficult on daily newspapers or on radio-television news programs because there is little time to examine issues with scholarly thoroughness. In recent years, however, the better newspapers often have put less emphasis on speed. They have been willing to hold up a story for an edition or two, or even a day or more, until additional facts can be gathered. These papers also make every effort to give reporters time to get the complete story so readers will not be misled by superficial information.

Editorial courage also can bring economic reprisals and terrifying personal anguish. When the schools in Little Rock were to be integrated a generation ago, the *Arkansas Gazette* editorialized firmly and almost daily that the courts had ruled in favor of integration and that the community should follow the law. The paper was denounced in vulgar language, the editors were harassed day and night, and an organized campaign cut the circulation more than 10 percent.

The schools were integrated, but the *Gazette* lost thousands of dollars in revenue and the editors suffered intensely from the insults and harassment. The publisher, J. N. Heiskell, received many awards, including the 1958 Pulitzer Prize for public service. Advertising revenue was not reduced, however, indicating that business interests either supported the paper's stand or felt they must advertise to function.

Such intense pressure has not occurred since on a middle-sized or large daily, but similar tactics have forced out some weekly and small daily publishers. During the height of debate on Vietnam war policy, many newspapers, editors, and reporters were vilified. Some of the attacks came from the White House itself. These assaults did not seem to cause loss of money, but they often meant serious personal distress.

The frictions that produced the Little Rock boycott are still with us. And even newspapers that try to report school integration events with absolute fairness and restraint sometimes have their reporters and photographers beaten, cameras smashed, and subscriptions canceled.

These pressures may seem remote to the young journalist, but they will soon appear and one must prepare to meet them confidently. The beginner practices reporting, writing, and editing, so he or she must also practice reacting to bribes—labeled gifts. And what would one do if a story cost the paper an advertising contract? What if a group of furious businessmen descended on the office? What if someone called from the White House to complain about an editorial? Unfortunately, most journalists have not prepared for such occurrences, and the first one can be unnerving. To become a capable and trusted editor, the professional must learn to resist pressures with confidence and skill.

Clarity needed

The conscientious editor makes the whole news picture clear as well as fair. But sometimes the news may not be clear to the editor either. The reporters may be unable to get complete information, some sources may have tried to mislead the press and the public, and the editor's own background may be inadequate to set the news in proper perspective. No newspaper editor can be sure of the accuracy of all the information received, nor can he or she usually be certain when attempts are being made to mislead. And no editor is so erudite that he or she can grasp the significance of every event or utterance. But every editor should strive to do the best job possible to make the news understandable. The reader expects and deserves to have events reported so they make sense.

The editor's job is to sift and organize the news so the reader does not have to struggle to get information. All kinds of distractions affect the reader. Television, radio, other papers, general noise, and conversation lure the reader's attention. Newspaper editors must make the product easy to read and worth reading. They accomplish this by an intelligent selection of news, careful interpretation of it, serious but sprightly editorial comment, good writing—and attractive placement of these items on the newspaper pages.

This is creative work, for it requires knowledge, imagination, writing skill, judgment, and an eye for design. An editor who combines these elements can create something significant—a paper that informs the public and guides citizens to intelligent decisions.

What about computers?

But won't computers replace human editors and make such idealistic goals passé?

It is true that the computer has swept through American newspaper plants, scattering typewriters, linotypes, lead pencils, paste pots, and copy paper. Reporters write on keyboards linked to computers; editors do their work on similar devices; and computers "set type" on a strip of film. The computer almost certainly will expand its power in both the newsroom and composing room. It already can be programmed to write simple stories and provide information on a certain mix of stories. It can review the number of stories sent to the printers and tell an editor how many inches of type are available.

So far, however, there is no indication that the computer can gather information, write it in fresh ways, and edit the material with all the subtle intelligence that the human brain can provide. But the stolid and unimaginative reporter or editor who does everything routinely quite likely, in years to come, could be replaced by a computer.

Perhaps the newspaper itself will be replaced by a super computer, so the reader may simply dial a number and the national news will pop onto the home TV screen. Another dialed number will produce the sports news and a third will bring forth some editorials. Maybe this will happen, of course, but most of us cling to some basic habits, and one of these habits is getting seven newspapers a week tossed onto our porches for about a dollar. And besides, if super computer comes, human editors will have to decide what goes into it.

Computers in perspective

The new technology can be so dazzling that the casual student may assume that the computer will make judgments, write most stories and headlines, and determine the layout of the paper. A closer inspection, however, might produce these four observations:

Computers are expensive.   So are programmers. Cheap programming could be provided, but it would result in a shabby paper, one without depth and sophistication which alert editors can give. Money-hungry publishers, alas, might seize upon computers to produce just that sort of dreary publication. But the quality paper, certainly for years to come, will find that human editors will produce a better product than any computer.

Most newspapers could improve without more machines.   Computers can store thousands of facts available for instant use, but using such machinery would be shipping in an elephant to kill a gnat. How many newspapers today make more than a minimal effort to collect facts which are not readily available—or want to spend the money, with present hands and equipment, really to dig for information? In getting full information on a story, newspapers should first spend money and people to check their own libraries, phone the public library, interview widely, send queries to press services, and so on. When these elementary methods to retrieve information prove inadequate, more sophisticated (and expensive) retrieval should be considered.

The computer, like the telegraph and the teletype, can be a great aid for the working editor.   If automated machinery is unlikely to emerge soon as the newsroom master, it can be a helpful servant. For example, even the experienced human brain is harassed in keeping track of the competing stories on a complex news day. But just as airline and hotel reservations become instantly available by pressing a computerized button, the whole array of world, national, state and local stories can be quickly recalled for human evaluators. Already, the wire services, Associated Press and United Press International, provide such aids to their computer wire services.

Human editorial judgment will remain essential to great newspapers.   In this generation, it seems unlikely that a robot will be created which can select and display news as well as a seasoned editor. The skill of a computer at chess-playing is limited by the brains of the chess-players who program it. Even if chess-players combine to create a master chess-player, one more skilled than any of them individually, this creation would not completely foreshadow a mechanical super-editor. For editing is less of a science than an art. It might be compared to poetry writing, and the poems and songs produced so far by computers have been remarkable but amateurish. Until computers can successfully make the subtle distinctions in word choice required of poetry, they will not be able to pull together into editorial choices all the variables which, consciously and subconsciously, mold the fine decisions as the editor works at his or her art.

Even as automation has advanced, so has our understanding of the complexity of news. Traditionally, the aim of journalism has been expressed in a three-part definition: to inform, to guide, and to entertain. While those goals still serve well enough for quick rule of thumb, any computer programming limited to them would be inadequate for the needs of the modern newspaper reader. In coming years, editors will have to weigh the news with at least nine purposes in mind, giving the edge one time to the serious, another time to the frivolous:

Goals for newsmen

To inform.   Transmitting the bare facts to people remains a major goal. They want, as fast as possible and in greater detail than broadcasting can give, the facts of life, like stock quotations, ball scores, election results, and contest winners.

To alert.   As watchmen, sentries, and runners have for ages brought vital news to leaders, the media of a democracy today have a role in alerting readers to what they need to know. To assume that the headline-skimmer is uninformed is an oversimplification. For example, over a few weeks a home-owner may note several headlines on house sales or mortgage rates and barely glance at the stories—yet he is alerted to trends which are important if he ponders selling or renting. Even the lack of war headlines from an area may "negatively alert" the reader that "all's well."

To interpret.   While the objective newspaper tradition of conveying only facts is still strong, for at least a generation editors have been emphasizing the need for interpretation. The facts alone may lie or distort. Someone must put them into perspective. For example, a Washington reporter may learn that a federal program for the poor has quietly been eliminated. But perhaps its end was contemplated when work was undertaken by another department sometime earlier. What is needed is an interpretation of what all the various departments of government are attempting to do about poverty.

A glance at any newspaper shows that opinion is no longer confined to the editorial page—it shapes many of the most important news stories, sometimes excessively.

To educate.   Some editors would argue that education is the same as interpretation, but other old-timers would say newspapering has nothing to do with education.* It is true that many interpretive stories—for example, on urban problems or on measures to overcome poverty—aim to convey an accurate picture of a situation, which is teaching. But many features besides interpretive stories, such as medical columns, science cartoon strips, and income tax pointers, are printed primarily as education. The "Newspaper in the Classroom" seminars sponsored by universities in cooperation with the American Newspaper Publishers Association underline these educational potentialities. One newspaper critic, W. H. Ferry, goes so far as to suggest that the whole purpose of the press is educational: "My view is that masscomm's social and cultural responsibilities are those of the largest and probably most influential educational system any society has known."[2]

To lead.   Newspapers inevitably lead, intentionally or not. The presentation of news leads readers to think and act about some things rather than others. A paper which emphasizes crime, scandal, and sex directs the attention of readers to such subjects. A more serious paper, with a diet of more important civic issues, directs community concern by its very act of establishing the agenda of discussion. Too often newsmen think of their leadership role as confined largely to opinion columns on the editorial page. In fact, headlines probably are more important in making both opinion leaders and ordinary voters sort out the vital issues. The Hutchins Commission in 1947 noted that one requirement of the press is to present and clarify the goals and values of society.†

---

*The mass media in developing countries, according to Dr. Wilbur Schramm of Stanford University, have three roles: to be watchmen, to be leaders, and to be teachers.[1]

†The name comes from the chairman, Robert Maynard Hutchins, of the Commisson on Freedom of the Press. The commission's suggestions have been largely ignored and, by now, forgotten.

To persuade.   While persuading is of course like leading, there can be static leadership which merely points a direction for concern, as thorough coverage of a pickpocket epidemic would direct attention to solving the problem. But there is also persuasive leadership, which includes arguing and cajoling to get citizens to act. This is a normal function of a good editorial page. When a newspaper crusades, as when it prints numerous items on a subject such as pollution, it is using facts to persuade.

To provide a forum.   The letters-to-the-editor page is the most obvious platform for different points of view. But a well-edited paper also has the purpose of seeing that all important shades of opinion on major issues are reported. One evil of the press in an authoritarian country is that the news presents only the official line, a monolithic view. Most American papers could do a better job than they do of giving a greater range of opinion instead of sticking to the popular or the view of the community's power structure.

To inspire.   A newspaper is not a church, but it can inspire. A good editorial stimulates a thrill of rededication. Even the news sections should contain some stories less important for their information and interpretation than for the bravery, courage, determination, or love they portray.

To entertain.   Obviously cartoons and gossip columns provide entertainment, but human interest stories and feature pieces entertain as well as inform. Life is not all drab, as the serious "big bad" news may imply, and editors should give their readers the amusing, the witty, and the whimsical.

Gatekeeping

The editor who puts out a paper which intelligently fulfills all these varied functions is a major figure in the community and in society. The term "gatekeeper" has been coined by some researchers to emphasize the editor's importance at a cutoff point where the decision is made to stop some items, to let a trickle of other news through, or to permit the flow of a story judged as important. In a 1949 study, Dr. David Manning White, now of Virginia Commonwealth University, analyzed the reasons a telegraph editor gave for rejecting copy and found them "highly subjective," colored by his personal experiences and attitudes.

All the research in this area supports White's findings in deciding what news gets in the paper and what gets discarded. One of the researchers, Dr. Walter Geiber of San Francisco State College, observed that "news is what newspapermen make it."[3] How do the editors make their decisions? Why do they disagree so vigorously on what is news? We clearly need to know more about what influences gatekeepers. And society needs better-trained editors who can attain maximum objectivity and who will know their audiences and facilitate intelligent communication to them.

Newspapers of quality

The emphasis on quality editors may seem to say that a newspaper need only hire competent people and the customers will flock to the newsstands to buy it. That is rarely the case. The production and sale of anything good usually takes time, so much time that the editors of a paper trying to do a conscientious job become discouraged. Its sales may stay small, while a third rate competing paper gains circulation. In other cases a newspaper staff may spend a great deal of energy, resourcefulness, and money to get some outstanding stories, then find that few people bothered to read them.

Rather than get needlessly discouraged, the editors must ask themselves in such cases if they have done as good a job as they thought. Perhaps they had overestimated the reader's knowledge. Were the stories really easy to grasp? Were the editors expecting that a story or two would bring quick reaction in circulation figures? Was the news displayed so the reader could hardly avoid the stories? Or was the paper so deadly serious, so lacking in any humor or sprightliness, that people found it ponderous and tedious?

If the editors with high standards are sometimes discouraged, they are often heartened. Thoughtful people in the community, sometimes called "the creative minority," frequently will praise the coverage of local, national, and world events. Public officials may mutter harsh words, but they usually will work better when aware that what they do is scrutinized carefully but fairly. The business community is especially responsive because advertisers like to put their ads in carefully-read newspapers.

What the public wants

Sometimes newspapers employ organizations that survey readership to "find out what the people want." Some successful editors suspect such surveys because people often consciously or subconsciously misrepresent their beliefs on a question. They also are skeptical of surveys because people tend to like what they are accustomed to. If they have been taking a quality paper for years, they tend to like quality. If they have been handed for years a diet of comics, agony columns, and other fluff, they will find quality hard to digest.

Editors who have drawn the greatest praise in the nation—men like Joseph Pulitzer, Adolph Ochs, E. W. Scripps—have had concrete ideas on what a newspaper should be. They produced that kind of paper and their kind of journalism was successful, both commercially and professionally.

Editors who turn out "what the public wants" usually produce an insignificant paper. Believing that the public is bored by anything important, they fill their papers with the trite and the trivial. This formula has been enormously profitable in the past. Circulations skyrocketed at the turn of the century on a news formula of love, lust, and lucre. The technique started to fade in the early thirties and today it is usually the serious, thoughtful, and penetrating newspaper that shows the best gains in circulation, advertising, and influence.

The most spectacular increase in circulation in the last twenty years has been made by the *Wall Street Journal,* a newspaper with three detailed, socially-significant stories each day, plus several valuable minor stories and, of course, full financial reports. The *Journal,* without pictures, comics, sports, or women's pages, has climbed to the second largest circulation in the United States behind the *New York Daily News.*

The *New York Times* and the *Washington Post,* both serious papers that spend lavishly to get the news, have made remarkable gains. The *Los Angeles Times,* with perhaps more columns of news than any paper in the nation, has soared to more than a million in circulation to become the dominant West Coast paper.

The more literate magazines, like *Columbia Journalism Review, Saturday Review, New Republic,* and *Atlantic* have either steady or spectacular growth. Interest in creative arts, such as painting, music, writing, has burgeoned so fast in the last two decades that the movement is called a cultural explosion. While the extent of this interest may be exaggerated, it should not be ignored. The newspapers in the last years of the 20th century, to meet public demand, must blend thorough reporting and intelligent commentary with an attractive format.*

These superior newspapers will have imaginative, knowledgeable, and demanding editors who will be looking for young journalists with a talent for intelligent reporting and editing. They also will be searching for someone to replace them in the future.

It is important for a democratic society that these superior papers not be only the dailies of New York, Washington, Los Angeles, or other huge cities. Dozens of medium-sized or even small papers now do a fine job of reporting the news of their communities and the world, and there is room for many more. These papers also are seeking people who can do the exacting and rewarding job of editing. Young people obviously have better chances of landing in key positions on these less-famous papers.

Anyone preparing for such a career would do well to consider President Kennedy's ideal editor, described at the opening of this chapter. The late Walter Lippmann, who spent sixty years as a journalist, reinforced Kennedy's concept, noting that the reliable and responsible professional seeks "to bring to light the hidden facts, to set them in relation with each other, and make a picture of reality on which men can act."

---

* Frothy periodicals may make great gains too, of course, and we do not suggest that quality is measured by circulation growth. Still, strong consumer demand for high quality books and magazines reminds the editor that many of these readers also want a high quality newspaper.

Fig. 2–1. The old. Editors on the foreign desk of the *New York Times* work at the horseshoe-shaped desk with paper and pencil and take directions from the slot person.

2 The copyeditor and copyediting

A few years ago it was fairly easy to describe the operations of the copy desk. Stories came on paper from reporters and the wire services. With a pencil, an editor corrected errors, sometimes shortened a story, and tried to improve the language. A headline was written, either typewritten or in longhand, and story and head were sent by a pneumatic tube to the composing room, where printers would set the stories and headlines into type.

A fair number of newspapers still function that way. But nearly every week newspaper trade magazines bring the news that another paper has signed up with the technical revolution. This means that old-fashioned pencils, paper, manual typewriters, and pneumatic tubes are steadily getting scarcer.

In their places have come two new systems. One of those systems has the newsroom dotted with boxes that look like television screens with a typewriter keyboard attached.

Reporters write their stories at those keyboards. As they type, their words appear on the screen in front of them. If they don't like what they write, the press of a button will take it away. The reporter wishing to rephrase a sentence pushes a few keys and the change is made. When the story is finished another key is pressed and the words leave the screen, apparently darting about the inside of a computer until the copyeditor turns on the set.

The copyeditor touches a key and the story appears on the screen. With a few signals from the keyboard, imprecise words or errant letters can disappear and some better words can be inserted. A sentence can be eliminated or the lead changed. When copyeditors are sure that they have improved the story properly, they can type out a headline; it appears on the screen, and all the words are then drained off the screen to appear on a strip of film, almost instantaneously, in the composing room. That strip can be pasted, with a dozen similar strips, onto a sheet of paper the size of a newspaper page. The sheet is photographed and a page plate is made. The plate, along with perhaps 60 others, is put on the press and the paper is printed.

Those television screens-with-keyboards are called CRTs (cathode ray tubes) or VDTs (video display terminals). They look so formidable that the beginner might approach them gingerly, fearing that one mismove will cause millions of dollars worth of damage. But the machines are reasonably durable and a person who can type can learn to operate them in a few days. Most veteran editors who have worked both the old and new systems say they much prefer the new.

Fig. 2–2. The new. Copyeditors at *Today,* of Cocoa Beach, Florida, work with Cathode Ray Tubes (CRTs) at an H-shaped desk.

The scanner

That's one new system. The other makes use of a device called a *scanner,* or an OCR (optical character reader). The reporter uses an electric typewriter, because it gives an even, clear impression. The typewriter is equipped with a few special symbols which instruct the electronic "eyes" as they scan the copy. For example, the delta sign (Δ) tells the scanner to make room for an insert. The same sign at the end of the insert shows that the insert is concluded. The copyeditor goes over this copy with a special marking pen. The editor can cross out words with this pen, but if inserts are made, the editor must put the copy into the electric typewriter and type the inserts into the copy.

When one is satisfied that the story is in good shape, one sticks the copy into a scanner and, presto, those "eyes" dart over the copy and out comes a strip of film containing the whole story. As in the usage of a VDT, the strip can be pasted on a sheet, ready for the final production steps.

Perhaps strangely, neither of these systems speeds operations in the newsroom. They probably even take a little more time than the old-fashioned methods. The saving is in the composing room, and a mighty big saving it is. Not so long ago it took a linotype operator about an hour to set a column of type. Some technical advances cut that time moderately. But the latest equipment requires almost no time to set type—and almost no workers to do it.

The new devices can perform some of the tedious jobs once done on the desk, and save some newsroom time. No longer do copyeditors have to figure out the length of the story or keep score on how much type has been sent to the composing room. The computer can

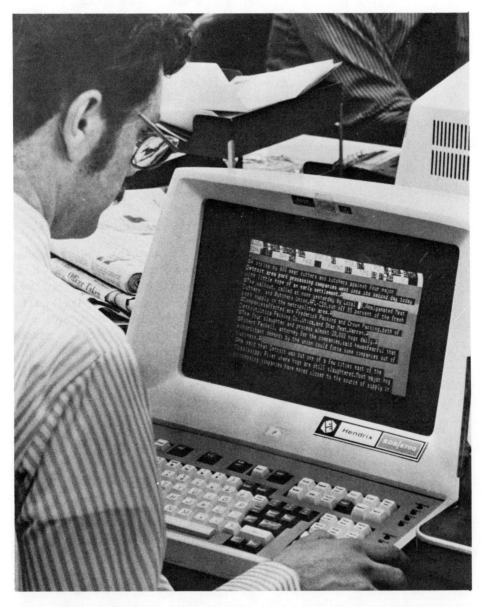

Fig. 2–3. Electronic editor. At the *Detroit News,* a copyeditor presses a few keys to alter a story glowing on his CRT screen.

do that. And if an editor forgets what one story is about, a couple of punches on his VDT keyboard will refresh his memory, for the story once more will leap onto the screen.

But whether the copyeditor uses a light pencil or a lead pencil, the job is basically the same. The task is to remove misspelled words, alter language, cut out redundancies, trim away surplus wording, or insert some more facts until the story is concise, accurate, factual —and appealing to the reader.

To attain this result the editor needs to combine an interest in the English language with an understanding of reporting, some knowledge of printing processes, a reasonably broad education, and a clear understanding of the newspaper's policy.

The path of copy

Regardless of the method of handling copy, all desks operate about the same way. They edit material from three, or possibly four, sub-editors.* The city editor sends copy from his city reporters. The state editor provides stories about events from the paper's circulation area outside the city. The telegraph editor delivers copy selected from the wire services. Some papers even have a fourth sub-editor, a suburban editor, who transmits news and features from the suburbs.

The person in charge of the copydesk is the *slot,* so called because he or she sits on the inside—in the slot—of a horseshoe-shaped desk or its equivalent. The slot's aides, the copyeditors, sit on the outside and so are known as *rim men* or *rim women.* (Copyeditors are also called *desk men* or *desk women* and *copyreaders.*) Figure 2-2 shows a typical arrangement.

The slot selects the rim person best able to handle a particular story. For example, a city council story may be read by an editor who once covered city hall. The slot also decides how it should be edited. On a paper-and-pencil desk he or she may write a curt phrase like "trim," "cut," or "slash" on any story. The slot may even mark "trim one-third" or may even jot down the number of inches the story should measure when set in type.

Copyeditors then understand that they must reduce the story to exactly that length. A copyeditor also has some of this executive power. The copyeditor may cut a story more sharply than ordered or even kill it, but will probably want to discuss the reasons for doing so with the slot. Others have already planned space for the copy and must know how many column-inches were trimmed.

Sometimes the slot will suggest a certain handling of a story, writing cryptically, "Trim out puffs" or "Bring fire angle to top." But not all orders from the slot are written. Since he or she is only feet away from the rim, the person in the slot may shove a story across with "Sharpen up that lead on this stuff of O'Hara's—it's too long. And move it along, ahead of that Latin story."

---

*The term "sub-editor" is descriptive but not much used in U. S. newsrooms. In Britain, however, "sub-editor" is common professional usage.

The notations by the slot include a symbol to tell the copyeditor what size headline to give the story. It may be simply "C" or "E" or "2/36." Any one of these may mean "two columns of 36-point Tempo heavy italic type." The editor knows the shorthand of the paper and can write the head accordingly. (Headlines are discussed more fully in chapter 4.)

If the newsroom is electronic, the slot has to operate differently, but not much differently. The slot types instructions on head size and story length into the "header" — various codes for the computer and the copyeditor that appear at the top of the story.

This editorial teamwork occurs at a single desk on medium and large newspapers. All local, state, and wire copy crosses this desk. Because stories from all three sources come from everywhere, the desk is called "universal." Only sports and women's news usually are edited at separate desks.

A few metropolitan newspapers receive too much news to use the universal desk system. They divide the flow of news into "city," "national," and "world" operations. Local, suburban, and state copy comes to the city desk, and most wire news and stories from special correspondents go to the world desk. But in this system sports and women still remain apart.

Small newspapers, of course, do not use enough copy to keep a full desk busy, so each sub-editor himself edits the appropriate stories from reporters or wire services. For example, the "city editor" may edit the copy written by one or two local reporters and himself, including sports stories, while a "telegraph editor" may handle international, national, and state news from the wire, as well as copy from correspondents in nearby villages. There then has to be an informal system of consultation so sub-editors know how much copy is flowing and what the top stories are.

No matter how simple or complex the system, editors must concentrate on improving copy. They tighten, point up, trim, polish. But they should *not* make over stories by altering every one so it will read as if they wrote it. Reporters seethe when clever phrases are made prosaic or novel leads are made routine. All editors should apply pencils with care, for they should encourage originality. The best newswriting is sprightly and varied. An editor who makes all copy read alike mechanizes writing; and as Dean Wayne Danielson of the University of Texas has observed, "If you write like a machine, you can be replaced by a machine."

The nature of desk work

The special qualifications of a copyeditor bring advantages. In most cases the pay is better. American Newspaper Guild contracts usually set the base pay of editors at least five dollars above the minimum salary for reporters. Salaries sometimes are pushed above Guild scale, frequently well above the minimums.

The way to promotion most often is by way of the rim person's chair. As copyeditors usually have been reporters, the combination of reporting and desk experience makes a journalist valuable for positions requiring more than one point of view. The first step for a copyeditor usually is over the desk into the slot. But it may be that the copyeditor will be boosted directly from the rim to such jobs as state editor, city editor, suburban editor, telegraph editor, or picture editor. The first promotion may even be to assistant city editor or assistant state editor. These jobs then prepare the copyeditor to move up to the more responsible and best-paid positions as editor, assistant to the publisher, executive editor, news editor, or even editor-in-chief.

Fig. 2–4. The city room. Reporters at the *Detroit News* write on CRTs, then send stories via the computer to the copydesk.

Even at the beginning, in the informal atmosphere of the copy desk, the copyreader is in good company. Most desks are populated by bright men and women with superior wit and humor who appreciate a well-turned phrase. Copydesk wisecracks are told all over the newsroom, and from time to time they show up, without attribution, in a local column. Most of the joking is done during the lulls that occur during the work day, for copy tends to come in spurts. After working at a good pace for an hour or so, an editor can take a few minutes to relax. During these breaks editors often spoof each other, rib the copy aides, who used to be called copy boys or copy girls, or even comment on the boss's foibles. Satirical pokes at local, state, and national stuffed shirts may start a serious discussion of world affairs.

If young journalists enjoy being up-to-date on current affairs and ideas, the copydesk puts them in the midst of news flow. On the small paper editors tend to be better informed on the full range of human events than anyone else in the community and thus have a special responsibility to stay up-to-date. On the large paper the desk person can become expert on a few specialties. Like the professor, he or she amasses knowledge on a favorite subject or two; but, unlike the professor, the desk person is not pressed to delve for the minutiae and to publish. Scholarship is an avocation to most editors. But desk persons have written books on their pet subjects and received the acclaim of scholars, and substantial royalties as well.

Though it provides great rewards, copyediting also includes some frustrations. Editing is sedentary, and the lack of physical activity bothers some people.* Egos also get little exercise, since the work is anonymous. The reporter can get a byline, but no one ever sees a story topped "Headline by Joe Guggenheimer." Copyeditors' fame rarely extends beyond the newsroom, so they have to be satisfied in large part by belief that he or she is doing an important job well. Editors find their egos strengthened most by the approving chuckles or praise from their associates or, best of all, from their bosses.

The person who enjoys being out where the news is made and hob-nobbing as a reporter with the big names may miss the excitement when brought to the desk. Though writing headlines and re-shaping stories has its creative possibilities, the copyeditor who is at heart a writer may be unhappy without the creative challenge of writing news and feature stories. Not all newspeople are cut out for this relatively unspectacular side of the editorial operation.

Perhaps the greatest and most surprising drawback in desk work is inactivity. While breaks can be stimulating, long slack periods can be depressing. This is particularly true on the biggest newspapers, where there are several editions and the staffs are large enough to cope with almost any emergency. By hard work the first two editions are taken care of, and subsequent editions rarely require many changes. There may be almost nothing to do for an hour or more, yet editors can't count the time as their own. If a slack period comes at the end of the work day, most slot persons let a few copyeditors go home half an hour early. If rim people can spend slack times reading magazines or books, they will turn a disadvantage into an advantage. Such people "get their reading done" on company time, and the paper gains from their widened knowledge.

Much of the negative side of copyediting can be eliminated by real appreciation from the desk person's editors and colleagues, a good principle for copyeditors when they move up the ladder to recall. Praise when the copyreader has made a complex story readable or turned out an exceptional headline is worth almost as much to him as a raise in pay.

The *St. Petersburg* (Fla.) *Times* underlined the value of accurate

---

* Physically handicapped journalists, however, often find their niche on a copy desk.

editing with a game of "killing enemy errors." "X-act Agent" buttons were distributed to 664 staffers, along with special blue pencils. The paper paid $25 to the one who circled the most errors. Perhaps the game was a corny gimmick, but it showed every reporter and copyeditor that management cared about quality.

Reporters who appreciate the efforts of editors boost the morale of the desk, as an example at the *New York Times* illustrates. A member of the *Times'* Washington bureau wrote a letter to the city room expressing appreciation for checking doubtful points with him. To the amazement of the desk crew, a breed accustomed to little praise, he wrote: "I read my story this morning with just the greatest pleasure, noting where, as always, you had smoothed some lumpy sentences, chopped apart some over-long ones, skillfully made a couple of internal cuts in exactly the right places and, in short, made the story better than the one I had written."

The alert professional

Whether working on small or large papers, editors have to keep tabs on themselves, for they can go stale on the job. A person who develops professional skill remains, it is hoped, a credit to the profession. But a lazy journalist can drift through several years, unaware of changes in newspapers, oblivious to undercurrents in world affairs, and unwilling to prepare himself for more demanding tasks. The job is a deadend for such a person.

The editors with the brightest future are readers. They read magazines and the best newspapers, and at least skim through the current books, while thoroughly reading some of the old ones. Their reading alerts them to change and to ideas. News almost by definition concerns itself with changes and ideas, and editors unfamiliar or uninterested in them become ineffective. They will gain neither the responsibility nor the respect of a professional.

Even competent editors can slip unconsciously into carelessness about the fine points of the job. They may allow slips in grammar because of letting slide the occasional few minutes necessary for review. A well-thumbed book on grammar shows that an editor is concerned with details of quality—and therefore probably concerned with quality in general.

A good desk person can obtain tips for quality writing and editing in three or four minutes of reading every day or so. One of the best sources is *Winners & Sinners,* "a bulletin of second guessing issued occasionally from the southeast corner of the *New York Times* News Room." This one-sheet paper recounts the journalistic blunders and triumphs of Timesmen. The *Cleveland Press* publishes a similar paper called *Tips and Slips,* and a medium-sized paper, the *Wilmington* (Del.) *Journal-News,* turns out *Hits & Misses.* These sheets help greatly in preventing editing mistakes. Books like Strunk and White's *Elements of Style* and Gowers' *Plain Words, Their ABC* (see Bibliography) prod the editor to make sure that copy uses words correctly and that the language is simple and direct.

The goal of the copyreaders is to be sure that the stories in the paper are in good, readable, accurate English. They look at the message and structure of the whole story. But they also fix all its minute parts. For example, they catch dangling participles, so this cutline would not get under the picture of a lost child: "Wearing only a diaper and rubber pants, police guessed his age at 12 to 14 months." The copyeditors should see that the police were more appropriately dressed.

They also block mixed metaphors, such as this quadruple one from a paper submitted by a journalism student: "This then is the key. The potential is pushing at the dam's gates. Given the proper catalyst, we may be on the threshold of witnessing an entire new era of journalism." With luck, maybe the key will keep the flood from getting through the door.

Verne English, long a copyeditor for Syracuse newspapers, kept a file of writers' boners the desk had caught. Here are samples, the kinds of things that the sharp desk person spots:

— Four juvenile boys admitted the theft.
— Dear licenses outsold marriage licenses.
— Passengers were treated to a mid morning concert shortly after noon.
— The General Electric Advanced Electronics Laboratory shot its last employee Saturday as the company's flu vaccination program ended.
— A post-mortem autopsy was performed.
— The hospital reported she was pregnant but the injuries did not effect it.

A visitor to a newsroom is often surprised that the paper ever comes out. "How can you keep everything straight?" "Aren't there all kinds of problems that take hours to solve?"

The answer, of course, is that all the jobs mesh. The result is a newspaper with nearly all the words spelled correctly, the main news events reported, all the space filled with a good blend of news, pictures, commentary, and advertising.

One reason so much work can be done in such a short time is that, except in slack times, no one on a newspaper staff spends much time in conversation. On many papers the top editors spend a half an hour a day in conference deciding how the main news of the day will be played. But the rest of the work is completed with almost no conversation during busy periods. Each person works quietly.

That picture may surprise those who imagine the newsroom filled with people screaming orders at one another. Actually the noise level is not much higher than in a bank. The reason for the lack of noise and conversation is that newsmen have a silent language.

The headline order, as mentioned before, comes to the copyeditor in the form of a written symbol. The slot marks paper copy with a string of other cryptic orders, like *kill, add, more,* and *jump.* Other symbols are little more than a scratch of a pencil. The editor uses all this sign language on copy so that the printers will know, without being told, what he or she wants done. The signs put on stories are understood in every composing room in the country. These terms often are unnecessary in the electronic newsroom. To be flexible, however, the beginner should know how to use all methods of handling copy, including the old pencil-and-paper method. These are the symbols once used on all desks and still used on hundreds of newspapers. The signs are understood in every composing room where old-style printers still function. The editor must use these symbols unconsciously, just as a touch-typist punches typewriter keys without thinking where the fingers go.

the symbols ~~common~~ *used* in ~~most~~ *many* newsrooms in the country may seem puzzling to the student at first but a few hours practice re moves their Mystery.

Start new paragraph:

Jones said he arrived at 10 a.m. Rogers

insisted that the time was 10:45.

Set in lower case instead of capital:

The Biology class met outdoors.

Capitalize:

Los Angeles--Governor Brown signed the tax bill.

The supreme court will hear the case at noon.

The supreme court will hear the case at noon.

Insert and delete:

He profesed a belief in gosts and the consensus

~~of opinion~~ was that he was sincere

Insert new word:

The bookkeeper *allegedly* spent the money at the races.

Separate elements:

Everything had been all right that morning.

Transpose elements:

Alabama

He only won two games.

Close:

She started as a copy reader and worked her way up.

Close, but leave space:

The fourth is freedom of the press.

Connect elements:

He said that ~~he saw the three men enter~~ ~~the building and that~~ the men were injured.

Insert period:

The U.S. team won the match.

The U. S. team won the match.

Insert comma:

The tour will include Ireland Scotland and Wales.

Insert colon:

Prizes were awarded in three categories fiction,

nonfiction and poetry.

Insert semicolon:

The winners were John McIntyre, for fiction Paul

Barnes, for nonfiction and William Ellis, for poetry.

Insert apostrophe:

The reporters story was praised.

Insert quotation marks:

The Golden Pheasant is a musical.

Insert exclamation point:

"Oklahoma" was a hit musical.

Insert hyphen:

Police claimed the thief was caught redhanded.

Insert dash (and exaggerate its length or frame it with short lines):

The bill passed 94 to 2 is the first of its kind.

Abbreviate:

Governor Otto Kerner signed the bill.

Spell out:

Wm. B. Zarfoss won the election.

Use figure instead of word:

The group represented twelve states.

Spell out figure:

He had 1,000,000 counterfeit dollars.

(Spelled out it would be one million.)

Let it stand as first written:

He pleaded not guilty.

Indent to left:

(The world Almanac gave the figure as

2.25 million.)

Indent to right:

(The Statistical Abstract of the U.S. listed the number as 28.)

Indent both right and left:

(The Denver Post reported that the lost men were rescued within hours of the disaster.)

Center:

Three Kick Goals

Let capital stand (for marking all-capital copy from Western Union or a news service):

WASHINGTON--SEN. HIRAM FONG, R-HAWAII, INSISTED ON THE CHANGE, AND HE WAS SUPPORTED BY THE UTAH DELEGATION.

Change from tabular to paragraph style:

The decision will give these grants to the following states:

Wisconsin, $14 million;

Utah, $7.4 million; and

South Dakota, $11 million

(Long tabulations require no more than one to two of these connecting lines. Mark the margin "Run In.")

Wisconsin, $14 million

Utah, $7.4 million

South Dakota, $11 million

Ohio, $22 million, *and*

Kentucky, $14.9 million

Let copy stand as written (if the typesetter may think the copy is mistaken):

The boy's name is Jakque.

The boy's name is Jakque.

("Folo copy" in the margin provides the same instruction.)

Italicize:

The girl said, "Nein, nein."

Set in bold face:

The reporter is a Phi Beta Kappa.

(If possible, hand-print corrections; otherwise clarify ambiguous handwritten letters.)

Underline:

Overline:

The paper editor's finished work will look like this:

williams

(SCHOOLS)

Three area school districts will get special state grants _totaling $2.5 million)_
to finance vocational education projects. ~~The grants will~~

~~amount to $2,500,000 dollars.~~

The three districts are Van Buren, Chatworth, and Lan-

caster. The funds will pay for special equipment, mostly ~~in~~
(to use in teaching)
~~the~~ auto mechanics ~~field~~. Each school ~~system has room for~~ _will install_ the

equipment _in_ ~~since~~ additions ~~to the school were~~ built last year.

~~The additions also contain other vocational education equip-~~

~~ment.~~

The superintendent of the Chatworth district, Homar C.

McTavish, said the equipment can be ~~delivered within 60 days~~
in three
~~and~~ in operation ~~with a~~ month ~~after that~~. "This means we will

be ready to use the machines in instruction by next fall," he

declared.
also
Other ~~school~~ officials ~~in the other~~ districts said they

would be using the equipment ~~in teaching~~ by the opening of

the school year.
$2.5 million)
_Of_ The ~~$2,500,000 is not split evenly between the districts.~~
(and Lancaster) (each, and)
Van Buren ~~gets~~ $9,000,000 Chatworth ~~$7,000,000 and Lancaster~~
gets $700,000
~~$900,000.~~

Practiced copyeditors can flash over copy—on paper or screen—ousting occasional waste phrases and correcting misspelled words. Few mistakes will get by them.

The copyeditor's goals

But this kind of editing, after a time, tends to be dull and even sterile. The mediocre editor works mechanically, catching minor errors while failing to detect the big ones, like inconsistencies and omissions of fact.

Excellent editors do not disregard the little flaws. They know that even a well-written story may have slight imperfections that distract the reader. The editor not only corrects the misspelled word and the redundancy but sniffs the whole story for completeness and accuracy, questioning its news value. Is it worth eight paragraphs as written? Should the story be thrown away as inconsequential? Should it be rewritten for more impact on the reader? Is the lead buried in the fourth paragraph?

Copyeditors who recognize that even the best reporter may blunder recognize that the same thing can happen to them. They may doze off and let an obvious mistake get into print. Editors must not only be skeptical of the reporter's accuracy but also be skeptical of their own ability to do everything right in what often has to be a hasty reading of a story.

Editing is an intellectual pursuit that requires meticulousness, careful analysis of content, judgment of story value in relation to other news, and a weighing of the significance of all news that gets into the paper. Many journalists find it satisfying to use their knowledge and skills every hour to make the news more understandable for thousands of readers.

3 Copyediting techniques

Copyeditors using the older methods toil with pencil, eraser, scissors, and paste. They scratch out some words, insert others, erase their own mistakes, snip apart a story and paste it together in somewhat different order. Sometimes they need to paste inserts into the copy.

This system has its good points. The slot gets to skim the story and may spot an error or two. A printer may notice a real boner and, after mumbling about those oafs in the newsroom, the printer will see that the correction is made.

In the electronic newsroom, however, it is unlikely that the slot will "call up" the edited version on the slot's VDT. So only machines probably will see the story after it leaves the rim. With VDTs and scanners, then, the copyeditor must be sure that the story is right. But couldn't corrections still be made? Yes, but it would mean starting all over, running the story through the VDT or scanner and resetting the type. That isn't why publishers pay $8,000 each for those VDTs.

As for editing itself, slot people agree at most points on what they consider good copyediting. They want stories to be "fixed up" but, unless the writing is bad, they don't want them butchered and rehashed. The copyeditor has to learn the technique of the proper amount of editing. He or she keeps an eye on all the minutiae, at the same time watching to see that the whole story fits and flows together to give an accurate general impression. The copyeditor combines good English and good sense with the paper's rules and traditions.

The leads of stories deserve particular attention, for a lead can make or break the reader's interest. If the lead doesn't click, the editor certainly should revise it.

A good copyeditor, unless squeezed by a deadline, reads each story at least twice. Often an error will show up in each reading, so the copyeditor must take great care to recheck all rephrasing. The new sentences inserted should be read two or three times to make sure that the corrections themselves are not in error.

The editor ought to ask finally, "Does this story make sense? Are there any inadequacies? Will the reader have any important questions? Does the story read smoothly? Are all the statements properly attributed? Is there any factual error?"

The desk person should also check to see whether the story rambles on for ten or eleven paragraphs of detail without getting essential information close to the top. This shortcoming often mars stories of strikes. The beginning usually reports who says what and how long the strike has been going on, but what the strike is all about may be buried or ignored.

The copyeditor should make the necessary changes and quit. This means keeping a pencil off clear and accurate writing. *Winners & Sinners* has warned editors not to change language for the sake of change. One issue noted:

> Itchy pencil . . . refers to occasional copy desk tinkering with copy for no apparent reason—a practice that sometimes makes the writing inferior, sometimes makes it outright wrong and always baffles the writer. If a holdup man takes a picture of his colleagues with a Polaroid Land camera and the reporter writes that in that way "he was able to avoid taking the incriminating film to the corner drugstore for developing" what is gained by changing the final quoted phrase to "elsewhere"? There is actually a slight loss in sense.
>
> If a reporter writes about a chimpanzee at the Museum of Natural History that "whizzed across its acres on a red tricycle" why should "acres" be changed to "halls," which loses the idea of vastness? If a correspondent writes that a "betting man could get a dime to a nickel from almost anyone in the Western delegations" about the break-up of the Geneva conference, is there any improvement in making it "could get a wager"?
>
> Although the damage wrought in these instances may seem minor, the reader has been deprived of colorful detail; moreover, the cumulative effect on reporters of such tinkering is discouraging. Changes have to be made in copy, to be sure, but be certain that when you make a change it is definitely a change for the better and not just the work of itchy pencil.

The job of editors, then, is to go over the copy to correct grammar, to cross out waste words and sentences, and to make the language more graceful. They should throttle clichés. Ambiguous phrasing should be hunted down and corrected.

Editors need a quizzical, skeptical approach if they are to catch errors. They must keep asking as they read, "Can this be right?" With this in mind, for example, they will question whether, as the story says, Edward Kennedy was born in California and the University of Michigan is in Kalamazoo.

The probing editor

Editors must check to see if needed information is omitted. A *New York Times* reporter once sent a note to the desk mentioning an editorial oversight: A story on a supersonic airliner gave only oblique reference—in the eleventh paragraph—to the name of the government agency which received the airliner designs. Knowing this kind of error should be caught by the desk, he wrote (in *Winners & Sinners*), "Every reporter is going to have an occasional lapse in fullest lucidity, and he would like to feel that he is securely backstopped. That, after all, is the copydesk's primary function."

If there is any doubt about the accuracy of changes in a story, the editor should check with the nearest authority—the writer of the story. The reporter might be asked, "Does this improve the meaning of the story? Have I made it clearer, or have I muddled the facts?" A reporter will be furious, and has a right to be, if copy is revised into error. It makes him look like a fool with news sources, and it embitters the staff when an accurate story is distorted by an editor who had no first-hand knowledge of the event.

Where a reporter has used an inappropriate word, the editor should find the right one. This requires familiarity with semantics to be sure that the words convey the intended meaning. For example, where the reporter has written "statesman," the word "politician" might be better.

There must be a steady watchfulness for libel. Every story that defames anyone—and many stories must defame—should be checked to see if the defamatory phrases can be used safely under law. Chapter 12 discusses in detail the legal pitfalls that always lurk near a copyeditor.

Hoaxes are another thing to contend with. A naive reporter may write a story that sounds like a dandy. The more experienced copyeditor, however, may recall that the same story ran a decade ago and was exposed as a fake. This story needs the oblivion treatment.

Unless editors are careful, a single story may get in the paper twice, causing merriment among readers. It is doubly amusing if the same stories get into the paper the same day. Occasionally, different reporters will write essentially the same story a few days apart. The writer of the second story should have read the paper more carefully. But such an oversight is no excuse for the copy desk to repeat the error. An alert desk must likewise kill outdated stories which did not make the paper. A story announcing last night's event as "tonight" is bad news for the participants, the frustrated audience, and the newspaper.

Editors also have to watch for advertising that masquerades as news. Since newspapers sell advertising, news stories should mention advertisers only when they make news. For example, if a meeting is going to take place at a hotel, the reporter has to say which hotel. This "advertising" is unavoidable and therefore permissible. Glowing descriptions of the hotel, however, should be crossed out of news copy.

It is even harder but more important to eliminate propaganda. All kinds of people try to sneak their points of view into the paper under the guise of news, and this is most apparent during election time when dozens of events are staged to attract attention. The editor should sift through all the fakery and try to stick to the issues in the reports that get into the paper.

Sometimes an inexperienced reporter will quote a news source too much and let the source misuse the news columns to further an individual or a cause. The editor gives this material its proper weight, which is sometimes nothing.

Eleven pointers

Double-check names. If the copyeditor has any doubt about the spelling of a name, someone should look it up, and be sure that a name is spelled consistently through the story. A person should not be Whelan in the first paragraph and Whalen in the second. The editor should watch for a common lapse associated with unusual names: The reporter uses a person's full name in the lead but mistakenly substitutes the first name for the last in the rest of the story. For example, the lead may refer to the president of Harvard University as Dr. Curtis Bok. From then on, however, he is Dr. Curtis instead of Dr. Bok. The copyeditor should catch this blunder.

Attribute facts properly. Almost anything that cannot be witnessed by the reporter should be attributed to some person. The "almost" is essential to remember because often stories contain facts neither observed by reporters nor found through records, and yet there is no attribution. Attribution is unnecessary when the source obviously is telling the truth. For example, it is silly to attribute to a university president the employment of every single faculty member. The university is not going to announce an appointment by a news release and then back out of it, so phrases like "the president announced" are unnecessary.

Produce clean copy. Stories sent to an old style composing room must be readable. Hurriedly scrawled editorial changes make the printer guess at the scribbles—and make wrong guesses—or force him to throw the story back to the desk. Either way the paper can lose accuracy or time. If the desk must make complicated handwritten changes, he or she should type out the most involved ones and paste the retyped material over the messy original. In the electronic newsroom, or course, computers ignore handwriting.

"Duck it." Sometimes an editor spots a minor misstatement in a story, and the reporter who wrote the story is not around for verification. Any other check might take fifteen minutes. The item is not worth that much time, so the editor "ducks it" by omitting the

statement. A story may say, "Jones, who moved here in 1958, has served on the county board for 17 years." The copyeditor may trust "17 years" but doubt "1958." How could Jones have won an election so soon? So the editor ducks the problem by changing the sentence to "Jones has served on the county board for 17 years."

Simplify language. Newspapers are written not for morons, but for people who want to get news and comment in easy-to-read form. Simpler words should replace involved ones like "inextricable," "dichotomy," and "tangential." Language even for an intellectual audience should be precise and readable, not pretentious.

Reporters sometimes get caught up in the special language or jargon of the fields they cover. Court reporters, for instance, may write "filed a demurrer," "stayed the execution," or "granted a continuance." Such terms may be hard for a layman to grasp, and the editor who thinks the story should interest the ordinary reader will either change the wording or send it back to the reporter for translation.

Recognize your own prejudices. Copyeditors need to double-check themselves to be sure they do not make decisions to chop one story and inflate another because of personal prejudice. Some editors who control newspaper content favor stories that concern their personal hobbies. A person who loves to sail may run an unusual number of stories about boats and the sea. Such prejudices are basically harmless, although they could make the paper look amateurish. Sometimes, however, an editor may intensely dislike a senator or fear that the nation is moving rapidly toward socialism. This person may edit the news to make the senator look foolish or to emphasize personal political views. This kind of editing is harmful and unprofessional. An editor must develop an attitude of detachment in handling the news.

Don't trust your memory completely. A copyeditor is often tempted to pencil into a story a fact as a way to improve the article. These facts should be inserted, however, only when the editor is absolutely sure of them. If one isn't certain, look up the information in the clipping file or a reference book.

Be sure copy is fair and tasteful. Balancing objective reporting and interpretation is a continual problem, but even if a story is primarily interpretive it should be fair. Snide, belittling comments should be removed.

Rebuttal from criticized persons should be included or run as a separate story nearby. Copy also should remain in good taste. Taste is difficult to assess, but most editors have a rule-of-thumb: A paper read by all kinds of people, including children, should soften or eliminate the most brutal or intimate details.

While this advice is generally good, it doesn't always work. As an illustration, some papers handle a sex offense by referring to a "morals charge." But such an all-encompassing term actually may be unfair to the accused, because the phrase covers a wide spectrum of sins. In such cases some editors try to be a little more specific without being salacious. Others simply do not print "morals" arrests except in cases when they can't avoid it, as when omitting such news about a public figure might bring a charge of covering-up for him or her. Editors would print news of so-called morals convictions, however.

Watch for Doublespeak. The art of using language to deceive has swollen so much in recent years that the term *doublespeak* has been adapted into English from George Orwell's *newspeak*. Much of this deception is unintentional—the speaker or writer was plain sloppy, as in the case of the senator who said, "We might ventilate the structure of campaigning." But much of the deception is deliberate. The military announces a "protective strike," to avoid saying *bombing*. Presidents talk constantly of "national security." Diplomats rattle off "balance of power." These terms either lack meaning or are intended to fool the public. The copy editor should oust such phrases and encourage reporters to challenge sources who spout doublespeak.

Scratch euphemisms. A beginning journalist learns on the first day of work that people *die, not pass away*. But "pass away" is a simple euphemism, and the dictionary bulges with more complicated ones. The State Department doesn't *fire* people, it *terminates* them. *Poverty* gets replaced by *low income; slums* become *inner city;* and *prisons* get named *correctional facilities*. The desk should serve as translators.

Myths must go. Sometimes through error or carelessness, a scrap of information gets passed as fact. As an illustration, some reporter once wrote that one-third of dog food sold in slums was consumed by human beings. This was not true, yet it was widely quoted about the country. Copyeditors, always skeptical, should ask frequently, "Who said so? Where did you get this information?"

Color and completeness

Copyeditors must always think of how to make the news readable. They point up the local angle whenever possible. They revive listless writing and chop out ponderous language to make sentences brisk and stories a pleasure to follow. On the other hand, they may have to add a phrase to make a story clearer or to tone down lurid writing. A good slogan is "make copy brisk but not brusque—vivid but not lurid."

The editor should make every reasonable effort to get a local angle high in the stories, because readers tend to pay attention to stories that mention local issues or people. Localization can be overdone, of course, like this:

```
The brother-in-law of a man who lived in Oshkosh in 1929 was

arrested today in Dallas on a charge of panhandling.
```

But if an Oshkosh native wins a Nobel Prize, the Oshkosh paper had better have his birthplace in the lead, not in the ninth paragraph as it probably came over the wire.

Localizing often requires some juggling of paragraphs. Sometimes it requires only a phrase inserted high in the story:

Fifteen cities *(including Peoria)* have been awarded million-dollar grants to

help relieve poverty.

In other cases it will require restructuring the story considerably, perhaps rewriting the lead or inserting paragraph seven after paragraph one. Feature writers have a habit of writing long introductions before getting to the heart of the story. An editor often can chop out whole paragraphs at the beginning of such pieces, as well as trimming the tail end of many news stories.

Whenever possible the stories should be organized to pinpoint the significance for the reader. Most of us read stories, as Wilbur Schramm has pointed out, because we want to be rewarded: We want to know what will affect our pocketbooks, to know what has happened to our friends and acquaintances, to know what might please us or upset us. The reporter writes stories with these ideas in mind, and the copyeditor fixes the reporter's oversights:

School *(property)* taxes will go up $1.5 million next year, the board of

education decided last night. *The new rate means that if a resident paid $200 in school taxes this year, he will pay $229 next year.*

Because editors know that every reader has certain areas of ignorance, they often explain what the reporter thought obvious. "Died of nephritis" needs an explanatory phrase. If the story mentions District IV schools, tell the reader, at least roughly, what District IV covers. If the story mentions Albert Einstein, add an identifying phrase. The story must remind as well as inform readers, and the brightest of them have gaps in their knowledge.

The reporter, as has been said many times, is the eyes, ears, hands, nose and tongue of the reader. If the reporter does not describe the look, the sound, the feel, the smell, or the taste of something that

Balancing the
reporter's judgment

needs these descriptions, the editor should get this information in the story.

But the copyeditor occasionally thinks that a reporter, striving for vividness, has given an incorrect tone. Perhaps the reporter unconsciously chose the words the editor thinks will sound snide to the reader. Words like *intellectual, radical, foreigner, dropout, or uneducated,* if used in a certain context, may be irritating to some readers. Context of words may alter the whole tone of the story. For example, a report of a speech may be filled with attributive phrases like "he roared," "Harrington thundered," and "he shouted." It is possible that the speaker did roar, thunder, and shout. But in print these words make the man sound wild, and he may not have been wild at all. He may simply have had a strong voice or he may have been trying to reach listeners sitting far behind the reporter's front row seat.

On the other hand, a reporter may turn in a biographical story filled with syrupy phrases that make a rather ordinary person appear to be a saint. The deletion of a half dozen adjectives in these cases usually makes the tone ring true. No one should assume, however, that the tone of stories need always be coldly factual. A funny incident should be reported in a funny way. A story on a political session may be irreverent. And a story on a funeral generally should be dignified and restrained.

The *New York Times* started a story on a St. Patrick's Day parade with: "Irishmen, regardless of race, creed or color, marched down Fifth Avenue today."

Sports writer Red Smith, covering a Democratic national convention, wrote, "The Democratic party last night was smitten with the jawbone of an ass."

A somber funeral story might include: "The senator's wife sat dry-eyed through the services, occasionally biting her lip to keep back the tears."

Of course every story should have the essential facts as well as the right tone. The reader is interested in the overall view of an event, but he or she also expects the story to answer reasonable questions. If the reporter doesn't have the answer, the story should say so: "Petersen's age was not learned."

Polishing pointers

Sometimes the editor can't revive a story. The sentences are long-winded, the quotes are ponderous, and the story seems to drone on. The copyeditor has to read each paragraph twice to get the foggiest understanding of what the writer was driving at. The story demands rewriting, and it should go back to the reporter or another staffer with specific instructions on how to improve it.

Quotations that look brief in copy take up an alarming amount of space when squeezed into a column width. The copyeditor can boil down long-winded quotations by combining material, omitting by ellipsis, or using partial quotes:

"The dam, which is designed to bring vast blessings to the people of Central Illinois and which will avoid terrifying floods, will cost $8 million and be built within two years," the governor said.

The quote could be paraphrased:

The dam will cost $8 million and take two years to build, the governor said.

Another possibility would be:

"The dam . . . will cost $8 million and be built within two years," the governor said.

Quotation marks do suggest authenticity, but too many of them make the report look patched together. Quotes are the seasoning of the story, not the meat.

Reporters who keep interrupting their own stories put the reader in a coma with the comma. An involved sentence that stitches facts together with commas needs editing:

The Tobiason boy, 8 years old and a fourth grader at the new Leal school, said that his mother, ~~the former Ann Davis who was Miss America 14 years ago,~~ had planned to pick him up at 4 p.m. at the school.

The reference to her former title, if essential, can be inserted elsewhere.

Other reporters string identifications of people throughout a story. This is noted particularly on the sports page. In the first paragraph the football player is simply "a halfback," in the second he is "the native of Florida," in the third "the 205-pounder," in the fourth "the Big Ten's leading ground-gainer," and in the fifth "the junior economics major." Such detailed identification, if used at all, should form a two or three sentence paragraph of background information.

Redundancies are harder to spot than quotes or identification tags, and they are more worrisome. They waste space and bring snickers from readers. Obvious ones like "killed to death" rarely creep into copy, but subtler ones like "widow of the late John Smith" are unsettlingly common. "Autopsy of the body" suggests that autopsies are performed on things other than bodies. "Graves of dead soldiers will be decorated" indicates that some soldiers are buried alive.

The correct use of words can raise interesting problems. A dictionary, of course, is a good guide, but sometimes a "correctly" used word will convey the wrong sense. An editorial writer once referred to a major religious denomination as a "sect." If connotation is ignored, this is a "correct" use of the word. But many readers were incensed, for they viewed the word "sect" as a term for little flocks that convene in abandoned stores.

Six more flaws to fix

Subject-verb disagreement.   It is not unusual to see a story with "the council *meet* today at noon" or "the group *is* going to take separate cars to *their* hotels."

Pronouns.   Whenever the copyeditor runs across *he, she, it,* or *they* he should check to see if the right person or thing is identified. If there is doubt, a suitable noun, not a pronoun, should be used.

Illogical dependent clauses.   Watch sentences like "A graduate of Harvard, he is the father of eight children." Being a father has nothing to do with attendance at Harvard.

Double meanings.   There is always someone around who will spot the secondary—and possibly racy or bawdy—meaning of a phrase. These double meanings amuse readers, but they detract from professionalism. As an illustration the *Philadelphia Bulletin,* on a food story, added this headline:

**A Leek in the Soup
Is Worth Two in the Garden**

Editorializing.   Any trace of personal opinion or a value judgment should be eliminated, unless the story is a feature or news analysis.

Unlikely quotes.   Sometimes reporters invent quotes and the unfortunate result is a sentence or two with a hollow ring. A baseball team manager noted for his linguistic errors, for example, may be quoted as saying, "We were in a desperate position in the third inning, but Bocko Jennings, our superlative third baseman, made what must be the best play of the year, allowing us to escape without damage." This unbelievable quote should be scratched and the facts put in as straight news: The manager said Bocko Jennings' spectacular play saved the game.

Occasionally, a reporter writes that more than one person said the same thing: "John Adams and Peter Farrel said, 'I think the foreign policy of the nation is clearly a menace.'" One of them might say it, but not both.

Series.   Check a series of several items in one sentence for a surplus verb. "He is a determined golf player, a collector of antique clocks and often reads a detective story at night." To clear up the awkwardness, the copyeditor could change it to: "He is a determined golf player and a collector of antique clocks. He often reads a detective story at night."

Rechecking details

The copyeditor obviously checks spelling and punctuation with particular attention to the placement of quotation marks and apostrophes. *Its* and *it's* always need a second look to see if they have been used correctly. Every possessive must have the apostrophe in the right place. The editor even does a little arithmetic to check totals given in a story. For example, if the reporter's copy states that two objects weigh three pounds and that each weighs eighteen ounces the editor should start asking questions. An editor must not hesitate to ask the reporter to double-check something that looks as though it might be wrong. If the story is from a wire service, a query to the wire service should resolve the doubt.

Saving space

When copyeditors rewrite extensively, they are tempted when handling paper copy to pencil whole new paragraphs between the lines of copy. This short cut usually turns out to be the hard way for the typesetter and proof-reader. Obviously, electronic copy doesn't have this problem. If any copy, paper or electronic, needs extensive revision, it should be returned to the reporter for a rewrite. The copyeditor, however, may try to rewrite a few sentences in such a story and discover that one new sentence includes the gist of three or four.

Any copyeditor must spend a good share of his time reducing copy—not because the slot person would not like to run more detail but because there simply is no room for it. Editing to save space means applying the scalpel, not the meat ax. Some copy butchers would merely whack off six inches from the story's end. The skillful editor, however, recreates. For example, he or she takes off the last two paragraphs, removes the fourth, combines two rather long sentences into one of moderate length, takes a phrase from two or three different sentences, and makes a long quotation into a short one. The marked copy below shows how the editor in such condensation leaves as much fact as possible, sacrificing only the least significant details.

The cutting may not seem like much, but it removed about six lines of copy. This means that the story is about an inch and a half shorter in type and may now just fill the allotted space. Furthermore, a dozen stories each shortened that much would make room for another eighteen-inch story.

The City Council ~~at a meeting~~ last *night* ~~evening~~ voted ~~by a~~ 9 to 5 ~~margin~~ to up the city's utility tax by 1 percent. *(3 per cent)* ~~The present rate is currently 3 per cent.~~

Mayor Hiram C. Stetler *said* ~~told reporters after the meeting that~~ he would not veto the *tax* ~~measure~~, so *it* ~~the new tax~~ will take *e*ffect the first ~~day~~ of next month.

The *levy* ~~tax~~ will apply to water, electricity, *and* natural gas bills ~~with~~in the city~~,~~ ~~limits~~.

The (three) per cent tax produce*d* ~~s~~ $1,234,000~~, in tax revenue. At least it did~~ this year. The extra (one) per cent is expected to raise $400,000.

Mayor Stetler said the *new rate* ~~extra revenue~~ will *yield* ~~produce~~ enough ~~revenue~~ to balance the budget *($8.8 million)* ~~which totals $8.8 million. The budget is~~ 4 percent higher than last year'~~s budget~~.

The *increase* ~~extra cost~~ is *caused by* ~~due to~~ the construction of a new fire station on the east side ~~of the city which will require putting~~ nine new firemen *will staff it.* ~~on the city payroll.~~

The city gets other ~~tax~~ revenue from taxes on property, licenses and fees, *and* ~~a state income tax refund, and a state sales tax distribution and motor fuel taxes collected by the state.~~ *state refunds on income, sales and motor fuel taxes*

Every newspaper should have a *style book*. This term does not refer here to a book on writing style but rather to a booklet put out by a newspaper telling how capitalization, abbreviation, and punctuation are handled in news stories for that paper. Reporters are supposed to follow this set of rules, or *style,* but sometimes they don't. The editor, to correct their errors, needs to be thoroughly familiar with the style book but willing to look up an obscure point whenever there is any doubt—or argument.

The consistency established by the style book prevents the meticulous reader from being annoyed when a story spells a proper name two or three different ways in as many paragraphs—or abbreviates a word one time and spells it out the next.

If a newspaper does not have its own style book, the editors may use a book published by another paper, such as the thorough one published by the *New York Times.* The Associated Press and United Press International have joined forces to publish a widely used style book. Since all copy from AP and UPI coming into newsrooms conforms to this style, it would be wasteful for a paper that used mostly wire copy to make many changes in it.

Accuracy of copy requires several other reference books. Two of them, a medium-sized dictionary and the *World Almanac,* should be at arm's length. The need of the dictionary is obvious. The *Almanac* is the poor man's encyclopedia. It gives an editor quick access to thousands of facts on recent history, dates, biographies, and records. Today a one-volume paperback edition of an encyclopedia is even available to save the editor from getting up to consult the multi-volume, recent set in the library.

A good, unabridged dictionary and the city directories should be close by. Most newspapers have such books in the middle of the newsroom where everyone can get to them quickly. In addition, some editors use a thesaurus to help find the right synonym for an awkward word in a headline or story.

The following essential but less frequently used books should be easily accessible in the newspaper's library or reference room (sometimes still called "the morgue").

Congressional Directory
Area telephone books
Various kinds of *Who's Who,* such as *Who's Who in the East*
United States Postal Guide
Blue Book or *Red Book* for every state the newspaper serves—to
   provide information about state government
Dictionary of American Biography
Current Biography
A grammar, such as E. L. Callihan's *Grammar for Journalists*
Facts on File
A complete, modern atlas, such as the *National Geographic Atlas of
   the World*
American Labor Yearbook

**Guidebooks
for accuracy**

A geographical dictionary, such as the *Macmillan World Gazetteer and Geographical Dictionary*

New York Times Index, and back issues of *Times* on microfilm

Statistical Abstract of the U.S.

International Motion Picture Almanac

King James and modern editions of the Bible

Poor's Public Utilities

Moody's Railroads

Encyclopaedia of the Social Sciences

Editor & Publisher Yearbook

Bartlett's Familiar Quotations

Yearbook of Agriculture

Various sports record books and military directories

A book on good usage, such as *Current American Usage,* by Margaret M. Bryant; *A Dictionary of American-English Usage,* by Margaret Nicholson (based on a famous English work by H. W. Fowler); *A Dictionary of Contemporary American Usage,* by Bergen and Cornelia Evans; or *Modern American Usage,* by Wilson Follett

The largest newspapers have even more reference books, and Dr. Eleanor Blum's *Reference Books in the Mass Media,* a paperback, lists all of them. Some are used so rarely that many newspapers don't need to own them. However, a telephone call or a quick trip by a copy aide to a public library can put an editor in touch with almost any reference book.

4 Writing headlines

Headlines have been compared to road signs, advertising slogans, and store windows. All these have in common the task of seizing attention and putting a message across swiftly. That is what a good newspaper head does. The first and most important purpose of a headline is to inform the reader quickly. The well-written head tells him immediately the gist of the accompanying story.

When it is said that we are a nation of headline skimmers, the tone is usually derogatory. The other side of that criticism, however, is that skimming heads is what makes possible rapid comprehension of the news, since literally no one can read all the stories that are processed each day. If the heads do their most important job—rapid summary—the careful skimmer will get the general drift of events; and yet the reader can slow up for a story that may be worth more careful reading.

A second important goal of headlines is also related to their billboard function. Headlines must sell. On newstands in competitive cities, front page headlines tend to sell one paper instead of another. In monopoly cities they may push a reader to buy a paper instead of skipping it. But on the inside pages of every newspaper, headlines "sell" the reader to start reading a story. Philosophically, the primary function of the free press in a democracy is not to make money but to inform citizens. But in our society the paper must be profitable to remain alive—and lively, so the head that sells is significant.

Related to both informing and selling is a third function: grading, or evaluating, the news. One head shouts that this story is important. Another suggests quietly that this one might be of some interest as well. Even the size and style of type help communicate to the reader the importance and quality of the news—whether it is a cataclysmic disaster or a pleasant afternoon tea. A more extensive explanation of how the editor evaluates news appears in chapter 6.

A final purpose of headlines is to stimulate the reader's artistic sense. Dull heads make a dull page. But graphic artistry is much more complex than merely replacing dullness with brightness. Headlines may add to the clutter of ugly or confusing pages. But when heads are well-written and well-placed in styles that have been thoughtfully designed, the pages are clean and good-looking. Indeed, the whole personality of a paper is set by the consistent use of heads day after day, and a sudden, drastic change in heads may make a subscriber feel that a familiar friend has moved away.

Hazards in heads

One of the newspaper's most vulnerable points is the headline. Readers may grumble about the way a paper covers the news, but often their complaint boils down to dislike of the heads used.

Simple inattention can make heads which read two ways, sometimes ludicrously. Here are two published examples which seem to speak of mailmen who are stolen and belts which are hurt:

**Stolen Postman's Truck
Recovered in N. Jersey**

**Couple Hurt
Seat Belts Aid
In Collision**

Often reporters complain that their stories were all right—and it was the heads that distorted. For example, in *Editor & Publisher* James Steed of White Plains, New York, complained: "For too long the reporter has had to explain to the public and his readership that 'someone back on the copy desk' makes up the headlines and if they don't match up with the story there is nothing the reporter can do about it." Steed pointed out that since newspapers print corrections on stories, they should likewise run "a correction when the headline conveys the wrong meaning." He urged that the anonymity and immunity be removed from the headwriter who "messes up a good story by putting the wrong tag on it."

Popular confidence in a newspaper can be seriously shaken by an attack on headlines. As an illustration, when Nelson Rockefeller was governor of New York he criticized a headline in the *New York Times* before the New York Council of Churches. He said the head, which appeared on page one, misrepresented his statement about a state lottery. Rockefeller, who had long opposed such a lottery, said he had explained to a reporter that if the people approved a lottery in a referendum and the legislature then passed a bill, he would study and possibly sign it. The *Times* editor used a short, punchy verb in the head over the resulting story:

Rockefeller Bows
On State Lottery

The secondary head, or deck, on the resulting story did qualify the main head with some of the governor's words:

Would Go Along Reluctantly
With 'Reasonable' Bill

But Rockefeller contended that the main head oversimplified his position and would be all that most readers would catch. Such attacks by public figures erode the public's confidence in newspapers. Admittedly, some headwriters do distort or bias the news, or they editorialize. But there are built-in dangers in headwriting even for careful copyeditors of goodwill. They have to struggle with the limitations of both space and brief words to convey a fair and accurate impression.

Perhaps oversimplification is the greatest threat in headlines. When the news is complex, the reporter often oversimplifies in writing a tight lead. The copyeditor's job is to polish and tighten that more, if possible. Then the task requires further condensation into a half dozen words or fewer for the headline. The subtleties inevitably get squeezed out, which was at the base of Rockefeller's complaint. All that the honest desk person can do is avoid distortion the best way possible, changing the angle if necessary in order to keep from oversimplifying.

A second danger in headlines is emphasis on a minor angle of a story. A common complaint of speakers is that a reporter takes some minor point, even an aside, and builds a big story around it. The fault is compounded if the head plays up this angle, perhaps in oversimplified form. What the speaker and audience both understood as almost a joke may, for example, be blazoned:

Blasts Communist Professors

Readers who were there—and perhaps the speaker's future audiences—will then be re-convinced that newspapers distort and sensationalize.

Distrust of headlines has caused many serious newsmakers to try to avoid distortion. They greatly fear that an unusual but insignificant point will be emphasized. Some of these people have telephoned city editors or managing editors to plead for a headline that reflects the heart of the story. Others have got magazines to put a serialized book into only two or three installments, so newspapers taking excerpts from the installments would have fewer chances to exploit the bizarre. Some editors are aware of the problem, and for complicated stories they will ask the reporter either to write the head or approve it.

Another danger in headlines is overplay. Too much emphasis on a story usually results from a bad choice of type, but vivid headline words may also overdramatize. Another factor is news flow. A story which would deserve a small one-column head inside on an ordinary day may be overplayed under several columns on the front page when news is dull. According to a tradition, which is passing, a few newspapers run a full-width banner head across the front page every day. (The *banner* is also called a *streamer* or *line*.) This tradition inevitably overplays some stories. A reader might suspect that some of the banners in figure 4-1 distort the news.

Underplay, of course, is also a threat. Admitting that there is no universal standard of correct play, fair-minded editors nevertheless acknowledge that some papers do not give certain stories the space or heads they deserve. This may be the result of policy or simply of ignorance—maybe the desk person does not realize that the coup in such-and-such a country really affects local readers. Some editors knowingly order small heads on racial riots in other communities, on the theory that large heads would "stir things up" at home.

DECATUR HERALD

Vol. 96— o 11   • •   DECATUR, ILLINOIS, MONDAY, SEPTEMBER 8, 1975   2 Sections   15 CENTS

Cans, Rocks Thrown at Guardsmen

 Chicago Tribune
THE WORLD'S GREATEST NEWSPAPER

Midwest Edition

Friday, September 12, 1975

18 Pages 2 Sections   20¢

'Teachers have lost respect'

Halt school strike: Daley

'Hoover lied on JFK' *Senator charges; asks reopening of inquiry*

Story below in Column 1

Chicago Daily News

State Edition

TUESDAY, SEPTEMBER 8, 1975 • 15 CENTS IN CHICAGO AND SUBURBS • 25 CENTS ELSEWHERE

Daley sneers at Singer 'tax'

Story below in Column 3

 # Boston police battle angry busing foes

PLEASANT
Mostly sunny mild Thursday. Chance of showers at night. High 70s. Low 50s. Maps tables are on Page 10. Part 2

MILWAUKEE SENTINEL

TODAY'S CHUCKLE
Salesman to housewife: "You should have seen what I saw next door. May I step in and tell you about it?"

24 PAGES 2 PART   THURSDAY MORNING, SEPTEMBER 4, 19   • • • • • FINAL

Mideast Accord Signing Set Today

RUSS TO SNUB PEACE PACT

Fig. 4–1. Banners. Though street sales are of declining importance, a number of newspapers still use banner headlines like these, clear across the front page, sometimes with other banners or streamers above or below.

Notwithstanding criticisms, most newspaper headwriters do a good job, day in, day out. They may often compose routine or dull heads, but they are accurate. Nothing better illustrates such good, ordinary headlines—unimaginative, perhaps, but fair—than the latest edition of any large daily.

Kudos for headwriting usually go to the writers who have a flair for saying the difficult with style. The head which draws the envy of other professionals usually displays unique imagery or wit. Neophytes who want to distinguish themselves as headwriters should try to develop a colorful way of putting things in a few words; they will sometimes write corn, but they may develop a valuable talent. The headwriter should probe nearly every story for something amusing or clever that can be brought up to a headline. In some instances, as for an obituary, it would be in bad taste. So would heads that make puns out of a person's name. But some real effort to be droll or even funny will produce an occasional gem. Here, for example, are several heads which play on words cleverly:

The Reign in Spain Is Plainly on the Wane

Tigers Get 9 Goose Eggs for Easter

British Doctors Vouch for Girth Control Pill

City Has Bumper Crop of Junk Cars

Greased Youth, Trapped in Duct 7 Hours, Slips into Police Hands

Fat Policeman Is Told to Render Himself Fit

When Star Trek fans were going to have a reunion in Chicago one newspaper headlined the event:

Star Trekkies to Relive Their Future

When an electrical storm knocked out a July 4 celebration in Washington, the *Post* head told the story:

**Substitute
Fireworks
Light Area**

In England years ago Prime Minister Harold Macmillan, for the second time, fired several cabinet officials. One paper shouted:

Mac the Knife Strikes Again

The grand champion headline appeared in the *New York Daily News.* President Ford in 1975 curtly rejected New York's appeal for financial aid. The *Daily News,* in 144-point type, proclaimed:

Heads of quality

FORD TO CITY: DROP DEAD

Modern head styles

Even before the words of a head are chosen, several other decisions face the copydesk. Normally the slot person or news editor makes these choices almost automatically. Chapter 9 takes up typographic points in detail, but here are some brief guidelines on modern practice.

Type face and size

Modern newspapers use head types which are clean and easily readable, as is apparent in figure 4-3. *Sans serif* types (without decorative lines, dots, and squiggles) are popular; so-called *modern* or *transitional* types—especially Bodoni—also are often employed because their sharp, bold lines are quickly grasped. Condensed type (squeezed so that many letters will fit into a column) was popular a few decades ago, but the trend is to larger sizes. This movement toward display types which are big, legible, and attractive complicates the problem for the writer who has much to say in little space.

Number of lines

The spread of horizontal make-up, which uses multi-column heads almost exclusively, brings wide use of the single line three or more columns wide. But two-line heads are by far the most frequent. Though three lines in major headlines are still common, probably less so than a generation ago, four lines are rare.

Width

The writer is helped, however, as papers shift to wider columns and use more "magazine style" heads. The traditional "Civil War head" of numerous parts was one column wide and, it seemed, almost a column long (fig. 4-2). Today only a few papers still hold to a tradition of frequent one-column heads. Headlines of two, three, and four columns are widely employed on most American newspapers. Use of two and even three heads of six and eight columns on a single page is common.

Style

Aside from the number and length of lines, several other elements set the style of an individual headline.

One factor is arrangement of lines. Should they be even on the left or should they step in on one side? Or should they be stepped in on both sides? The answer will determine how modern or streamlined a head looks. The *stepped* head, in which succeeding lines of about the same length are stepped over to the right, is still used. But the *flush left* head—all lines evened up at the left—has been most popular for decades now, because it can be written more speedily.

If the first line is full and another line or two are stepped in to make a trapezoid shape, the head is called an inverted pyramid. This style is usually used as a subordinate part of a heading, but it sometimes stands alone as the main head.

Lines of varying length are not always set flush left, with ragged right edge; instead, centering each line can make an effective head. This style is not much used in this country but is common abroad, as in the London *Daily Telegraph*.

Stepped Head
Takes Lines of
Equal Length

Flush Left
Lines Can
Vary a Bit

Centered Head
Finds Little
Editorial Support

Inverted Pyramid Style
Rarely Used In
Main Head

Another question of style concerns capitalization. The two older forms are "all caps"—with every letter a capital—or "caps and lowers," the conventional capitalization of book titles. But the *lower case* head, which appears to be growing in popularity because of speed of setting and reading, uses only one capital letter—for the first word. Except for proper nouns, other words are entirely lower case—that is, small letters—for quick reading.

ALL CAPS SEEM
TOO BOLD
TODAY

Caps and Lowers
May Soon Be
On Uppers

Lower case rises
to prominence
in U. S.

The other most obvious variable in determining the shape or appearance of the head is the number of parts. Accompanying the main head may be one or more smaller headings to lead the eye down into the story. These parts of a headline are called *decks* (or sometimes *banks* or *drops*). The strong trend has been toward the single deck, especially in one-column heads. The *Wall Street Journal* and the *New York Times* are the only major papers that cling to the

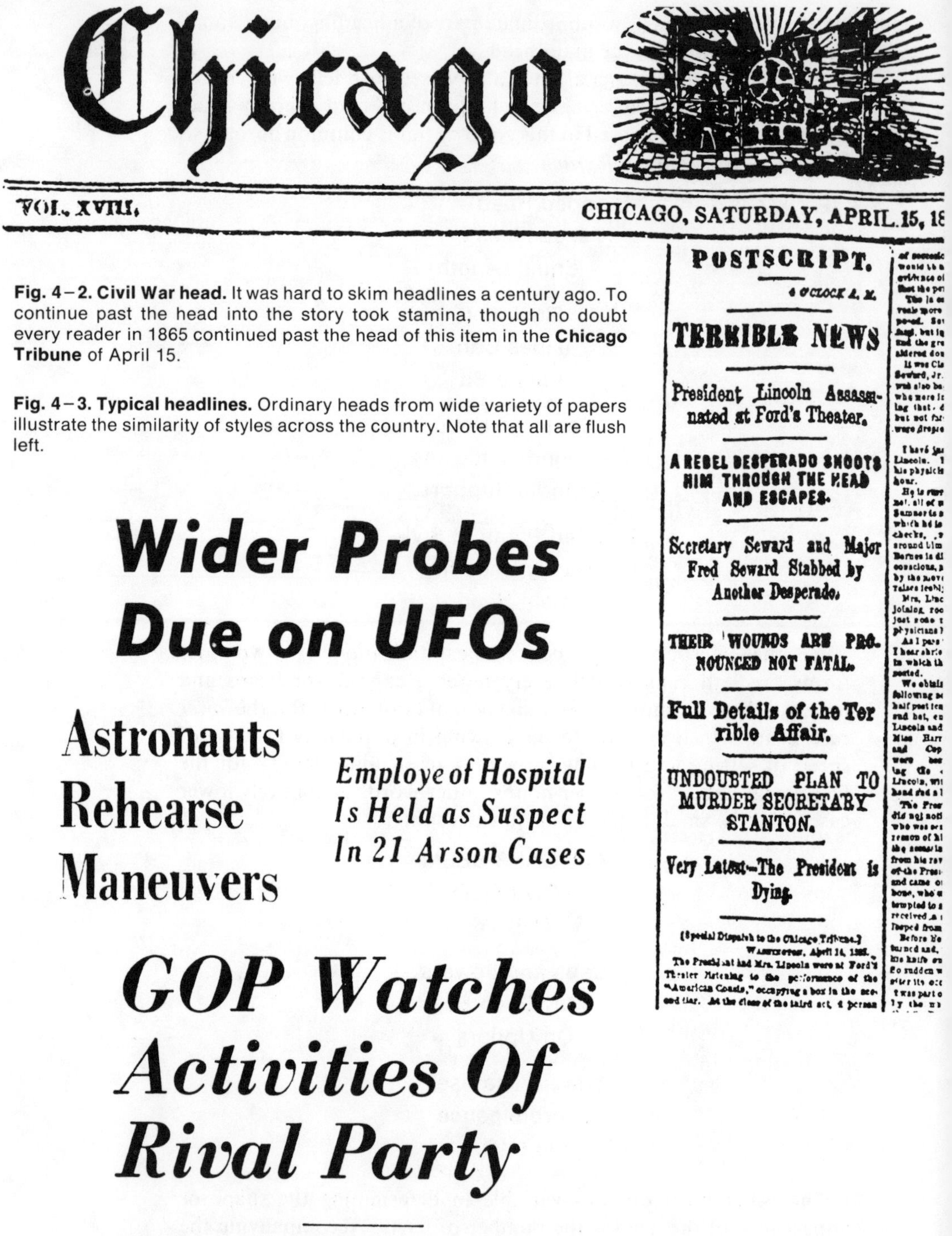

Chicago

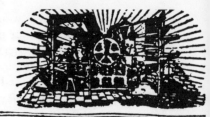

VOL. XVIII. CHICAGO, SATURDAY, APRIL 15, 18

POSTSCRIPT.

4 O'CLOCK A. M.

TERRIBLE NEWS

President Lincoln Assassinated at Ford's Theater.

A REBEL DESPERADO SHOOTS HIM THROUGH THE HEAD AND ESCAPES.

Secretary Seward and Major Fred Seward Stabbed by Another Desperado.

THEIR WOUNDS ARE PRONOUNCED NOT FATAL.

Full Details of the Terrible Affair.

UNDOUBTED PLAN TO MURDER SECRETARY STANTON.

Very Latest—The President is Dying.

(Special Dispatch to the Chicago Tribune.)

WASHINGTON, April 14, 1865.

The President and Mrs. Lincoln were at Ford's Theater listening to the performance of the "American Cousin," occupying a box in the second tier. At the close of the third act, a person

Fig. 4–2. Civil War head. It was hard to skim headlines a century ago. To continue past the head into the story took stamina, though no doubt every reader in 1865 continued past the head of this item in the **Chicago Tribune** of April 15.

Fig. 4–3. Typical headlines. Ordinary heads from wide variety of papers illustrate the similarity of styles across the country. Note that all are flush left.

Wider Probes
Due on UFOs

Astronauts
Rehearse
Maneuvers

Employe of Hospital
Is Held as Suspect
In 21 Arson Cases

GOP Watches
Activities Of
Rival Party

Only Republican Interest
Centers on Comptroller

use of heads with three or more decks. Typically the story is told in the first part, or *top,* and further detail follows in the second part, which is sometimes called simply *the deck.* (See fig. 4-4.)

As decks have declined in popularity, the *kicker* has become popular. It is a head of from one to several words, frequently with an underlining rule centered above the main head or to the left of it. Writing of decks and kickers will be considered later in this chapter.

In summary, a head in small type, narrow measure, with several decks of stepped lines looks old-fashioned. The modern head tends to be in a large and clear face, flush left and several column wide, in lower case, and accompanied by not more than one subordinate deck.

U.S. Boosts Aid for Refugees' Education
Administration Bows to Pressure but Cranston, Riles Call Rise Inadequate

Some Fathers Find Loafing Worthwhile

Jobs Pay Less Than Welfare

Fig. 4–4. Use of decks. Subordinate decks are used in various ways in relation to the main head or deck.

Head schedules

If the head writers had to ponder all these decisions for every headline, they would never get out a daily paper. Even on magazines, where longer deadlines permit debate on head decisions, many choices are routinized. On newspapers, the editors select few head styles for regular use and put them into a list or *head schedule.* This listing of headlines facilitates the choice of head and also provides a coding which permits fast communication with the printers. (See fig. 4-5.)

The typical head schedule is a graduated listing of big heads down to little. For example, a 48-point head may be called "A," a 36-point "B," a 30-point "C," and so on. Then the copyreader has only to write the letter to instruct the printer. (A "point" is one seventy-second of an inch. Seventy-two point type, then, is one inch high. Thirty-six point is a half-inch. Other details will be explained in chapter 9.)

With each heading on the schedule—or in the copyreader's memory—must be the "head count," the number of characters or units in a line. Normally this count refers to the maximum number of letters which will fit into one column, and the copyreader writes lines with a count a little below that; if the head is two, three, or more columns, one gets the count by multiplying by two, three, etc. (How copyeditors count fat and thin letters will be discussed later in this chapter.)

Here, for example, is the top of the head schedule for the *Roches-ter* (N. Y.) *Times-Union:*

Name	Character Count	Type Size Indicated
No. 2	9	(36-point Bodoni)
No. 3	10-1/2	(30-point Bodoni)
No. 4	11-1/2	(24-point Bodoni)

This means that the large No. 2 head permits up to 9 letters and spaces in a column. For two columns the count is obviously 18—perhaps a bit more, because the copyeditor gains the space of the rule between columns. The No. 3 head has slightly smaller type, so 10-1/2 units of this fit into a column. And so on. (On the copy, two lines after the number, like an equals sign, indicate a two-line head, and three lines a three-line head. Thus 4= is a two-line No. 4 head.) Or in multi-column heads a 2/36/2 would mean two columns, 36 point, two lines. A 3/36/2 indicates a head that is three columns, 36 point, two lines.

The parenthetical indication of type size in the *Times-Union* schedule is unusual. But even if a schedule does have a reminder of type size, it is important that the copyeditor memorize the faces and sizes of the heads.

In fact, too often the whole head schedule is not in print. The authors have worked for three large dailies that had no formal printed head schedules. Copydesk staffers keep the schedule in their heads, and a newcomer must learn the heads and counts from them. The better practice is to have examples of the heads run off on proof paper, distributed to concerned staff members, and posted near the copydesk.

The newcomer to a copydesk naturally learns and follows the heading system in use. To revise the head schedule takes the judgment of journalists familiar with the personality of the paper. Sometimes typographers may aid in a complete redesigning of the type dress. The general rule is to choose types which harmonize, and that usually means sticking to one family of type. The regular face is used in different sizes, and more variety is introduced by using italic, bold face, ultra-bold, and condensed versions of the basic face. Sometimes a second style of type will complement the basic one, as, for example, sans serif with a modern face. Use of three or more faces leads quickly to chaos.

Too many head sizes also will disrupt the schedule. A dozen probably will suffice for most stories. The head schedule becomes too lengthy and complicated for practical use if jammed with every head ever used. The desk then has to be prepared, and have the liberty, to create different arrangements of type for features and other special needs. Using that *Times-Union* schedule, for example,

Fig. 4–5. Headline Schedule. This is a partial headline schedule from the *St. Louis Post-Dispatch*. Single-column headlines are numbered. Multi-column headlines are made from the samples at left. Numbers in parentheses show the maximum number of characters possible per column. (The type faces are reduced to provide a manageable illustration.)

72-point (4)

Fine

72-point Italic (4)

Still

60-point (5)

Limit

60-point Italic (5)

Born

48-point (6)

Policy

48-point Italic (6)

Police

42-point (7)

Soldier

42-point Italic (7)

Confer

36-point (8)

Arrested

36-point Italic (8)

Confuse

No. 1—30-pt (9)

Policemen Caught in Cross Fire

No. 2—24-pt (11)

$5700 Gone From Offices At Stix Stores

No. 3—24-pt (11)

Switch Crews Strike Here

No. 4—18-pt (14)

Steamfitter Fund Study to Resume Monday Morning

No. 1 Ital—30-pt Ital (8)

Escaping Men Face Rifle Fire

No. 2 Ital—24-pt Ital (11)

New Officials Inaugurated A Day Later

No. 3 Ital—24-pt Ital (11)

$5700 Gone From Offices

No. 4 Ital—18-pt Ital (14)

Steamfitter Fund Inquiry Halted

a copyeditor could write a four-column headline of two lines in 36-point Bodoni, with a 24-point kicker in Bodoni Roman or Ultra. Only brief instructions to the printer would be required beyond the head schedule code.

A knowledge of type enables the copyeditor to write offbeat headlines. While one must take care not to introduce confusion and ugliness, the imaginative deskperson can create variety and freshness with unorthodox new heads, such as those in figure 4-6.

Basic rules for heads
Label heads

Many of the world's papers have accustomed readers to heads which are mere labels. A London paper, for example, may proclaim in 18- or 24-point type, "Parliamentary Debate" or "Death at Chamonix." Most American readers find such label heads dull, but an editor overseas can argue with some point that they do not give the whole story away. There may even be some tendency in the United States, as newsstand competition diminishes, for the American editor to use more label heads. Some editors see no point in insisting on heads with verbs on certain feature stories. So they use verbless heads, much like magazine article titles. The *Village Voice* in New York runs heads like these:

Wills: His and Hers May Not Be Theirs

In the absence of a will, state law determines who are one's heirs. And, legal heirs are not necessarily the people closest to the deceased.

He Led Two Lives

Heroin Bust Climaxes Five-Month Ruse by State Police Sergeant

The *Biggest* Lovers of Smallness *Are Making* Much of Little

Fig. 4–6. Off-beat heads. The copyeditor who knows his head types can create unorthodox headlines such as these, which are probably not on a head schedule.

The Return of the
Show Biz Gypsies

Down and Out at the City University

The main stream of American head-writing, however, emphasizes the punchy, dramatic, summary headline. American readers would immediately sense something wrong if they met this headline:

Punchy heads

The Congressmen Were in a Disagreement
On the Housing Legislation

It is wrong because it is past tense; it has no active verb with subject; and it has several articles. Furthermore, most of the words are too long for a conventional head.

Americans feel much more at home if they see the subject summarized this way:

Solons Split
On Race Bill

This head is in the present tense; a concrete noun is followed by a strong, active verb; and the articles have been sliced out. This same example, however, has some weaknesses of headwriting. "Solons" is *headlinese,* or jargon, which many copydesks frown on. "Split" may be read here as a verb in the past tense or an adjective, and it doubtless overstates the debate which the reporter discussed. And while "race bill" has punch, it introduces an oversimplification and perhaps even connotations which the more complex language avoids.

The severe space restrictions for headlines bring forth dozens of short words that the headline writer weaves among longer words so the heads will fit. Stewart Benedict, a copyeditor for the *Jersey Journal* in Jersey City, wrote for *Editor & Publisher* this spoof of the copy desk's short-word vocabulary.

Q.—So you work as a copy reader?

A.—Yes.

Q.—What does your work involve?

A.—Fix copy, write heads.

Q.—Are you considered a sort of executive?

A.—No. Aide.

Q.—If things go well, how do you describe your day?

A.—OK.

Q.—And, if they go badly, what emotion do you experience?

A.—Ire.

Q.—But, if you aren't quite so angry, what is your state of mind?

A.—Irked.

Q.—And if you're only slightly irritated?

A.—Miffed.

Q.—After work, when you drop into a bar to unwind, what do you do?

A.—Parley.

Q.—But, if you don't run into any of your friends to converse with at the bar, what do you do while you're having a drink?

A.—Mull.

Q.—What is your marital status, sir?

A.—Wed.

Q.—And how would you describe your wife?

A.—Top gal.

Q.—Do you and your wife ever have any disagreements?

A.—Tiffs? Sure.

Q.—What do you do about your concerns?

A.—Air them.

Q.—And what is the next step?

A.—Close them.

Q.—Do you have any children?

A.—One tot.

Q.—How would you describe your abode?

A.—Fine site.

Q.—But, back to your work. What's the first thing you do on getting a piece of copy?

A.—Eye it.

Q.—Suppose you get a story so badly done that it seems hopeless?

A.—Kill it.

Q.—But, if it can be salvaged, what do you do to the reporter?

A.—Flay him.

Q.—And what does he do to his story then?

A.—Alters it.

Q.—Do you find that your work has any drawbacks?

A.—Unquestionably. The limitations incumbent upon me to eschew polysyllabic vocabulary and linguistic esoterica are inhibiting. Frequent animadversion about my inability to transcend these aforementioned restrictions has, I fear, produced in me a somewhat pessimistic Weltanschauung. A consolation, however, is my perhaps utopian expectation that some hitherto anonymous philanthropist will establish a periodical in which only sesquipedalianisms will be tolerated.

Q.—Uh—check. Thanks.

A.—30.

Abbreviating   How do copyeditors decide what to put in the abbreviated key sentence which is the headline?

As reporters try to get the gist of the story into a lead which summarizes the event, headwriters boil that sentence to fit the count on the head schedule. In theory, at its simplest, they switch the sentence into the present tense and eliminate articles and time-place references. The remaining skeleton is typically subject, verb, and, perhaps, direct or indirect object.

Following the example above, let us say the wire carries this lead:

WASHINGTON—Congress today launched debate on the controversial bill providing for an expansion of racial integration in housing.

This lead might become a two-line head:

**Congress Debates
Housing Bill**

But since the second line is a little short, one writer might stretch it a bit by juggling grammar:

**Congress Debates
Bill on Housing**

Another might prefer to add information:

Congress Debates
Race Housing Bill

It can be objected that this head is rather general and imprecise, but the objection applies to the lead as well. The head properly condenses the lead.

Some slot people would contend that the first words of the head should carry the main punch of the story. "Congress" is dull. So they would ask the copyeditor to substitute a more powerful word:

Race Housing
Bill Debated

But this makes the verb passive, and other editors would argue that the verb must be active. Most would object to the adjective separated from the noun.

Rules and reality

This difference illustrates two points about headwriting: (1) "Inviolable" rules sometimes collide head-on, and a choice has to be made as to which is more important; (2) since tastes of copydesk chiefs vary, the headwriter has to be alert to the dictums and prejudices of each particular boss.

In the American fashion, headlines "give the story away" so skimmers can decide what they want to read in detail. But "feature heads," another whole category of headlines, give only a hint of the story. In magazines, of course, these are simply "titles." Such heads do not summarize but rather try to capture interest. They may lack verbs or subjects, as sometimes mere fragments arouse the reader's curiosity.

Traditional headlines usually go on spot news stories. Feature-head treatment best fits material like the human-interest story or the personality sketch. It may pun. It may twist a common phrase or aphorism. It may employ alliteration. As we said earlier, such heads require imaginative or witty desk people. They can also apply their talent to the occasional straight news story when a traditional summary head doesn't provide insight into the story. A clever, catchy head may do the job. Some editors, to describe this situation, have a slogan: "If you can't tell it, sell it."

An example of the "sold-not-told" head could be

Ah, There, Doomsayers!
You Forgot $42 Million

Creating the headline

"Almost anything goes" is the motto for the writer of feature heads. But copydesk traditions are quite firm about news headlines. Beginning copyeditors have to have the rules firmly in mind before they can decide which ones may be broken safely.

The previous discussion suggests the two cardinal rules of the news headline:

1. State (or imply) a complete sentence in the present or future tense.
2. Eliminate all articles and most adverbs and adjectives.

The first rule notes that to imply a complete sentence, as with an infinitive or an understood verb, is permissible:

Chancellor to Speak
At Senior Dinner

Guerrillas Aiming
for April Victory

Usually the subject of the sentence is vital to a headline, but sometimes the alert slot person will accept a head that clearly implies the subject. Here are borderline examples:

Discusses GOP
Industrial Plan

Enjoins Strike
In Second Day

Beware of heads that seem to command action from the reader. This one sounds like a plea rather than a report:

Hit Democrats'
Housing Proposal

Some editors, to whom such headlines are anathema, suggest that too much permissiveness may lead to the ridiculous:

Beat Grandma
And 3 Babies

The second rule, banning articles, also has exceptions. Sometimes a head reads and fits better with an article:

Judge Charges Teen-agers
'On the Loose' at Night

Beyond these two cardinal rules lie five other guidelines for headwriting. Most of them stem from our discussion of good and bad heads and are given here more or less in descending order of importance.

Major rules

Be accurate.   If necessary, sacrifice color and drama in a headline to avoid leaving an erroneous impression.

Accuracy may force the copyeditor to sift the story for the kernel of the news. Of course if the lead is buried, the good copyeditor revises the story so the major news at the top then draws the head from the revised lead. But an interpretive news story may properly start with a less pointed lead than a spot news story; then the headwriter has to grasp the full meaning of the story and try to summarize that accurately.

Here, for example, is the lead of a story in the *New York Times:*

> ALBANY, April 24—Evidence that the Legislature is embroiled in its adjournment rush is visible and audible this week.
>
> Absent members are being voted "aye" by the leadership to pass favored bills. Legislators cannot get copies of bills even as the bills are being passed, lobbying is rampant and many legislators have dropped all pretense of parliamentary politeness and are literally snarling at each other. . . .

The *Times* copyeditor summarized the whole piece with this head:

Tension Rises as Windup Nears at Albany

Be specific and concrete.   "One-eyed thief" is better than "robber" or "man"; "3,000 bales" is better than "cotton." One of the problems in the above illustrations about an interracial housing bill was to be more specific than just "bill." Increasingly, it is difficult to write heads that tell the story on complicated economic issues, international tensions, or environmental legislation. A single word like "economy," "accord," or "nature" rarely gets across what the subject is about. Vague, abstract words make headlines without punch. But blunt words which fit may bias.

Use strong verbs.   Avoid jelly words like "discuss" and "indicate" and forms of "to be." As in good news story style, use strong verbs in the active voice—*slash, pinpoint, reveal, assail, hit, kill.* Some otherwise good words have been used so much that good editors avoid or ban their use; these include *rap, sift, probe* and *flay.* Remember that verbs must be accurate as well as active. So perhaps *assail* should be replaced by *criticize,* or *denounce* by *chide.*

Start with the news.   The first line of the head should tell the reader what he wants to know immediately. A short noun followed by a short, active verb will usually do:

Pope Decries . . .

Teachers Revolt . . .

U.S. Shifts Lead . . .

Of the five w's used in the lead, the top line of the head summarizes the *who* and *what*.

But sometimes the body acting is less important and newsworthy, at least in a label-word, than is the body acted upon. So, as indicated already, "congress" and "legislature" as the first word of a head probably will have less pulling power than the tag for the legislation passed, as for example *pollution bill* or *teen draft act*. Though such a subject forces the verb into the weaker passive form, strength can still be given, as with *debated, argued,* or *killed*.

Punctuate correctly. Some beginning headwriters mistakenly cut out punctuation marks as well as articles. As figure 4-7 shows, punctuation is the same in heads as other copy, except that the period almost never ends a headline. Commas are often necessary, as in other writing. Semicolons join independent clauses, but a semicolon in the middle of a line splits the reader's attention. To save space and improve appearance, single quotation marks may replace the traditional double ones. The dash has many good head uses, but since words are not split at the end of the line in the heads of the well-edited paper, hyphens appear only between words.

Whether periods mark a head abbreviation is a question of the paper's style; it may Y.W.C.A. or it may be YWCA. Sometimes a paper will use periods in one group of initials but not in another, according to a tradition which the person must learn. Similarly, abbreviation is according to style. *Prof.* without the name, *yr.,* and *Dept.* are typical abbreviations that many newspapers would ban. But *Dr.* and *Rev.* and *Co.* (with appropriate names) or *Pct.* or *U.N.,* would be used without hesitation. Nicknames, like "Rocky" or "Jerry" as well as first names alone or initials only—like "FDR," "Abe" and "Teddy"—are taboo on some papers, though frequently used by others.

Shot by police, wounded youth faces charge

Fig. 4–7. Punctuating headlines. Punctuation, as in these heads, follows the conventions of English sentences, without the ending period.

SMITH SEES TALKS NEAR 'A CLIMAX'

Mrs. Dittler, 97, Dies in Hospital; Services Monday

Jersey Will Spend $30-Million on Rails

All sorts of other traditions and preconceptions hedge the major rules. One paper may avoid the verb "eye" in heads; another will use names of only the most prominent personages in headlines. But all agree that numerals may be used in heads, even to begin a line (See fig. 4-7.)

Most editors would further agree on these five minor rules: *Minor rules*

Don't split.   "Splitting" a head means dividing a natural grouping of words by the end of a line. The most heinous split puts the "to" of an infinitive at the end of one line and the verb on the next:

**Mayor Promises to
Study Rent Frauds**

Splitting prepositional phrases is almost as bad. But it is also poor practice to sever "have" or "will" from the rest of the verb, or separate an adjective from the noun it modifies. (To keep headline writers sane, editors usually allow splits in decks or between the second and third lines of a three-line head.)

Don't repeat.   A good headline, like a good sentence, avoids simple-minded repetition. **Fair Manager Tells Plans for Fair** obviously is awkward. Copyeditors also should skip awkward repetition of sounds, as in **Legislators Eye New Racing Legislation.**

One of the greatest temptations is to repeat a word from the head in the deck. Even use of a synonym sounds strained, so the deck should usually reveal a second angle.

The subject of the top head may be implied in a deck that starts with a verb. If the subject is omitted in the top, however, it must begin the deck. The following head is wrong because "investigators," not "wild animals," is the subject of "charge":

*Charge Cages
Old, Filthy*

**Wild Animals in Deplorable
Condition, Say Investigators**

This head properly handles the omission of subject:

*Probers Charge
Zoo Coops Filthy*

**Claim Wild Animals
'In Deplorable Condition'**

Don't overpack.   It is good advice to try to get many ideas into a head; good practice avoids padding and thinning. Yet one can cross a line where the head becomes so packed with ideas that the reader has trouble translating it. Piling up nouns as modifiers makes awkward heads. **State police investigators** is clear to most. **State police traffic toll investigators** is more difficult, but **State police major highway traffic toll investigators** is impossible.

Don't use headlinese.   Good English is best. As indicated already, headlinese is the language of overworked words. They may be the short, punchy verbs, so some editors object to even *hit* and *gut* as headlinese. Certain nouns, such as *cops* and *tryst,* are overworked and slangy. Stay alert to usage; when a word becomes a cliché, avoid it.

Homely words become headlinese when used for their size and not their sense. One of the most infelicitous such uses is "said" for "termed," "called," or "described as." Those who employ this poor English can argue that it is short for "is said to be," but the mind swirls at fitting in the missing words, as in this head from an Eastern paper:

Red Bloc
Trade Said
Beneficial

Called counts only one and one-half characters more than *said* and in this instance would have fit. (Words like *called* or *labeled* are considered attributive words. They indicate to the reader that someone is making a statement. Without such words the headline would become a flat statement, like **Red Bloc Trade Beneficial**, which would be an *editorial* head appropriate on the editorial page but not over news stories.)

Don't be ambiguous.   Mushy words leave mushy meanings. The many legitimate meanings of a single English word make the writer's job difficult. The verb *will,* in faulty context, may appear to be a noun, which one reader may mistake for "determination," another for "legal document," or vice versa. Humor sometimes results from unexpected double meanings.

Roberts Will Suit
Stalls over Horses

Precision is essential in heads, as illustrated by earlier discussion of Rockefeller's reaction to "bow."

Making heads fit

Fitting the letters of a head to a given space is simply a question of figuring out how many of a certain size will go into a line and choosing words with no more than that number.

In the long single line of six or eight columns, this is easy. Here one quickly determines (perhaps by counting heads in old papers) that so many letters will fit; usually it is thirty-five or more, and this means the editor has space for six to ten words. He or she adds, drops, and changes words, finally coming out with about the right total.

The problem becomes more difficult when the head must fit the space of only a column or two. The reason is not only that there is room for fewer letters but also that letters vary in width; a short space increases the importance of those variations.

Most small letters do not vary much in width. So they are simply counted as one character or unit. Some letters are wider, and regardless of the exact variation, this greater width is figured out at 50 percent for counting purposes. The small *m,* for example, is counted as 1-1/2 units, half again as big as an *a* or *b*. On the other hand, some narrow letters—such as *i*—count 1/2. Most punctuation marks also count 1/2.

Capital letters, of course, are generally wider. In the cap-and-lower head which predominates today, therefore, the basic count is 1-1/2 units for most capitals. The wide ones, *M* and *W,* count as 2, and the narrow ones, *I* and *J,* are 1.

A space must of course be allowed between words. It may be counted 1/2. Some copyeditors like to count space between words as 1 because they then feel able to crowd in more letters. But for a tight count, 1/2 is acceptable.

Here is a table for quick reference which shows "the counts" for the characters in a typical case of type:

	Count
Lowercase Letters	
All except f,i,l,m,t and w	1
f,i,l,t (remembered easily by lumping the four letters into the word lift)*	1/2
m and w	1-1/2
Uppercase Letters	
All except I,J,M and W	1-1/2
I and J	1
M and W	2
Miscellaneous	
&	1-1/2
All figures except 1	1
$ % ? " #	1
1 and . , - : ; ! ' ( )	1/2
Space between words	1/2

*In some faces *j* also counts 1/2.

The counts in this table will work for most head types used by newspapers. The copyeditor new to a paper will find out quickly whether it applies to the faces used there. The *t* may have to be counted 1 rather than 1/2, since it runs wider in some faces. The miscellaneous symbols such as the dollar sign and ampersand may vary from the count given; but they appear in a small minority of heads, and adjustment can be made when they do. Some changes may be made in the table to fit the fonts in use, and other quirks of individual faces can be kept in mind. The *Syracuse Post-Standard,* for example, uses one sans serif type with a very narrow *J* and *r*, so heads which count a shade over the maximum will sometimes, in fact, fit.

Note in these lines how the width of the letters actually varies, in spite of identical counts:

MWQ	**IJS**	**mwq**	**fijlt**	**Bodoni**
MWQ	IJS	mwq	fijlt	New Times Roman
MWQ	IJS	mwq	fijlt	Universe

Awareness of such shades of difference may help a copyeditor, pushed against a deadline, to decide to send a tight head to the composing room with a minimum of fear it will have to be sent back for rewriting.

Copyeditors work out their own schemes for rapid counting. Take, for example, this head, used by a Western daily:

Drug Offers
Leprosy Hope

The letters of the first line count this way:

D   r   u   g   O   f   f   e   r   s

1½ 1   1   1   ½ 1½ ½   ½   1   1   1

The beginner will probably count this simply by adding one number at a time: "1-1/2, 2-1/2, 3-1/2, 4-1/2, 5, 6-1/2, 7, 7-1/2, 8-1/2, 9-1/2, and 10-1/2." But the experienced editor knows that a space followed by an ordinary capital counts 2. Two *f*'s can be grouped as 1.

D   r   u   g   O   f   f   e   r   s

1½ 1   1   1   2   1   1   1   1   1

So a person can count more rapidly: 1-1/2, 2-1/2, 3-1/2, 4-1/2, 6-1/2, 7-1/2 plus 3 *(e, r,* and *s)*, or 10-1/2. Another way is to count all the letters and spaces as one: 11. If the count available is 12 or 13, no further counting is necessary. But for precision, a copyeditor can take the 11, add 1/2 for the capital *D* and subtract 1 for the *f*'s, and he gets the correct answer, 10-1/2.

To mutter "1-1/2, 2, 3-1/2, 4-1/2. . ." or to make all kinds of marks above or below a head wastes time. It is much quicker to count everything as 1 and then make the adjustments required by the thin or fat letters. In many cases a fat letter will balance a thin one, leaving the count unchanged. Beginners should learn to count at least by twos and even by fives. "Drug Offers," at a glance, counts 5 ("drug" plus a space), 10 (adding "offer"), and 11 at the last letter.

Also, since many names are in the news often, one should glance at the name and know what the count is. For example, "Burger" and "Kennedy" are frequently in headlines. One counts 6-1/2, and the other 7-1/2. By adding a count for the space, the editor can add 7 to the rest of a "Burger" head and 8 to the rest of the "Kennedy" head.

The count we have been discussing so far applies to heads that mix caps and lowers. All-cap heads are harder to read but easier to count. Papers that still use them use a different counting system.

An easy rule is: all capital letters except four count 1; M and W are now 1-1/2, and I and J are 1/2. Punctuation marks also have varied counts, though most marks are 1/2.

Graphically, the phrases of a headline are lines put together in simple designs. Obviously these designs should be chosen to please the eye. Similarity of type is important. For example, lines of very large and very small type clash. The two or three lines of a deck all should be of similar lengths. In the stepped head, for example, lines that vary no more than a unit or two will create the symmetrical design on the left rather than the unbalanced example on the right:

Making heads attractive

<pre>
          xxxxxxxxxxxx
           xxxxxxxxxxxx
            xxxxxxxxxxxx

          xxxxxxxx
          xxxxxxxxxxxxxxx
            xxxxxx
</pre>

The flush-left head was invented to overcome the problems of writing the lines to very nearly the same length, and it is true that attractive heads can be written where the lines in these heads vary three or even four units. Some papers permit more. However, too great a variation makes a flush-left head ugly too. Compare the attractiveness of these two examples:

<pre>
          xxxxxxxxxx
          xxxxxxxxxxxxxx
          xxxxxxxxxxxx

          xxxxxxxx
          xxxxxxxxxxxxxx
          xxxx
</pre>

Some editors argue that the all-cap line is more attractive than the caps-and-lower because the full-height letters create a clean, straight line on both top and bottom. Most papers still use a few all-cap headlines, but they favor mixed upper and lower case letters for legibility because we are accustomed to seeing them mixed in all our reading. To maximize readibility the usual practice is to capitalize first words of lines and all other words except articles and preposi-tions. Admittedly, such lines are ragged on top. Several recently redesigned papers have gone to a head which is mostly lower-case. Whether this very readable style of head is more attractive, because streamlined, than the more traditional kinds is a matter of taste. It does give a writer a bit more room.

While the simple, flush-left head is by all odds the most popular today, newspapers are not completely standardized in the United States. Heads can be pyramids, inverted pyramids, or centered styles. Headwriters, like magazine editors, also create special forms, especially on feature materials. The full-box head is no longer very' popular, but the three-quarter box is occasionally used. Sometimes double or shaded rules (Ben Day) are used instead of simple hair-lines or one-point rules; frequently words are inserted into the top rule, kicker-fashion. (See fig. 4-8 for examples of box rules and un-usual headline shapes.) A great advantage of cold type is that a great variety of heads can be constructed with those strips of film.

In addition to rules and boxes, black-and-white designs or shaded illustrations are often part of standing heads. (See fig. 4-9.) Usually these heads run the same day after day. But space requirements shift, and to adjust a permanent heading a copyeditor must know the type used. The *Rochester Times-Union,* for example, has a daily feature made up of short personality items. Under a three-sided box which may be three or more columns wide is the word "People" in 42 Ultra Bodoni. Each day there is a new 18-point Bodoni head alongside this word, two lines inverted-pyramid style.

Fig. 4–8. Boxed heads. Rules are used in a number of ways to dress up heads, with the three-sided or three-quarter box expecially popular for leading the eye into the story. Note the kickers cut into top rules and the varied headline shapes. (The deck of the **Wall Street Journal** head (right) is a hanging inden-tion, a shape now rare on American newspaper pages.)

The Hello Business:
Welcomers Abound
For Moving Families
• • •
But Business, Not Friendship,
Spurs the Visits by Women;
Bargaining With the Milkman

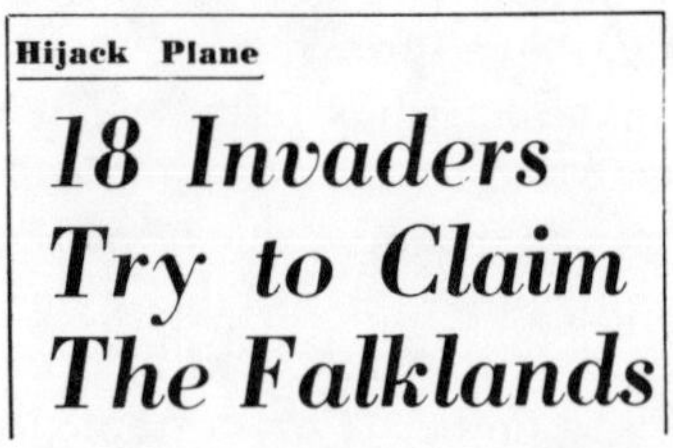

Hijack Plane

18 Invaders
Try to Claim
The Falklands

Fig. 4–9. Standing heads. Regularly used headings, often with a cut, are kept ready for quick insertion. Note that simple, clean, uncrowded heads are the most attractive.

ON-THE SCENE . . .

In Louisville

From the bookshelf

Dropping in on the Indians . . . . By Rhea Jane

News Digest   Sunny and Cool

Instructing the printer

Since each paper has its own system for preparing heads, the new copyeditor has to inquire about local rules. However, certain procedures are the same for all papers.

On paper-and-pencil desks, heads may be written at the top of copy or on a separate piece of paper, but a newspaper's procedure generally calls for writing the head on the story if the type is small. This is why the reporter has been instructed to start typing a story a third or a half of the way down the first page. If the copyeditor can quickly write the simple head above it, then the compositor can, without changing typesetting machines, set the head at the same time the story is set. For example, the smallest head on most papers is a single line of the body type set in bold face. It would be foolish to put such a head on a separate piece of paper and make the printers assemble head and story from separate galleys.

Nevertheless, most heads cannot be set on the machine which sets the story. On papers with limited facilities a printer may have to set the big heads by hand; typically, however, a machine specially suited for casting big sizes of type will be used. Either way, the copyeditor must prepare some heads for such necessities.

It is conceivable that, on a slow operation, the stories could all be set and then passed elsewhere for setting of the heads. But it is clearly much faster and more efficient to have printers working on stories and heads at the same time. For bigger heads, therefore, the copy desk typically writes out the head on a separate sheet of paper. A key word, or *slug*, is given to the story, and this same slug is put on the paper with the head. Finding these slugs in the galleys of type, the printer can assemble the proper head with each story. (The slug line is then thrown into the discard, or *hellbox*, since it has served its communications purpose. In the electronic composing room it is snipped off with a scissors and put in a wastebasket.)

Aside from the slug, the other main communication to the printer is of course about the style and size of type. Where there is a headline schedule, this information is generally given simply as the head number. For example, a copyeditor might jot "Astro" and "#2" on a story about astronauts. The copyeditor would write the same coding on the paper with the Number 2 astronaut head. (See fig. 4-10.) The slug on both story and head would then look like this in the proof:

Astro # 2

Some papers, particularly smaller ones, do not use the slug system to identify copy. They use guidelines, which are the first word or two of the headline itself. For one-edition papers the guideline saves a little time, because the slug does not have to be set on each headline. The Astro story, for example, could have been slugged MOON, CAPSULE, HEIGHT or anything else. But in the guideline system the word ASTRONAUTS would have to be marked on the top of the copy. Note the differences:

(ASTRO)

Slug system:

*2 / Astronauts seek
Space Platform*

Guideline system:

*2 / Astronauts seek
Space Platform*

When copyeditors go beyond the head schedule to create other headings, they must give concise but clear instructions to the printer. If they want a single, centered line of 24-point Ultra Bodoni, they write:

24 Ultra Bod. Cent

For two lines of 30-point Cheltenham, flush left, capitals and lower case, in a box made of rules, they may write:

*30 Chelt. fl left clc ═
3 col. box*

or even more simply:

30 chelt | *Astronauts Seek Space Platform*

The headwriter can quickly learn the shorthand of different shops. "Ultra" may be enough without "Bod." or "B" because the printer knows that the only "ultra" type used is Bodoni.

The application of the rules and guidelines may be demonstrated with the handling of an illustrative story. The slot person marks "C" at the top of copy which begins with the lead:

Writing a headline

> WASHINGTON—Both liberals and conservatives in Congress detect a sudden national mood of anxiety over the economy.

The story adds several events and comments which have contributed to the uneasy feeling among the people.

The copyeditor checks the head schedule, unless it is memorized, to find the requirements of a C head: three flush-left lines with a maximum count of 13-1/2. Mentally, the lead gets skeletonized into headline form: "Lawmakers report feelings of anxiety over nation's economy." But that leaves out the report that the change in mood is sudden. So the sentence is rephrased to make it "Lawmakers report sudden anxiety over nation's economy." So the headline writer jots down:

> **Lawmakers Find**
> **Sudden Anxiety**
> **Over U.S. Economy**

But the first line counts 15, the second is just right; the last is far too long. There is no good, short substitute for "lawmakers" so maybe a longer word would work. And it is hard to believe many would be worrying over any other nation's economy, so why not skip "U.S.?" So the revision comes up:

> **Congressmen**
> **find economy**
> **worries nation**

The slotperson may not like it, for the head does not take care of the report that the concern is sudden—and the head starts out weakly. So a rewrite is tried:

> **Nation Found**
> **Suddenly Upset**
> **Over Economy**

The head writer realizes that the head doesn't say *who* found the nation in that shape but it does reveal that the anxiety is a new feeling. The writer could decide if the last head is best. The slotperson may approve it—or send it back for still another try.

Developing the knack

Illustrations can be misleading because they may imply that the creative process is absolutely straightforward. Some headlines come easily and naturally and fit the first time, but often copyeditors have to ponder several possibilities. They should try to put the whole head together at once and make space adjustments afterward. If they tinker to make the first line perfect before going on to the rest, they will likely find it impossible to fit other lines to the first line.

Flexibility is most important. The copyeditor should try not to get the mind "locked in" on a particular wording. If a pet phrase doesn't work after a bit of trying, the head writer should stop wasting time with it and use a new approach. The key statement of the lead may have to be abandoned and the writer rethink what the story is trying to say.

Three pointers

Here are three pointers on the knack of writing heads, probably in the order the copyeditor will use them.

Try for good short synonyms when the head doesn't fit. Since English has many short verbs, these can probably be juggled more easily than others: e.g., *criticizes, assails, slaps, raps, quits.* Sometimes a slight loss in clarity is unavoidable when substituting, as when "School Superintendent" becomes "School Chief." Initials and nicknames can be used, though good desk procedure requires that they be immediately clear to readers and that they not become too numerous. (Such means may be the only feasible way to distinguish among news figures with the same name; in a city with a a mayor named Rudolph Hammerhill, headwriters would use "Rudy," "Ham," "Mayor," and other such codes to communicate the right name quickly.)

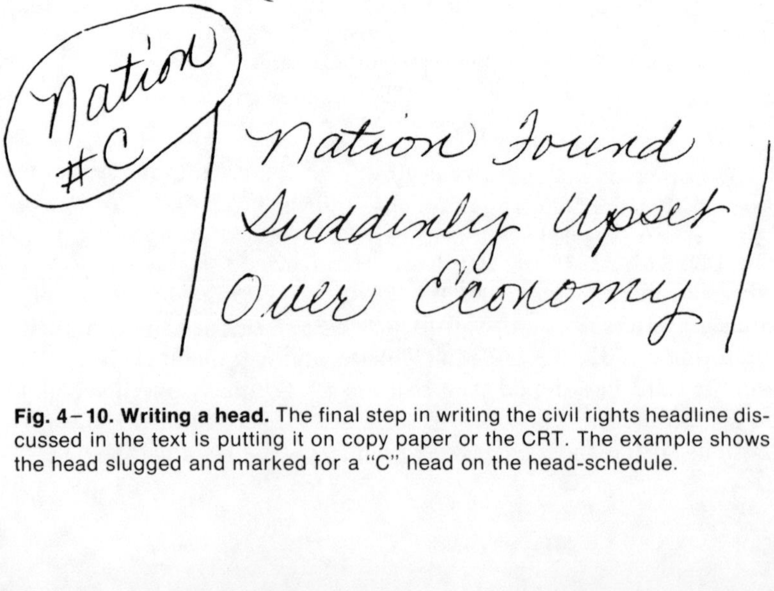

Fig. 4–10. Writing a head. The final step in writing the civil rights headline discussed in the text is putting it on copy paper or the CRT. The example shows the head slugged and marked for a "C" head on the head-schedule.

Reverse the head if the first subject-verb pattern doesn't fit.

**Rogers Sees
Venezuela Revolt**

will fit if changed to

**Venezuelan Revolt
Seen by Rogers**

Look for a new angle. In the "mood" story above, perhaps the head writer would be forced to try something different, coming up with

**Jobless rise
seen causing
wide anxiety**

Some editors think a two- or three-line head does not tell enough of the story. So they add another deck or two. See. Fig. 4-11.

Decks and kickers

Television's Trials
TV Industry Is Feeling
Government Pressure,
But the Money Rolls In

Fairness of News Questioned,
Cigaret Ads Face Banning,
Licenses Are in Jeopardy

Station Prices, Profits Rise

CHANGE ON SCHOOL LEVY

Missouri House Approves Proposed Change in Constitution to Aid in
Raising Funds—Approval by Voters Is Required
Before It Goes Into Effect

WELFARE NOD

Program Clears Legisla-
ture, Goes to Governor
for Signature

AN EMERGENCY CLAUSE

Tax and Budget Bills
Must Be Acted on
Before Midnight

Bulletins

Fig. 4–11. Two or more decks. The subordinate unit of the typical two-part head, often called simply "the deck," comes in varied styles and shapes. A few papers still use them.

Traditionally, the lower deck of an ordinary single-column head is two or three lines in inverted pyramid style:

xxxxxxxxxxxxxxxxxxx
xxxxxxxxxxxx
xxxxxxx

Graphically, it is important in the three-line deck to have the lines step in evenly, as in the step head. Head schedules give counts for the full column width, and the top line is written to fill; simply counting letters is usually satisfactory with deck sizes and counts. If the top line is 32, the full count, the second line might be 24 to 26, and the third line should then be 16 to 18. Or the second line could be 20 and the third line 8 to 10. If either the second or third line is too long or too short to provide even steps, the head will be ugly.

Content, of course, is an even more important consideration in the second deck. It should not merely repeat the top. The deck should point up or develop a new angle. The rules for keeping it active and compact are the same as for top decks.

Care should be taken that the headline reads clearly when read straight through. The lower deck may begin with a verb, but the subject then is understood to be the same as that of the top. In figure 4-12 "Black Politicians" is the subject of both the top and the lower deck. A shift to "Moynihan" as the subject in the deck would be a blooper of the same genre as a dangling participle.

BLACK POLITICIANS OPPOSE MOYNIHAN

Say He Is 'Not Acceptable' as a Senate Candidate

Fig. 4–12. Subject of deck. Space can be saved by using the subject of the main head as subject of the deck.

A less common form of deck—the hanging indention—is somewhat easier to write than the inverted pyramid:

xxxxxxxxxxxxxxxxxxxx
xxxxxxxxxxxxxxxx
xxxxxx

The top line fills, and the second line should be two or three characters shorter. The third line then can vary all the way from a few letters to the same length as the second and still be attractive. Otherwise, rules for the pyramid deck apply to this deck.

Since mid-century, the most popular lower deck by far has been the brief, flush-left head. Usually it is two lines, with the right side ragged. Though the number of words available is usually much more limited than in the old-style, inverted-pyramid deck, the content rules are the same for both; the editor constructs it just as the flush-left head is constructed. (See fig. 4-13.)

**Blast Kills
3 at Toledo
Steel Plant**

500 Flee Plant
As Fire Roars

**'Hidden'
jobless
on rise**

▽   ▽
*Rate upsets
labor office*

**Cost of Living
Up Sharply
During July**

Automatic Pay Rises
Increase Concern
Of Administration

ASSEMBLY BACKS CAREY PROPOSAL TO ASSIST CITY

Measure Is Sent to Senate,
Where Anderson's Support
Could Signal Passage

The Perini Caper

Leads That Fizzled,
And a Fatal Shootout,
Frustrated the FBI

Suspect in $1.1 Million Theft
Was a Charming Convict
Who Specialized in Banks

Party Chatter—and a Clue

Fig. 4–13. Popular deck styles. These examples show the popular styles of decks for single-column heads.

Another subordinate head is the kicker. Almost all newspapers use this device of a little head above the main head, though research shows that kickers are seldom read. They do, however, provide a ribbon of white space above the head and thus help attract attention. So they should be kept short, to maximize the white space, and their wording should stir interest with a new angle or touch. Words that would make a good, crisp flush-left second deck probably also will make a good kicker, but it should be a little more striking or dazzling than the typical deck. Sometimes dropping the verb will do the trick, for labels are more readily accepted in kickers. A conservative kicker looks like a regular head:

Detectives Spot New Evidence

But a kicker can deliver more punch:

Mysterious Time Bomb

A quote draws attention to the main head:

'I Was Framed!'

To emphasize that not all news is bad, the *Denver Post* regularly employs a little all-cap kicker, "GOOD NEWS," sometimes in red. Papers also use kickers to indicate columns or regular features. (See fig. 4-14.)

ALL'S QUIET
A Feeling Of Relief In Cicero

GOOD NEWS TODAY
CU Receives $674,000 Grant

MOVIES
Suspenseful Terror Stalks Murder Yarn

OIL MAY HAVE COME FROM SHIP
Mystery Goo Hits Beaches

Theories crack
Market antics still puzzling

Fig. 4–14. Kickers. Typically underlined, the kicker is widely used and often replaces the deck. It may give more information in verb—head form or simply add a word or two of identification. Though the type face of the kicker may virtually match the head or be markedly different, it usually represents a shift to italic or caps.

As the flush-left head and kicker have flourished, the crossline has virtually died out. This headline element is a single column-wide line, typically in caps, that appears with four or more decks, usually sandwiched between two inverted pyramids. Copyeditors on the few papers which use crosslines can quickly pick up their rules, but it may be generalized that this form summarizes a new angle with a present-tense verb, just as other subordinate decks do.

Subheads and jumpheads

One form of head, widely used both yesterday and today, is the *subhead*. Ordinarily it is simply two or three words of boldface, the same size as the body type, in the body of a story.

There are two schools of thought about handling the body of a story. One group of editors wants to break it into short "takes" with subheads every three or four paragraphs. The paragraphs not next to subheads may be set boldface and indented. The other school contends that such typographic devices tend to make stories harder rather than easier to read. These editors advocate long, unbroken stretches of body type, with few subheads. The spread of horizontal makeup patterns, which reduce the amount of unbroken gray body type, supports the second school. Many papers, of course, will choose a middle ground and use a moderate number of subheads.

Rules for the subhead are much the same as for major heads —present tense, no articles, active voice, and so on. Some papers permit a simple label of two words, because their primary concern is to break up type. Research shows their major practical value is this graphic purpose; still, at least for a minority, well-written subheads can help a reader find parts of a story that stimulate him to read the whole piece.

Except on rare occasions, the subhead should refer to the paragraph immediately following. Few things frustrate a careful reader more than to have curiosity piqued by a good subhead and then have to search down two or three paragraphs to find this angle.

The copyeditor usually writes the subhead right in the copy at the appropriate place. Then the copyeditor marks the margin "sub" or "ffclc" (full face caps and lower case) or simply "BF" (boldface). He or she may use brackets to indicate centering, but printers usually follow subhead style unless directed otherwise. (See fig. 4-15.)

The declaration contained, apart from the pledge by the two countries to abjure force, various steps toward normalizing their relations.

Peoples Kept Apart

However, except for the withdrawal of troops to positions held before fighting broke out and an exchange of ambassadors, there has been no other significant progress. The peoples of the two nations still live

---

countries to abjure force, various steps toward normalizing

their relations. *Peoples Kept apart*

However, expect for the withdrawal of troops to posi-

tions held before fighting broke out and an exchange of

Fig. 4-15. Subheads. The typical subhead is written into paper copy this way. A designation such as "BF" or "ffclc" may be used instead of "sub" to indicate boldface is to be used. An editor using a CRT types in any subheads.

As type sizes have increased, subheads have grown bolder. Some stories, especially in wide measures, may be broken up with two-line flush-left heads in 12-, or 14-, or even 18-point bold italic.

Dingbats—typographic designs such as round dots (bullets) or stars—sometimes accompany a subhead. White space is another important break-up element—around subheads, with dingbats, and sometimes simply by itself. These attention-getters should be used with restraint, for too many will annoy rather than attract the reader.

A number of papers make the first two or three words of a paragraph boldface caps with a break of white space or three bold dots and space just above this paragraph. (See fig. 4-16.) A few papers, in special sections, use the magazine-style printing device of *initial letter* to kick-off major feature stories. This device is a beginning capital several points bigger than the text type and may even be used to start paragraphs in the body of articles, especially on editorial pages.

State Department and White House.

Weary of Work Going for Nought

The arrangement has been zealously adhered to by the President. There has been no break over a fundamental policy issue. Goldberg,

accept offers of help in crossing the border.

* * *

One Cuban woman recalled her stay in Mexico City with

descent in the area. Most speak Russian.

Sister Ships at Dock

The Fedor Litke and the Alexy Chirikov are 300-foot sister ships built to

mountaineers, will name nine men.

To Write Constitution

The a s s e m b l y will be charged with turning out a

said the revolutionary teenagers are under direct control of the Mao-Lin faction.

PAPERS BACK DRIVE

It went on to say that "until very recently 'anti-Mao ele-

tion already taken has moderated the growth of bank credit.

ACTION EXPLAINED

"However, in view of increasing pressures on prices stem-

would have to be amended to permit the h i g h -r i s e buildings on the waterfront.

● Jack V. McKenzie, former data processing man-

learned to listen to the strident voices.

NOR DID HE ever manage to convince the black community that he was con-

of advances would be kept to narrow bounds.

THE STRONG performance of blue chips was cited as one of the reasons why

moves with real estate dealers prove unsuccessful.

● ● ●

KING SCHEDULED a strategy meeting for tonight to evaluate today's activities and

Fig. 4–16. Subhead styles. While the typical subhead is probably still boldface caps and lowers, centered, newspapers use many other devices to break up copy, as illustrated. Some papers are dropping subheads. But where they do, copyeditors must be sure to use horizontal make-up to keep the strips of type short, or to work out other methods to prevent the columns from looking gray, old-fashioned, and forbidding. Note in the bottom row how the importance of division increases, left to right, by the addition of boldface, space, and dingbats.

Stories continued inside the paper need some heading for the continuation, or *jump*. Formerly the *jump head* was the front page head, or very like it. Modifying this tradition, some papers now use a smaller head for the jump. It typically has a "better count" than the one on the front page, and the copyeditor may be able to get ideas and precision here which were abandoned in writing the major head. (A reverse-plate "logo"—white letters on a dark gray background—sometimes helps the eye spot the jump.)

The jump word is often a single key word. It may be employed with a jump head, but more often it stands alone. Like the slug, this word should distinguish the story from all others that day. The jump word is set in larger type or caps; and a box, rules, or white space should make it easy to spot. (See fig. 4-17.)

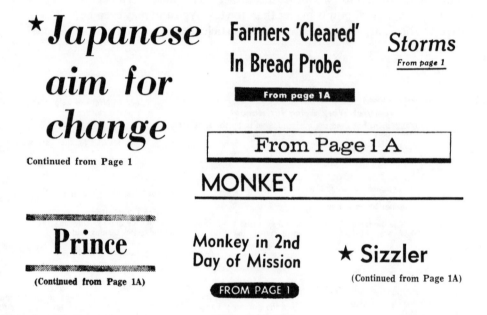

Fig. 4-17. Jumps. Editors have developed ingenious heading devices for inside pages to help readers find continued stories. Regular heads are often used to emphasize the news content of these pages. Many editors also use a gimmick, such as a reverse plate, so that the reader's searching eye can spot the jump quickly. A slug word, perhaps with rules, is especially attention-getting.

This discussion of headlines has moved from theory to the nuts and bolts of head counts and then to the lowly subhead and jump head. A copyeditor may similarly leave broad principle behind and become involved in the minutiae of quick writing and fast counts—"anything that fits." Professional editing, however, keeps to the high purpose of the newspaper. Even though a head must fit a space and flag attention, its main purpose is to inform quickly and truthfully. And the best headwriter produces such accurate heads so regularly that applying ethics becomes as habitual and automatic as counting *m* as 1-1/2.

5 Makeup

Good news coverage, news selection, editing, and headline writing are four of the five essentials of an excellent newspaper. The remaining element of excellence is good typographical design—the choices of type and the placement of type and pictures. *Makeup* is the designing process; *layout* and *dummying* are part of makeup but the terms are loosely used to refer to the whole process.

Good design attracts readers and makes their reading easier. A well-designed newspaper encourages readers to look at every page. They will find that their eyes do not have to squint to read the material and that the various blocks of type are arranged in a pleasing way.

There is no set way of doing this, any more than there is a set way of painting a picture. Yet as painters learn to understand form, color, and highlights, designers of newspapers learn the principles of readability and attractiveness. They use findings in art and psychology to test intuitions about what makes pages appealing. Researchers have found that today's reader won't take the time to read small type, so body type sizes have been increased to 9- or 10-point on the better designed papers. Researchers have also discovered that moderately large headlines of both capital and small letters are easier to read than those in all caps. The better papers, then, use headline types that are easy to see, but are not so large they shout at the reader. Many papers, as noted in the previous chapter, have put all headlines in lower case, capitalizing only the first word and any proper nouns. These moves reflect our total experience with print and handwriting: words are made up mostly of small letters. Designers believe we are more content following familiar patterns.

Modern newspaper designers, in general, have decided that much typographical ornamentation hampers readership. To separate stories from one another, they reject stars, dashes, asterisks, and cutoff rules in favor of ribbons or blocks of white space. This trend toward "clean" layout also has eliminated most headline decks.

The reverse-6

Some researchers have found that the eye tends to scan a page in a line that resembles a reversed number 6. The reader looks toward the upper left of a page first, shifts across to the right, to the lower right, to the lower left, and then loops to the center of the page.

Why, then, do newspapers put their best stories in the upper right, the number two position? Custom, or habit. For years newspapers ran banners on page one. When reading English, people move their eyes from left to right. When they finish reading the banner, their eyes are at the right of the page. Editors argued it was foolish to send the reader back to the left to read the story, so the story "read out" of the banner down the right column. Most papers have nearly given up the banner but still cling to putting the lead story in the upper right. A few have discarded the idea and make up page one with the main story at top left and other strong material at the lower left.

Though many papers cling to the upper right lead, almost all exploit the rest of the reverse-6 findings. Strong typographical display in the lower right and lower left, including the placement of pictures in those positions, support stories with multi-column headlines centered on the page. These stories hold the eye at the end of its sweep around the reverse-6.

Some researchers discount the reverse-6 theory. They contend that readers start reading a newspaper page as they start a book page, at the upper left. Their eyes then tend to move diagonally across and down the page until they reach the lower right, where they expect to turn the page. This diagonal theory assumes that the eye is lured right and left, up and down, to see all parts of the page, rather than moving in a straight line. Defenders of the diagonal theory argue that major headlines or pictures attract the eye out of the diagonal path.

No matter what the theory, all agree that attention should be given to placement of good-sized heads, blocks of copy, and pictures in every section of the page. Generalizations about makeup are usually based on the complicated front page, but they hold good for an inside page, depending on how much space goes to advertisements. (See figs. 5-1 through 5-15).

Strengths of
horizontal makeup

The grasp of new information about eye movement and design principles led to an introduction of what is called *horizontal* makeup. Previously, blocks of type and headlines invariably moved down a column. Now they can move across the page, sometimes taking up a rectangle of space only three or four inches deep but four, five, or even eight columns wide. This method not only attracts the eye but also facilitates the placement of type. Instead of restricting body type to only one column, the horizontal method allows it to be juggled in many different measurements. For example, body type under a five-column head may be two inches deep in the first three columns and four inches deep in the last two. It can even be jockeyed from one column to another so it all fits the page.

The opposite of horizontal, or course, is *vertical*. Most papers a century and more ago ran all stories with single column headlines for reasons related to the fastest presses of that day.* Body type went steadily down under the head to the bottom of the page. When a story ended at mid-page, another single column headline and story began beneath it. A story that reached the bottom of the page with some part left over was continued, or jumped, to another page.

Vertical makeup suited the fast presses but not the reader's eye. The many ribbons of vertical lines made the paper look narrow and skinny. The bottoms of vertical pages looked washed out and dull. Vertical makeup also highly restricted the placement of type, because all body type for one story had to go in the one column. If it did not fit, the only solution, except for jumping, was to throw away part of the story.

Horizontal makeup, which is now easy to use with modern presses, means a fairly long story can appear complete on one page, without a jump. While the stories often are long, they do not seem lengthy. The few inches of copy in each column encourage the reader to skim the whole story rather than to stop with the first few paragraphs. The avoidance of jumps is desirable because readers get impatient at having to turn from page one to page twenty-one and back to page one again. Only the most determined readers will make that double jump.

Some years ago newspaper designers took a careful look at the American newspaper and realized that the narrow columns looked jammed with type. The reader had to focus carefully to read the stories. And a rather simple test showed that most readers did not read one line at a time. The narrow, 11- or 12-pica column was a trifle long for one glance and not quite long enough for two. (Since a pica is one-sixth of an inch, a 12-pica column is two inches wide.) So the six-column—or *optimum format*—newspaper was born. The columns widened to 16 picas (two and two-thirds inches), which allows rapid, comfortable reading and permits better head counts— resulting in more accurate headlines.

Two other modern styles increase readability by providing more space between columns. The *W-format* divides the front page into six columns of 11 picas and a seventh of 16 picas. The leftover half column is distributed in white space to divide the columns. Similarly, the *seven format* has seven columns of copy on an eight column page. The extra column allows the news columns to be separated by a full pica of space.

These changes provide more openness on the pages and are in line with the growing tendency of newspapers to report the news in greater detail. Page one of the six-column paper can use two or three

---

*In 1848 the New York newspapers began using a type-revolving press invented by Richard Hoe. Cylinders with curved iron beds circulated the type itself at high speeds (in anticipation of today's solid stereotype plates). Wedge-shaped column rules held the type in place, and any break in those rules would send the type flying all over the room.

pictures and five or six stories. This method leaves plenty of good stories for the inside. Readers now sense that they are getting a lot of information for their money—and they are. Most users of this format try to put out a newspaper that looks like a big magazine and gives readers both the news of the *day* and the news of the *times.* That is, readers get, clearly spread out before them, the news of the previous twenty-four hours. In addition, they receive information about trends in local and world events that may have been going on for the last three months or the last three years.

Basic goals of makeup

While *optimum, W-format,* and *seven column* are relatively new terms for makeup, some older descriptive phrases deserve attention. Applying labels is difficult because one category shades into another. Those who actually do the day-to-day job of designing pages may rarely use the names of the categories, if they ever heard of them, for editors make up pages by judgment or "feel," not by labels.

Everyone concerned with makeup does refer frequently to *balance.* The term is so common that it has come to describe a particular kind of makeup. In this system the typographic display on one side of a page balances, or nearly balances, a similar display on the other side. In the early days of newspapers, only the top of the page was balanced, but eventually the whole page fell into this pattern. A picture often occupied the exact center, with headlines of equal size on either side. At the bottom would be a double-column headline on one side and another double-column head on the other. The idea was to achieve perfect symmetry (See fig. 5-1.)

Perfect balance, however, has serious drawbacks. In judging the day's news, editors usually decide that one story is clearly better than all others. They want to say so by giving it the biggest headline. But in *balance* they must give the same headline display to a lesser story.

Strict balance has another shortcoming. The eye finds it hard to focus on anything so exactly proportioned. A balanced page calls attention to a pattern but not a point. Every cluster of type is tempered by another exactly the same. Some critics have contended that looking at a balanced page is a bit like looking at a checkerboard.

For these reasons formal balance has been replaced largely by *contrast-and-balance,* or *imbalance,* or *dynamic balance.* This method of many names includes balance but not exact counter-balancing. A two-column picture may balance a three-column headline in the adjoining quarter page or quadrant. Or a two-column headline may adequately balance a three-column head. In this system, the lead story is clearly the lead, as it has the biggest headline. Most American papers now use this kind of makeup because it provides a certain symmetry, a focal point for the eye, and an opportunity for the editor to give special emphasis to some stories. (See figs. 5-2 through 5-11.)

THE MILWAUKEE JOURNAL

44 Pages—4 Sections | *96th Year; Founded 1882* | Tuesday, January 17, 1978 | *© 1978, The Milwaukee Journal* | Latest Edition ††

Many Feel Rate Bias of Insurance Firms

(c) New York Times Service

Washington, D.C. — Irma Carroll, widowed after 28 years of marriage, decided to switch auto insurance companies when her insurer, Geico, closed its local office and she figured that "a widow might need a little more help."

So she went to a store, asked how much an auto insurance policy would cost, and was told "about $189."

"Everything went all right," she recalled, "until they got to whether I was married or single, and I said I was a widow. And she said, 'Oh, my God,' in this case it will go up about $200."

Mrs. Carroll is one of many consumer, government and industry witnesses ready to testify before the Citizens and Shareholders Rights subcommittee of the Senate Judiciary Committee, which is investigating reports of discriminatory practices by insurance companies.

Sen. Howard Metzenbaum (D-Ohio), chairman of the subcommittee, opened the hearing Tuesday by saying Congress must reconsider its 1945 exemption of the insurance industry from federal antitrust laws.

Insurance underwriting manuals obtained by the subcommittee show that agents writing standard auto and homeowner insurance policies are instructed to reject applicants because of their occupation, sex, marital status and other factors that the manuals concede are subjective and unsubstantiated.

Beauticians and manicurists (unmarried) are considered poor risks. So are musicians, farmworkers, professional athletes, waiters, cooks and military personnel under 25. So are those with divorces, particularly men.

The Continental Insurance Companies manual observes, that without any data, the firm is convinced that persons in-

Turn to Rates, page 7, col. 1

Their Collie Proves He's a Dandy Tracker

South Deerfield, Mass. —UPI— At an age when most dogs are content to curl up in front of a fire and bask in the affection due their advanced years, Dandy is still chasing the ladies.

The 10 year old wily collie just returned from a 125 mile, 49 day trek from Preston, Conn., to South Deerfield.

"He's a wanderer. You might call him a real woman chaser," Lyman W. Griswold of Greenfield, Mass., the dog's owner, said Monday. "That's probably what got him lost down there in Connecticut."

Griswold said his collie got lost while he was visiting friends in Preston Thanksgiving Day. And until he limped into South Deerfield last week, that was the last time the dog was seen.

Somehow Dandy made the trip on his own steam, not much the worse for wear.

Snow, Rain, Winds March Across US

UPI and AP

Bad weather gripped most of the nation Tuesday as a parade of at least three storms marched from coast to coast.

In the West, a howling windstorm Monday ripped off the roofs of a high school gymnasium in Sacramento and a baseball park in Tracy, Calif. The swollen Russian River forced evacuations in California's Sonoma County, and high water near Red Bluff, Calif., drove rattlesnakes out of their lairs and into trees.

A second storm ranging from the Rockies to the Ohio Valley and as far south as Texas snarled traffic and closed schools. Louisville, Ky., reported 16 inches of snow Tuesday, a record for the city. Kentucky state police called Interstate 65 an ice skating rink. Farther south, Tennessee and Georgia had sleet.

In the East, a third storm spread snow across Pennsylvania, New Jersey, Delaware, Maryland and Virginia Tuesday. The National Guard was called out to help restore power to 100,000 suburban New York City customers as the storm headed north into New York and New England.

The storm battering the Midwest and Great Plains appeared to cause the most havoc. Wisconsin, however, escaped the blast as the storm passed to the south of the state, socking Illinois and Indiana.

Hundreds of schools were closed across the Midwest Tuesday, and motorists slowed to a crawl or went skidding into ditches in Kansas, Oklahoma, Missouri, Arkansas, Illinois and Indiana.

Evansville, Ind., was buried in 13 inches of snow Tuesday, and the University of Evansville, schools and industries were closed.

In Illinois, Cairo, at the southern tip of the state, was hit especially hard, with 15 inches of snow. Police gave rides to pedestrians, and businesses closed.

Managing Editor Jay Scott of the Cairo Evening Citizen said only three employes of the afternoon newspaper had shown up by midmorning Tuesday and that it was uncertain if the paper would publish.

The storm caught Springfield, the Illinois capital, without salt because a salt carrying barge was stuck in a Mississippi River lock at Alton, Ill. Street crews used hot sand to clear intersections.

Both houses of the Mis-

Turn to Weather, page 2, col. 8

Maier Blasts Times Story on Joblessness

By Charles J. Sykes
of The Journal Staff

Attacking The New York Times for what he called a slur on the City of Milwaukee and blasting the Labor Department for poor presentation of unemployment statistics, Mayor Maier released a detailed study Tuesday on the problems of nonwhite unemployment in Milwaukee.

Maier's study claims that Labor Department statistics, as reported in The Times, exaggerated the problem in Milwaukee and misrepresented the official figures on nonwhite unemployment.

The mayor's study also concluded that the problem of nonwhite unemployment here could be traced not to racial discrimination but to the division of the metropolitan area between suburbs and central city.

Conference Called

Maier's study, which was scheduled to be unveiled at a press conference Tuesday afternoon, charges that The Times article, which said Milwaukee had the highest nonwhite unemployment in the US, ignored such important and related figures as the number of persons who have given up the search for work. Milwaukee has the third smallest number of such discouraged workers among nonwhites of the cities surveyed, Maier said.

With that factor included, he said, Milwaukee has only the eighth highest nonwhite unemployment rate among the nation's 16 largest cities, with an unemployment rate of 21.7%, compared with rates of 31.1% in St. Louis, 29.3% in Cincinnati, 28.6% in Newark, 28.6% in Pittsburgh, 23.5% in Detroit, 22.5% in Kansas City and 22.4% in Miami.

Refiguring Data

Maier also said The Times article included the entire metropolitan statistical area and not just the city.

If only city data are included, Maier said, Pittsburgh has

Turn to Mayor, page 5, col. 1

On, Wisconsin

An Editorial

Beware of Pushing Feeble Student Out the Door

Look what they're planning in Connecticut. Then look again. A new "opportunity" for students to get out of high school a couple years early by passing some tests isn't necessarily an opportunity at all. Wisconsin ought to be wary of charging off in the same direction.

Connecticut next fall will join California and Florida as states allowing students who are below the normal compulsory attendance age to leave school. They will have to pass the nationally standard (but none too rigorous) General Educational Development Test, plus a new test being developed for Connecticut.

This latter test gives concern, for it is being designed to measure "life coping skills," such as making change with money and filling out a consumer complaint. An official says it will provide "an alternative to a high school degree for students who are likely to drop out."

An alternative, or an open door? It's no secret that some educators would like to just get rid of apathetic, trouble making students. That's easier than developing (and paying for) meaningful educational alternatives for them.

We have no objection to — indeed, we welcome — a trend toward more *individual* evaluation for admission, graduation and promotion through the grades. That makes far more sense than mere chronological age. But such a system should adhere to respectable standards of intellectual competence and include an array of learning alternatives to meet the abilities and interests of different pupils. Little is gained if dropping out is facilitated through use of tests that merely offer an illusion of proved competency.

DUCKS IN FLIGHT — Hundreds of ducks took to the air when the car ferry Badger entered Milwaukee's Harbor after a trip across Lake Michigan. The ducks congregate in large numbers on the expanses of open water created by the boat's path through the ice.

—*UPI Photo by Ralph Schauer*

1 Year After Gilmore: Gallows Doors Still Shut

UPI, AP, Washington Post

Salt Lake City, Utah — One year ago Tuesday convicted killer Gary Gilmore nervously told a Utah State Prison firing squad, "Let's do it" — and the riflemen shot him dead.

Opponents of capital punishment predicted that Gilmore's death, brought on by his refusal to appeal his first degree murder conviction, would set off a wave of executions across the United States.

But the death of the 36 year old Gilmore remains as the only legal execution in the United States in 11 years. And, although he died on Jan. 17, 1977, Gilmore continues to haunt Utah's courts and the lives of the people who dealt with him.

"There are not many people like Gary Gilmore who volunteer to stand up and be shot," said Shirley Pedler, executive director of the American Civil Liberties Union in Utah, which is planning a candlelight vigil on the anniversary of the execution.

"We all predicted there would be a rash of executions," she said. "I am delighted we haven't killed anyone in the intervening year. But that just means the legal process is terribly slow. There is still a move to execute people."

Says Joel Berger of the NAACP Legal Defense and Educational Fund:

"Even the most advanced

Turn to Penalty, page 7, col. 1

Gary Gilmore

Bingo Players Line Up Despite Slim Chances

By Mildred Freese
Journal Consumer Affairs Reporter

Since Bingo Nite began, Gary Miller and a neighbor, Edith Johnson, say they have been in every Kohl's Food Store in the Milwaukee area at least once. Miller figures he has probably spent about $100 on gas and on extras he buys when he goes into the store. Of course, he added, the things that he buys are cigarets and other things that he will use.

Miller won $1 twice and extra tickets on Bingo Nite nine times, but that's not close to breaking even.

He's trying. Each day he and a friend keep trying to get winning numbers.

Woman wins first $1,000 prize. Story on Page 1, Part 2

It bothers him a little that somebody who is not trying as hard as he is might unknowingly throw away a winning number. They apparently are interspersed among 13 million tickets.

In their game promotion, Kohl's Food Stores are committed to redeeming 75 tickets for $1,000. But if some tickets are not turned in, there will not be that many winners, a Kohl's spokesman said.

Miller started playing because he had enough time and needed a new project. He crushed both arms in a punch press accident in 1970 and is not employed. Now the bingo

Turn to page 7, col. 1

Retiree Wins Age Bias Case

A Brookfield man who was forced into early retirement by an Illinois firm has been awarded more than $156,000 in damages by Federal Judge Myron L. Gordon.

The decision was issued in favor of Harold W. Buchholz after a trial without a jury conducted by Gordon.

The judge ruled that the Symons Manufacturing Co. violated federal laws against age discrimination when it forced Buchholz out of his sales job in 1974.

Buchholz was then 62.

The company denied that Buchholz was forced out because of age and claimed that his work was unsatisfactory. Gordon said evidence showed a clear pattern of illegal discrimination and that he believed statements by Buchholz, not those of corporate officials.

Buchholz worked for the firm at its headquarters in Des Plaines for several years before being transferred to the company's Waukesha office as an account manager.

He received several commendations for exceeding sales quotas, but starting in late 1972, officials began transferring his accounts to younger men and referring to his imminent retirement.

Buchholz protested that he had no plans to retire, but his objections were ignored.

On Feb. 1, 1974, all of his accounts were taken from him and he was told that if he did not retire, he would be fired.

Buchholz testified that he

Turn to Suit, page 6, col. 3

The Weather

National Weather Service

Milwaukee — Occasional cloudiness tonight and Wednesday, periods of light snow near lake; low tonight around 20 near lake to 10 inland; high Wednesday in teens to lower 20s.

Hour	5	6	7	8	9	10	11	12
Temp.	20	20	20	20	21	21	22	25

Wisconsin — Partly cloudy, cold tonight, occasional periods of light snow near lake; lows −5 to −20 most sections, mostly cloudy Wednesday, chance of snow northwest, partly cloudy, chance of light snow southeast; highs 5 to 15 most sections.

Weather map, Page 6, Part 2.

In The Journal

Amusements, Movie
Ads ....Pages 2-3, Accent
Business News ....Page 10, Part 2
Deaths ....Page 2, Part 2
Movie Review .....Page 3, Accent
Opinion ....Pages 8-9
Picture Page ....Page 4, Part 2
Spectrum ....Page 5, Part 2
Sports ....Page 7, Part 2
TV-Radio ....Page 6, Accent

Consumers Must Pay More for Energy

Energy: A PERSONAL VIEW

By Paul G. Hayes Journal Science Reporter

Like it or not, the price of US petroleum and gas must rise. But not for the reasons the oil and gas companies say.

They want the profits. They say they will use them to develop domestic supplies. But they don't just mean oil and gas, which are insufficient for our long term needs.

They also mean uranium, coal and other forms of energy. They intend, in short, to expand their control over domestic energy supplies. And that's dangerous.

With big oil owning larger shares of coal and uranium, the companies could make sure the price of one fuel would not undercut the price of another.

Our only protection would be greater public regulation through large watchdog agencies.

Nonetheless, the prices of petroleum and gas should rise. And the reason they should rise is to dampen our outrageous consumption and to prompt serious energy conservation.

In that regard, it wouldn't make any difference whether the prices rose through taxation, as the Carter administration proposes, or through decontrol, as the industry wishes.

From the consumer's point of view, it would be good if supply and demand could set the prices of fuels. Among other things, that would eliminate the waste and irrational compromise that always accompany publicly controlled prices.

The ideal solution, in my opinion, is to decontrol the prices of oil and gas, but also to order the large oil companies to divest themselves of their holdings in other fuels.

Our present low prices are an irrational response to our growing dependence on foreign oil and a wonder to other industrial nations, who tax their fuels heavily, and to OPEC nations, who supply us with half our oil.

"A nation running an enormous (trade) deficit in order to avoid proper energy prices, and in order to keep the temperature of its homes and offices cooler in summer than in winter, does not make economic sense to the rest of the world," the London Times editorialized recently.

Federal controls keep the price of US oil below the world price. Natural gas sold across state lines costs a fraction of its value, but more expensive gas is inefficiently burned in electricity generators in producing states.

Natural gas distributors, including the Wisconsin Gas Co., still reward big users with rates based on the principle of the more you use the less it costs. Electricity is still hawked along those lines, although that's changing in Wisconsin.

In effect, the cost of petroleum has been dropping in the US recently insofar as prices haven't increased as

Turn to Energy, page 6, col. 5

Fig. 5–1. Semi-modular. The *Milwaukee Journal* blends modules with balance in this issue. Note that the *Journal* clings to the eight-column format with column rules.

Today in Sports Plus | The countdown to Super Bowl XII | Profiling Tom Sanders, the coach of the Celtics | How to get there —via snowshoes | Reviewing college hockey, basketball

Guide to features

ARTS/FILMS	19	ECONOMY	24
BRIDGE	30	EDITORIALS	14
CLASSIFIED	39	HOROSCOPE	30
COMICS	29	LIVING	17
CROSSWORD	29	SPORTS	33
DEATH NOTICES	38	TV/RADIO	31

Lottery number, Page 30

The Boston Globe

's no escape
FRIDAY—Snow, low 30s
SATURDAY—Snow mixed with rain
HIGH TIDE—2:07 a.m. 2:27 p.m.
FULL REPORT—PAGE 30

Vol. 213, No. 13© 1978, Globe Newspaper Co. FRIDAY MORNING, JANUARY 13, 1978 Telephone 929-2000 Classified 929-1500 Circulation 929-2222 80 Pages—20 Cents

Indochina intrigue: What's with that yacht?

By Thomas Oliphant
Globe Washington Bureau

WASHINGTON — The terse dispatch from Indochina three months ago yesterday was ominous:

"Two gunboats fired on a US yacht off Vietnam, rammed the vessel and then apparently seized three Americans aboard in the first such incident since the US freighter Mayaguez was captured in 1975, US officials said yesterday."

Would there be a retaliatory bombing raid? Would the Marines be sent? Was a serious crisis in the offing?

Yesterday, US and Vietnamese officials confirmed, the 39-foot craft, the Brillig, and its three crew members were finally permitted to set sail from Vietnam after a three-month confinement.

Against the ominous background of the first official word of their seizure, it was a strange 90 days. Vietnamese officials said virtually nothing about what had happened; US officials were similarly quiet. Nor was there any orchestrated outcry from the crew's families or from American politicians.

There was a simple reason for all this tiptoeing — drugs.

For the first 80 days of the Americans' confinement, for all the world knew, their imprisonment was a mystery; the word "drugs" was never mentioned officially. But in private, it hung all over the case like a wet blanket.

The silence was broken on Christmas Eve in a dispatch from the official Vietnamese News Agency. In addition to saying the boat and crew would be released shortly, the dispatch charged the Brillig had been carrying a large number of "marijuana boxes."

VIETNAM, Page 6

ICE AGE — Forced by an incoming tide to retreat, Michael Dyer leads Sarah Willwerth over the rocks after viewing ice formations left by the cold spell on the rocks at Singing Beach in Manchester. (Globe photo by Ulrike Welsch)

New state rule eases path to minority hiring

By Norman Lockman
Globe Staff

Gov. Michael Dukakis has signed a new state civil service rule which will give appointing officials the option of hiring minorities and women applicants not at the top of the lists.

The rule, signed without fanfare on Monday, was approved 4-1 by the Civil Service Commission. It permits the state personnel director to forward to appointing officials the names of the top three minority candidates on the appropriate civil service list as well as the top three candidates overall if the personnel director decides that minorities or women are underrepresented in the job being filled.

Now, only the top three candidates overall can be forwarded.

The rule change removes what many state and municipal officials have complained is the main stumbling block in meeting affirmative action program goals, according to Amelia Miclette, chairman of the Civil Service Commission.

At present, minorities are significantly underrepresented in civil service jobs. Affirmative action programs are designed to accelerate the hiring and promotion of minorities, women and other protected groups in areas where discrimination has been proved to exist in the past.

Failure to meet affirmative action goals can jeopardize federal grants in some cases, and in Massachusetts, Boston, Springfield and several smaller cities have come under pressure to comply or lose funds.

Miclette said the rule will take effect about March 1. The time lag will be used to print and mail explanations of the rule to state hiring officials, mayors, boards of selectmen, legislators and city and town clerks, she said.

The rule is called the "3 plus 3 plan" or "Certification of Other Eligibles." The appointing official is not required to choose a minority candidate when the 3 plus 3 plan is used; he simply has the option.

The plan was written by Wallace H. Kountze, the state personnel administrator, who got the idea from personnel officials in the state of Washington. Massachusetts is the second state to promulgate such a rule, according to Kountze.

The rule change was necessary because minorities and women applicants frequently do not place high enough on the eligibility lists to receive consideration, he said.

The civil services tests now being used, Koutze continued, "cannot be said to be a thoroughly fair device for ranking candidates solely on the basis of differing scores."

Impact of the new rule could be wide because in Massachusetts state civil service rules extend not only to state employees but also to employees of most cities and towns.

Kountze said the rules change can be used as a vehicle to begin to successfully implement affirmative action plans, "all within the confines of the civil service laws."

POLITICAL CIRCUIT

The real Dukakis is a manager

By Robert Healy
Globe Staff

Michael Dukakis is a 1978 politician. For years politicians have been saying, "Don't label me," but Dukakis is a political man who cannot be labeled.

He is not a liberal. He hates spending, despite what he said in his State of the State message Wednesday. He is not a conservative because of what he did say in the State of the State message.

He is a manager — some say not a very good one and point to the tax department and that is a problem. But his record is not a bad one.

Like most managers, Michael Dukakis tries to read almost everything, which is impossible, and he tries to manage almost everything, which is also impossible. He has a rather low threshold for intellectual ferment although he would be the last to admit it.

Managers simply do not have a high tolerance for ferment because ferment is never resolved to anyone's total satisfaction. It's messy rather than tidy and above all else Michael Dukakis is tidy — a clean-desk type.

Bearing that in mind, Michael Dukakis' management has probably taken him close to where the people of the state are today.

POLITICAL CIRCUIT, Page 15

Mideast assassination campaign feared

By William Beecher
Globe Washington Bureau

WASHINGTON — Diplomatic sources say there is reason to believe the murders of a moderate Palestinian in London and of a British journalist in Cairo were linked to the same group and could represent the start of a campaign of assassinations throughout the Mideast.

The sources say that the killings of both Said Mammami, a close friend of Palestine Liberation Organization (PLO) leader Yasser Arafat, and David Holden, Mideast correspondent for the Sunday Times of London, are believed to be the work of a radical PLO splinter group based in Iraq and led by Abu Nidal, alias Sabri Al-Banna.

They suggest it would not be surprising if some counterassassinations take place on behalf of those determined to show the radicals that political murders are a dangerous game that two sides can play.

Ironically, the sources say that Israeli counterintelligence agents are providing some discreet protection on the West Bank to prominent Palestinian mayors and other leaders thought to be in favor of a moderate course in the negotiating process.

Mammami was an outspoken leader of moderation in the PLO camp and met from time to time with Israeli leftists interested in promoting an Arab-Israeli settlement long before the dramatic November trip to Jerusalem of Egyptian President Anwar Sadat. Hammami was gunned down in his London office earlier this month by someone who had an appointment with him.

Holden, one of the most experienced Mideast reporters was intercepted and killed somewhere between the Cairo airport and the city in mid-December.

Well-placed sources here say that both murders were believed to have been meant as object lessons to moderate Palestinians thinking of cooperat-

ASSASSINATE, Page 12

IN THIS CORNER

For Tut, they stand and wait

By Alan Richman
Globe Staff

NEW ORLEANS — Not to be confused with the Football Hall of Fame, the Museum of Art here is displaying the treasures of Tutankhamun, boy pharaoh of Egypt. Tutankhamun died in 1325 BC, even before the time of George Halas, and was buried with more pomp than a Super Bowl halftime show, if such a thing can be imagined.

On Nov. 27, 1922, British archaeologist Howard Carter entered the tomb of Tutankhamun. Five months later mysterious events started to occur.

The British earl sponsoring the expedition died. His dog was possessed with a howling fit. And thus was born the legend of the curse of the tomb.

Now a mysterious event grips New Orleans. It has been labeled Tut Fever. It is everywhere.

It is bigger, far bigger, than the Super Bowl.

The Super Bowl is expected to draw 60,000 visitors to New Orleans over the three-day weekend. These people will spend about $15 million.

The exhibition of 55 treasures from the four-room tomb of Tutankhamun opened on Sept. 15. Already nearly 900,000 persons have seen the exhibit, some of them standing in line as long as 20 hours to gain entrance.

King Tut's coffin

TUT, Page 8

You can save on loans that save on energy

By Jean Dietz
Globe Staff

A total of 115 savings, commercial and cooperative banks and credit unions across Massachusetts will offer interest rate reductions up to 2 percent to homeowners seeking loans for energy conservation.

The voluntary program, described by Gov. Michael S. Dukakis yesterday as "the nation's first," also is expected to increase business for the state's growing alternative energy industry as well as small companies in the home-improvement field.

Solar hot water heating systems and other solar energy systems including space heating and passive solar heat are included in the program.

More conventional heat-saving improvements on the list include insulation of walls or attics, storm windows and doors, furnace and oil burner changes, clock thermostats, weather-stripping and caulking.

Dukakis noted Massachusetts has one of the highest percentages of older homes in the nation. More than 60 percent of the state's housing was built before 1940, after which insulation became more common.

INSULATE, Page 25

President Carter calls for a question at yesterday's news conference. (AP photo)

Congressman under probe asked for new US attorney — Carter

By Stephen Wermiel
Globe Washington Bureau

WASHINGTON — President Carter disclosed yesterday that a Democratic congressman who is reportedly under investigation by a Republican US attorney in Philadelphia asked him late last year to expedite the removal of the prosecutor.

Questioned several times during his 30-minute news conference about Attorney General Griffin Bell's decision to replace Republican US Attorney David W. Marston, Carter said, "Rep. Joshua Eilberg (D-Pa.) called me and asked that we look into it.

"My only involvement in it at all was to expedite the process," Carter said. "As far as any investigation of any members of Congress, however, I am not familiar with that at all."

Eilberg and Rep. Daniel Flood (D-Pa.), according to informed sources, are both under investigation by Marston in connection with allegations of irregular financing for an addition to the Hahnemann Hospital in Philadelphia.

Eilberg is vacationing until Jan. 19, according to an aide, who said no member of the congressman's staff would comment. Flood has said he is not aware of any investigation and has not tried to have Marston removed.

MARSTON, Page 13

Carr fails to show at bail hearing

By Susan Trausch
and Joseph Rosenbloom
Globe Staff

Embattled commodity options dealer James A. Carr has suffered a "complete collapse" and is under psychiatric care in New Jersey, his attorney said yesterday when Carr failed to show up for a bail reduction hearing in US District Court. Thirteen states and the federal government now have moved against Carr and Lloyd, Carr & Co.

Federal officials here said they have been unable to confirm attorney Walter J. Hurley's statement of Carr's condition and whereabouts or to locate Carr.

In other developments yesterday:

—US District Judge Joseph L. Tauro agreed to reduce bail for two Carr associates arrested with Carr on Tuesday — Vice President James Brien and sales manager Ralph R. Zolla — but declined to reduce Carr's bail.

— Representatives of Lloyd, Carr charged the government with trying to harass them out of business and announced they had hired F. Lee Bailey's law firm as counsel.

— Massachusetts Secretary of State Paul Guzzi, appearing with Harry

OPTIONS, Page 25

Fig. 5-2. Balanced modular. The *Boston Globe* provides neat rectangles for many stories and, across the bottom, balances one module with another. Note picture borders.

Los Angeles Times

LARGEST CIRCULATION IN THE WEST, 1,020,987 DAILY, 1,309,677 SUNDAY

VOL. XCVII   SIX PARTS—PART ONE   120 PAGES   FRIDAY MORNING, JANUARY 13, 1978   CC†   Copyright © 1978 Los Angeles Times   DAILY 15c

STAN MARSH 3

Artful Texan Mesmerizes Oddball Buffs

BY NICHOLAS C. CHRISS
Times Staff Writer

AMARILLO, Tex.—Just when everyone thought that eccentric Texas millionaires were a thing of the past, as outdated as longhorn cattle drives and rusty six-shooters, along comes Stanley God Bless America Marsh 3 to prove it just ain't so.

What more fitting place to find this scion of Texas' petroculture than in Amarillo, the conservative blue-sky land that looks like Marlboro country, where men are men and sometimes still have to prove it.

Stanley Marsh 3 proves it by doing as he damn well pleases. That makes him stand out like a sore thumb in this sometimes short-on-culture part of the nation, particularly because he is an art aficionado.

But Marsh, 40, is many times a millionaire and has the oil and gas money to go his own way. Of course, he is more than just an art lover. He also loves fun, and attracting attention, and doing outrageous things.

Not long ago he and a group of friends flew to the Yukon wearing boy-scout uniforms with short pants. "We wanted to see if we would be taken for sissies," he said. They ended up in a tussle in a bar and were thrown out, boy-scout uniforms and all, he added.

Marsh's family helped settle the countryside hereabouts. His great grandfather, Andrew Jackson Marsh, deserted the Union Army in 1863, fled prison, moved south, married, had a family, left his wife, stole the church funds, and ran off with the maid. He did not marry her, however, Marsh said in an interview at Toad Hall, where he and his patient wife, Wendy, and their five children live.

Marsh, who writes his nickname, "God Bless America," as part of his name, is most famous for having commissioned a monument to the United States in the 1950s called the Great American Dream. It consists of a line of 10 Cadillacs sunk halfway into the ground, hood-first, on the city limits of Amarillo.

His brother surprised him one Christmas by giving him a red Volkswagen buried halfway up the doors in the front lawn of Marsh's house.

Marsh is also known in some circles as the creator of the world's largest phantom soft pool table. But more of that later.

"Stanley Marsh?" a female art patron at the Amarillo Art Center said, perking up, a smile spreading across her cheeks. "He's a little . . . well it's just a pose, you know. But he really can be serious. If you visit Amarillo and don't see Stanley Marsh 3, you really don't see Amarillo."

Marsh has attracted widespread attention in this conservative city for his flamboyant ways. Toad Hall attracts sportswriters, art critics, far-out artists, automotive reporters, out-of-work cowboys, and even society people from the East Coast. The hall is an elaborate stone house on a 10,000-acre ranch that once was in the country.

But urban sprawl is changing all that now. The city is encroaching. So when Marsh saw a residential development beginning to spring up not far away, he rented a sign on the highway to announce that the world's largest poisonous snake farm was being built there.

Today, most Texas millionaires are much more serious and quiet about

Please Turn to Page 26, Col. 1

CAR CRUSHED BUT ALL SURVIVE—Dump truck rests on auto, its five occupants—four college students and associate professor—still inside after crash in Whittier. A fireman cuts open car, after truck was removed, to reach a victim. All were rescued and hospitalized along with truck driver. An official said it was a near miracle that no one in car was killed; it was crushed to about 3 feet.

Story and additional photo in part 1, page 3.

Times photos by Mike Goulding and Joe Kennedy

U.S. Decries Red Influence in West Europe

Firmly Opposes Posts in Government for Italian Communists

BY OSWALD JOHNSTON
Times Staff Writer

WASHINGTON—The Carter Administration spoke out firmly Thursday against Communist participation in the next government in Italy and declared that "Communist influence" should be reduced in any West European country where it exists.

In a statement aimed at bolstering the resolve of democratic parties now on the brink of a government crisis in Italy, the United States firmly disputed the claims of Italian Communists that they are democratic.

In substance as well as in style, Thursday's statement from the State Department was a throwback to the previous administration, when Secretary of State Henry A. Kissinger frequently issued warnings of the dire consequences if Communists were allowed to share power in the government of any U.S. ally in Europe.

A statement to "clarify" the Carter Administration's generally softer view of West European communism had been expected ever since the U.S. ambassador in Rome, Richard Gardner, returned here this week to urge such a course. But the statement read by the State Department spokesman was more forthright in its warning than had been expected.

It was learned that the statement initially drafted Wednesday in the State Department to express U.S. "concern" at the impending political crisis in Rome was rewritten during an afternoon meeting at the White House to sharpen its language.

Specifically, the interagency group responsible for the statement wished to avoid any ambiguity that would allow the Italian Communists, who have had long experience playing by the rules of Italian electoral policies, to claim that a standard Carter Administration warning against "non-democratic" political influences could not apply to them.

Accordingly the statement made the point more clearly than it had been made before in this Administration that Italian Communists and the other Western European Communists are, in the eyes of the United States, alien to Western democratic traditions.

"The United States and Italy share profound democratic values and interests," the final version of the statement read, "and we do not believe that the Communists share those values and interests."

Typical of the Italian Communists' public image on this score was a recent statement in the party newspaper L'Unita by party chairman Luigi Longo to the effect that the Communist Party, "since it represents a third of the electorate, cannot fail to be regarded as an essential part of Italian democracy."

Administration officials believe that Longo, as a rule, gives a more accurate picture of his party's structure and aspirations when he theorizes on the necessity for Italy's Communists to remain strictly Marxist-Leninist in character.

"The Russian Revolution has been the greatest work that has ever been done," Longo told an interviewer late last year. "Can you imagine what the situation in the world would be, supposing that this great economic, political, military—yes, also military—and ideological force no longer existed?"

Please Turn to Page 10, Col. 1

President Admits Democrat Sought Marston's Ouster

BY RONALD J. OSTROW and ROBERT SHOGAN
Times Staff Writers

WASHINGTON—President Carter acknowledged Thursday that a Democratic congressman linked to an investigation conducted by the Republican U.S. attorney in Philadelphia had called him to urge the swift replacement of the prosecutor.

Under questioning at a nationally broadcast press conference, the President said he was unaware that his caller, Rep. Joshua Eilberg, had been a subject of the probe.

But he confirmed that he intended to remove the prosecutor, David W. Marston, who has already gained convictions against a number of prominent Philadelphia Democrats and, according to well-placed sources, is pressing an investigation into allegations of political corruption involving both Eilberg and another Democratic Pennsylvania congressman, Daniel J. Flood.

Carter said that when Eilberg phoned him about two months ago to ask that "the replacement process be expedited," Atty. Gen. Griffin B. Bell, "had already decided to make the change. As far as any investigation of members of Congress, however, I'm not familiar with that at all, and it was never mentioned to me," the President said.

Bell told reporters later Thursday that he had first heard only the night before that Eilberg was under investigation. At a hastily called press conference at the Justice Department, Bell said it was against department policy to disclose whether Eilberg or Flood were subjects of the probe.

But Bell said that under department procedures he would have

Please Turn to Page 20, Col. 1

Smog Inspection Stations to Be Built in L.A. Area

State Will Require Tests of Emission Systems on Used Cars Before They Can Be Sold, Quinn Says

BY ROBERT A. JONES
Times Staff Writer

California will construct a series of smog inspection stations in the Los Angeles area and, beginning early next year, will require the inspection of emission control systems on every used car before it can be resold, Air Resources Board chairman Tom Quinn announced Thursday.

The new inspection stations, which will cost an estimated $34 million annually to operate, will replace the current system of certifying smog devices on used cars at private garages and service stations.

Speaking at a luncheon meeting of the Los Angeles Barristers Club here, Quinn said the state-run facilities will be far more effective in reducing emissions from old cars and, possibly, could lead to an annual inspection of all automobiles in the South Coast air basin within several years.

Over the last two years, the ARB has operated an experimental inspection program in Riverside County to test its effectiveness and the reaction of motorists. This program, which Quinn referred to as "Phase I," has been highly successful and has been received enthusiastically by Riverside drivers, he said.

The new program, which Quinn called Phase II, will require the construction of 15 stationary inspection stations and two mobile units. It will begin in January, 1979, and if successful will lead to Phase III, an inspection of all cars each year.

ARB officials said they expect about 35% of the 1.2 million cars sold in the Los Angeles area each year will fail the test and require some repair. However, they said, the cost of such repairs should average $21 and in no case exceed $50.

In a speech at times highly critical of past smog control programs, Quinn said continuing air pollution "stands as a monument to incompetence in government." In the Los Angeles area, Quinn identified oil refineries, power plants, and older autos as the major remaining sources of air pollution and he said the ARB plans to attack all three over the next several years.

The reductions in smog from the new inspection program will make it well worth the estimated cost of $2 million annually for each inspection station, he said. The ARB estimates that by 1980 the system will result in reductions of 30,000 pounds per day of hydrocarbons, 200,000 pounds of carbon monoxide and 15,000 pounds of nitrogen oxides.

The inspection stations will be built throughout the South Coast Basin, which includes Los Angeles, Orange, Riverside, San Bernardino, Ventura and Santa Barbara counties. The sta-

Please Turn to Page 30, Col. 1

British Firemen End Long Strike

Accept 10% Pay Hike After Nine Weeks Off

BRIDLINGTON, Eng. (AP)—Britain's firemen Thursday voted overwhelmingly to end their nine-week-old nationwide strike and accept a 10% pay raise, considerably below what they had demanded.

The decision, made at a stormy union delegates' meeting in this seaside resort, was a major victory in the Labor government's campaign to hold down pay increases in order to fight inflation.

"We were starved into going back to work," said union official Terry Segars. The union has no strike fund, and the 33,500 strikers lost an average of $1,000 each in pay during the walkout.

They will return to work Monday, relieving the 18,000 servicemen who have handled fire fighting duties throughout Britain since the strike began Nov. 14.

The firemen had demanded an immediate 30% boost in their average wage of $118 for a 48-hour week. The deal they accepted Thursday gives them a 10% annual raise retroactive to Nov. 7, and additional raises over the next two years, boosting their average pay to just over $190 a week. In addition, the 48-hour week will be reduced to 42 hours.

The overwhelming approval—more than 3 to 1—strengthens the hand of Prime Minister James Callaghan's government in getting other unions to

Please Turn to Page 6, Col. 1

Italian Premier Seeks a Way to Keep Reds Out

BY LOUIS B. FLEMING
Times Staff Writer

ROME—Italian Prime Minister Giulio Andreotti, under mounting pressure to increase the power wielded by the Communist Party, Thursday was considering a number of options but none that would give the Communists cabinet seats in a new government.

One way or another, Andreotti's 18-month-old government is expected to fall in a matter of days for lack of support in Parliament.

The Communists, second only to Andreotti's Christian Democrats in the 1976 election, are demanding a so-called government of emergency that would be made up of members of the six leading parties. This would mean that Italy would have Communist cabinet ministers for the first time.

The Communists are supported in the creation of such a government by three other parties, actively by the Socialists and the Republicans, and with qualifications by the Social Democrats.

Andreotti's Christian Democratic Party, which has governed Italy since World War II and remains the nation's largest party, officially has rejected a government of emergency with Communist participation but has agreed to see if the other parties will settle for anything less. His minority government now relies on the support of other parties to pass its legislative programs.

Andreotti's principal leverage in the crisis negotiations comes from the threat of general elections which none of the major parties wants. Elections this spring are opposed by the majority of political leaders because

Please Turn to Page 10, Col. 1

President Labels Economy Strong but Asks Tax Cuts

BY GRAYSON MITCHELL
Times Staff Writer

WASHINGTON—While describing the national economy as "basically strong," President Carter Thursday renewed his call for a sizable cut in personal and corporate taxes later this year to maintain the current rate of economic growth.

In his first full-scale news conference of the new year, the President also predicted that the deadlocked Senate-House committee considering energy legislation would soon resolve its differences and produce compromise legislation "in which we can take pride."

The President said present projections called for continued economic expansion during the first half of this year, with no precipitous rise in either inflation or unemployment. But he said the projections also showed that by the end of the third quarter in October, the rate of economic growth is expected to lag, making a tax cut necessary.

"We are not trying to deal with an economy that is tottering or on the verge of collapse or in any danger," Carter said. "We have basically a very strong national economy."

Carter is expected to propose a $25 billion tax cut in his State of the Union message to Congress Jan. 19.

Administration officials had said previously that the reduction was needed to help offset recent Social Security tax increases and the effects of shrinking consumer dollars due to inflation.

The President used the occasion to emphasize again the importance of oil conservation to a healthy national economy and to rally support for his energy program.

Please Turn to Page 17, Col. 1

FEATURE INDEX

THE WEATHER

National Weather Service forecast: Considerable cloudiness today and Saturday with an increasing chance of light rain. Highs both days in the low 60s. High Thursday 65; low, 51.

Complete weather information and smog report in Part 3, Page 13.

CHICAGO, ST. LOUIS JUDGES

Two Top FBI Candidates Known for Their Integrity

BY NORMAN KEMPSTER and LARRY GREEN
Times Staff Writers

WASHINGTON—In the wood-paneled world of the federal courts where they have spent most of the last decade, William H. Webster and Frank J. McGarr are known as men who would never condone "black bag jobs" or any of the other questionable practices that have tarnished the reputation of the FBI.

"If anyone asked him to do anything illegal or to overlook something that was illegal, he'd tell them to shove it right up their rear end," a fellow judge in Chicago said of McGarr. "He's beyond reproach, a man of great integrity."

"I think he would be a tough law enforcement man, but at the same time I think he would make sure that the legal rights are protected of anyone who might be investigated by the FBI," James Meredith, chief judge of the U.S. District Court in St. Louis, said of Webster.

McGarr, a district judge in Chicago, and Webster, a circuit judge in St. Louis, have emerged as the front-runners in President Carter's year-long search for a new FBI director. The President is expected to decide soon, perhaps as early as Monday, on one or the other as the successor to the retiring Clarence M. Kelley.

On the surface, Webster and McGarr have much in common. Both are Republicans. Both tend to be somewhat conservative. Both have close ties to the Midwestern cities in which

Please Turn to Page 21, Col. 1

Fig. 5–3. Balance. The *Los Angeles Times* consistently balances one story with a similar one on the other side of the page. The paper rarely uses big headlines.

The Weather

Today — Sunny with increasing cloudiness, high near 40, low in the 20s. Chance of precipitation 30 per cent. Friday—Mixed rain and snow, high near 40. Yesterday: 3 p.m. AQI: 21. Temp. range: 34-16. Details, C2.

The Washington Post

Index

Amusements	B13	Food	E 1
Classified	C14	Metro	C 1
Comics	Weekly	Obituaries	C12
Editorials	A26	Sports	D 1
Fed. Diary	C 2	Style	B 1
Financial	D 9	TV-Radio	B12

Inside: The Weekly

101st Year No. 38 © 1978 Washington Post Co. THURSDAY, JANUARY 12, 1978 Phone (202) 223-6000 Classified 223-6200 Circulation 223-6100 Higher beyond Metropolitan area See Box A2 15c

HEW Opens Campaign to Cut Smoking

Califano Eyes Tax Incentives, Warnings; Industry Fires Back

By Thomas O'Toole
Washington Post Staff Writer

Declaring war on "Public Health Enemy No. 1," Health, Education and Welfare Secretary Joseph A. Califano Jr. announced a campaign yesterday to ban smoking in airliners, toughen restrictions on smoking in federal buildings and strengthen health warnings on cigarette packages.

Calling it the most sweeping effort ever to break the habits of the nation's 55 million smokers, Califano said the Federal Trade Commission will consider a recommendation to empower the government to set maximum levels of tar, nicotine and carbon monixide in cigarettes.

Califano also said that he and Treasury Secretary W. Michael Blumenthal will study whether to recommend an increase in the eight-cent federal excise tax on each pack of cigarettes and a lower tax on cigarettes with reduced tar and nicotine contents.

"People who smoke are committing slow-motion suicide," said Califano, who gave up smoking 2½ years ago. "Research since the 1964 Surgeon General's Report [linking smoking with lung cancer and heart disease] has proven that smoking is even more dangerous than we originally believed; it accounts for even more disease and disorders than we realized 14 years ago."

Califano's campaign against smoking was attacked almost immediately from both sides of the issue. The House of Representatives in Kentucky, a tobacco state, called for his resignation, and the American Tobacco Institute denounced his program as an intrusion on Americans' civil liberties.

"Secretary Califano's 'stop smoking' campaign appears the personal product of a prohibitionist mentality," said institute Vice President William F. Dwyer. "I have to wonder whether the secretary's plan will deny federal assistance unless and until the applicant files an affirmative stop-smoking plan attached to an anti-tobacco impact statement."

On the other side, John Banzhaf, director of Action on Smoking and Health, said Califano "has labored mightily and brought forth a mouse." Dr. Sidney Wolfe, director of the Ralph Nader-affiliated Health Research Group, said the $23 million proposed by Califano for an anti-smoking campaign in fiscal 1979 is not enough.

"If the government can spend $250 million to combat a non-existent disease like swine flu," Wolfe said, "it should spend at least that much on smoking."

White House press secretary Jody Powell endorsed Califano's campaign at the same time he said the government would not go so far as ending

See SMOKING, A10, Col. 1

United Press International

Flanked by FBI official, left, and lawyer William Hundley, Tongsun Park meets reporters in Seoul. Story A16.

Godwin Bequest: No Tax Rise in Budget

By Megan Rosenfeld and Bill McAllister
Washington Post Staff Writers

RICHMOND, Jan. 11—In his final speech to the Virginia General Assembly, departing Gov. Mills E. Godwin said today he is proposing a budget for the next two years that will not require any tax increases but will provide only limited state support for the Metro subway system in the Washington suburbs.

Godwin said his $9.1 billion budget for the 1978-80 biennium, an increase of nearly 20 per cent over current spending, would give the state "continued momentum." But he warned that there is little unallocated money in his proposal and that there are "unmet requests" from state agencies excluded from the budget that total $470 million.

In a nearly 50-minute speech that often was a reprise of themes Godwin had developed during his eight years as governor, he also told the 140 legislators to be wary of excessive federal government influence and urged them to keep the state on its conservative course.

He said he will not make a decision on the controversial issue of state funding of abortions for indigent women before leaving office on Saturday, thus leaving the choice to the legislature. He also counseled the legislators to find a "workable solution" to the problem of Virginia cities' annexation of adjoining county land, which he called "this major problem of our time, the fate of the core city."

If the Assembly does not deal with the annexation issue, he said "we have before us in the nation's political

See GODWIN, A25, Col. 1

Legislative sessions open in Maryland, Virginia. Page C1.

Willard Hotel to Change Hands Today

By Martha M. Hamilton
Washington Post Staff Writer

Title to the historic Willard Hotel on Pennsylvania Avenue will pass today to the U.S. government and the Pennsylvania Avenue Development Corp., which is expected to ensure the hotel's renovation and reopening.

The once-elegant hostelry at 14th Street and the Avenue, which has fallen into disrepair since its closing in 1968, will be purchased by the government-sponsored corporation with a "good-faith" deposit of $4.55 million. The eventual full purchase price will be decided in negotiations with the Willard's private owners.

The U.S. Court of Claims ordered the purchase a year ago, and the agreement on the initial payment was filed last week with the court. Title is expected to change hands formally today in a real estate closing procedure.

With the closing and the subsequent transfer of the title, the development corporation will be able to ask developers for bids to renovate and operate the hotel. "Our intention is not to sit on this property, but to get it back into active use," said PADC director William A. Barnes.

PADC officials said a developer could be selected as soon as six months from now, which might allow reopening of the hotel within two or three years.

Once lavish lodgings where presidents lived and history was made, the hotel encountered financial difficulty in the 1960s and finally was closed in 1968. The hotel escaped scheduled demolition at one point; instead its contents and decorations were auctioned off. Since then, vandals, time and weather have taken a further toll on the building, which stands three blocks from the White House.

On Jan. 26, 1977, the Court of Claims ruled that the United States

See AVENUE, A22, Col. 3

Jobless Rate Hits Three-Year Low Of 6.4 Per Cent

By James L. Rowe Jr.
Washington Post Staff Writer

Unemployment fell dramatically in December to a three-year low of 6.4 per cent, the Department of Labor reported yesterday.

The rate in November, originally reported as 6.9 per cent, was 6.7 per cent, the department said.

President Carter called the decline "good news for the country," and took quick credit for a good deal of the improvement.

Carter, at a session with reporters and the chairman of the Council of Economic Advisers, Charles L. Schultze, said the effects of the public works and public service employment programs he backed last year are finally being felt.

Despite the quick self-congratulations at the White House, it is clear that the deep decline in the December unemployment rate came as a surprise to most analysts, including those in the administration.

Only last month presidential spokesman Jody Powell all but wrote off the administration's chances of reaching its goal of driving down unemployment to 6.5 per cent by the end of 1977. "It's not likely to be there," he told reporters then.

Commissioner of Labor Statistics Julius Shiskin said yesterday that the performance both in December and in 1977 as a whole was "truly remarkable." Last month 410,000 people found jobs, according to the Labor Department's survey of a sample of 47,000 households. Over the year, 4.1 million Americans gained employment, a postwar record.

Another Labor Department survey, of employer payrolls — which is less inclusive but more reliable on a month-to-month basis than the household survey — also showed a big pickup in jobs in December and in 1977 as a whole.

The December performance also indicates that earlier unemployment reports—which had shown the jobless rate stuck between 6.9 and 7.1 per cent from April through November—probably masked what has been a steady improvement in the nation's economy throughout the year, Shiskin told the congressional Joint Economic Committee.

The problem is with the adjustment the department makes in the unemployment rate each month to account for seasonal ups and downs in employment and joblessness. When the department revised its adjustment formula, as it does every year, it found unemployment had declined gradually throughout the year, rather than being stuck on a plateau through November, then falling sharply.

The dip in unemployment should strengthen the President's hand in pressing Congress to hold down spending, and it may be an indication

See JOBS, A8, Col. 1

REP. AL ULLMAN
. . . warns of "overheating" economy

Ullman to Press Smaller Tax Cut, But Earlier Start

By Art Pine
Washington Post Staff Writer

The chairman of the House Ways and Means Committee said yesterday he plans to press for a much smaller tax cut this year than the $25 billion President Carter is proposing, and will push to make it effective July rather than waiting until October.

Rep. Al Ullman (D-Ore.) said in an interview he does not believe the tax cut should be any larger than is needed to offset new federal energy taxes and Social Security tax increases. Private economists now estimate that these will total $15 billion to $16 billion.

At the same time, Ullman came out in opposition to most of the remaining "tax reforms" that aides say Carter will propose. These include elimination of two foreign tax breaks for multinational corporations and a limit on deductions for such business expenses as "three-martini lunches."

Ullman also said flatly that Carter will not be able to push through any kind of comprehensive welfare "reform" plan. Ullman said he's working on a proposal to alter the welfare system on a step-by-step basis over the next three to five years.

While the chairman's positions aren't always followed precisely by the committee, he nevertheless is one of the most influential spokesmen in Congress on tax issues.

Ullman said he fears that too large a tax cut may risk "overheating" the economy and bringing on a new round of inflation. And he warned that load-

See TAXES, A9, Col. 1

Carter news conference live on TV today at 2:30 p.m.

Nonwhites Form Alliance

Challenge to S. Africa

By Caryle Murphy
Washington Post Foreign Service

JOHANNESBURG, Jan. 11—Leaders of the three major nonwhite groupings in South Africa held an unprecedented meeting today and formed an alliance to establish a nonracial state.

Top representatives of the Zulus, the country's largest black tribe, Coloreds and Indians called for a convention in March to "formulate a common strategy against apartheid" and to draft a new constitution for South Africa.

The meeting marked the first time that political leaders have met across racial lines in South Africa at such a high level and represented a significant challenge to the white-minority ruled country. A union of 19 million blacks and 2.7 million Coloreds (persons of mixed race) has always been feared by the whites who have hoped that in any confrontation the Coloreds would side with the 4.3 million whites.

Any successful alliance would upset the government's plans to proceed with its policy of apartheid (racial separation), by setting up homelands for the blacks and separate parliaments for the other major racial groupings.

There is considerable question whether the government would allow any such alliance to come into exist-

See SOUTH AFRICA, A16, Col. 4

Military Leaders Of Israel, Egypt Begin Sinai Talks

By Thomas W. Lippman
Washington Post Foreign Service

CAIRO, Jan. 11—The military leaders of Israel and Egypt today opened direct negotiations on conditions for Israeli withdrawal from the Sinai peninsula and its return to Egyptian control.

With all ranking military men of the two nations in attendance, the talks got underway with both sides expressing the hope that peace can be attained.

Before the session began, however, Israeli Defense Minister Ezer Weizman held a 50-minute conversation with Egyptian President Anwar Sadat, presumably to discuss the thorny issue of Jewish settlements in the Sinai and Sadat's demands for a complete withdrawal of all Israelis, civilian and military.

Weizman was taken directly from Cairo airport upon his arrival this morning to the Egyptian President's retreat at Aswan. No details of their meeting were disclosed but it was learned that it took place at Sadat's initiative, something the Israelis interpreted as a hopeful sign.

The military talks here are a direct result of the recent summit diplomacy by Sadat and Israeli Prime Minister Menahem Begin. They are to be accompanied by political talks that will get underway next week in Jerusalem involving the foreign ministers of Egypt and Israel and U.S. Secretary of State Cyrus Vance.

A United Nations representative also was to have attended the Jerusalem talks on the political aspects of a Middle East settlement. But it was announced today that the United Nation has backed out of the Jerusalem meeting.

See MIDEST, A13, Col. 1

Not Prohibited by Regulations

12 Double-Dippers Work for Police

By Milton Coleman
Washington Post Staff Writer

Last February, a District of Columbia police dispatcher retired after 20 years of service on the city's force. Shortly afterward, the same policeman was rehired by the same police department in virtually the same capacity, as a dispatcher, according to a police official.

On the surface, the officer, whose name city police officials will not disclose, appeared to be taking a pay cut, since the salary of a patrolman-dispatcher was $18,562 and the salary of a civilian dispatcher was $14,431. But in fact, he was getting a pay increase of 22 per cent because in addition to his regular pay, he was receiving annual retirement benefits of $10,764—a total income of more than $25,000 a year from the D.C. government.

There are 11 other D.C. policemen in similar situations, who in addition to collecting pension payments for serving 20 years on the force receive paychecks of as much as $21,000 a year as civilian employees of the D.C. Police Department.

"We don't have any control over it. It's not prohibited by civil service regulations," said Insp. Roland W. Perry, director of finance and management for the department. "The city is not losing anything because they would be paying his retirement anyway . . . The only thing it's doing is reducing the job market."

"I'm not defending it," Perry said. "But on the other hand, you've got a guy with at least 20 years experience that you can bring into the position. You're getting the benefit of his 20 years of experience and it's not costing any more."

City officials say that the policemen are given no special preferance in filling the vacancies.

The existence of the 12 police offi-

See POLICE, 24, Col. 2

Decontrol Urged to Increase Jobs

NAACP Hits Carter Energy Plan

By Austin Scott
Washington Post Staff Writer

The NAACP has begun circulating on Capitol Hill an energy policy statement calling for deregulation of prices on new oil and gas and also criticizing President Carter's national energy plan.

The statement by the nation's oldest civil rights organization was drafted by an 18-member task force that included a number of blacks who hold executive positions in the oil and gas industry.

It conforms to the spirit of a declaration by NAACP board chairman Margaret Bush Wilson last November for a partnership among "big government, the big minority and big oil. . ."

The statement criticizes Carter's energy plan for taking "a pessimistic attitude toward energy supplies for the future," and for emphasizing conservation in an attempt to cut energy use.

It also says a "major portion" of the money Carter wants to raise through new taxes on energy should be plowed back into the industry for expansion, one of the principal goals of the energy companies and their congressional allies last year, rather than rebated to taxpayers as Carter proposed.

The chairman of the task force that drafted the statement was James Stewart, a veteran of almost 20 years on the NAACP board of directors, and a retired assistant to the vice president of the Oklahoma Natural Gas Co.

Stewart said he tried to find people for the task force "who have a knowledge" of both the NAACP and the industry.

"It's a little confusing to people that we would be supporting the aims and objectives of much of industry,

See NAACP, A10, Col. 1

H. LYNN WOMACK
. . . was "bookish child"

A Pornographer's Rise, Fall

Fifth of a Series

By James Lardner
Washington Post Staff Writer

H. Lynn Womack, in his time, has won friends and influenced people.

A woman who was one of his students in the mid-1950s, when he was an assistant professor of philosophy at Mary Washington College in Fredericksburg, Va., was so impressed that she spent the next 17 years helping him run his adult book empire here.

At the end of their association, she was indicted on obscenity charges (later dropped) and forced into bankruptcy. But far from blaming Womack for her troubles, she wants to point out how badly he has been treated over the years by the press. Story after story, she complains, has described him as a "fat, gay albino" rather than as a "charming, dynamic, thought-provoking man."

Even Womack's probation officer, otherwise a very law-and-order sort of fellow, found Womack so persuasive that prosecutors said he gave "less than objective treatment" to Womack the convict.

A few years ago, by his own ac-

THE SEX INDUSTRY

count, Womack, a white-haired, white-complexioned man of 56 who appears to weigh at least 300 pounds, was the fourth largest pornographer in America.

Although he has two ex-wives and a daughter who graduated from Vassar, Womack also is a homosexual—a discovery he says he made at age 27.

See WOMACK, A24, Col. 1

Fig. 5 – 4. Imbalance. While the *Washington Post* usually leads with a strong story to the right, it also uses a variety of modules on the rest of the page.

"All the News That's Fit to Print"

The New York Times

CITY EDITION

Weather: Rain, windy and mild today; rain and mild tonight, tomorrow. Temperature range: today 32-46; yesterday 23-37. Details, page 59.

VOL. CXXVII .... No. 43,831 — Copyright © 1978 The New York Times — NEW YORK, WEDNESDAY, JANUARY 25, 1978 — 25 cents beyond 50-mile zone from New York City. Higher in air delivery cities. — M + 30 CENTS

MRS. ABZUG AFFIRMED BY COURT IN CONTEST ON HOUSE NOMINATION

BURDEN THEN ENDORSES HER

Opponents Embrace in an Emotional Moment, but He Won't Rule Out a Possible Primary Fight

By FRANK LYNN

Bella S. Abzug was reaffirmed as the Democratic nominee for the House of Representatives in the 18th Congressional District yesterday in State Supreme Court in Manhattan. The action came after weeks of political campaigning by Mrs. Abzug followed by nine days of legal maneuvering against the initial winner, Carter Burden.

Moments later, Mr. Burden embraced her in a rare display of emotion by both of them, and he endorsed Mrs. Abzug.

Despite the embrace and the endorsement, Mr. Burden said he was not foreclosing a primary challenge of Mrs. Abzug if she is elected on Feb. 14 for the interim term to the House seat vacated by Mayor Koch and then seeks a full two-year term in the general-election campaign.

Despite the Democratic disarray over the nomination, Mrs. Abzug starts out the abbreviated campaign for the Feb. 14 special election as the favorite largely because of a 3-to-1 Democratic enrollment margin in the district.

The Republican Threat

However, the Republican candidate, S. William Green, is already waging a strong and well-financed campaign, and Mr. Burden cited the possibility of the Democratic squabbling helping Mr. Green if it continued into higher courts.

"I've decided not to appeal—this has gone on long enough," said Mr. Burden as he left the courtroom. "I don't want to see Mr. Green elected. Now is the time to join ranks."

He quickly added: "I'm holding wide open the possibility of a primary."

The two candidates had spontaneously embraced inside the courtroom just after Justice Alvin F. Klein ruled in Mrs. Abzug's favor; then embraced again and kissed outside the courtroom.

Then, at the behest of photographers, Mrs. Abzug and her husband, Martin, and Mr. Burden and his wife, Susan, posed together outside the courtroom and on the courthouse steps overlooking Foley Square.

"A lovely Christmas card," said Mr. Burden.

The smiles and embraces served as a striking counterpoint to the tension

Continued on Page 36, Column 4

Associated Press

GETTING ACQUAINTED: G. William Miller, left, named to head Federal Reserve Board, talks with Senator William Proxmire, chairman of Senate Banking Committee, before hearings on his confirmation. Details, page 43.

Saudi Increase In Output Seen By Schlesinger

12 Million Barrels Daily Forecast for 1980's

By STEVEN RATTNER
Special to The New York Times

WASHINGTON, Jan. 24—Secretary of Energy James R. Schlesinger said today that Saudi Arabia, the world's largest oil exporter, planned to increase productive capacity modestly between now and the early 1980's and was not now planning further increases to meet the gains that might occur in world oil demand.

The Saudis should be able to produce about 12 milllion barrels of oil a day on a sustained basis by about 1983 or 1984, according to Mr. Schlesinger, compared to about 10 million at present. This general scenario was independently confirmed by sources close to the Saudi Government, although they suggested that sustainable production could reach 12.7 million barrels a day by 1982.

The question of how much oil Saudi Arabia will be able to produce in the 1980's has been hotly debated in energy circles of late because of the central role that the country is expected to play in meeting increased demand. A basic change in the supply of Saudi oil relative to demand could cause upward pressure on oil prices.

Warnings Reiterated

In his remarks today, Mr. Schlesinger reiterated warnings of a severe world oil supply problem in the 1980's, which the Administration has used as a major justification for its National Energy Plan, now stalled in Congress. Again today, the Energy Secretary termed adoption of the plan "our highest priority."

Although 12 million barrels of oil a day from Saudi Arabia would likely be sufficient to meet the demand in the early 1980's, Mr. Schlesinger indicated today—and is supported by a number of private economists—that the demand could outstrip that level within a few years.

An additional 2 million barrels a day of production could be achieved by the mid-1980's, the Energy Secretary said today, but no decision to do this has yet been made. Other sources said that while no formal decision on a further expansion had been made, the added

Continued on Page 49, Column 1

SOVIET SPY SATELLITE WITH ATOMIC REACTOR BREAKS UP IN CANADA

U.S. KNEW OF TROUBLE DEC. 19

Moscow Cooperated as Craft Began to Decay Mysteriously in Space—Secrecy Imposed to Bar Panic

By RICHARD D. LYONS
Special to The New York Times

WASHINGTON, Jan. 24—A crippled Soviet satellite carrying a nuclear reactor re-entered the earth's atmosphere and disintegrated over northwestern Canada today, 12 days after the United States and the Soviet Union had joined in a secret cooperative effort aimed at minimizing possible radioactive contamination and averting public panic.

Intelligence sources said the spacecraft was a naval reconnaissance satellite of a type that the Soviet Union has used for 10 years to spy on the movements of the United States fleet.

The sources said the nuclear reactor aboard Cosmos 954 was used to generate electricity that powered an ocean-scanning radar, whci htracked surface ships, and radios that beamed their number and position to Soviet ground stations.

'First Such Crisis'

"The real significance of this episode is that this was the first nuclear-related crisis in space, and it brought forth Soviet cooperation and informal preparations to deal with a potentially serious situation," a White House official said.

The fact that the satellite was carrying a nuclear reactor and was mysteriously decaying was known to the United Stater as early as Dec. 19 but was kept secret because, in the words of one White House security adviser, "We were trying to head off a re-creation of Mercury Theater."

The reference was to "War of the Worlds," the famous radio broadcast of Orson Welles's Mercury Theater in 1938 in which Martians were reported to have landed at Glover's Mill, N.J. The result was near hysteria among many Americans who had not realized that the Halloween program was fictional.

Two American spacecraft bering radioactive power sources have disintegrated upon accidental entry into the atmosphere. If such mishaps have befallen Soviet craft before yesterday, they have not been publicized. [Page 9.]

Soviet Envoy Queried

According to White House aides, on Jan. 12 Zbigniew Brzezinski, President Carter's national security adviser, asked Anatoly F. Dobrynin, the Soviet Ambassador, for details about the Soviet space flight because United States tracking stations were reporting that the satellite was on a strange orbital path.

"We were pretty sure that it was coming down and we wanted the Russians to provide some details about what was aboard," was the way in which one Presidential adviser put the situation.

The following day Mr. Dobrynin presented Mr. Brzezinski with some technical specifications about the satellite, including its nuclear generator. Further conferences were held over the next few days and more information exchanged.

In the ensuing days, the United States warned its allies in the North Atlantic

Continued on Page 8, Column 2

KOCH DISBANDS PANEL IN DISPUTE OVER ROLE

Transport Advisory Group Hears News After It Is Made Public

By MAURICE CARROLL

Mayor Koch dismissed his transportation advisory panel yesterday in a letter that was made public before those who were ousted saw it.

The panel, after challenging his appointment of Anthony Ameruso as Transportation Commissioner last week, considered disbanding, but decided to stay in business and sent the Mayor a polite letter of criticism that ended with the hope that "our future role will be meaningfully defined by you."

Yesterday the Mayor meaningfully defined it. He abolished the panel.

"I intend to do the interviewing myself," he wrote.

Taxi Post Still Open

Still to be picked in the transportation field are the chairman of the Taxi and Limousine Commission and some deputies to Mr. Ameruso.

Those are the main jobs for which the "search" process is incomplete. The 17 other talent-search panels that Mr. Koch named have made their reports and gone out of business, according to his office. But the transportation search was still on when the searchers were dismissed.

"And he released this to the press and didn't tell me," said Sally Goodgold, co-chairman of the advisory group, when a reporter telephoned the news to her at her Manhattan home.

The other co-chairman, Joel Harnett,

Continued on Page 54, Column 4

Califano Asks Emphasis on People Rather Than Cities in Aid to Poor

By DAVID E. ROSENBAUM
Special to The New York Times

WASHINGTON, Jan. 24—Joseph A. Califano Jr., the Secretary of Health, Education and Welfare, has proposed a fundamental change in the way the Federal Government tries to help the nation's poor.

In a memorandum to President Carter circulated throughout high levels of the Administration, Mr. Califano argued that the Administration was placing too much emphasis on developing a master plan for aiding the nation's cities.

Instead, he wrote, "We should place our primary emphasis on people in distress rather than places in distress, and channel our efforts accordingly."

More Appropriations Urged

He suggested that individual strategies be devised and tailored to the special needs of particular communities, that a new office be established in the White House to coordinate all the government programs designed to help the poor, and that "substantial increased appropriations" be made available to finance the new effort.

The memorandum has not been made public, but a copy has been obtained by The New York Times.

It could not be determined whether the President had seen the memorandum or, if he had, what his reaction to it was. But Administration officials said that Mr. Califano's standing within the Administration was so high that his views were bound to be considered carefully.

Mr. Carter is scheduled to outline his Administration's urban policy in a special message to Congress this spring. That policy is being developed largely by an interdepartmental group headed by Patricia Roberts Harris, the Secretary of Housing and Urban Development.

Neither Mr. Califano nor others in his department have actively participated in the group's work. His memorandum was seen by some in the Administration as an attempt to get his own views across to the President so that they could be weighed against those of Mrs. Harris's group.

Mr. Califano refused last weekend to discuss the memorandum publicly. One of his aides said, however, that the Secretary meant the memo as a supplement

Continued on Page 35, Column 1

The New York Times/Chester Higgins Jr.

AND NOW, THE SLUSH: Warmer temperatures melted city's snow making walking messy and tricky.

INSIDE

Egyptians Rebut Begin

Cairo's press, responding to charges of anti-Semitism from Prime Minister Menahem Begin of Israel, says Egypt is anti-Begin, not anti-Semitic. Page 3.

Report on Marston Case

A Justice Department inquiry has concluded that neither the President nor the Attorney General acted to obstruct justice in the Marston case. Page 12.

Pension Fund Money Running Out For Fire Dept. in New York City

By CHARLES KAISER

The New York City Fire Department Pension Fund is running out of money and, for the first time, its expenses will exceed its income this year. Unless an agreement is reached soon on additional contributions by the city, the firemen's union, or both, the fund will have to start selling its stocks, bonds and other assets to pay firemen's pensions.

"That would be a disaster," said one city official.

According to an unpublished report by the State Insurance Department, 15 major law changes and dozens of minor ones that sharply increased retirement benefits for some New York City firemen contributed to the underfinancing of their pension fund.

The changes in the law—some made as long as 15 years ago—are detailed in the highly critical report, which was sent to the pension's trustees last June.

Letter From Superintendent

While a covering letter from Thomas A. Harnett, then the State Insurance Superintendent, demanded that the trustees respond within 10 days, they never have. Insurance Department officials said yesterday that was the reason the report had not been released, but a copy was obtained elsewhere by The New York Times.

The trustees have requested and received a series of postponements of that 10-day deadline while trying to resolve the fund's fundamental problem: Its long-term liabilities now exceed its assets by at least $750 million.

According to both city and union experts the $750 million is not needed right away to keep the fund solvent. Rather, it represents the additonal funds that will eventually be needed to finance all of the pension fund's accrued benefits for both its current and retired members.

The reason for the deficit is a 20-year impasse between the city and the union over who would increase contributions and by how much to keep the pension fund solvent.

State Constitution Cited

Firemen's pensions range from about $9,600 to $15,000 a year, depending on their term of service, how much overtime they earned and whether they receive disability pensions at three-quarters of their former pay Last year, 590 officers and men retired from the force, and a total of 6,222 are currently receiving benefits from the fund.

The union has repeatedly cited a section of the State Constitution that states that pension benefits shall neither be diminished nor impaired" during the term of a worker's employment. The union contends that an increase in contribu-

Continued on Page 59, Column 5

Associated Press

Zbigniew Brzezinski, left, national security adviser, and Adm. Stansfield Turner, Director of Central Intelligence, at the White House yesterday.

Congress Studies Bill to Require Judicial Scrutiny of Some Spying

By DAVID BURNHAM
Special to The New York Times

WASHINGTON, Jan. 24—Congress is considering legislation to focus judicial light on one of the most secret activities of the Federal Government: the electronic surveillance of people in the United States who are suspected of being involved, directly or indirectly, in intelligence activities for a foreign power.

Many experts agree that the proposal is one of the most significant bills pending before Congress. Already approved by the Senate Judiciary Committee and subject to hearings by the Senate Intelligence Committee beginning next week, the legislation has generated disputes over several key issues.

The legislation had first been proposed by the Ford Administration and then was adopted in a modified form by President Carter. It is one outgrowth of the disclosures in 1975 and 1976 of widespread investigative abuses by the Central Intelligence Agency and the Federal Bureau of Investigation in the name of national security.

The bill is only part of the efforts to regulate intelligence and counter-intelligence operations. Today President Carter signed an executive order reorganizing intelligence agencies and limiting their activities. [Page 14.]

Together with the pending electronic surveillance measure, the order is expected to develop into "charter legislation" that would describe and circumscribe the agencies' responsibilities.

Because of the dense secrecy surrounding both the broad techniques of surveillance and specific counterintelligence investigations, the electronic spying legislation can be fully understood only by the small number of House and Senate members who have received secret briefings.

"The smartest lawyer in Washington

Continued on Page 14, Column 1

De La Roche Pleads Insanity in Murders Of All 4 in Family

By ROBERT HANLEY
Special to The New York Times

HACKENSACK, N.J., Jan. 24—Harry De La Roche Jr. killed his parents and two younger brothers as charged, but was legally insane at the time, his lawyer said today in an abrupt change in his defense that seemed to startle the judge and prosecutor.

The defense counsel, John R. Taylor, had devoted considerable time during the trial attacking the admissibility and credibility of the 19-year-old Montvale youth's original confession to all four murders. Mr. De La Roche had testified that he killed only his brother Ronald, 15, in a fit of temporary insanity after Ronald killed his parents, Harry Sr. and Mary Jane, and his brother Eric, 12, following a fight with his father about marijuana.

The judge, James F. Madden, said from the bench that Mr. Taylor's shift had left him confused.

After a luncheon recess, Judge Madden let Mr. Taylor change his defense because he found that Mr. Taylor had previously notified the Bergen County Prosecutor's office in writing that the defense would be insanity. That document never specified how many murders the insanity defense would apply to.

However, Mr. Taylor's repeated suggestions out of court and his constant line of questioning bolstered impressions that the insanity defense would be limited

Continued on Page 33, Column 1

Fig. 5 – 5. Balance. The *New York Times* shifted to a six-column format in 1977 but has stuck with the old-fashioned balanced makeup with all-cap headlines.

Biggest Food Section In Town - 21 Pages

Coupons, Recipes, Shopping Advice Starting on Page 21

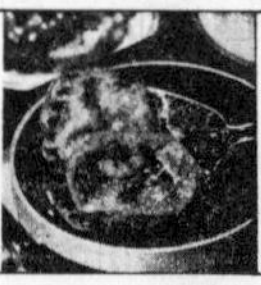

A Comeback Story: Augie Pantellas

He KOs Isaac Vega In 1st Fight in 6 Months

Page 45

Benny Goodman Fans Relive the Good Years

Clarinet Still Mellow At Anniversary Concert

Page 41

Late Sports, News and Stocks

The Evening Bulletin

WEDNESDAY, JANUARY 18, 1978

FIFTEEN CENTS

Sadat Breaks Off Peace Talks

Good Evening

PARTLY CLOUDY TONIGHT — PARTLY CLOUDY TOMORROW

Partly cloudy and colder through tomorrow. Lows around 20, highs around 30. (Details on Page 63.)

Very Classy, Fellas

Two men, one of them armed, robbed a Long Island fish store. They ignored the cash register. Instead, they hayled out 1,000 pounds of lobster tails and 800 pounds of shrimp. Total value: $5,000.

Wildwood Fire

A dozen small shops on Wildwood's boardwalk were destroyed in a fire that raged into the early hours today. Although the fire threatened some larger establishments, firemen managed to contain it to the small shops, between Cedar and Oak aves.

Snow Crushes 3 Roofs

The roofs of three large Connecticut buildings — including Hartford's Civic Center Coliseum — collapsed in the early hours today under heavy snow and ice. Roofs also fell at a supermarket in Manchester and a factory in Jewett City. There were no injuries reported, but officials were probing the factory rubble looking for a missing workman.

Sugary Health Threat

A heart researcher says our sugar-rich diet could be a cause of high blood pressure, claiming the sugar combines with salt to trigger the problem. Salt has long been known to cause such problems; this is the first time sugar has been named. The finding was reported by Dr. Gerald Berenson of the Louisiana State University School of Medicine.

Money for College

A lot of parents may not believe it, but the Congressional Budget Office says family income has risen faster than college costs in recent years. College costs rose 75 percent from 1967 to 1976, a report says, but median family income was up 89 percent.

A $200 Bounty

Victor Periu, a Brooklyn deli owner who shot three would-be robbers, has been cited by a gun club that honors persons who shoot hoodlums. Many persons won't accept the awards from the club, the Federation of Greater New York Pistol and Rifle Clubs, but Periu says he didn't mind the award — a plaque and $200.

Long Island Blackout

Some 100,000 persons on ice-laden Long Island were still without power early today, the aftermath of a weekend ice storm that initially turned out the lights for 340,000 persons.

Order in the Court

Superior Court Judge Harry F. Brauer dismissed a prospective juror from his Santa Cruz, Calif., courtroom with this admonition: "You can't serve on a jury in this court. You don't pay any attention to anything I say at home, and there is no reason to believe you would listen to anything I would say here." So he directed his wife, Georgia, to report to another courtroom.

— *Ralph Frattura*

The Education Of a Public Man

Fourth in a series of excerpts from Hubert H. Humphrey's book appears today on Page 54.

And Then Came The Sun

That unfamiliar stuff outside your window today was sunshine. The U.S. Weather Service says we can expect some more tomorrow. But Friday may be another snow story.

Heavy rains drenched the Greater Philadelphia area last night, turning yesterday's snow into slush, flooding streets and highways and stalling cars in puddles.

The rain became a light drizzle early this morning and finally ended by the morning rush hour.

Dry and cold weather is expected to prevail for the next several days. Temperatures will dip below freezing

How did you cope with the storm? For the school kids, it was great fun. For drivers, a case of the horrors. Story on Page 4.

tonight, though, which could turn unmelted slush into treacherous ice.

The weather outlook includes a chance of snow again on Friday, but a spokesman for the National Weather Service said the possible storm was too far in the future to know whether any accumulation can be expected.

The stormy weather that has buffeted the area has dropped nearly two and one-half inches of precipitation since last Firday. Between three and eight inches of snow fell on the area yesterday, bringing total snow accumulations to between five inches in parts of the city and 12 inches in some suburbs for the last five days.

Service on four trolley routes was disrupted this morning as a result of the rain.

Wet motors disabled many trolleys on Routes 10 (running from 63d st. and Malvern ave. to center city), and 15 (operating from 63d st. and Girard ave. to Richmond and Westmoreland sts.

A SEPTA spokesman said there were no trolleys available to replace the idled ones because of a fire in

Please Turn to Page 4

Bulletin Photo by Joe Palfo

George McKain, of South Philadelphia, prepares to go home from work in the slush after parking his car in a lot at 17th and Ludlow sts. Mural on building features monster-size flowers.

Minister Called Home

Bulletin Wire Services

Cairo, Egypt — President Anwar Sadat has ordered his foreign minister to break off talks with Israel in Jerusalem and return home, Egypt's information minister announced today.

The official Egyptian statement said Egypt's foreign minister was ordered home because it "became apparent from the declarations of the prime minister of Israel and its foreign minister that Israel insists on presenting partial solutions that cannot lead to the establishment of a just and lasting peace."

The dramatic announcement, broadcast by Cairo radio, was made without warning. It said the ambassador was to return "immediately."

Earlier, in Jerusalem, a serious diplomatic incident at a state banquet overshadowed today's resumption of negotiations between the Israeli and Egyptian foreign ministers.

Israeli Prime Minister Menahem Begin made a toast at a state dinner last night, comparing self-determination for the Palestinians to Adolf Hitler's land-grabbing policies during the 1930s.

Egyptian Foreign Minister Mohammed Kamel chided Begin for "bringing his work" to a social event — a public banquet covered by scores of reporters. In a sharp public snub, Kamel omitted the customary toast to peace.

The negotiations already were marked by sharp disagreement on basic issues.

But an Egyptian journalist with close ties to President Anwar Sadat said only intervention by Secretary of State Cyrus Vance could save the talks.

Kamel's hardline demands at the opening conference session and Begin's reply made clear that neither the Israelis nor the Arabs are prepared to compromise on the chief issues blocking a peace agreement.

Moussa Sabry, editor of the newspaper Al Akhbar, said "there can be no way out of this basic difference (on the Palestinians) except by means of an American (compromise) draft ... American presence, therefore, is essential to prevent the talks from collapsing."

The rival draft declarations show wide differences, particularly on the issues of the Palestinians and Israeli withdrawal from occupied Arab territories.

Both Egyptian envoys and officials in Vance's party said they expected Begin's toast at the banquet to be nonpolitical in nature and they were surprised when he began talking about issues at stake in the negotiations.

"Peace cannot be established if Israel were to restore its former aggression-provoking lines of June 5, 1967," Begin said.

He then compared a future, independent Palestinian state to Nazi Germany of the 1930s.

Please Turn to Page 2

Klenk Charges Marcase Job Cover-Up

By LOU ANTOSH
Of The Bulletin Staff

Philadelphia school district employes altered official records and engaged in a "cover-up" in the construction of the sun porch at the summer home of Schools Superintendent Dr. Michael P. Marcase, says City Controller William G. Klenk.

In a report issued today, Klenk also charged that "favoritism" was used in the rehiring of Michael Pilla, a school district employe who was laid off last June, then hired back after he helped build the Marcase sun porch.

A sharply-worded report by Klenk's top investigator, Nicholas J. Pitts, termed "an obvious abuse of the use of public funds" the fact that one school employe was paid his school district wages for building the porch and another was hired back by the school system after building the sun deck.

Such use of public funds, the report continued, "is not proper and should not be tolerated."

The 12-page report, sent to the Board of Education, said the cover-up involved alteration of pay and attendnace records of Samuel R. Piselli, a $23,330-a-year roofing supervisor whom Marcase has described as a friend and lodge brother.

Marcase, asked if he was aware of any cover-up in the matter, said "Of course not."

"I don't think there was any wrongdoing," Marcase said in a phone interview today. "I know there wasn't any wrongdoing on my part. These men offered to do the work for me. They were my lodge brothers."

He said he paid $2,000 out of his pocket for materials to build the sundeck and to have a local contractor dig holes for the sundeck's footings.

"If I was about to rip off anyone I sure botched it," Marcase said. "I had an estimate from a local contractor to build the deck for $2,700. I sure didn't save much letting my friends help me."

He said Piselli had 40 vacation days coming to him when he worked on the

Please Turn to Page 8

Warren Hesitated To Head JFK Probe

Washington — (UPI) — In the days following the assassination of John F. Kennedy, Chief Justice Earl Warren initially declined to head a presidential commission to investigate the slaying, newly released FBI documents showed today.

There was no indication why the chief justice refused the appointment, but Supreme Court justices historically have avoided taking other assignments in the government.

But Warren changed his mind almost at once, the memos showed, and the appointment of the commission of seven public servants was announced on Nov. 29, 1963, six days after Kennedy was slain in Dallas.

Warren's hesitancy was revealed in one of 8,150 pages of FBI communications with the Warren Commission. These — and 50,604 pages of censored raw FBI files — were released today under terms of the Freedom of Information Act.

A memo, dated Nov. 23, 1963, from one high FBI official to another, reported that Attorney General Nicholas Katzenbach had informed the FBI that "the chief justice has declined to commission."

"He (Katzenbach) does not know who may be selected as a replacement," the memo said.

But later the same day, the White

Please Turn to Page 2

Today's Contents

Bridge....... 53	Focus/ Food 21-40
Business...15-17	Horoscope... 63
Chat......... 17	Lottery...... 59
Classified Ad Index .. 54	Mr. Fixit 40
Crossword... 57	Obituaries 10,52, 54
Dear Abby... 26	Seek & Find . 56
Editorials ... 18	Sports 45-50
Entertainment 41-43	TV, Radio ... 20

131ST YEAR, NO. 280
PUBLISHED EVENING AND SUNDAY
•BULLETIN CO. 1978 PHILADELPHIA, PA.
19101 • 215-662-7550

NEARLY EVERYBODY READS THE BULLETIN

Twenty/Twenty Game
Winning Numbers, Contest Rules On Page 60.

A Carter Switch On Marston Issue?

The Carter Administration indicated today it was softening its position on the removal of U.S. Attorney David W. Marston in Philadelphia.

A spokesman said this morning, "We are waiting for the three-man team to ascertain and assess what is going on in Philadelphia regarding the U.S. Attorney there."

"We do not intend to impede or obstruct justice and whatever action we take on the removal of Mr. Marston will be done with that intention," said Rex Grannum, assistant press secretary.

Meanwhile, another Carter Administration spokesman said Marston may be retained indefinitely if the

The nation's press comes to the aid of Marston, as editorials from around the country are critical of Carter, Page 18.

Justice Department decides he is needed in ongoing corruption investigations.

The official, who declined to be named, said Marston would probably remain in the post until the investigations are completed, perhaps for several months.

There have been indications by White House and Congressional sources that President Carter may suc-

Please Turn to Page 5

Fig. 5–6. Mixed style. The once-staid *Evening Bulletin* of Philadelphia splashes a long story reference box in column one plus a few stories surrounded by white space.

The two faces of a Chinatown tong

By Raul Ramirez
and Larry D. Hatfield

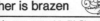

One is benevolent —the other is brazen

The recent Golden Dragon massacre that left five people dead has focused attention on the activities of the Hop Sing Tong, the secretive fraternal organization that owns the Chinatown building where the restaurant is located.

Police and other sources point out that some tong members and associates have been on the fringes of Chinatown turmoil for years.

The bullets and shotgun pellets that killed five innocent bystanders and wounded 11 others Sept. 4 at the Golden Dragon were thought by authorities to be intended either for members of the "Hop Sing Boys" gang at a table in the back of the restaurant or for their friends, members of the Wah Ching gang sitting nearby.

In addition, Kin Chuen Louie, 20, a well-known leader of a group involved in Chinatown extortion and a top Hop Sing Boys figure recently was gunned down on a Telegraph Hill street by an unidentified assassin. Earlier, another young Hop Sing affiliate, Bill Wong, was shot outside the Hop Sing Tong headquarters on Waverly place in what police said was a gang-related assault.

Tong elders adamantly deny that the organization has links to Chinatown youth elements that have been involved in more than three dozen killings in the past decade, or that the Hop Sing Tong has ties to gambling or other illegal activity.

—Turn to Page 28, Col. 1

San Francisco Examiner
MONARCH OF THE DAILIES
Vol. 1977, No.49 ☆☆ 777-2424 SUNDAY, OCTOBER 23, 1977 50¢ METRO AREA 75¢ ELSEWHERE PREVIEW EDITION

Today

Topic A

CHINATOWN'S SECRET SOCIETIES — the tongs — are portrayed by their spokesmen as benevolent organizations whose admittedly bloody history is a thing of the past. Police believe otherwise, and they have been watching tong activities for years, looking for connections to extortion and gambling up and down the coast. **Page 1.**

City/State

PRINCE CHARLES is making San Francisco the last stop on his whirlwind tour of the United States, and almost everyone is looking forward to getting a glimpse of the world's favorite heir-apparent. **Page 1.** Except local Irish activists. **Page 18.**

JUSTICE WILEY MANUEL is the California Supreme Court's first black member, and he's a natural as a role model — but he hopes that aspect of his success isn't defined in terms of race. **Page 4.**

A THIRD YEAR OF DROUGHT in California isn't expected by most weather experts, but they caution that we should be prepared for the worst. **Page 1.**

The Nation

THEY CALL THEMSELVES the "Crabgrass Brigade," eight congressmen who've banded together in an effort to form a suburban caucus in the House of Representatives. They say half the country lives in the suburbs and pays a good share of federal tax dollars without getting enough in return. **Page 5.**

The World

"THE GOVERNMENT JUST couldn't stand the heat and decided to rid itself of its severest critics" is one explanation of the South African government's ban on two newspapers and a number of opponents. The government minister of agriculture said of one such government opponent: "We must get rid of such bastards." **Page 19.**

"OUR WAR HERE IN NORTHERN Ireland is a poxy, petty, stupid, insane little war when you think of places like Beirut or South Africa," said one of the two people who won the Nobel Peace Prize for their efforts to bring peace to their country. Since they think their war is petty, they plan to give their prize money to other causes. **Page 27.**

Sports

FANS, the newly formed sports consumer protection group, officially begins operation Nov. 1, and its director says the first obstacle it must overcome is ridicule. **Page 1C.**

Business

A PALO ALTO COMPANY has developed a new technique for storing information using lasers and a glass disk that it says can preserve much more information than other electronic systems. **Page 10C.**

Editor's report

The curious Mr. Carter

By William Randolph Hearst Jr.
Editor-in-Chief, The Hearst Newspapers

NEW YORK — Within a few days it will be one full year since a majority of American voters selected a relatively little known former governor of Georgia to lead our country for four years.

How much better have we come to know our President, Jimmy Carter, during the succeeding months? Many feel — and I share the view — that we know very little more about him than we did when the so-called "Carter Groundswell" burst upon the scene in Atlanta in those months before the convention.

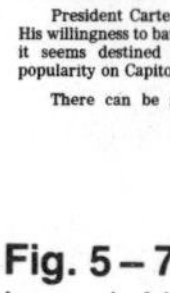

W. R. Hearst Jr.

But something even more upsetting seems apparent: Jimmy Carter is in trouble. He is in trouble with the voters, with members of Congress, with vast segments of the business community as well as the investing community and even with some members of his own elite inner-circle.

President Carter's energy program is a shambles. His willingness to battle the full power of Congress over it seems destined to further weaken his political popularity on Capitol Hill.

There can be no question that the President's

—Turn to Page 2B Col. 1

Prince Charles, decked out for a tour of a Cleveland steel mill

AP Photo

Articulate, intelligent — in a word, he's a prince

By Ivan Sharpe

First, you should know that Prince Charles probably will be exhausted when he arrives at San Francisco Airport Thursday. And second, the chances of the world's most eligible bachelor squeezing in any romance during his four days here look very slim.

This is for those immodest others who have been besieging the British consulate here with day-and-night phone calls and letters pointing out the virtues of their daughters.

"I can assure them that Prince Charles will not have one second free to indulge in any kind of amorous interlude," British consulate spokesman Donald Stokes said.

The prince's rigorous schedule will, no doubt, also disappoint other seekers of royal attention, such as the flat earth folks, various religious cults, psychic groups, mystics, weirdos and someone who wanted to share a good old Yankee hot dog with him.

The imminent arrival of the 29-year-old Prince of Wales is stirring more interest than any royal visit here in a dozen years, in the opinion of Stokes, who has seen them all.

—Turn to Page 18, Col. 1

Yerba Buena delayed again— until mid-1978

By Donald Canter
Urban Affairs Writer

Construction of San Francisco's Yerba Buena Center convention hall, already delayed six years by lawsuits and other near-fatal calamities, will have to wait some more.

The latest groundbreaking date for the project, tentatively set for the end of this year, will be postponed again, at least until the middle of 1978 by the most optimistic estimates, the Examiner learned.

The reason for the latest delay is concern by legal advisers that the $85 million worth of bonds needed to finance the 290,000 square-feet underground facility will not be saleable unless a new federal environmental study for the entire 87-acre Yerba Buena renewal area is prepared.

Because of that concern, city officials next week will ask the U.S. Department of Housing and Urban Development to prepare such a report because substantial planning changes have made a previous environmental impact statement on Yerba Buena out of date.

HUD spokesman Dirk Murphy said it will take his office "from five to nine months" to do the job. This includes a mandatory minimum 90-day period during which the initial draft is circulated for public comment

Murphy said the assumption that the process may not be completed until the end of June "is not unrealistic."

How fast the work proceeds will depend largely on what extent the federal government, which finances a major chunk of urban renewal, can rely on data being gathered for yet another environmental impact report (EIR) that is now nearing completion.

That EIR is required by state law for all projects believed to have a major impact on the environment.

—Turn to Page 8, Col. 1

Smog: Are kids the victims?

By Carl Irving

Children who breathe heavy doses of automobile-polluted air may have a harder time in school than their clean-air counterparts, according to a report by the state Air Resources Board.

The report also says the children should expect to suffer a higher incidence of breathing problems, have less athletic ability and face the prospect of higher medical costs throughout their lives.

Because children are smaller, breathe more quickly and generally have more sensitive lungs than adults, they more often will be hurt by air pollution, the study shows.

"It used to be, a kid would have had to stagger and gasp for breath before he'd be rated as a victim of air pollution," says a member of the state Department of Health. "Now we've come to realize the effects can be far more subtle."

The pollutants studied include sulphur dioxide (emitted from refineries and plants using fuel oil), smog (generated mostly by cars), carbon monoxide (also from vehicles) and lead — 95 per cent of which comes from vehicles.

—Turn to Page 8, Col. 1

For sale: Good old Gorda, lively ghost town

By John Todd
Examiner Staff Writer

GORDA— "People pull into the filling station here and ask 'is the road windy all the way?' I say 'yup.' I give it to them hard."

Bill Gomez, who pumps gas here, was talking.

Gorda is the coastal point midway between San Francisco and Los Angeles, perched on a ledge by Highway 1 about 70 miles south of Carmel. The town, in the lap of the towering Santa Lucia Mountains and overlooking the Pacific, is for sale.

Gomez sips his beer and continues:

"Some people I get a real kick out of. Some are so happy to see this country. Others think it is a drag.

"People ask how far it is to the Hearst castle, or how I can get back to 101. One day when the fog was hanging off the coast this guy said 'Gee, it must be nice when you can see the other side. I couldn't believe it. The other side of the ocean!

"When they ask what time does the fog lift, I always say '1:15' and they drive out happy."

About 20 people live here. They all work either at the station, the store or the restaurant, Sorta Gorda. The owner is a Los Angeles contractor, Larry Anderson, who bought the lonely nine-acre site 20 years ago. He now wants to sell it for $950,000.

A real estate flyer reads, "We proudly present Gorda. Overlooking the blue Pacific, it is an entire town, self-supporting and brimming with charm and dollar potential.

"Potential is the operative word here. Tenants presently live a kind of Dogpatch existence. Yards could be cleaned up. Rents could be raised. The gas station is old and crummy looking, but a competitor would probably build a new one."

—Turn to Page 16, Col. 1

Manchester's saloon, a popular watering hole

A hard look

Forecasters putting their money on rain

By Alan Cline

At first glance, the word from the long-range weather forecasters appears optimistic.

Few of the experts are predicting a third year of drought for California. The odds against it are said to be 50 to 1.

Rainfall predictions for the coming season range from 70 per cent of normal, from a private forecaster hired by the state, to 160 per cent of normal, by a University of California climatologist using comparative records.

Even the forecasters caution that their field is new and unproven. But there are other promising signs for the coming winter.

Ocean conditions are different from the last two years — some telltale warm currents have disappeared.

Early rains, absent last year, have returned to the Pacific Northwest. The first river flood warning in 19 months was issued in late September for the Smith River in the state's northwest corner.

But while hoping for the best, state and federal water managers are planning for the worst, noting the state has had droughts that lasted five and six years.

To add substance to that pessimism, a federal report issued Friday in Washington indicated that, if the drought continues, California, despite expenditures of $8 billion for water projects, could wind up short by 3 billion acre feet of water annually by the year 2000.

"We look at the optimistic forecasts for this winter, but we certainly cannot operate on those predictions," says Don Miller, chief of the state drought center in Sacramento. "Until we get those storms, we're in a drought."

—Turn to Page 26, Col. 1

San Francisco Sunday
Examiner & Chronicle

Sunday Scene, Travel, Want Ads, California Living, Comics in 2 parts

Fig. 5–7. Modular. The *San Francisco Examiner* uses a collection of rectangles, some of them boxed. Note the story above the nameplate.

The Courier-Journal

26 Pages   ••••   Louisville, Friday, January 14, 1978   Newsstand 15¢   Home delivery 80¢ week

Copyright © 1978, The Courier-Journal

Byrd announces he'll support canal treaties

By RUDY ABRAMSON
© L.A. Times-Washington Post Service

WASHINGTON — Senate Majority Leader Robert C. Byrd of West Virginia announced yesterday that he will vote for and actively promote ratification of the Panama Canal treaties.

Although his decision had long been expected by opponents of the treaties, Byrd's formal declaration helped the Carter administration in its uphill fight to win approval of the agreements. The pacts are expected to be sent to the Senate floor in the next few weeks.

"The basic question to be considered is whether these treaties are in the best interest of the United States," Byrd told a news conference in his Capitol office. "I believe that the weight of the evidence argues convincingly that they are.

"It is particularly important for our relations with Latin America and should

open a new era of mutual trust and cooperation in inter-American relations," he said. "Given the history of the canal and the principles of our country, the treaties are in our interest, and ratification is the right step to take."

The agreements would turn over control of the U.S.-built waterway to the Panamanian government by the year 2000 and would ensure the U.S. right to defend the waterway's neutrality.

Byrd said his reservations about the agreements were cleared up by a statement of understanding worked out between President Carter and Panama's leader, Gen. Omar Torrijos, in October.

The statement — issued after Torrijos met with Mr. Carter at the White House — declared that U.S. ships have the right to go to the head of the line for canal passage in time of emergency and that the United States has the right to use military force, if necessary, to assure neutrality of the canal after the year 2000.

Byrd said that, while he was personally satisfied by the unsigned October statement, practical politics requires that the substance of the statement be formally attached to the treaties.

Before making his announcement, Byrd called Senate Minority Leader Howard H. Baker Jr. of Tennessee, who was visiting South America, to tell him what he planned to say.

Byrd told reporters that he and Baker will work together to resolve objections blocking ratification.

During a visit to Panama last week, Baker indicated he would support the treaties, which were signed Sept. 7, if the issues of priority passage and U.S. assurance of canal neutrality are settled to his satisfaction.

Baker's vote is viewed by the administration as vital.

The Senate Foreign Relations Committee has scheduled three more days of hearings on the treaties and is expected to begin floor debate in February.

See BYRD
Back page, col. 4, this section

In a flurry

National Weather Service

LOUISVILLE area — Cloudy, chance of light snow or flurries through tomorrow, 30 per cent chance today. High today, low 20s; tomorrow, teens. Low tonight, 8 to 15.

KENTUCKY — Cloudy, chance of occasional snow or flurries through tomorrow. Accumulation less than an inch. Highs today, 20s; tomorrow, teens. Lows tonight, 8 to 15.

INDIANA — Chance of snow flurries today, variable cloudiness tomorrow. High today, low to mid-20s; tomorrow, teens. Lows tonight, 5 to 15.

TENNESSEE — Mostly cloudy through tomorrow; chance of scattered snow and snow flurries west today. Highs both days, 20s. Lows tonight, teens.

High yesterday, 28; low, 25.
Year ago yesterday, High, 35; low, -1.
Sun. Rises, 7:59; sets, 5:46.
Moon. Rises, 11:25 a.m.; sets, midnight.

Weather map and details, Page C 9.

Staff Photo by Paul Schuhmann

Blazing a cold road

The coal unloaded at the Louisville Gas & Electric Co.'s Cane Run plant in Louisville must be compacted to break up the frozen lumps of coal. The frozen coal is just one problem that area utilities have to contend with when the mercury takes a plunge. (Story, Page B 6.)

Carroll to seek $2.2 million for mine program

By RICHARD WHITT
Courier-Journal Staff Writer

FRANKFORT, Ky. — Gov. Julian Carroll's budget will include $2,244,900 for the state's often criticized strip-mining and reclamation program.

The new money will be used to hire an additional 248 employees, including 140 inspectors. And some of it will be used to increase the number of district offices in the Bureau for Surface Mining Reclamation and Enforcement from six to nine.

In addition to the inspectors, 35 more engineers will be hired, approximately doubling the size of the inspection and

Other stories about the legislature, Page B 1.

engineering staffs, a source in the Department for Natural Resources and Environmental Protection said yesterday.

The source would not allow his name to be used because Carroll's budget, although complete, is not scheduled to be released until Tuesday evening.

The new money would be spent to bring Kentucky into compliance with the new federal strip mine act. If it

doesn't comply, the state stands to lose about $20 million a year in federal funds set aside for reclamation of orphan lands (unreclaimed strip mines).

Money set aside in Carroll's budget will allow the department to operate for two years, the source said.

Interim regulations of the federal program go into effect next month. And this General Assembly is expected to pass legislation this session to bring Kentucky laws into compliance.

But Carroll may have to call a special session of the legislature next year to act on the permanent federal program,

the governor's office confirmed yesterday.

"We're facing the possibility of a special session in order to comply with the permanent regulations," said Carroll's press secretary, Gary Auxier.

The problem, Auxier said, is that the permanent regulations are not expected to be completed until August.

It would cost taxpayers about $7,400 a day to conduct a special session of the legislature, according to one estimate. Meanwhile, Robert D. Bell, secretary

See CARROLL
Back page, col. 2, this section

In shooting of trooper

Faulkner receives 15-year sentence

By BEN JOHNSON
Courier-Journal Staff Writer

Michael B. Faulkner was sentenced to 15 years in prison yesterday in the shooting of a Kentucky state trooper last September.

Bullitt Circuit Judge C. V. Sanders sentenced Faulkner, 23, of Indianapolis, to 15 years for first-degree assault and to concurrent one-year terms on three other felony charges.

"I have to live with this the rest of my life," Faulkner said after the sentencing. "It was just a human response. I responded the wrong way. I was too scared; I was just scared."

Faulkner pleaded guilty last Friday to all counts in Sanders' court. The pleas came as a result of last-minute plea bargaining to reduce a charge of attempted murder for the shooting of Sgt. Herbert Gibson, 38, of Elizabethtown. Gibson is partially paralyzed and undergoing treatment at the Institute for Physical Medicine and Rehabilitation at Jewish Hospital in Louisville.

A factor in his guilty plea, Faulkner told a reporter yesterday after the sentencing, was that he would be eligible for parole in two years. Had he been convicted of attempted murder and given the maximum 20-year sentence, he would not have been eligible for parole until he had served eight years. He will be credited with the four months he has already served in jail.

"That state trooper has a family and I'm really sorry that he's lost to them,"

Faulkner said. "But I have a family, too. I want to get back to my fiancee and two kids. I'm lost to them. I just wanted to make it easier to get back to my family."

(His lawyer said no one has been able to verify that Faulkner does have a family. No friends or relatives were among the 15 spectators in the courtroom in Shepherdsville yesterday, Faulkner said.)

Yesterday's sentencing ended another chapter in the Faulkner saga. It initially involved more than 200 county, state and local police officers in a high-speed chase Sept. 2, 2 minutes after Gibson was shot in the throat. Gibson had ordered Faulkner to pull his car over and was trying to question Faulkner about $20 reported taken from a service station customer.

Faulkner was captured three hours later after wrecking a stolen car he was driving while trying to crash through a police roadblock.

The saga continued with the largest police manhunt in Jefferson County history after Faulkner escaped Sept. 13 from a psychiatric testing facility at Central State Hospital. He was captured in Louisville the next day by an off-duty city police officer.

He was indicted by the Bullitt County Grand Jury Oct. 3 for attempted murder; receiving stolen property for the car he was driving at the time of the shooting; theft by unlawful taking for stealing the car he eventually wrecked;

Staff Photo by Robert Steinau

Michael B. Faulkner talks with reporters before his sentencing yesterday by Bullitt Circuit Judge C. V. Sanders. Faulkner told a reporter, "I'm really sorry about what happened, that the man (Sgt. Herbert Gibson of the Kentucky State Police) got hurt."

and escape for fleeing the Central State Hospital facility. On Oct. 21 he pleaded innocent to the four original charges.

Yesterday, Faulkner stood before Judge Sanders, his shackled legs slightly apart, his hands on his hips or crossed on his chest at times and at his sides at others. His small, boyish frame was lost in the baggy gray jail jumpsuit he wore. Sanders sat behind a slightly elevated

bench, looking straight ahead at Faulkner.

Faulkner's court-appointed public defender, Charles Sanders, had filed a motion for probation. (Judge Sanders is lawyer Sanders' father, a situation permissible under Kentucky law.)

Before ruling on the probation matter,
See FAULKNER
Back page, col. 1, this section

Japan agrees to cut its trade surplus in pact with U.S.

By WILLIAM CHAPMAN
© L.A. Times-Washington Post Service

TOKYO — Japan and the United States moved to avert a trade conflict yesterday by reaching an agreement that included Japan's pledge to open its markets to increased U.S. imports while trying to reduce Japanese exports to the United States.

The agreement came after more than five months of negotiations. U. S. and Japanese representatives said it marked a new era of peaceful commercial relations between the two countries.

Robert Strauss, the special U.S. trade representative, told a news conference that the agreement marked a major change of direction on the trade front.

"We haven't solved all the problems but we have defined them and we will begin a new process which will strengthen our relationship," he said. He conceded that the agreement would not eliminate the protectionist movement in Congress, which seeks to cut back sharply on Japanese imports that compete with U.S. products.

Strauss said, however, that "those protectionist forces would have raged much stronger" if the agreement had not been reached.

The agreement was concluded in an unusual bargaining session about 2 a.m. at a Tokyo dinner party given by U.S. Ambassador Mike Mansfield. Both sides had indicated late Thursday that there might be no agreement.

Japanese negotiators had complained that the United States was demanding too many specific promises. The Japanese said they were reluctant to commit their country on paper to a policy of eliminating trade surpluses and accepting the possibility of deficits in coming years.

The United States has complained for months about Japan's growing trade surplus — expected this year to range between $10 billion and $12 billion.

Sources on both sides said that shortly before 2 a.m. yesterday the Japanese representatives made new concessions that made an agreement possible.

According to a joint statement, Japan promised to reduce its balance of trade surplus considerably and said it would strive to wipe out the surplus completely in the future. It formally agreed to accept a deficit in its current accounts if such a deficit should occur. It also promised to reduce tariffs and make other changes to give foreign countries the same opportunities to sell in Japan as Japanese firms have in overseas markets.

Strauss called the agreement "a more far reaching result than I had anticipated."

The key phrase was one that pledged Japan to a policy of achieving "equilibrium," or an end to the current accounts surplus Japan had refused dur-

See JAPAN
Back page, col. 4, this section

Inside today

What has 4 corners and was born in North Carolina?

There is a Frankenstein monster loose in college basketball and Kentucky coach Joe Hall and Louisville coach Denny Crum would like to stomp it out. What is it? See sports editor Billy Reed's column, Page C 1.

When you're hot . . .

Ricky Skaggs is taking his bluegrass fiddle from the Lexington area to join Emmylou Harris and the Hot Band in Los Angeles, and will embark on a European tour with Miss Harris next month. In Accent.

Accent	B 4-5	Opinion page	A 4
Classified ads	C 9-10	Racing entries	C 8
Comics	C 11	Show clock	B 5
Deaths	C 12	Sports	C 1-8
Dimension page	A 5	Today's briefing	A 2
Marketplace	B 6-8	TV, radio	B 2

Vol. 246, No. 14

Sunday

Former Playboy favorite enjoys 'Pajama Tops'

June Wilkinson, six times featured in Playboy, would like to outgrow her "Pajama Tops" image, but the actress-wife of pro football quarterback Dan Pastorini, tells critic Gregg Swem she is having fun playing the bedroom farce at the Derby Dinner Playhouse in Jeffersonville. In Lively Arts.

Meat packer packs up

Farmers in southern Kentucky were shocked when a major meat-packing firm collapsed recently, but those involved say the firm's downfall illustrates the often unpredictable nature of the packing industry. In Marketplace.

A tale of two courts

Most Supreme Court watchers, civil libertarians in particular, view the Warren Court as uniformly liberal and see the Burger Court as a starkly conservative disaster. An analysis shows those watchers to be off base. In Outlook.

Fig. 5–8. Modular. The *Courier-Journal* puts its best story atop the page at the left, then uses modules for the rest, including index and Sunday promotion boxes.

Parents' guide to teen-age sex

Why your children are more sophisticated than you were — Lifestyle

Dr. King's children today

A rare interview — Page 14

Super Bowl Preview

Everything you need to know to watch the big game — Sports

Chicago Tribune

Midwest Edition

Sunday, January 15, 1978

131st Year—No. 15 © 1978 Chicago Tribune 10 Sections

60¢

Perilous U.S. border crossing

By Louie Gonzalez

Special from the Oakland Tribune

OAKLAND, Cal.—They have been characterized as a class of people spreading like a cancer across the country, depleting the resources of America. They are known as wets, wetbacks, mojados, ilegales, undocumented workers, and illegal aliens.

But no matter what you call them, they are victims of hardship, brutality, exploitation, and violence as they expend every ounce of their energy to reach for something better.

Who are these people? Why do they do what they do?

For four days, I became an illegal alien to find out.

BY THE TIME I arrived in the interior of Mexico, I could not have proved I was either a Mexican citizen or an American citizen. By leaving all identification in the United States, I had literally become a man without a country, an illegal alien traveling in Mexico.

My plan sounded simple enough—fly to Guadalajara from Tijuana, return to the border town by third-class bus, cross the U.S. border as an illegal, and if successful, get illegal help from smugglers for a passage to Oakland, Cal.

At the very least, I knew I could be apprehended by the U.S. Border patrol or harassed by the Ku Klux Klan. There was also the possibility that in attempting to cross the border I could be robbed on either side. But the odds for the latter seemed against all that.

I AND OTHER illegals also ran the risk of "disappearing," buried by American or Mexican bandits in some unidentifiable grave in one of the canyons southeast of San Diego near Chula Vista, victims of greed or cheap thrills.

As I stared out the window of the Mexican bus and surveyed the countryside shrouded in darkness, these facts made prospects seem grim. While these thoughts ran through my mind, I did not know that I would experience that violence and put my life in the balance twice in a battle for survival.

The jarring of the old red bus jolted me back to reality. It was almost 24 hours since I had slept and more than six hours since I had left Guadalajara. A beautiful Sunday sunrise with inky blackness giving way to irridescent pinks and reds promised a pleasant beginning to the trip.

EVENTS OF the day before had been put behind me: I had purchased a tourist card from a San Diego travel agent for $2 with a tearful story that "My grandmother is dying in Mexico." After all, I had no documents proving who I was.

"Ah, you are an American citizen," the Mexican immigration officer at the Tijuana Airport commented as I presented my tourist card for inspection. "Yes," I replied. That was the last English word I spoke as I left with his warning not to lose that card.

From now on, I knew all vestiges of

Continued on page 20, col. 1

"I was an illegal"

Thousands of illegal aliens cross into the United States from Mexico every night. Louie Gonzalez, an Oakland Tribune reporter, posed as one and made the hazardous trip. First of three articles.

Susan Clark: She wants new image

Actress Susan Clark wants to change her tomboy image. After working her way through 15 movies without attracting much attention, she became an overnight success with two television films, "Babe" and "Amelia Earhart." Now she's afraid she might be typecast, so she wants sexier roles. The bottom line for an actress, she says, is, "Will the truck driver in Iowa want you?" An interview is in the *Magazine*.

African editor's flight to freedom

Donald Woods, the white South African editor banned from public writing and speaking because of his antigovernment statements, made a dramatic escape recently to neighboring Lesotho. Step by step, Woods describes how he secretly hitchhiked 185 miles and then swam a river to reach freedom. In *Perspective*.

South Florida: A warm feeling

Though southern Florida may not qualify as a tropical area, it's usually warmer there than anywhere else in the continental United States. And certainly it's a lot warmer than Chicago in mid-January. Travel editor Kermit Holt tells what it's like to be in the Florida sun on a day like this. And travel writer Horace Sutton picks America's 10 top hotels. Both reports are in *Travel*.

'77 U.S. income form less taxing

The new federal income tax forms are easier to fill out and prettier to look at. There's more room on the pastel blue or pink tax returns and the language has been simplified so that you no longer need a college education to understand the instructions. All that's required now is the reading level of a high school sophomore or junior, reports Leonard Wiener in *Business*.

Index

Weather

CHICAGO AND VICINITY: Sunday: Partly sunny; high near 20 F [-6 C]. Map, other reports on Page 27.

No hope for peace pact: Sadat

Begin has given nothing, Egyptian leader says

CAIRO [UPI]—President Anwar Sadat said Saturday he had "absolutely no hope" of reaching agreement on the basics of a peace pact with Israel and that Israeli Premier Menahem Begin had given him nothing in return for his recent peace initiative.

In an interview published two days before an Egyptian-Israeli foreign ministers meeting aimed at sealing a joint "declaration of principles" for Middle East peace, Sadat said:

"I declare now, I have absolutely no hope that such a declaration will be issued and, therefore, we will have a different strategy." He did not elaborate.

In his sharpest attack yet on Begin, the Egyptian president told Cairo's October Magazine: "Begin gave me nothing. It was I who gave him everything. I gave him security and legitimacy and got nothing in return."

"I WANT TO be frank without making others angry," Sadat said, commenting on Begin being a guerrilla leader against the British in Palestine as a youth.

"My peace initiative is not the [Jerusalem] King David Hotel which Begin blew up in his youth [as a protest against British presence]. He cannot blow up this intiative without destroying himself and others for hundreds of years to come."

October editor Anis Mansour, a close friend of Sadat and the man who conducted the interview, said the president had sounded "sad, as if he regretted the [peace] moves he had made."

Sadat spoke in the past tense of his hopes to offer Moslem prayers in a liberated Sinai next year. Returning to the Israeli negotiating stance, he said, "The old concept about everything [concerning the Arabs and Middle East peace] has resurfaced in Israel."

SADAT SAID HE was "not sorry for what I did," but repeated recent pledges that, "If I fail, I will turn over my post to somebody else, and he will have to complete this [peace] mission or decide on something else or some other method."

Sadat also implicitly returned to earlier statements that the duration of a oral nonaggression pact he sealed with Begin in Jerusalem depended on Israeli negotiating concessions.

Egyptian President Anwar Sadat

"Israel is sowing the wind and therefore will reap the storms, as the Bible says," Sadat told the weekly magazine.

He compared Israel's stand to that of Syria, which has been spearheading hard-line Arab opposition to his peace moves.

THE EGYPTIAN leader said he had traveled to Jerusalem Nov. 19 "to escape being swallowed by Syrian verbal acrobatics in order to enter into the same thing with the Israelis. I consider the labrynthine method of both [to be] the same."

Earlier Saturday, Egypt said the deadlocked talks on military aspects of a peace plan would resume in Cairo next week despite disagreements on the key issue of Israeli settlements in occupied Sinai.

An official announcement carried by Egypt's Middle East News Agency said the talks, which stalled and recessed Friday, would restart next Wednesday and "continue discussing issues on the agenda concerning Israeli withdrawal from Sinai and other outstanding questions."

The announcement tempered pessimism expressed by many Egyptian officials over the Cairo talks. When the talks recessed, there was no immediate indication when they might resume.

AP Wirephoto

Gracious widow

Mrs. Muriel Humphrey waves to a small group of well wishers as she boards Air Force One Saturday morning to accompany the body of her husband, Hubert, to Washington. President Carter sent the plane to Minneapolis to fly Humphrey's body to the capitol to lie in state. The former vice president died of cancer Friday at his home in Waverly, Minn. He was 66. An obituary and more photos are on page 26.

Rep. McClory failed to reveal land and stock in ethics report

U.S. REP. Robert McClory [R., Ill.] failed to list a $27,000 investment in a federally financed housing project on his congressional ethics statements filed from 1969 through 1975, a Chicago Tribune investigation has disclosed.

McClory, ranking Republican member of the House Judiciary Committee, also failed to report a financial interest in two Waukegan banks during the same period.

Such disclosures to the House Committee on Standards of Official Conduct are required of congressional members by House Rule 44, which was passed in 1968.

McCLORY DID NOT make the required disclosures until 1976, when 44 House members petitioned the committee on standards to investigate Rep. Robert Sikes [D., Fla.] on several charges, including failure to disclose certain holdings.

Sikes subsequently was reprimanded by the House for failing to disclose stock in a defense contracting firm and in a bank on his ethics statements.

During several interviews conducted over a space of days, McClory progressively changed his position from stating that he originally disclosed "everything that was required to be disclosed," to "maybe we took a more generous interpretation of the rule than we should have," to "in the past I didn't volunteer anything . . . Now I have taken a position of disclosing."

McCLORY'S INVOLVEMENT in the Waukegan housing development—held

Continued on page 8, col. 1

Tribune reporters Chuck Neubauer and William B. Crawford Jr. and reporter Ray Gibson of the Suburban Trib have spent the last four weeks sifting through documents relating to business dealings in Lake County, where a grand jury is investigating allegations of political corruption. This is their report.

Warning: Tobacco politics may waste money

By Jack Fuller

Chicago Tribune Press Service

WASHINGTON—There is one tobacco habit Health, Education, and Welfare [HEW] Secretary Joseph Califano's new $23-million war on smoking probably won't cure.

It belongs to the federal government, which spends millions of dollars a year inspecting and grading tobacco and administering a loan program that runs into hundreds of millions of dollars to support the price of the crop.

Asked last week whether he intended to do anything to dilute the government's involvement with tobacco farmers, Califano said that he was not going to tilt at that particular windmill.

LIKE THE windmills in "Don Quixote,' this one had a face—and the face wore the unmistakable grin of Jimmy Carter.

According to Department of Agriculture figures supplied to congressional critics of tobacco price supports, the federal government in 1976 spent $15.1 million administering a program that gave $315.8 million in loans to tobacco farmers.

Those loans are granted by about a dozen farmers' cooperatives. The amount each farmer receives is based on price and projected production quotas.

The farmer pledges his crop as collateral on the loan if he cannot sell the tobacco on the open market at the support price.

"TOBACCO FARMERS are extremely good about paying back their loans," said Roxy Burris, a staff assistant to Rep. James P. Johnson [R., Colo.], who opposes price supports.

In the last three years, for example, the federal government's Commodity Credit Corp. has not lost any money on these loans, although the administrative costs of the program are borne by the taxpayer.

In addition, the government spent $5.9 million in 1976 paying for tobacco inspection and grading [cotton is the only other commodity that gets this special treatment], and $5.1 million on tobacco research.

It administered a $15.8 million Food for Peace program to loan money to poor nations to buy United States tobacco and another $81 million for loans to richer nations for the same purpose.

"THERE IS NO better example of the schizophrenia of government than its approach to tobacco," said John Banzhaf,

Continued on page 7, col. 3

Millions of Americans and almost a million Japanese have signed up for supplemental insurance that covers treatment for cancer. Story on page 13.

Fig. 5 – 9. Braced modular. The *Chicago Tribune,* still conscious of street sales, uses a big banner on nearly every edition but also displays a few modules most days.

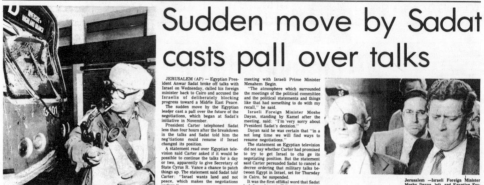

The Daily Pantagraph

Snow likely
Thursday snow likely, high in the middle 20s. Thursday night, snow likely, windy and turning colder, low 12 to 18. (More weather on page B-10).

133rd Year.—19th Day | Bloomington-Normal, Ill., Thursday, January 19, 1978—40 pages | 2 sections | First Edition 25c

Crashed

Boston —A workman surveys damage to the front of a Boston underground trolley car that collided with another Wednesday at the Arlington Street station on the Green Line. Several injuries were reported. (AP Laserphoto)

Sudden move by Sadat casts pall over talks

JERUSALEM (AP) — Egyptian President Anwar Sadat broke off talks with Israel on Wednesday, called his foreign minister back to Cairo and accused the Israelis of deliberately blocking progress toward a Middle East Peace.

The sudden move by the Egyptian leader cast a pall over the future of the negotiations, which began at Sadat's initiative in November.

President Carter telephoned Sadat less than four hours after the breakdown in the talks and Sadat told him the neg'tiations could resume if Israel changed its position.

A statement read over Egyptian television said Carter asked if it would be possible to continue the talks for a day or two, apparently to give Secretary of State Cyrus R. Vance a chance to patch things up. The statement said Sadat told Carter: "Israel wants land and not peace, which makes the negotiations useless."

An Israeli cabinet statement charged that Egypt "was under the illusion that we would surrender to demands that at no ime were acceptable to Israel" and accused Egypt of "astonishing intransigence" in the bargaining.

Vance, who has been attempting to bridge the gaps between Israel and Egypt in private talks with the negotiators, told reporters he does not believe the talks have reached an end.

"I've been through a lot of international negotiations," he said. "I've seen ups and downs in the past."

The Egyptian announcement caught Vance by surprise. He was planning a dinner Wednesday night for Egyptian Foreign Minister Mohammed Kamel.

"It will be for the president to decide what and how the next stage will take place," Kamel said after a 90-minute meeting with Israeli Prime Minister Menahem Begin.

"The atmosphere which surrounded the meetings of the political committee and the political statements and things like that had something to do with my recall," he said.

Israeli Foreign Minister Moshe Dayan, standing by Kamel after the meeting, said: "I'm very sorry about President Sadat's decision."

Dayan said he was certain that "in a not long time we will find ways to resume negotiations."

The statement on Egyptian television did not say whether Carter had promised to try to get Israel to cha ge its negotiating position. But the statement said Carter persuaded Sadat to cancel a decree ordering that military talks between Egypt in Israel, set for Thursday in Cairo, be suspended.

It was the first offi8ial word that Sadat had planned to cut off direct contact with the Israelis entirely, although there was speculation to that effect after Kamel's recall.

Those talks will reconvene Saturday, the statement said.

The talks between the Israeli and Egyptian foreign ministers, the highest level negotiations between the two countries so far, began Tuesday and soon were deeply divided over Palestinian rights to a homeland and Israel's 11-year occupation of Arab lands.

The talks were "continuing in a vicious cycle," Egyptian Information Minister Abdel Moneim el Sawy said in announcing the breakoff on Cairo television.

Sawy said Sadat ordered Kamel to return "immediately" because "it became apparent from the declarations (of Israeli leaders) that Israel insists on presenting partial solutions that cannot lead to the establishment of a just and lasting peace."

Informed of the Egyptian annoucement, Vance went to Kamel's hotel room, but their meeting ended abruptly when Vance was called out to answer a phone call from National Security Adviser Zbigniew Brezezinski in Washington.

Sawy, his face grave as he read the recall statement over Egyptian television, said Egypt's demands — for total Israeli withdrawal from Arab lands and self determination for the Palestinians — have not changed.

Sawy said Sadat has called an emergency session of the Peoples' Assembly, Egypt's parliament, for Saturday to "place before the representatives of the people all the facts of the situation.

It was from that same rostrum that Sadat launched the historic quest for peace that brought him to Jerusalem Nov. 19 for a first dramatic meeting with leaders of the nation his country fought in four wars.

Face press

Jerusalem —Israeli Foreign Minister Moshe Dayan, left, and Egyptian Foreign Minister Mohammed Kamel appear before newsmen as they leave Premier Menachem Begin's Jerusalem office Wednesday prior to Kamel's sudden departure back to Egypt. (AP Laserphoto)

Roof collapses on civic center

Photo on A-2

HARTFORD, Conn. (AP) — The coliseum roof of Hartford's three-year-old Civic Center collapsed under heavy rain and snow Wednesday, injuring no one but dealing what Mayor George Athanson called "a serious blow" to hopes for downtown revival.

Athanson called the Civic Center, w'ich cost $70 million and was the focus of a major urban renewal effort, "the focal point of the new beat of Hartford."

The flat, 1,400-ton roof of the 10,000-seat arena crumpled without warning at 4:19 a.m., just hours after 4,800 basketball fans had left the arena.

Initial assessments were that repairs would take 1½ to two years, and Arthur Lumsden, president of the Greater Hartford Chamber of Commerce, predicted business losses of between $15 million and $20 million a year.

Four maintenance and security workers near the arena escaped injury.

But Hartford's investment — psychological as well as financial — in the Civic Center as the focus of downtown renewal fell into jeopardy.

Like civic centers i8 other cities, Hartford's new home for sports, shopping and conventions was seen as the way out of the urban decay of recent decades.

Its 2½-acre roof was heralded as an innovation — it stood only on its four corners with no supporting walls between, and was raised into place in one piece.

Investigators were studying the remains to determine whether the sheer weight of the snow and drenching rain that followed caused the colapse — or if there were other factors.

At least three ot er roofs in Connecticut collapsed during the storm, one of them killing a man at a Jewett City factory.

Gov. Ella Grasso said her reaction was "tremendous sadness to see this tangled wreck, and fervent thanks to God that no one was inside at the time."

"The state is committed to helping a beleaguered city that has tried so valiantly to make the Civic Center the heart of its rebirth," she said.

Deputy Mayor Nicholas Carbone said a new, possibly bigger coliseum would be built, but he added that existing and planned city programs won't be scuttled by the collapse.

The city had about $30 million in insurance on its part of the building, including furniture and fixtures, Carbone said.

The coliseum, which is owned by the city, was built independently from the shopping section and an office complex.

"The initial shock is similar to a town that has had a heart attack," said John Gillespie, president of the Luettgens Ltd. department store in the retail section.

Inside today

Abby	B- 8	Opinion	A- 4
Amusement	A-10	Porter	A- 8
Births	A- 6	Sheinwold	B-11
Comics	B- 4	Shulsky	A-13
Deaths	B-19	Sports	B- 1
Farm	B-20	Television	A-11
Heartline	A-13	Today	B- 5
Markets	B-20	Weather	B-10

Carter phones Sadat

WASHINGTON (AP) — President Carter telephoned Egyptian President Anwar Sadat Wednesday and urged him to continue the search for a Mideast peace despite a dramatic breakdown in direct Egyptian-Israeli talks.

The 10-minute phone call was announced by White House Press Secretary Jody Powell, who declined to provide any information about the conversation.

Immediately after Powell spoke, however, an American official who asked that he not be identified told reporters:

"I would just encourage you all not to overreact to the situation and view it with excessive alarm."

It was this official who said Carter urged that Sadat "keep the negotiating process and the progress toward peace going."

This informant said Sadat expressed to Carter his concern about the course the peace quest had taken but restated his own desire for peace.

Sadat dramatically broke off talks with Israel in Jerusalem and called his foreign minister back to Cairo, accusing the Israelis of deliberately blocking progress toward peace.

The American official who talked to reporters here said: "It is not our view that either the Egyptians or the Israelis desire termination of the discussions or of the progress that has been made."

He said Carter had no plans to telephone Israeli Prime Minister Menahem Begin.

Judge from St. Louis named FBI director

WASHINGTON (AP) — President Carter has chosen U.S. Circuit Judge William H. Webster to be the next FBI director, administration sources said Wednesday night.

Webster, 53, of St. Louis won a strong recommendation from Attorney General Griffin Bell and Carter agreed with Bell's choice, the sources said. The White House was expected to make the formal announcement Thursday.

Webster must win Senate confirmation before taking over the FBI from Director Clarence M. Kelley, who is scheduled to retire Feb. 15.

The choice of the Missouri judge and former federal prosecutor ends the administration's year-long search for an FBI chief willing to serve a 10-year term, the maximum permitted by law.

Bell had insisted on a 10-year commitment, to provide the bureau with continuity in leadership as it continues major changes in its operations and recovers from disclosures of past wrongdoing.

Webster's friends and professional colleagues described him as intelligent, fair-minded and witty. They said he plays an intense game of tennis and that he's more moderate in his politics and philosophy than his short haircut and conservative style of dress would suggest.

A Republican, he dabbled in Missouri party politics several years ago, but has refrained from political activities since he was appointed a federal district judge in 1971 by then-President Richard M. Nixon.

Two years later, Nixon promoted him to the 8th Circuit Court of Appeals which handles cases from several midwestern states.

The President and Bell chose Webster over U.S. District Judge Frank McGarr of Chicago. Bell had narrowed the field to those two after Carter's first nominee, U.S. District Judge Frank Johnson of Montgomery, Ala., bowed out last November because of continuing health problems.

Kelly, who had been scheduled to retire the $57,000-a-year post at the first of the year, agreed to stay on until Feb. 15 after Johnson withdrew.

In nearly a decade of public life, Webster has attracted little criticism.

Judge William H. Webster

Some civil rights lawyers suggest that if there is a weakness in his record, it is in that field. But others say they found Webster fair even when they lost cases in his courtroom.

Farmers return to Washington

WASHINGTON (AP) — Pickup trucks, vans, buses, campers and tractors full of farm families protesting low prices for their crops returned to the capital Wednesday to present their case to Congress members.

They were starting a week of lobbying and picketing.

South of Washington, state and county police reported two incidents of violence, including shooting by undetermined persons, as tractors enroute to Washington blocked traffic and later rammed a police-car barricade.

A trooper received minor injuries. Three Virginians were arrested and charged with a variety of crimes, including reckless driving and leaving the scene of an accident.

Agriculture Secretary Bob Bergland, traveling in the Midwest, said again that it would be a mistake to meet the protesters' demands by government fiat rather than changes in market conditions.

Capitol and Washington police officials said they had no firm count of the number of demonstrators because they were so scattered, many attending Agriculture Department meetings, visiting Congress members, and sightseeing.

Demonstrators plastered police squad cars and motorcycles with "We Support Farm Strike" bumper stickers without incident.

Many members of Congress returning for the start of the 1978 session Thursday were greeted by small groups of farmers in the corridors, rallied by the American Agriculture movement, which organized a national farmers' strike that began Dec. 14.

Only 19 tractors out of at least 50 that were expected made it to the Capitol for the opening rally.

They were supposed to park on a side street, according to their demonstration permit, but the lead tractor — from Butler, Mo., — tried to go up a broad sidewalk that circles the Capitol plaza.

Capitol Police Capt. G.H. Abernathy, stood in front of the tractor surrounded by roughly 600 protesters, and told the men driving it to stop. After three tense minutes, the tractor backed up and parked on the street.

Assistant District Police Chief B.D. Crooke Jr. and a city lawyer gave the group a special permit on the spot to drive their tractors two miles through the heart of the city to the White House and back, as long as the crowd stayed on the sidewalks.

The strikers' main goal — "100 percent of parity" — was the favorite slogan for the signs and banners that dotted the crowds on the Capitol grounds.

One hundred percent of parity is theoretically the level at which the farmers would have the same buying power their predecesors had in 1910-14.

The parity index was 66 percent a month ago when the demonstrators first brought their case here, aiming their protest then at President Carter.

Anti-smog breakthrough made in burning high-sulfur coal

TULLAHOMA, Tenn. (AP) — Scientists have achieved an anti-pollution breakthrough that could permit America to burn high-sulfur coal for power within a decade and get 50 percent more electricity from it.

The experimental process reduces nitrogen oxide, a major component of smog, to levels far below federal standards, they said.

"This is the last scientific breakthrough we required," Dr. John Dicks of the University of Tennessee Space Institute said in a telephone interview Wednesday.

"We believe this will allow us to start a demonstration plant, which should culminate in the commercialization of MHD within the next 10 years," he said.

Magnetohydrodynamics (MHD) involves burning coal at abnormally high temperatures, improving the efficiency of the combustion.

Discovered by Michael Faraday in 1831, MHD posed some serious technological problems. But the space institute built the nation's only coal-fired MHD plant in the early 1970s for experimentation.

Last May, Dicks announced a first breakthrough, treating the coal with potassium.

He said the potassium merged with the sulfur, coated the fly ash, and could be spun out of the exhaust in a cylinder using centrifugal force. Tests showed that 95 percent or more of the sulfur could be removed without using a costly scrubber, Dicks said.

"That left only $ problem with nitrogen oxide," Dicks said Wednesday. "And the solution to that came very early and very easily.

"The way we achieved this is to burn the coal with very low amounts of oxygen, then to complete the combustion later by adding oxygen at much lower temperatures," he said. "It is the nitrogen-oxygen combination that has been causing the trouble."

In early tests, nitrogen oxygen had been running about 2,500 parts per million, Dicks said. But with the new process, he said it dropped to 20 parts per million.

"That is well beneath our standards," James Wellburn of the Environmental Protection Agency said in a telephone interview from Atlanta. EPA regulations require that new coal-fired power plants emit no more than 525 parts per million.

"We feel there is a possibility of applying this method to more conventional power plants," Dicks said. "It may not be necessary to restrict it to MHD. But it will take further work to determine whether that will be feasible."

Dicks said the two anti-pollution breakthroughs will allow MHD plants to burn plentiful, high-sulfur coal from the East Coast.

"We expect that MHD will be able to produce power 50 per cent more efficiently in the first generation, and that later generations may be able to achieve 60 per cent efficiency," he said. "Early development within the next 10 years could enable us to save many billions of dollars by the end of the century."

Ford agrees to recall

WASHINGTON (AP) — Nearly a quarter-million 1975 Ford and Mercury automobiles will be recalled to correct a faulty emission control system, the Environmental Protection Agency said Wednesday. The ForJ Motor Co. agreed to recall the 240,000 vehicles because the cars contain a faulty switch in the exhaust gas recirculation system, the EPA said.

Fig. 5–10. Imbalance. Nearly every element on the *Daily Pantagraph* in Bloomington, Illinois approaches balance with another element on the opposite side.

Cool

Low in 40s, high in low 60s today. Mostly NW winds 10-15 mph. Data, map 2-A.

St. Petersburg Times

Florida's Best Newspaper

COLLATERAL LOANS
A.P.R. 7 ½ %
First
Gulf Beach
BANK AND TRUST CO.
Phone 360-5581
Member Federal Deposit Ins. Corp. — Adv.
Equal Opportunity Lender

VOL. 94 — NO. 181 66 PAGES ★$ ST. PETERSBURG, FLORIDA, SATURDAY, JANUARY 21, 1978 .... 20 CENTS A COPY

Snow cripples East

Florida travelers snowed in
— Story, Page 1-B

Northeast sports are out
— Story, Page 1-C

UPI

Commuters make their way to a Long Island subway station after snow forced them to leave their Long Island Railroad train at Jamaica Friday.

Compiled from UPI, AP wires

A huge winter storm paralyzed much of the East Friday. Major cities were isolated, airports shut down, roads closed, rail service halted and the wheels of American commerce came to a virtual standstill.

New York City slowed to a crawl amid huge white drifts, with skiers poling themselves down the storied streets of the Big Apple. Boston, Philadelphia, Pittsburgh, Washington and Baltimore were hobbled by deep snow.

Ohio, Kentucky, Pennsylvania, Maryland, New Jersey and most of New England lay beneath a deep blanket of snow.

THE STORM ALSO struck deep into the South. Snow and ice crippled Virginia, Tennessee, Mississippi, Alabama and Georgia.

Schools and businesses shut down by the hundreds from Mississippi to New England.

The death toll from a series of storms that swept from Texas to New England this week climbed to 47 with the latest assault.

Here is a summary of how the storm affected various sections of the country:

New York

Thirteen inches of snow — whipped into road-blocking drifts by 40-mile-per-hour winds — brought New York to a halt. All schools were closed, government offices, businesses and industries shut down and Wall Street was desolate.

Major commodities exchanges shut down and the New York Stock Exchange — the mecca of American commerce — opened two hours late at noon. **Story, Page 8-A.**

New York Mayor Edward Koch declared a state of emergency, prohibiting travel on major highways by all vehicles except those equipped with snow tires or chains. Bus service and most subway service was cut off and the Long Island Railroad, which carries more than 100,000 commuters daily, shut down.

ONE YOUNG woman who went to work on skis had little competition in her ride down the usually crammed Third Avenue. Another slid gracefully across 42nd Street. The skiers were all over town, and sporting goods dealers reported skis were selling fast.

See STORM, 6-A

Times DIGEST

FSU survivors may be hypnotized, Page 1-B

Sparkman says he won't run for re-election

Democratic Sen. John Sparkman of Alabama, who served in Congress for 42 years, told his Senate colleagues Friday that he has decided against running for re-election this year. He gave no reason for retiring but noted he will be 79 years old at the end of his present term on Jan. 3, 1979. Sparkman is chairman of the Senate Foreign Relations Committee. Sen. Frank Church, D-Idaho, is considered the most likely replacement as chairman.

Three recalls announced

The Transportation Department announced the recall Friday of some 1978 Ford Fairmonts and Mercury Zephyrs. An estimated 185,000 of the vehicles may have a wiring problem that could result in total loss of electrical power. Also recalled were about 5,000 1972-78 Ford trucks for replacement of engine cooling fans that may crack and more than 131,000 1969-1972 Toyota Mark IIs for repair or replacement of fuel tanks that may be damaged by corrosion.

Jaworski: Some violated rules

The House ethics committee investigation of alleged South Korean influence-buying shows a small number of sitting congressmen violated House rules and some may be "criminally culpable," special counsel Leon Jaworski said Friday. Jaworski, briefing junior House Democrats, mentioned no names and gave no description of misdeeds. But it was the first time he reported firm evidence of wrongdoing by anyone now in Congress, and made clear he will recommend disciplinary action.

Pakistan hijacker overpowered

A hijacker who threatened to blow up a Pakistani International Airlines jet was overpowered early today in Karachi, Pakistan by the airline's president and the plane's crew. One person suffered a bullet wound in the scuffle with the hijacker, authorities said. The gunman hijacked the plane Friday on a domestic flight to Karachi. The hijacker said he was suffering from cancer and demanded $2-million to pay for treatment.

INSIDE THE TIMES TODAY

Bell fires U.S. Attorney Marston

GRIFFIN BELL
. . . final decision.

By MARTIN DYCKMAN
St. Petersburg Times National Correspondent

WASHINGTON — David W. Marston, the corruption-busting U.S. attorney at Philadelphia, was fired by Atty. Gen. Griffin Bell Friday despite a torrent of public support for the Republican prosecutor.

Marston himself broke the news, his face tense after a nearly two-hour meeting with Bell. "The attorney general announced his decision of last week to fire me was final," he said.

Marston, who answered Bell's summons to a meeting here still hoping that Bell would allow him to finish his term, said he was fired purely because he is a Republican and the Carter Administration is Democratic.

"**HE (BELL)** said we have a system and he has to accept it," Marston told reporters. ". . . I don't agree with that. Before I got there they had a system too in Philadelphia and I didn't accept that system. I threw it out and eliminated politics . . ."

Marston said Bell conceded that the Administration found no fault with his record in office.

In his 18 tumultuous months, Marston, 35, had supervised a sensational string of indictments and convictions of powerful Pennsylvania politicians. And he was reported to be investigating two Democratic U.S. representatives from Pennsylvania, Joshua Eilberg and Daniel J. Flood.

President Carter admitted at a press conference last week that he had passed on to Bell a request from Eilberg to "expedite" Marston's dismissal. And, though the Administration insisted it had meant to replace Marston all along, a landslide of public support for Marston fell on the White House.

Through Thursday, according to the White House press office, there had been 8,599 telegrams and letters and 1,030 telephone calls favoring Marston to only 3 letters and 2 telephone calls endorsing his removal.

Presidential press secretary Jody Powell said in Atlanta that he did not know whether Bell consulted with Carter before moving against Marston.

See MARSTON, 4-A

DAVID MARSTON
. . . disappointed.

Carter seeks tax cut, curbs on wage and price increases

By JIM LUTHER
Associated Press

WASHINGTON — President Carter asked Congress Friday for a $25-billion tax cut to sustain economic growth and called on labor and business to hold down wage and price increases in an effort to control inflation this year.

The tax cut, aimed mainly at offsetting increased Social Security taxes, would become effective on Oct. 1 and benefit 96 per cent of all taxpayers. A four-member family earning $15,000 a year would realize a tax reduction of $258.

By 1980, Carter advisers predict, the tax cut would result in creation of nearly 1-million jobs. And if the economy needs them, the President promised, he will consider proposing additional tax cuts in the future.

IN AN ECONOMIC message to Congress elaborating on ideas contained in Thursday's State of the Union message, Carter followed the tradition of his predecessors by painting a generally rosy picture of the economy.

The President abandoned an earlier goal of reducing inflation to 4 per cent, settling instead for a reduction of one-half percentage point per year in inflation and wage increases. Administration officials said the inflation rate has averaged 6.0 per cent in the last two years. Over the same period, the increase in hourly earnings has averaged 7.3 per cent.

Thus in broad terms, the Administration's inflation goal for 1978 is about 5.5 per cent, and the wage target is about 6.8 per cent.

Carter also appeared to concede it would take a minor economic miracle to meet his pledge of balancing the federal budget by 1981.

See ECONOMY, 6-A

Living costs up in '77

By SARA FRITZ
United Press International

WASHINGTON — Consumer prices rose 6.8 per cent in 1977, the Labor Department reported Friday, pushing the inflation rate up 2 percentage points during President Carter's first year in office.

The December increase of 0.4 per cent reflected some moderation in the price situation as the year drew to a close.

The December rate compared with a 0.5 per cent increase in November and 0.3 per cent increases in August, September and October.

THE CONSUMER Price Index was 186.1 in December, meaning that goods and services costing $100 in 1967 now cost $186.10.

The 1977 annual rate of 6.8 per cent showed a dramatic acceleration over the 4.8 per cent rise in prices during 1976 — Gerald Ford's last year in the White House.

Prices rose 12.2 per cent in 1974 and 7 per cent in 1975.

Rising food prices were blamed for accelerating inflation in 1977. This trend actually has cooled somewhat since the early winter months of last year when food and fuel shortages were driving prices up at a double-digit rate.

FOOD PRICES jumped 8 per cent in 1977, led by a 47.8 per cent rise for coffee. Medical costs climbed 9 per cent; fuel oil and utilities 10.7 per cent.

In December, food rose a bare 0.2 per cent — reflecting a decline in egg, coffee, dairy and poultry prices. This trend suggested a national farmers' strike was having little impact at the grocery.

Sadat, right, thanked Vance for U.S. effort in keeping peace hopes alive in the Middle East but told a news conference Israel must be ready to withdraw from occupied territories.

AP

Sadat: More talks now would be useless

By THOMAS W. LIPPMAN
Washington Post

CAIRO — President Anwar Sadat said Friday that it would be "useless" for Egypt to resume peace talks with Israel until the Israelis commit themselves in principle to withdraw from the occupied territories.

In strong language, he made clear that his decision to pull the Egyptian delegation out of this week's talks in Jerusalem was not just a negotiating ploy. The talks are off, he said, until the Israelis understand that they cannot have both peace and the territories.

HE SAID, "The door to peace is not closed." But his comments left the strong impression that the entire fabric of the negotiations has unraveled and it will take dramatic changes to stitch it back together.

With Sadat and Prime Minister Menahem Begin of Israel now moving away from negotiation and back into long-distance polemics, no such changes appear imminent, at least not without strong action by the United States.

Sadat was speaking at a joint press conference with Secretary of State Cyrus Vance after they met for two hours at the president's rest house on the Nile River, north of the capital.

When Sadat and Vance emerged from the house onto the lawn to see the press, Sadat did not wait for the questioning to begin. He spoke a few words of appreciation for the U.S. role in the negotiations and then plunged into his response to criticism from Begin in the past two days.

Referring to Begin's speech in the Knesset (Parliament) Thursday in which he called some of Sadat's proposals "preposterous," Sadat said, "anyone who reads his speech can feel that I was right, because they want land, they want security, they want everything and they are not ready to understand that peace cannot be achieved except if it is built on justice.

See MIDEAST, 4-A

Fig. 5 – 11. Modular. Big modules are used by the *St. Petersburg Times,* a paper that uses color photographs or charts on nearly every front page.

On Today's Editorial Page
Still A Long Way To Go
editorial
The House Leaders' Package
Editorial

ST. LOUIS POST-DISPATCH

FINAL
★ ★ M
Latest Stock Prices
Pages 13A and 14A

VOL. 99 NO. 324 Copyright 1977, St. Louis Post-Dispatch FRIDAY, NOVEMBER 25, 1977 SW 15¢ Suggested HOME DELIVERY $3.90 a Month

Who's Whooo..

Britain's Top 500 Ghosts

©1977, New York Times News Service

LONDON, Nov. 25 — England, which tends to believe in them, has just published a Who's Who of ghosts.

It lists alphabetically about 500 of the most widely reported apparitions from an estimated total ghost population of 25,000 in England and Wales. They range in age from a Bronze Age man to a jail matron who died in 1970, and in prominence from Henry VIII to a nameless man in a bowler hat who haunts the No. 1 Runway at Heathrow Airport.

The book is one of dozens on the subject published in London in recent years as part of a revival of interest in the supernatural.

Jack Hallam, the author of "The Ghost Who's Who," calls Britain the most haunted island in the world. He figures that at least 25,000 supernatural occurrences of some type have been reported in England and Wales alone, not counting the thousands of Celtic ghosts in Scotland and Ireland.

A survey a few years ago found that six million Britons would acknowledge having seen an apparition of some kind. Hallam estimates that 20 per cent of the population believes in ghosts, whether they have seen one or not.

The author, a retired picture editor of the Sunday Times and one of many British authorities on ghosts, discussed the British fascination with them the other day at his home

See GHOSTS, Page 8

Palestinian Moderates Invited To Cairo Talks By Egyptians

Compiled From News Services

CAIRO, Egypt, Nov. 25 — Egypt has decided to invite Palestinian leaders living in Israel and Israeli-occupied lands to visit Cairo for talks on a Middle East peace, a move aimed at undercutting the Palestine Liberation Organization.

The ruling political party, the Arab Socialist Party of Egypt, made the decision yesterday at a meeting called to discuss President Anwar Sadat's breakthrough visit to Israel last weekend.

Sadat's agreement with Israel that there would be "no more war" between their nations has drawn bitter attacks from the PLO, Syria and other hard-line Arabs.

The Egyptian Socialist Party did not specify which Palestinians would be invited to Cairo but it appeared the party was trying to establish contact with Palestinians more moderate than the PLO.

"It is time that all honorable Arab forces raised their voices to defend their right to a just peace," a party statement said. "It is the duty of all Arab peoples to show solidarity with the Egyptian people . . .

"Palestinian leaders are urged to shoulder their responsibility ... (by participating in) the Geneva conference in order to realize a just peace and set up a Palestinian entity," the statement said.

Israeli Defense Minister Ezer Weizman said Israel would allow those invited to go to Egypt, but reaction from the Palestinians concerned was mixed. At least two mayors rejected the move as an attempt to "outflank the PLO."

Egypt's acting foreign minister, Butros Ghali, said Sadat on his trip to Jerusalem had convinced Israeli leaders that the Palestinians should not be left out of an overall Middle East settlement.

Sadat and the Israelis discussed an "appropriate formula" for the participation of Palestinians in the Geneva peace conference, he said.

Ghali said the United States would continue to play "an important and positive role" in the Mideast peace process, but that it would be somewhat diminished.

"After Sadat's visit to Jerusalem, the proportion has changed," he said. "Now the two opponents, Egypt and Israel, hold the cards — and I will add the Palestinians."

Andrew Young, the U.S. ambassador to the United Nations, rose to support Egypt yesterday in the General Assembly, praising Sadat's trip to Jerusalem as a demonstration of rare vision.

"Peace seems closer to our grasp," Young said, urging the parties involved in the Middle East dispute to "capture the mood of peace."

Young asked assembly members to agree to a moratorium on extreme statements and on the passage of resolutions "to score pyrrhic victories."

His request followed an attack by

See TALKS, Page 8

FINAL CURTAIN AT A TRAGEDY: As the Miami Dolphins ran up the score against the Cardinals yesterday, the crowd at Busch Stadium thinned out, so that there were a lot of empty seats when the final dismal 55-to-14 outcome was announced. There are more sorrowful details on Page 1D. (Post-Dispatch Photo by Robert C. Holt III)

Moderate Blacks Back Smith Plan

Compiled From News Services

SALISBURY, Rhodesia, Nov. 25 — Moderate black nationalists gave qualified support today to Prime Minister Ian D. Smith's offer to steer Rhodesia to black majority rule in one-man, one-vote elections.

Smith did not mention a date for elections. A spokesman for one moderate black leader, the Rev. Ndabaningi Sithole, called Smith's offer a "decisive move which paves the way for black and white Rhodesians to sit down together and work out a blueprint for Zimbabwe which will bring peace and prosperity to our land."

Zimbabwe is the African name for Rhodesia. Sithole heads a faction of the African National Council.

Jeremiah Chirau, leader of the moderate black Zimbabwe United Peoples Organization, said Smith's acceptance of majority rule could mean the end of guerrilla fighting. He appealed to black nationalist guerrillas to "come home peacefully," calling them "misguided young men who think that the path of violence can lead to anything constructive."

Both moderate black leaders operate from within Rhodesia. There was no immediate word from black nationalist guerrilla leaders operating from Zambia and Mozambique.

Smith told a press conference yesterday that the British-American peace plan had failed, but said he believed that an internal agreement between his white minority government and moderate black leaders would end Rhodesia's bloody five-year-old guerrilla war.

Chirau, who leaves tomorrow on a trip to the United States and Britain to boost international support for his organization, told a group of white farmers in the town of Marandellas, about 50 miles south of Salisbury, that whites would not enjoy privileged status in a black majority-ruled Rhodesia.

"Most of Zimbabwe's people are black so you must understand that there can be no question of the continuation of the privileged position which the white section of the community has enjoyed for so long," he said.

However, Chirau said existing Rhodesian security forces should be retained, white-led but including about four-fifth blacks in the lower ranks. The suggestion was an apparent reference to Smith's insistence on a secure future for the white minority.

"With all parties inside the country agreeing to come together to discuss a future constitution based on majority rule, the terrorist war should cease," Chirau said.

Joseph Masangomai, spokesman for Bishop Abel Muzorewa's African National Council, said in a published interview that he welcomed Smith's offer but that it was just a first step. Masangomai said that several "non-negotiable conditions" were still outstanding, including a general amnesty for political detainees, an end to political trials and suspensions of detentions and executions.

Smith said that he had invited Muzorewa, Sithole and Chirau to talks on the changes.

He said that he expected a preparatory meeting to be conducted next week and that negotiations could produce results "in a matter of months."

Smith did not invite the leaders of the Patriotic Front, whose guerrillas are

See RHODESIA, Page 4

FBI Proposed 'Targeting' Radicals Here

By ROBERT ADAMS
A Washington Correspondent
of the Post-Dispatch

WASHINGTON, Nov. 25 — The St. Louis FBI office devised a plan in 1969 to scare two St. Louis radicals away from politics by making them think that heavily armed, right-wing Minutemen were after them, FBI papers show.

"It is felt that this action would be more than a harassment," the St. Louis office wrote as it tried to promote the idea. It asked FBI headquarters for permission to send the radicals copies of literature published by the Minutemen.

On the literature, the FBI had drawn small human figures — apparently to represent the students — with what could be taken as rifle targets on them. Headquarters vetoed the plan.

The scheme surfaced among the 52,600 pages of FBI documents on its counterintelligence program — Cointelepro — made available to the Post-Dispatch and other news organizations this week under the Freedom of Information Act. The FBI's program was designed to disrupt black militants and the New Left organizations.

The papers show that former Missouri state Rep. Richard N. Marshall of Webster Groves secretly exchanged information with the FBI about student radicals in the late 1960s. In a telephone interview, Marshall acknowledged his role and said he had no regrets.

The documents show also that the Springfield, Ill., FBI office suggested trying to use U.S. Rep. Thomas F. Railsback, R-Ill., as an outlet for disseminating derogatory information about radicals. Railsback said that he never participated in such a scheme nor was he ever asked to.

The "Minutemen" scheme was outlined in a memo from the St. Louis FBI office to headquarters dated Jan. 22, 1969.

The memo noted that two activists in the St. Louis area—whose names were blacked out in the copies given to the Post-Dispatch — "have recently expressed concern to established (FBI) sources" about "potential activities against them by the Minutemen."

The Minutemen organization was a heavily armed group of ultra-conservatives who talked about an armed struggle to save America from subversives. Its leader, Robert DePugh, was at that time being sought by the FBI.

DePugh and an assistant had been convicted in 1966 of violating the Federal Firearms Act. Later in 1969, a secret arsenal of more than 100 rifles, kegs of explosives, and other weapons was found at Minutemen headquarters.

Fears by the students about the Minutemen appeared to be groundless, the FBI noted. Nevertheless, the FBI set out to exploit those fears as a means of frightening the radicals away from politics. One of the radicals was described as a leader of the St. Louis branch of Students for a Democratic Society.

As part of the plan, the FBI obtained two copies of a Minuteman paper branding the United Nations as communist. On one, FBI agents drew a small human figure with a circle and cross-hairs on the chest. The initials "M.L." — presumably those of one of the radicals — were written underneath.

On the second copy, the FBI drew a small stick-figure enclosed in a circle, with a black dot in the center. The initials "R.F." were written underneath.

Another piece of Minuteman matter the FBI planned to send anonymously to the radicals spoke of "our socialist enemy." It said that "any means necessary is morally justified to defeat the enemy . . ."

The St. Louis FBI office said the two radicals were "both sensitive, introspective individuals." It said they "might consider curtailing their New Left activities somewhat if they thought their actions were opposed by the Minutemen."

The Memo ended: "This action would not entail any embarrassment to the Bureau."

On Jan. 29, 1969, however, FBI headquarters said no. Headquarters noted that the Minutemen, themselves, might be the subject of investigation by local authorities. It was "not desirable," headquarters said, "that the Bureau enter into any activity that would complicate or confuse this investigation."

Former state Rep. Marshall, a Webster Groves lawyer, is a Republican. During his six years in the Missouri

See FBI, Page 9

Legionnaires' Disease Case In County

By ROGER SIGNOR
Of the Post-Dispatch Staff

The latest confirmed case of Legionnaires' disease in Missouri is a 43-year-old St. Louis County man who recovered from the illness last month, the Post-Dispatch has learned.

State health officials would not disclose the man's name. He became ill in late September and was hospitalized with a high fever and pneumonia, said Dr. John Jacobson of the state Division of Health.

It was the fifth reported case of Legionnaires' disease in the state and the second in St. Louis County, Jacobson said in an interview. The other county victim was a 45-year-old man who became ill with pneumonia in May. He recovered also. He was the first confirmed case in the state, Jacobson said.

The second case was a 51-year-old man last May in Douglas County. A 59-year-old man and a 41-year-old man, both from Sedalia, were the other two Missouri cases. All three patients had

See DISEASE, Page 8

friday

local

DIVORCE LOGJAM: Uncontested divorce cases are taking longer to settle in St. Louis County under a new arrangement for them to be handled by magistrates. Page 4B

business

INFLATION is still a threat, despite encouraging consumer price reports, says columnist Bill Kester. Page 12A

features

AFTER THE FEAST IS OVER: Consult CALENDAR, the Post- Dispatch weekly entertainment guide for places to go and sights to see. The Doobie Brothers are featured in the centerfold.

WOMEN ON THE MOVE: For four days in Houston, delegates to the National Women's Conference forged resolutions to identify the barriers to their full participation in American life. Page 3F

Chance Of Snow

Official forecast for St. Louis and vicinity: Chance of snow flurries late today; clearing and much colder tonight with the low in the teens. Winds becoming northwesterly. Partly cloudy and cold tomorrow with the high in the low 30s. Quite cold Sunday with the low in the teens; warmer Monday and Tuesday.

SWOON OVER MIAMI
POST-DISPATCH WEATHERBIRD REG. U. S. PAT. OFF.

Other Weather Information on Page 2A

sports

SACKING OF ONOFRIO: The University of Missouri is hoping to find a new football coach by Christmas after the Thanksgiving Eve sacking of Al Onofrio. Page 1D

in today's
POST-DISPATCH
south/west
area news
in Sections B & E

inside

68 Pages	
Business	12-14A
Calendar	1-20C
Classified Advertising	8-16D, 4E
Editorials	2E
Everyday	1-10F
News Analysis	3E
Obituaries	8D
People	5A
Religion	7F
Reviews	4, 5, 9F
St. Louis	1E
Spectator	5F
Sports/Weekend	1-7D
TV-Radio	8F

Old College Try

Booths Jam Convention Center As Schools Vie For Students

A POST-DISPATCH EXTRA

By VICTOR VOLLAND
Of the Post-Dispatch Staff

Squatting on a stairway outside the new St. Louis Gateway Convention Center, Patty Kennedy and Kelly and Kristie Pasco, three high school students, pored over their accumulated stacks of colorful folders and fact sheets on various colleges and universities.

Inside, in the hangar-like expanse of Exhibit Hall A, was a bewildering, supermarket-style jam of information booths representing more than 200 colleges, universities and career schools, some from as far away as Alaska, Mexico and Switzerland.

At one booth, two students were listening intently to the sales pitch of David Ralston, area representative for Xavier University of Cincinnati.

"Well, my boyfriend's at Westminster," a pretty young girl in blue jeans said to an admissions counselor at the nearby William Woods College booth. The counselor took the opening to explain the merits of the women's liberal arts school, other than its closeness to the all-male Westminster College in Fulton, Mo.

The fourth St. Louis National College Fair last week was what is known in trade circles as a buyer's market.

"A few years ago, colleges could afford not to be represented because they had tons of applications," said Stephen M. Lefebvre, a coordinator

See COLLEGE, Page 6

TARKIO COLLEGE

OUTREACH: Harold Kocher (left) and Jack Schmidt of Tarkio College talk to a prospective student. (Post-Dispatch Photo by Wayne Crosslin)

Fig. 5–12. Modular. The *St. Louis Post-Dispatch* uses big modules at the bottom, with borders, and less dramatic ones on the rest of the page.

Minneapolis Tribune

Thursday January 12, 1978

Volume CXI
Number 213
$ ¢

1A

4 Sections

20¢ Single Copy
Lower price for home delivery

Copyright 1978 Minneapolis Star and Tribune Company

Jobless rate drops to 6.4%

By Edward Cowan
New York Times Service

Washington, D.C.

A strong burst of employment expansion in the last two months of 1977 caused the national unemployment rate to drop to a year-end 6.4 percent, the Bureau of Labor Statistics reported Wednesday.

The surge in jobs and some statistical revisions of unemployment data together produced a fourth-quarter unemployment rate of 6.6 percent, the target posted by the Carter administration last summer and unofficially abandoned as hopeless in the autumn.

President Carter grasped eagerly at the brightening in an unemployment picture that had been gray for months.

"I think the slow impact of the programs we put into effect that was disappointing for a while is now beginning to show up," the president said.

Carter asked his chief economic adviser, Charles Schultze, if the administration's proposal to cut taxes by $25 billion in 1978-79 still is necessary. Schultze said that it is, emphasizing that the reduction would not take effect before Oct. 1, when the economic upswing, now 33 months old, is expected to be running out of steam. Administration economists have predicted strong increases in industrial activity and consumer spending in the early months of 1978.

The bureau reported that the number of people with jobs rose by 409,000 in December, following an extraordinary jump of 950,000 in November. In all, employment in

Jobs continued on page 4A

Staff Photo by Donald Black
State troopers accompanied surveyors across a field on the farm of Dennis and Nina Rutledge, who were arrested along with six other power-line opponents Wednesday.

8 arrested in power-line protest

By Roberta Walburn
Staff Writer

Lowry, Minn.
The strong winter sun was sinking behind the hills late Wednesday afternoon as the man and woman stood in the middle of a snow-covered field.

A small group of invited guests huddled in the cold. Photographers were ready for the ceremony.

An official was ready too. "Are you man and wife?" he asked the couple.

"Yes," said the man. "I do," he quickly added with a laugh.

And Dennis and Nina Rutledge, ages 35 and 34, were pronounced under arrest by a state trooper. They were charged with obstructing legal process for standing in front of a surveyor working on the controversial high-voltage power line in Pope County.

Six other power-line protesters were arrested yesterday on the Rutledge farm one mile east of Lowry. Most were friends of the Rutledges.

The eight arrests came at the end of a day that started with about 200 protesters, superbly

organized, taking a stand that forced a temporary halt by one surveying crew.

But by the afternoon the presence of 150 state troopers in rural Pope County caused tension to set in and disrupt planning.

Protesters entering their Lowry headquarters yesterday morning were greeted by a large sign carrying the agenda for the day. The first item read: "Meeting to plan action not to talk about how bad the line is."

In past meetings, protesters have rambled on

Power line continued on page 4A

Dennis Rutledge

It's moving time as police receive election desserts

By Tom Davies
Staff Writer

The corridors of the Minneapolis Police Department were more treacherous than ever Wednesday, and it had nothing to do with criminals.

The day started with the police federation criticizing the appointment of a woman to head a sensitive division and ended with a well-known policeman calling the new chief a buffoon.

And that's not mentioning the administration's continuing hassles with the transfer of its political cronies and enemies — hassles

that are not likely to end before one captain holds four different jobs in less than three weeks.

The biggest flap of the day was caused by Lt. Gary McGaughey, who has spent much of his time working on prostitution. McGaughey had recently been transferred from the organized crime unit, considered a plum position, to an investigative unit at one of the precincts, considered the pits.

The transfer angered McGaughey, who began to fight back Tuesday by sending letters to Mayor Albert Hofstede, Chief of Police Elmer Nordlund, city councilmen and others demanding an explanation.

At the same time, he said some pretty unpleasant things about the chief and the latest takeover of the administration by DFL-oriented police officers. The difference yesterday was that he said those things in print.

Nordlund, the DFL-oriented Minneapolis Star columnist Jim Klobu-

Police continued on page 4A

Almanac

January 12, 1978
12th day; 353 to go this year.
Sunrise: 7:50. Sunset: 4:54.

Today's weather

Light snow

Cloudy with light snow is the forecast for the Upper Midwest today and Friday.

Predicted high temperatures: Twin Cities, 16; Minnesota, ranging from 8 to 22; North Dakota, 20; South Dakota, low 30s southwest to the teens northeast; Wisconsin, low 20s.

Details on Page 7B.

Count your blessings

Egotistical author anonymously entered 'a bookstore and asked how his latest book was doing. "Oh, my," the clerk said, "I wish I had a hundred of that book." How many do you have? the author asked. "Four hundred," replied the clerk.

Arts	7B	Editorial	6A
Business	8-10A	Sports	1-4D
Comics	6B	TV, Radio	9B

Tribune telephones	372-4141 News/General 372-4242 Classified 372-4343 Circulation

Per-diem lifts pay of legislators

By Steven Dornfeld and Steve Brandt
Staff Writers

With the help of more generous per-diem expense payments, members of the Minnesota House managed to boost their average compensation to $17,800 in 1977.

Members of the Senate, meanwhile, averaged $15,900 in salary and expense payments.

In 1975, the last year that the Legislature had to assemble the state budget, House members collected an average of $13,500 and senators an average of $12,900.

The salary collected by each legislator is $8,400 a year. However, legislators traditionally have given themselves per-diem payments for every day they are in session or attend to committee business.

For the 1977 session, the DFL-controlled House and Senate increased this payment from $33 to $48 a day for outstate members and from $25 to $40 a day for metropolitan members. For the interim, the time between sessions, they raised it from $33 to $48 a

Pay continued on page 4A

Califano announces drive to get U.S. smokers to quit

New York Times Service

Washington, D.C.
Federal officials Wednesday opened a new drive to encourage Americans to stop smoking cigarettes.

Joseph A. Califano Jr., secretary of the Department of Health, Education and Welfare (HEW), announced a series of actions and proposals aimed at reducing the number of Americans who smoke, now estimated at 53 million.

"Last year smoking was a major factor in 220,000 deaths from heart disease; 78,000 lung-cancer deaths, and 22,000 deaths from other cancers," he said, adding that "these facts mean that people who smoke are committing slow-motion suicide."

Califano outlined his proposals in a speech to the National Interagency Council on Smoking and Health. His major points included:

■ Asking the major broadcasting networks to increase antismoking announcements, which have dropped off sharply since cigarette advertising was banned from radio and television in 1971.

■ Urging that education programs dealing with smoking dangers be set up in every American school.

■ Banning smoking in most public areas of HEW buildings and segregating smokers' work areas.

■ Seeking to extend the rules in HEW buildings to the 10,000 other federal buildings run by the General Services Administration.

■ Endorsing the action taken two months ago by the Civil Aeronautics Board that banned cigar and pipe smoking on commercial airliners and supporting the CAB's proposed rule to ban cigarettes.

■ Examining with the Treasury Department the federal policy on

Smoking continued on page 7A

Officials believe fire victim was 'ornery' recluse, Joe

By Tom Davies
Staff Writer

By the time firemen arrived, the fire was only smoldering in the back of a truck. They didn't know it then, but it was a house fire and the occupant was dead.

The old delivery truck had been abandoned years ago near the Mississippi River, on the banks in front of 330 SE. Main St. For the last few years, it had been home for an elderly recluse known as "Joe."

The Hennepin County medical examiner couldn't say for certain Wednesday if the man who died in the fire was Joe. The body had been severely burned, fire officials said, and identification will be very difficult.

If the victim was Joe — and police and fire officials believe it was — then he will be remembered more than missed. Joe, it seems, had one distinctive quality — a horrible disposition.

"He was the kind of guy," a police detective said yesterday, "who would just start screaming curses at you if you said 'Hello.'"

Joe, the detective said, would mumble curses as he passed you on the street. The police are so aware of Joe because they ran into him often.

Joe always carried a knapsack with him, police said. He always carried rocks in that knapsack, keeping them handy to throw at passing cars.

The police were called to check about those reports often, but they never knew why he threw the rocks.

"Just out of orneriness, I guess," one policeman said.

One of the reasons the body at the morgue is considered to be Joe's is that he was not known to invite visitors to his 8-foot room in the back of the truck. There was a well-worn path to the truck, Joe.

Fire continued on page 7A

State city goes from riches to rags

By Eric Black
Staff Writer

Becker, Minn.
There's a boom or bust economy at work here, and it just went bust.

A couple of years ago the Becker City Council was merrily planning how to spend millions of tax dollars the city would receive from Northern States Power Co. (NSP), which built a $368-million generating plant here.

The tax boom enabled Becker to pave roads all over the city, install a new water system, build an addition to its municipal building, buy a bunch of new equipment for its fire department, hire a second policeman and retain a professional planning consultant.

Tuesday night the council was considering selling its snowplow to get its hands on some extra cash

and wondering how it could squeeze a few more dollars of profit out of the municipal liquor store.

Because of a state law that was recently called to the attention of the Sherburne County auditor, the council has to cut the general operating fund of its proposed 1978 city budget by 92 percent.

Some people in Becker think an old feud with Elk River, the Sherburne County seat, is responsible for their current budget problems, although county officials say they're just enforcing the law. The Becker city attorney hopes to get the law amended during the state legislative session that starts next week.

The law, which was enacted in 1921 to prevent Iron Range towns from annexing iron mines for tax purposes, limits a city's tax revenues to $143 per person.

Becker continued on page 4A

Minnesota

Becker

Twin Cities

Fig. 5 – 13. Modified modular. The *Minneapolis Tribune* uses bold headlines on several stories and often breaks stories out of the modular mold. Bottom is anchored strongly.

Schools:
Why busing works for the 'Thunderbirds'
Page 13

SPORTS
Bulls brawl to fourth straight win
Sports, Page 18

Chicago Daily News

THURSDAY, JANUARY 19, 1978

State Edition 25¢
15¢ City and suburbs

© 1978 BY FIELD ENTERPRISES INC.

Sadat stops peace talks

My Years with Mayor Daley

How Daley gave LBJ the 'kiss of death'

Mayor Daley and President Johnson in Chicago in 1968.

By Jane Byrne *as told to Kathleen Begley/2d of 4 articles*

I got my first glimpse of how far Mayor Daley's power extended in March of 1968 when he was talking to me in his office about my new job as commissioner of sales, weights and measures.

At that time, Mayor Daley was on record for supporting President Lyndon Johnson to the death. But I believe he was hoping even then that Bobby Kennedy would make a run for the Presidency.

Anyway, while I'm sitting in his office, the phone rings and Mayor Daley takes it in another room.

The next thing I hear is "Yes, Mr. President, so good to hear from you." President Johnson apparently was calling to get the mayor's opinion on his chances of carrying Chicago if he ran for a second term. Well, he got the kiss of death as far as I was concerned. "Well, Mr. President, there are good years and bad years and I don't think this will be a good year for the national ticket in Chicago," I overheard Mayor Daley saying.

"But I'm backing you all the way, Mr. President," the mayor continued. "It doesn't matter that you can't win here."

President Johnson obviously got the message. He announced shortly thereafter that he was not going to run for re-election. I'm sure he checked around in a few other cities, but I firmly believe that that conversation with Mayor Daley was the deciding factor.

"Daley is Chicago, Chicago is Daley." That's what all the presidential

Turn to Back Page, this section

Chief delegate to negotiations in Israel is called home.

By Jay Bushinsky
Special to The Daily News

JERUSALEM—President Anwar Sadat has ordered the chief of the Egyptian delegation to peace talks with Israel here to return home.

Foreign Minister Mohammed Ibrahim Kamel is expected to leave Israel within hours. It is not clear whether the delegation will leave with him. Sadat's order referred specifically to Kamel.

U.S. spokesman Hodding Carter III said "we have learned" of the order from Cairo recalling the foreign minister "and are seeking information.

"The talks are effectively stopped," he said.

An hour after the announcement on Cairo radio, the Israeli Cabinet was called into an extraordinary session.

(A Middle East news agency said Sadat took the action because of Israel's attitude and behavior at the first meeting of the political committee which had been set up in an

Turn to Back Page, this section

Cost hike perils the 'deep tunnel'

By Terry Shaffer

The Sanitary District's deep tunnel sewer project may never be completed because the estimated cost of the project has escalated out of sight, according to a federal report.

Congress has been asked by its own investigative branch to re-evaluate the entire project and consider less costly, less ambitious alternatives.

A copy of a 36-page report, restricted to official channels but obtained by The Daily News, sets a new projected cost for the Tunnel and Reservoir Project (TARP) at a staggering $7.3 billion and recommends that Congress "evaluate this program and consider less ambitious goals."

Deep tunnel blasting called hazard. Page 16

The report by the General Accounting Office (GAO), which has been given to the Sanitary District, the Army Corps of Engineers and the federal and state environmental protection agencies for comment, also reports that there is no federal policy nor any precedent for federal administration of such a huge public works project

Some contracts awarded

The report warns that, because the project is broken down into more than half a dozen phases or related projects, funding would be granted on a piecemeal basis. This eventually could force Congress to fund the whole plan or face the alternative of stopping construction short of com-

Turn to Back Page, this section

Circle Campus center studied

The University of Illinois is considering building a 12,000-seat sports and concert center at Circle Campus here, university trustees were told Wednesday.

The $7.5 million hall might be financed by a bond issue to be carried by income from events at the hall. A $7 million theater and arts building with an auditorium at Circle could be paid for the same way. A third project on a long-range shopping list at Circle is a $6 million building for student counsellors and deans.

The same list includes a $5.4 million student union addition and a $5.2 million parking building at the university's Medical Center here.

Another crack on Ryan L line

High atop a snorkle, a workman checks for new cracks in the Dan Ryan L span Wednesday. (Daily News Photo/John Tweedle)

Trains halted, then resume service after officials say new crack is not significant.

By Tom Page Seibel and Larry S. Finley

Service on the CTA's Dan Ryan L line was shut down temporarily again Wednesday after inspectors discovered a small crack in the steel support structure near where three cracks were discovered earlier this month.

Full service was resumed after two hours when it was determined that the new crack posed no danger.

City Public Works Comr. Marshall Suloway ordered service resumed after he inspected the new crack near 18th and State, along with another flaw in the steel that he described as a "scratch."

Suloway said that while the previously discovered cracks were "signifigant" the new crack was "insignifigant."

"They aren't even minor cracks," he said "They are insignifigant cracks—flaws in the steel."

The new 7-inch "hairline" crack was discovered Wednesday morning by two CTA inspectors examining the supports under the 4-story-high elevated line about two blocks from the cracks found Jan. 4 at 18th and Clark. The Ryan line was partly closed for 10 days while those repairs were made.

Leo Cusick, chief operating officer for the Regional Transportation Authority, said that he was not alarmed by the report of a new crack.

Discovery of the small crack , he said, "shows the CTA's continued vigilance" in inspecting the span. An RTA engineer was at the scene assisting in the evaluation of the problem, he said.

Auto traffic on 18th St. between Clark and State was shut off by police during the inspections.

A spokesman for Rock Island Lines, whose commuter trains run

Turn to Back Page, this section

Taxi audit firm offers to resign

By Diane Monk

A top executive of Arthur Young & Co. angrily offered his firm's resignation as auditor for the City Council's taxi fare investigation during a boisterous meeting Wednesday of the council's special taxi committee.

John Schornack, a managing partner, made the offer while responding to charges that his firm's selection as auditor was predetermined.

Schornack said:

"If anyone on this committee, or outside of it, can present and substantiate any evidence to support the allegations and innuendoes regarding the openness and fairness of the process by which we were selected, or regarding our independence, our integrity, or our qualifications to conduct an audit in the highest standards of professionalism, Arthur Young is prepared to resign this assignment immediately."

Vrdolyak may face second quiz by taxi grand jury. Page 3

However, Ald. Martin Oberman (43d) refused to retract his charge that the selection was "predetermined." Oberman added, "If Young wants to resign, that's up to them."

The committee ignored Oberman's charges and it was clear as the

Turn to Back Page, this section

Insight / Monroe W. Karmin

The real Carter stands up with conservative message

WASHINGTON—This week, the real Jimmy Carter will stand up.

Thursday he will deliver his State of the Union message to a joint session of Congress. Friday will come his economic message. Saturday, his tax message. Monday, his budget.

These proclamations will establish the President as a fiscal conservative who wants to control federal spending so that he can stimulate economic growth by cutting taxes.

Carter will propose a $25 billion tax reduction, two-thirds for individuals and one-third for business, to be enacted this year. What may or may not be mentioned is that the President wants to make room for a second tax cut later on, perhaps in 1980 when he's up for reelection.

"Yes, he'd like to be able to cut taxes a second time," confides a top administration official. "The form of that second tax cut will depend on economic conditions at the time."

To accommodate a second tax cut, the President will do his best to gain control of federal spending in the new fiscal 1979 budget. That won't be easy because of uncontrollable, built-in increases.

Expenditures will rise to approximately $500 billion, up from this year's $459.8 billion. The deficit will come close to, if not exceed, this year's $58.5 billion, which means Carter will lose ground in his effort to balance the budget by fiscal 1981.

In fact, a balanced budget may be a lost cause for the President's first term. "He's tiptoeing away from that promise," says an informed source.

Carter will try to make the retreat with grace. He'll point out that the reason he was unable to reduce the new deficit substantially was because he's giving $25 billion back to the voters in the form of tax reduction. At his press conference last week, the President said that tax relief was necessary to compensate taxpayers for the increased Social Security taxes this year, to keep the ecomony growing smoothly beyond mid-1978, when it's feared some softness may set in, and to compensate for inflation-induced wage increases which push families into higher tax brackets.

The President will emphasize that the fiscal 1979 budget, the first one he has prepared from scratch, is a "tight" one, with no new major

Turn to Page 4

Today in the News

Stock prices climbed Wednesday as the Dow Jones average of 30 blue-chip industrials was up 7.28 points to close at 786.30 in moderately active trading on the New York Stock Exchange. Page 24

In response to the heavy mail received in recent weeks with comments, The Daily News is expanding its letters section on Thursdays and Mondays. On today's editorial page, readers comment on several subjects, including jobs and the Loop L. Page 10

Ron Hunter is Channel 5's No. 1 anchorman and a journalistic joke to many of his colleagues. They say he lacks credibility as a journalist because of his demeanor off camera, according to Frank Swertlow's column. Page 17

FBI files released Wednesday shed new light on communications between the Warren Commission and the FBI. Marina Oswald's comments to the FBI, Earl Warren's reluctance to head the commission and other facts also are released. Page 2

Striking miners, who have been off the job for six weeks Downstate and across the coal belt, face unpleasant times until miners and coal operators agree on a new contract. One Downstater, 81, tells his story of working in the mines since 1914. Page 5.

Index

		Business	21	Harris	10
		Cappo	23	Landers	14
		Comics	8	Nightingale	20
		Crossword	16	Obituaries	26
		Deaths	26	Royko	3
		Editorials	10	Schulian	18
		Ent'rtainm'nt	17	Sports	18
Action	15	Everyday	13	Swertlow	17
Anderson	11	Fischetti	10	TV List	16
Bridge	16	Geyer	11	Weather	16

Weather

Snow likely and continued cold, highs in teens and low 20s. (Digest on Page 16)

Fig. 5–14. Dark Modular. Before it folded, the *Chicago Daily News* used heavy borders to separate its modules. Note the centered headlines.

Fig. 5–15. Modified circus. Few American papers cling to circus makeup. European papers don't use it much either but *Le Soir* in Paris comes close.

Another makeup style is called *focus* or *brace*. The names suggest the heavy focus of attention at the top and the way the big headline at the top is "braced"—or supported—by sizable heads beneath it (fig. 5-12). The big headline and its satellites dominate the page. Few newspapers use this style because it may suggest that, except for the number one story, nothing much is going on. The style also lacks aesthetic appeal, since nothing attracts the eye except the big type at the top of the page.

Circus, the opposite of brace, scatters big headlines all over the page. Its detractors sometimes call circus the "Gee Whiz" method. Half of the front page stories are headlined as though each were an advance on the Second Coming. A few of the heads will even be in color. For years the *Denver Post* had a makeup that might have been considered Seven-Ring Circus, but its makeup has been modified now to only One-Ring Circus. The *Post* still is the leading exponent of circus in the United States. Traditional circus is now the province of foreign newspapers (fig. 5-15), but even there it is declining.

Laying out a circus page is difficult. Any doubters might try to squeeze several stories, most with multi-column heads, on a page with two or three pictures. Since few stories are to be jumped in the circus plan, the problems are evident.

Critics of circus contend that the makeup job is more time-consuming, and therefore more expensive, than it is for other styles, and that the reader becomes jaded in the typographical excitement. They also argue that circus makeup does not jibe with the trend for news detail and that it tends to cram all the good stories on page one, leaving only culls for the inside. The better editors try to draw the reader through the whole paper by putting at least one significant story on each page. For these reasons, circus makeup has nearly disappeared from the American newspaper.

The newest page makeup goes under the name of *modular*. It takes blocks of type—modules—and stacks them in what is intended to make a pleasing and readable design. Each block is a big rectangle. These rectangles of type are arranged along with pictures, also rectangles, of course. Nearly all heads are wide: three to eight columns.

Such pages have appeal and are easy to read. One shortcoming, however, is that many good stories are not long enough to form a rectangle that would take, say, 25 inches of space. A tiny rectangle would look out of place. Another drawback concerns the system's inflexibility. When a page is laid out in such symmetry, a late-breaking story disrupts the plan. The editor, faced with designing the page over again, may decide to forget the fresh information.

Further goals of makeup

While makeup aims primarily to give the reader an attractive newspaper, it has several other functions. One is to reflect the newspaper's personality. The *New York Times,* a serious paper, would be unwise to adopt a frivolous design. Its makeup has been undergoing liberalization, but the paper still radiates a no-nonsense approach. Much of this serious impression stems from typography, for the type and the layout indicate tradition and formalism. On the other hand, the design of the *Chicago Daily News* suggests not a "paper of record" but a paper filled with alert, lively, clever writing. Newspapers that cling to the policies of Love-Lust-Lucre have page designs to match: headlines and pictures scream for attention.

Another function of makeup is to tell the reader what editors consider the most significant stories of the day. As noted in chapter 4, headline size does most of this job. The bigger the head, the more important the story. But not always. A short story on page one with small but special typography tells the reader that this story is short but important.

Placement, then, cues the reader. A story on page one rates high. On the split page—the first page of another section—it also rates. But if it is three paragraphs on page sixty-nine, the reader realizes the editor considers the item little more than a space filler.

Makeup should provide other aids for the reader. The various sections—editorial page, comics, sports, etc.—should be in about the same place every day so the reader doesn't have to hunt for them. Related stories, such as reports on state legislative activities, should be grouped. If this is not possible, a "reference," or "refer" (pronounced "reefer"), can be inserted in the story. (See fig. 5-16.)

Elgin teachers approve contract, will return to classes Tuesday, Page 14.

Fig. 5–16. Refer. This device in a story alerts the reader to related but secondary stories on inside pages.

Another goal of makeup is to provide variety. Unless the makeup varies, at least slightly, every day, it lulls readers into thinking that they saw the same thing yesterday. The main picture may be in the first two columns one day and in columns three to five the next. One day there will be a banner and the next two lines of five-column headline for the lead story.

Typography should enhance the appearance of the paper, but never at the expense of misrepresenting the importance of the story. Readers used to banners that signify nothing will learn to underestimate headlines that are really important. Readers are just as ill-served if a story of considerable significance is underplayed.

Some papers use typographical devices to have fun with the news, if there is anything funny about it. In a way, the makeup in these papers pokes fun at events, and even jabs at the conduct of political and educational figures. The *Chicago Sun-Times* frequently pulls off this kind of humor with its makeup, as shown in figure 5-17.

WEATHER
Mostly sunny and continued cold Thursday. High 6 to 12. See Page 96.

CHICAGO
SUN-TIMES

FINAL
TURF EDITION

Vol. 16, No. 275   Phone 321-3000   THURSDAY, DECEMBER 19, 1963   120 Pages—7 Cents

We're FrOzen

7 Days Of It; 3 More To Go

A two-dimensional record for a December freeze was set in the Chicago area early Thursday as below-zero temperatures marked the weather's turn from cold to colder.

It was the longest and deepest December freeze in these terms, said the weather bureau—seven straight days of zero or subzero temperatures. The previous such record for the month was five straight days in 1945.

With the mercury still on its early morning descent Thursday, the temperature was 9 below at O'Hare Airport and 7 below at Midway Airport, where the official reading is taken. Lower readings were reported in suburbs, where the weather bureau expected the mercury to reach 15 below.

There were prospects that the record might be extended indefinitely.

A long-range forecast envisioned low temperatures near zero for Friday, Saturday and Sunday.

While Chicagoans mutter-

Sea of ice greets motorists on Cicero Av. near 55th after water main break. (Sun-Times Photo by Larry Nocerino)

Other pictures on Page 2

ed with the cold's deepening bite, Muskegon, Mich., struggled through a 24-hour storm that dumped 34 inches of snow and threatened to pile up at least three more inches.

Mountainous drifts rose in near-blizzard conditions to block streets and create emergencies in the Lake Michigan industrial-port city's area of 100,000 residents.

With the storm, Muskegon's December snowfall records for one hour, 48 hours and one week were rewritten.

In the Chicago area, the cold was blamed for the bursting of two water mains.

A break in a 30-inch main under 55th, between Cicero and Lamonte caused the Chicago Transit Authority to reroute bus traffic in the flooded area.

Water pressure was reduced in a one-mile radius of the break. But no water shortage developed anywhere in the area served by the main, said Thomas Allen, acting engineer.

als Ward urged special precautions against fire because of the difficulty of moving firefighting equipment. Snowplows kept Muskegon's main arteries passable, but few side streets were cleared.

Turn to Page 2

How 'Perfect' Kidnaping Failed

By Sandy Smith
Sun-Times Correspondent

LOS ANGELES—The Federal Bureau of Investigation has learned that Barry Worthington Keenan, 23, planned the $240,000 ransom kidnaping of Frank Sinatra Jr. as a perfect crime.

An FBI probe revealed the abduction was plotted over the last six months by Keenan, son of a Los Angeles stockbroker.

An obsession for money impelled Keenan to polish his plans for the kidnaping until

he believed the crime was so perfect that he never would be caught, The Sun-Times learned.

Several times since June, Keenan and his co-conspirators stalked the 19-year-old singer in an attempt to kidnap him.

In one instance, they were prepared to snatch Sinatra when he appeared at a night club here. For undisclosed reasons, their plans went awry.

Keenan finally put his plan into action Dec. 8, kidnaping Sinatra from a motel at Lake Tahoe, on the California-Nevada border.

The abduction showed flashes of cunning but it was far from perfect. The FBI seized Keenan and his partners, Joseph C. Amsler, 23, and John K. Irwin, 42, soon after they collected the ransom from film star Frank Sinatra Sr.

Young Sinatra was released unharmed Dec. 11. Within 48 hours, all of the ransom except $6,000 was recovered, and the three conspirators were jailed on kidnaping charges.

A wrangle among the Sinatra kidnapers over the $240,000

Turn to Page 48

SURPLUS OF MINUSES

Unofficial temperatures in suburban communities early Thursday:

Arlington Hgts.	-5	Harvey	-2	Naperville	-6
Aurora	-4	Highland Park	-10	Oak Lawn	-5
Barrington	11	Hinsdale	-7	Oak Park	-4
Berwyn	-7	Homewood	-7	Park Forest	-9
Blue Island	-8	Joliet	-10	Park Ridge	-10
Calumet City	7	La Grange	-10	River Grove	-9
Des Plaines	tie	Lake Forest	-4	Skokie	-4
Downers Grove	0	Maywood	-10	West Springs	-7
Elgin	12	Melrose Park	-5	Wheeling	10
Gary	-8	Morton Grove	-9	Whiting	-7
Glencoe	12	Mount Prospect	-6	Wheaton	-6

Fig. 5–17. Imagination. An imaginative layout person can add zip to the front page with a humorous touch, as when Chicago was hit by ten days of bad weather.

It is easy for editors to get so enthusiastic about newspaper design that they let makeup overshadow content. They concentrate on how the paper looks, not on what the words or pictures tell. Their newspaper makes a good first impression. Readers eagerly pick it up because it looks so delightful. But their delight changes to disgust if they find the news play clumsy, the stories disjointed, and important items buried or even omitted. Editors infatuated with appearance may refuse to change one day's makeup when a breaking news story demands it. They are so smitten with page design that alteration cannot be tolerated. They may even sketch a design and then look for stories that might match the diagrams.

News before beauty

Makeup always should be an adjunct to news coverage. Editors must first consider the news. They must select it, weigh its merits, and decide what stories are most important. Then they will decide the typographical display of the most important stories and pictures. No matter how clever the makeup, the editor must be willing to scrap or revise it whenever news events demand. Revising makeup is itself a skill, and we cover it separately in chapter 11.

The process of designing each day's page is called *dummying*. The editor uses a diagram called a dummy to send the printers instructions on where the type and pictures are to go. Some papers refer to the dummy as a "map," and the description is apt. The printer looking over the dummy is really reading a "map."

Dummying

The blank dummy is usually a sheet eight and one-half by eleven inches of columns with measurements, signifying inches, at the sides. (See fig. 5-18.) The news room gets dummies for all inside pages from the advertising department, which has placed the ads in the dummy. The news department fills the remaining space with news and pictures.

The task of dummying is easier if the editor knows almost exactly the length of each story. Computers provide this information. Where reporters write their stories on paper they often are told to write each line a certain length so four lines of typewritten copy will equal one inch of type. The number of lines, divided by four, equals the number of inches of type. Headline space is easy to tabulate. If a headline is 24-point, three lines equal one inch. If a story with the 24-point head takes up eight inches the total length, obviously, is nine inches. The editor simply provides nine inches of space on the dummy.

Several editors usually prepare various dummies on a big paper. The sports editor and the women's editor will dummy their pages. The city editor probably will do it for his section. The state and suburban editors will handle a few, and the news editor or slot person probably will lay out page one plus several other pages. On some newspapers the telegraph editor, who handles wire news, makes up page one and other major pages.

The wire service budget, or "news digest," lists the important stories to be filed that day. It gives editors an early view of what state, national, and world stories will be available. If a newspaper puts any local or regional news on page one—and every paper should—the person dummying the front page will have to confer with the city editor and state editor to see which of their stories may warrant front page play. From the telegraph editor comes information on what unexpected stories arriving on the wires are worthy of special attention. Available pictures are inspected and a mental note is made on pictures which might arrive by deadline.

The editor then makes a series of decisions almost automatically. The day's best story is picked and a headline assigned. The editor reaches the decision by comparing the merit of the story to top stories on other days. If the story is unusually good, it gets bigger display than an average lead story will receive. If it is less worthy it will draw a smaller headline, and the editor will mumble, "Nothing much going on today."

From then on, the editor quickly sketches where pictures will go and, holding all the major stories in mind for comparison, decides which story ranks No. 2. A head to that story is assigned and dummied-probably near the top at the left but perhaps under a picture. The "play" of No. 2 depends on how far it ranks in news value behind No. 1 and how attractive the headline on No. 2 will be. No. 3 story may get a three-column head at the lower right. No. 4 may get a two-column head and be placed in the lower left. These decisions get made while the rest of the main stories are kept in mind.

From then on the priority system is a bit blurred. The other stories may be unconsciously rated "good," "fair," and "expendable." Five stories may about tie for fifth place. The editor may put three or four of these onto page one, until all the available niches are filled. The rest and other good stories can be saved for inside pages where "fair" and even "expendable" stories may appear.

Beginners in dummying tend to put all display at the top. They methodically march down the page, filling the space with lesser stories until they hit the bottom. The result is that the top of the page looks good but the bottom looks ragged: covered with minor, one-column stories.

This tendency of beginners reveals their limited vision. They work with one story at a time and do not consider or even see the whole picture as they select the news. They need to think of *all* major stories as they sketch makeup.

The skilled editor looks at the available stories and mentally roughs out the makeup for the front page, putting the key stories at various spots on the page. This means that stories with good-sized headlines land at the top right, the top left, in each of the lower quarters of the page, and beneath pictures that have been dummied at the top. As a result, five or six important spots are filled and the open space will be filled in later. While the number of ways the job can be done is not limitless, a good designer guards against having only four or five basic patterns. Like some musical composers, the designer strives to weave seemingly infinite variations on basic patterns. The variations can be supplied by several typographical devices.

Boxes. These can be both ruled and "sideless" (set off with white space only). Boxes can be single-column, double-column, or even eight-column.

Typographical devices

Wide measure. This is type set wider than usual, probably one and a half columns to divide into two wider columns under a three-column head.

"One-up." Five columns of type, for example, go under a six-column head. The extra white space between columns attracts attention. Sometimes the top of the page has a one-up with seven columns of type under an eight-column head.

Headlines with kickers. The extra ribbon of white space above the head makes the headline stand out to attract the reader.

Ben Day borders. These gray strips may go around a whole story or only at top and bottom to call attention to it.

Centered headline. A centered headline in a page of heads set flush left makes an effective contrast.

Art work. A little sketch inserted into stories relieves the monotony of solid type.

Unruled columns. Eliminating the rules between the columns of a story with a multi-column head unifies it. Only a few papers these days, however, use column rules.

To supplement these devices, an editor may put a six-column head over a story at the bottom of the page; the next day each lower corner may get a two-column head. To draw attention to the lower left, a picture may be used on some days and a three-column head on others. (A wide variety of typographical display appears in the illustrations of front pages.)

The editor does well to dummy the front page with variations in mind. Thus, the tentative sketch of the first five stories in the dummy might look something like figure 5-18. If the dummy of these five is satisfactory, the editor sifts through second-level stories—the ones that are good but not outstanding—and fills the rest of the space with them. All the type must be arranged so no gaps are plugged with dinky fillers, and there should be few jumps, especially jumps of only an inch or two. If readers take the trouble to hunt up a continuation and then find only two sentences, they surely will be irritated.

For layouts that neatly fill the page with stories the editor must juggle type, shorten some stories, and move others. Sometimes it means that a story intended for page three must be switched with a story planned for page one. If both stories have about equal news value, the transfer is easy. But sometimes the shift forces alteration of the editor's original judgment of importance.

Fig. 5–18. Makeup process. The news editor may put the best story upper right and a big picture upper left. Another good story may go under the picture, a third under the top story and still another at the bottom.

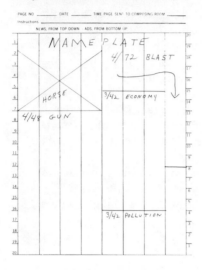

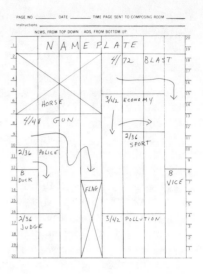

Fig. 5–19. Makeup process. The editor finishes by blocking in other stories to fill the page and to achieve informal balance of elements.

Fitting stories to space

Makeup would be easier if there were an endless number of good stories four, seven, twelve and sixteen inches long. Then the editor could readily choose the right one to fit a certain hole. The story desired for a specific place, however, is almost invariably too long or too short. Three choices remain: Select another story; shorten or lengthen the one in hand; or shorten an adjoining story to make room for the one that didn't fit. Editors usually don't have the time to lengthen stories, so they keep shortening, choosing, and juggling until the full page looks like fig. 5-19.

The dummy should provide only basic information on picture placement (shown by crossed lines plus an identification word), headline size, slugline or guideline, and how multi-column stories move from one column to another. Any other mark on the dummy makes instructions confusing. For example, it is usually unnecessary to note whether heads are roman or italic type, although good papers do use a mixture of both. It also clutters the dummy to draw all kinds of lines indicating that type goes to a certain point. Under a single-column head, the printer will know that type is to be placed there so it is unnecessary to make any mark in that area. Leave it blank. The little arrows on multi-column stories tell the printer exactly where type is to go.

The job of fitting the copy to the available space in a limited time requires a system. Most papers work the system something like this: Each editor is assigned to fill a certain number of pages. He or she then reviews the stories that passed over the desk and takes note of the stories expected by deadline. Often the editor tells reporters what length to write their stories, and they must tell the editor if a story is "running long"—that is, longer than anticipated. Such information enables editors to begin dummying their pages, making minor—and sometimes major—adjustments as the news develops.

Copy Control Sheet

Slug	head size	page	length
council	#1	3	8
peace	4/72	1	18
President	3/42	4	12
Gov.	6/42	2	17
goat	#2	1	4
race	2/36	6	11

Fig. 5–20. Copy control sheet. With a form like this, the copyeditor can keep a list of stories by slug, head size, page placement, and length.

Makeup guidelines

When editors instruct a copyeditor to cut a story to a particular length, they either speak across the copydesk or write the headline size and the desired story length on the copy and simply hand it to the copyeditor. The copyeditor then trims a story by peeling away a few phrases without eliminating the basic information. More extensive cutting will require pulling out paragraphs here and there or perhaps whacking off the last six.

The editor keeps tabs on the stories sent to the composing room by listing them on a *copy control sheet* (fig. 5-20), unless the computer does this automatically. Memory on what stories are still coming can be refreshed by referring to a list of assignments and to the wire service news digest.

Anyone making up pages should keep in mind the knowledge of typography accumulated by researchers. For a newspaper to gain maximum impact with the reader, most experts in typography advise certain guidelines in makeup. Here is a list of negatives:

Avoiding pitfalls

Avoid letting headlines "bump."   Heads should be separated vertically by body type so each one stands clearly by itself. This sometimes is impossible at the top of page one.

Don't "tombstone."   Heads of similar type face side by side resemble grave markers in old cemeteries. (See fig. 5-21.) Even contrasting type faces side by side tend to deaden the page.

Avoid "squint-size" headlines.   The reader should never have to squint to read headlines. Twelve-point heads are all right on one- and two-paragraph stories, but a longer story ought to have a bigger head. Multi-column heads should be at least 30-point, unless there is a corner above an ad to fill on an inside page.

Don't restrict the type beneath multi-column heads to neat squares or rectangles.   Makeup gains variety if, for example, the body type in column one is four inches, in column two six inches, and in column three five inches. The chance to switch type from one column to another under a multi-column head also makes the job easier. (True, some typographic experts urge that type under heads be squared off. It is not suggested here that makeup people go too far in varying lengths of type under multi-column heads, or do it too often; certainly they should be aware that there is a danger of producing a ragged appearance.)

Never crowd the page.   To ensure a fair amount of "air," body should not stand without a subhead every few paragraphs.* Neither should headlines take up every millimeter of space nor cutlines be jammed against their pictures. On the other hand, too much air gives the reader the feeling that he bought a piece of fluff.

Stop body type from forming ponderous blocks.   Several subheads or some little sketches should break up the gray. Or type should spread over several columns. This way the reader notes only four or five inches of type in each column and doesn't think the reading job will be arduous. Even an editor, upon seeing a long story in print, tends to say, "That looks good. I'll have to read it when I have more time." It never gets read.

Avoid top heavy or bottom heavy pages.   Top or bottom headlines so big that one area overpowers the rest of the page are only appropriate if the paper's policy is to have brace makeup.

No headline should "cry wolf."   If a story is of little consequence, let the headline admit it. A reader justly feels cheated if the head grossly exaggerates the story's value.

Repress dingbats.   Most stars, asterisks, dashes, and rules can be scrapped. The most typographically advanced newspapers have eliminated column rules and do not end stories with dashes. It is clear to the reader when the stories end, and a little ribbon of white space usually does a better job of separating stories than a rule ever did.

---

*Some papers are dropping subheads because many persons do not read them. But great care must be used to keep strips of type short, by emphasizing the horizontal, if there are no break-up devices.

Don't let a story escape its headline. Tucking the last few lines of a story someplace in an adjoining column is sloppy editing. It confuses the reader and makes the type look sidetracked. Keep the story under the shelter of the head.

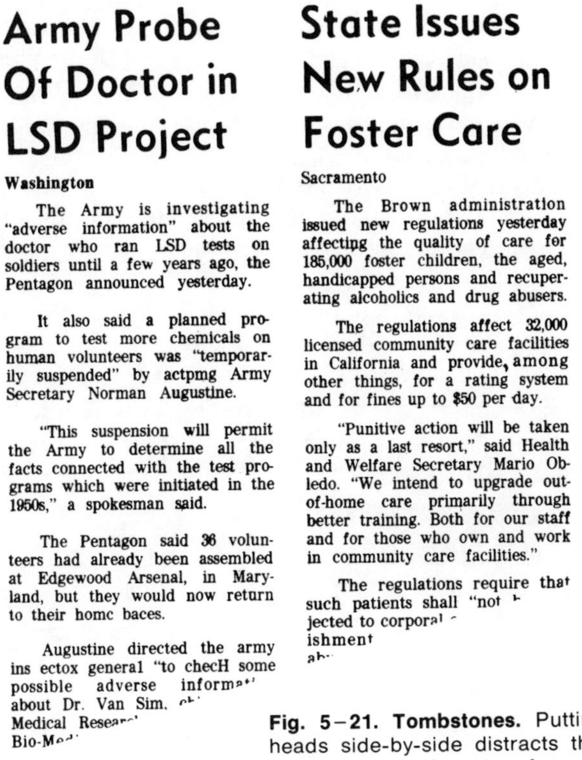

Army Probe Of Doctor in LSD Project

Washington

The Army is investigating "adverse information" about the doctor who ran LSD tests on soldiers until a few years ago, the Pentagon announced yesterday.

It also said a planned program to test more chemicals on human volunteers was "temporarily suspended" by actpmg Army Secretary Norman Augustine.

"This suspension will permit the Army to determine all the facts connected with the test programs which were initiated in the 1950s," a spokesman said.

The Pentagon said 36 volunteers had already been assembled at Edgewood Arsenal, in Maryland, but they would now return to their homc baces.

Augustine directed the army ins ectox general "to checH some possible adverse informa... about Dr. Van Sim, ... Medical Resear... Bio-Me...

State Issues New Rules on Foster Care

Sacramento

The Brown administration issued new regulations yesterday affecting the quality of care for 185,000 foster children, the aged, handicapped persons and recuperating alcoholics and drug abusers.

The regulations affect 32,000 licensed community care facilities in California and provide, among other things, for a rating system and for fines up to $50 per day.

"Punitive action will be taken only as a last resort," said Health and Welfare Secretary Mario Obledo. "We intend to upgrade out-of-home care primarily through better training. Both for our staff and for those who own and work in community care facilities."

The regulations require that such patients shall "not ... jected to corpora... ishment ...

Fig. 5–21. Tombstones. Putting similar heads side-by-side distracts the reader, whose eyes tend to stray from one to the other.

Taking positive steps

Other rules accentuate the positive.

Try to put associated stories together. Otherwise insert a "refer" somewhere near the beginning of the major story. This can be a simple statement, such as the "Elgin teachers . . . " of fig. 5-16 or a slug, such as "President Calls Plan Silly. Story on A9."

Liven the corners of the pages. They can look like dead space unless strong typography is planned to give them life.

Choose headline type faces that contrast but don't conflict. Perhaps this harmony of type can be explained by comparing it to harmony of dress. A man who wears a plaid jacket with a horizontally striped shirt and a diagonally striped tie may find the combination overwhelms the eye. Type faces should impress the reader as pleasantly symmetrical.

Use few type faces. A paper displaying half a dozen different type faces can be as upsetting as a woman wearing an orange hat, a blue blouse, a brown skirt, a purple scarf, yellow shoes, and a green coat. The editors of the *Los Angeles Times* fill that huge paper with only two type faces. For contrast, type is varied in size and font (roman and italic).

Inside pages

Some editors take pains with front page makeup but throw together the inside pages. The reader may get the impression that the inside is a snarl of words not worth reading. So good editors work nearly as hard on the inside pages as on page one.

Newspapers with good inside pages continue the reverse-6 system, which means that each page has a strong left side with a good-sized headline or a large picture in the upper left. The rest of the page offers such variety that no story, except perhaps a tiny one used as a filler, will be lost. (See fig. 5-22.)

Fig. 5–22. Reverse-6 inside. The box at the top left of this inside page attracts the reader's eyes first, but vision soon gets lured to the other stories at the right and bottom.

Anti-Communists

Military restructuring is sought in Portugal

© New York Times News Service

LISBON — A move to drastically reduce Communist influence in the highest spheres of Portugal's armed forces has begun concurrently with negotiations for a new centrist cabinet.

While the complicated bargaining that is expected to produce a new government by the end of the week captured most public attention, a more discreet struggle that could determine the control and direction of the Portuguese revolution was taking place within the military.

With the first defeat of the Communists registered last weekend with the removal of Premier Vasco Goncalves from positions of responsibility, those who opposed him are now understood to be confident they can completely remake the organs of power within the armed forces.

In their view, the military plays a major role in foreign and domestic policy so a new government in which two major anti-Communist forces, the Socialist and Popular Democratic parties, are expected to be amply represented will be effective to the extent that it receives military backing.

A committee has been appointed by the present high council of the revolution to draw up a plan for restructuring the military. New elections from top to bottom to reflect majority opinion appear to be favored.

This opinion is felt to have been flouted by Goncalves and those around him, particularly since the strong shift to the left after an abortive rightist coup in March.

As a way of introducing democracy and the free play of ideas into the armed forces, assemblies of officers and men were formed toward the end of last year and were capped by a General Assembly of the Armed Forces.

Under an agreement the armed forces made with the principal political parties before the elections for a Constituent Assembly last April, the council is to remain in power along with the armed forces General Assembly for three to five years. The council is given the power to define foreign and domestic policies and to oversee their execution.

The agreement is to be consigned in the constitution now being drawn up by the assembly. But among some of the military there is a move afoot to go beyond the removal of Communist influence from the armed forces and remove the military itself from politics. It is not yet clear whether this trend has majority support even among so-called moderates who feel they have a role still to play in the revolution.

Meanwhile, the outgoing Goncalves government approved a measure last month that would give workers' committees control of all firms with more than 50 employes, the Communist-controlled daily Diario de Noticias reported today.

The decree has not been published in the official government journal yet and could be scrapped by the still-unformed government of Vice Adm. Jose Pinheiro de Azevedo, which is expected to be less Communist-oriented than Goncalves'.

The newspaper's page-one display evidently was intended to win worker support for the measure before Azevedo takes office.

Report of try on Sadat's life called 'untrue'

Associated Press

CAIRO—An Egyptian government spokesman denied a radio report from Iraq yesterday that an attempt had been made last week to assassinate President Anwar Sadat of Egypt.

The spokesman termed the broadcast by the Voice of Palestine in Baghdad as "untrue, a lie and rubbish."

The report also was discounted by U.S. officials in Washington who described the Voice of Palestine as "very unreliable."

The broadcast from Baghdad claimed that gunmen opened fire on Sadat in Alexandria after the signing of the new Sinai interim agreement with Israel.

The Egyptian spokesman also described the radio in Baghdad as unreliable and added that it doesn't represent the Palestinian people.

The head of the Voice of Palestine in Cairo said the radio in Baghdad represents a group of mercenaries who have nothing to do with the Palestine Liberation Organization, headed by Yasir Arafat.

In addition to the Voice of Palestine in Cairo and Baghdad there is one in Damascus, Syria.

The Baghdad report, attributing its information to "well-informed diplomatic sources," said Sadat was taking a walk in his palace garden with a number of aides, including Foreign Minister Ismail Fahmi.

Sadat and Fahmi reportedly fell to the ground when the shooting started. Then Sadat reportedly crept behind a tree while his guards fanned out in an unsuccessful attempt to seize the attempted assassins. Two of the guards were said to have been wounded.

MF

A Celebration

Kay Morrisse
Area Directo

You know, it
overweight.
That's a cha
glad you dii

'WEIGHT WATCHERS' AN

(The combine

New army chief, Lebanon troops to act as buffer

© New York Times News Service

BEIRUT—Premier Rashid Karami announced yesterday that a newly appointed commander of the army had been ordered to station troops between the warring northern Lebanese towns of Tripoli and Zgharta.

Karami said the forces would not enter the two embattled towns. Security in Tripoli, which is largely Moslem, and Zgharta, predominantly Christian, will continue to be the responsibility of local authorities.

The premier said that the current army commander, Maj. Gen. Iskandar Ghanem, had been given a "leave of absence" to take up an unnamed diplomatic post. His replacement is a little known colonel, Hanna Saeed, who was promoted to major general.

Saeed, a Maronite Christian like Ghanem, is considered noncontroversial.

Eight days of fighting in the port town of Tripoli and the villages and olive groves in the hills to the east of the city have taken a heavy toll of casualties—estimates of the dead exceed 100, with many more reported wounded.

Visitors to Tripoli, which was relatively calm yesterday, said hospitals were jammed with unattended wounded and that many Christian-owned stores were gutted and looted.

But gunmen were reported to have continued to trade fitful barrages of rocket, mortar and heavy weapons fire.

Brooks Tangy Catsup

Now appearing at a supermarket near you.

Grant
KNOWN FOR
NOW THRU SAT., SEPT

Fig. 5—23. Neat fit. The *Louisville Courier-Journal,* using wide columns, slips three stories, each well-separated, into a small inside page hole.

Annapolis graduate is seeking amnesty

SAN DIEGO (AP) — The Navy dismissed agent Grant Kimball from the service because the 1966 graduate of the Naval Academy refused to return to Vietnam in act of conscience, his attorney says.

Now Kimball, 30, wants the Presidential Clemency Board to overturn his dishonorable discharge.

A spokesman for the board said Kimball is the only Annapolis graduate among 16,000 persons seeking amnesty. His case may be considered within a few weeks, the spokesman added.

Technically, Kimball was dropped from the Navy because he pleaded guilty to unauthorized absences from Vietnam in 1970.

"I wasn't so much disenchanted with the Navy," he said of three years of active duty that included submarine assignments and a tour aboard the guided missile destroyer Decator in the Gulf of Tonkin off North Vietnam. "But I became absolutely opposed to the Vietnam War. I refused to fight in it."

In September, 1969, he applied for special status as a conscientious objector.

Kimball was ordered to report to Travis Air Force Base near San Francisco for an assignment helping plan air strikes along the Cambodian border, he recalled.

Twice he refused, remaining at a Navy base in the San Francisco Bay area. He was charged with desertion and disobeying direct orders. He tried to resign, "for the good of the service," he said, but was turned down because of the pending court martial.

Attorney J.H. Toms said he believes the Bureau of Naval Personnel "maneuvered Lt. Kimball into a position where he either would have to go to Vietnam in violation of his conscience or else fail to obey the orders and be court martialed."

Although Kimball agreed to a guilty plea to lesser charges, Toms said it was the only choice other than jail.

Civilian firms have turned him down because he has listed his dishonorable discharge on employment applications, Kimball said.

The Naval Academy awarded him an engineering degree, and he has worked the last year as a computer programmer for a small digital equipment company in San Diego.

CL
Ki
126 S.
Open Da

A CARSONS BUDGET

Fig. 5—24. One hole, one story. The *Chicago Sun-Times,* a tabloid, uses horizontal makeup to fill the five-column hole.

Thousands of U.S. troops in Mideast seen possible

By Thomas B. Ross

Sun-Times Bureau

WASHINGTON — The cadre of 200 U.S. civilian technicians who are to monitor the new Egyptian-Israeli truce line in the Sinai could expand into a force of thousands of U.S. military men before there is a final Middle East settlement.

Pentagon officials estimate that each additional Israeli withdrawn from Arab territory will involve a few hundred more monitors and that a complete pullback to the 1967 lines could entail the stationing of as many as 10,000 U.S. troops in a buffer zone.

Sec. of State Henry A. Kissinger has conceded privately that the 200 technicians in Sinai could become a precedent for a larger presence in future agreements. He also has declared that a U.S. force along Israel's final borders is not out of the question.

Israel insisted on the U.S. technicians as an absolute condition for making the second Sinai pullback, and many high-ranking Israelis now are pushing for a security treaty with the United States backed up by U.S. troops.

The demand for U.S. personnel represents a major reversal by the Israelis, who previously have argued vigorously against any super power presence, either Soviet or U.S.

But the implication of the new Israeli policy is that it will demand a major U.S. troop commitment — not a token force — if Israel is to take the risk of withdrawing from the Sinai and particularly from the Golan Heights and the West Bank.

In testimony and confidential consultation with members of Congress, Kissinger and other U.S. officials have avoided specific projections of how large the U.S. presence ultimately might be.

But they have not sought to deny that substantial commitments may have to be made in view of the unappealing alternatives. In brief, the administration argument is as follows:

To maintain access to Arab oil without recurrent embargoes and major price increases the United States must induce Israel to make successive withdrawals from territory taken from Egypt, Syria and Jordan in the Six-Day War, ultimately back more or less to the 1967 borders.

But Israel is not likely to make such a sacrifice in its defense perimeters without firm security guarantees from its only major ally, the United States. The guarantees are sure to include the outright grant of military and economic aid Kissinger offered $2.5 billion year to get the latest agreement and ultimately a major U.S. military presence.

The unappealing, politically difficult alternatives are:

(1) Conciliate the Arabs by cutting off aid to I s r a e l and forcing it to fend for itself a course of a c t i o n that could muster only scant support in Congress.

(2) Apply massive energy conservation and increase in gas prices to make the U.S. economy less dependant on Arab oil — a program that has proved equally unacceptable to Congress.

As the alternatives come into clearer focus, administration officials are convinced Congress and the public will accept a larger U.S. presence as the least unpalatable.

There already are 36 U.S. military men in the United Nations emergency force in the Sinai. The force, now down to some 5,000 men from an original 7,000 in early 1974, is composed mainly of troops from Canada, Poland, Finland, Sweden, Senegal, Indoesia, Ghaha, Australia and Peru.

Kissinger insists that the 200 U.S. technicians will play a role similar to that of UN peacekeeping forces and totally unlike that of the first U.S. advisers in Vietnam.

The Israelis thoroughly agree, pointing out that the technicians have been endorsed by both sides in the Middle East dispute, whereas the advisers in Vietnam were violently opposed by one side and only tepidly supported by the other.

Ultimately, however, U.S. forces will be in direct contact with the Palestinians if the forces are deployed along the final peace lines, particularly on the West Bank. And it is unlikely that Israel will settle for UN troops as an alternative.

After the 1956 war, the Israelis believed they had a firm commitment from the United States to keep open the Straits of Tiran. But when the late Egyptian President Gamal Abdel Nasser ordered the UN force out of the Sinai, the world organization complied and the United State did not intervene.

Before Israel withdraws again to its borders at that time, it surely will insist that a major U.S. force be on the ground, as in Western Europe and West Berlin, as a deterrent to a possible Arab attack — even as a hostage to prevent it.

Fig. 5–25. Inside switch. The *Sun-Times* often switches from a six-column paper to three wide-measure columns to emphasize an inside story.

Bribe suspect ailing

TOKYO (AP) — The influential right-winger accused of taking a $7 million payoff from Lockheed Aircraft was rushed to a hospital Friday after his condition worsened, authorities reported.

Yoshio Kodama, 65, had been ordered to testify next Monday before a legislative committee investigating Lockheed payoffs in Japan. Kodama failed to appear for the committee's first hearing last week, and his doctor said he was unable to testify because of the aftereffects of a stroke.

Fig. 5–26. The Chicago Daily News occasionally sets a short story wide measure, puts an Ultra Bodoni head on it, and uses Oxford rules top and bottom.

Variety for inside pages follows the guidelines outlined for page one: no tombstoning, a blend of roman and italic heads, a picture or two, and some of those change-of-pace techniques like boxes and Ben Day borders. (See figs. 5-23 through 5-26.)

Most inside pages lack the flexibility available on page one, because ads may fill as much as 90 percent of the space. If copy does not properly fit the news hole of the page, either the story will have to be cut after it has been set in type or two or three shorts will have to be added to make up a deficiency. Such last minute makeup takes time and often cripples a page.

Fitting copy to the news hole on a page can be done quite simply ahead of time. The editor totals the available space. It may come to thirty-two inches and there may be room for a four-column head —that is, ads fill four columns to the top and other ads fill a large amount of the page. The editor may put a four-column head on one story that will take up seventeen inches. That leaves fifteen. A nine-inch, two-column story might be placed beneath the four-column and a six-inch, single column story inserted. The result can be seen in fig. 5-27. Note that the four-column story is not "squared-off."

An inside page with a little more space for news can be seen in fig. 5-28. To aid in the explanation, "roman" and "italic" have been added to the headline symbol.

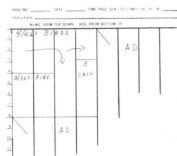

Fig. 5-27. Dummy problem. The ads planned for this page leave little space for news yet the editor has fitted three short stories and kept the heads clearly separated.

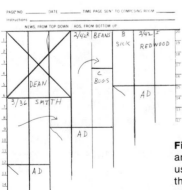

Fig. 5-28. Inside picture. With a big picture and varied heads, the inside pages can make use of front page design techniques, even though the bottom of the page is occupied with ads.

Pictures in makeup

Editors making up pages on a big newspaper usually have a large selection of photos from wire services and from staff photographers. Even if there are only a few really good pictures on a given day, the editor tries to avoid printing any poor art and aims for a large proportion of excellent photographs. The average quality is kept high this way, even though the number of pictures may have to be reduced some days.

Some papers have a rigid policy on art: There must be a picture on every news page. This restriction frequently forces the editor to use poor pictures. A better policy would be to have a picture on every page if a good photograph is available. Some of the better-designed papers that try to mix art and news are not bothered if several pages lack art. Their editors believe that a solid page of type is better than one diluted with a photographic cliché—the presentation of a trophy or the handshake of two grinning people.

Increasingly, editors are willing to print a few pictures that have no direct bearing on the news, pictures published for beauty, not news content. The *Christian Science Monitor* has been a leader in printing this kind of photograph, and nearly every issue has two or three stunning pictures. The handshake shot is dull, but few can overlook a photo of striking beauty.

The makeup editor

The term "makeup editor" may suggest a person who dummies the pages and controls the placing of news. Not so. Although this person may make frequent appearances in the news room, headquarters are in the composing room.

The makeup editor makes the necessary little last-minute adjustments that fit all the stories, ads, and photos on each page. Suppose a story planned for sixteen inches really measured sixteen and one-half. The makeup editor then checks a proof of the story to see if four lines can be cut without damaging the story's meaning. These expendable lines are called "bites." The printer is told, "Bite it here." The printer then throws hot type in the hellbox (or cold type into a wastebasket).

The makeup editor's biggest job, however, is keeping everything straight in a developing story or during a major change in deadline. In these cases stories may be cut drastically or "time copy"—really timeless—may be inserted. New dummies may be sent from editors in the newsroom. Sometimes the makeup people will have to peer at hot type itself to tell the printer where to cut stories and how to juggle type. Cold type, of course, is as easy to read as the newspaper itself.

It should be noted that the job of makeup editor varies with the size of the paper. A paper that usually runs less than fifty pages would not have enough work for such a person. And on a big paper the makeup editor usually does not supervise the makeup of special sections. The sports department will send a copyeditor to the composing room for perhaps half an hour to check the makeup on sports pages. Individuals from the financial, women's, and editorial page departments will do the same for their sections. Still the makeup editor on a big paper has plenty to do.

On medium-sized and small papers each sub-editor goes to the composing room to make sure the pages get put together the desired way. Each of them may spend no more than thirty minutes at the task. Printers, following dummies, may have the pages nearly ready by the time the editor arrives. Only a few adjustments may be required or worth the time of both editor and printer. On small papers, the managing editor, who may write editorials as well as manage the news operation, may also be the one who dummies the key pages and supervises their makeup.

Whoever goes to the composing room to make up should remember not to touch type without permission of the printer. That prohibition is a printers' union rule and a reasonable one. Editors would not like a printer messing with their papers, so editors should not interfere with the printers' work.

Persons supervising makeup should have proofs of the stories in their section so they can refer to them quickly and mark any changes on them. And, most important, they should listen to advice from printers. Since most printers are intelligent people who take pride in their craft, they can often suggest ways out of a problem. The makeup editor should accept with thanks the good suggestions and reject gracefully the ones not so good.

Future makeup

When a newspaper staff decides to try improving typography, it probably should make changes gradually. Readers are creatures of habit who, if confronted by a revolutionary makeup, may rebel. So most papers revamp their makeup piecemeal. The headline type faces are altered, and a few months later the body type is modernized. The nameplate may be next, but each shift comes only after the readers have adjusted to the preceding change.

Staffs of a few papers, however, have decided to make all the changes at once, figuring that the sudden alterations will dramatize for the readers the alertness and modernity of their paper. "Why cut off the dog's tail an inch at a time?" they ask. Each method has its merits, but most editors take the gradual approach. Substantial changes, regardless of how sweeping, should be accompanied by a news story announcing them. The paper may even use pictures to contrast examples of the new and old. The reader then sees the improvement and perhaps will recognize his newspaper as more than a fusty old relic frozen in tradition.

Most typographers look at today's best-designed pages with satisfaction. The type is easy to read; white space separates headlines from stories, and nothing looks crowded. The design pleases the eye.

No one should believe, however, that perfection has been attained. Editors must stay alert to borrow the typographical changes other editors make. They need to find new ways to get the reader to read and to understand what he reads. Of course, what the reader absorbs should be worth absorbing.

Editors must also study the findings of psychologists, communications specialists, and newspaper researchers. While some findings will be of little value, they will find some pearls that will help them help the reader. More thought and study on how human beings respond to the printed page will stimulate hundreds of fresh ideas to help the modern reader both survey and absorb the news.

6 News evaluation

Deep in American folklore is the idea that when a man bites a dog, it's news. The notion accurately emphasizes that the unusual and interesting are one aspect of the news. A small (and probably declining) segment of the press sees only this aspect in its "gee-whiz" evaluation of events. This one-dimensional "definition" of news perhaps subtly influences what American readers expect of their newspapers. Yet how can editors imbued with such a man-bites-dog philosophy consider their periodicals to be bona fide *news*papers?

The bizarre conflict of the mythical man and dog becomes, at a more sophisticated level, the idea that news is conflict. During the last generation editors have given the big play to stories of conflict—the foreign leader threatening the world, the aspiring candidate "flaying" the President, the mayor scrapping with a city councilman.

Front-page headlines tend to make the world look even more belligerent than it is, and yet, in a sense, news interest declines where there is no clash of views or armies. Peaceful government operation, like placid marriages, are considered normal and routine—and dull. If classes go routinely for a college student, he or she writes home, "No news." But if a professor is fired, or if students demonstrate against a dean, the student's interest perks up; that's news!

Journalism students, many of whom will edit the news the rest of this century, may well ask if the public is jaded with conflict news. Intelligent readers know that a dog fight is not really as important as the medical advances made possible through research with dogs. They have had their fill of conflict in Asia, the Near East or anyplace else. Research indicates, furthermore, that long reports of war or bickering are not read as well as most editors assumed.

Through habit, some editors make up pages as if bombings and threats of bombings were the most important of news. Certainly conflict is significant; yet readers hunger for news of the relief or end of conflict—perhaps just because peace is uncommon. Journalists, the *Saturday Review* once complained, too often consider only bad news real news, so for a time the magazine ran a column of "good news." Newspaper editors might find a hint here.

Though sometimes editors act as if the choice of news were decreed by the stars, it is men and women who make the decisions that make "news." They base their decisions on theories and intuitions which are subject to analysis and criticism. What are these foundations for decisions? Is news the bizarre or the hopeful, the story of conflict or of the meaningful?

What, after all, is news? There is no more critical question for the editor to consider.

The nature of news

News is *current information of interest to readers* (or listeners or viewers). That definition is not meant to be a legalistic pronouncement but a stimulus to thinking about events. The concept "news," like the concepts "mental health" or "spirituality," is more easily recognized than precisely described. That first brief statement is meant to center attention where the editor's attention must be centered: on the reader's concern to be informed more than on the source of information or the incident itself.

The deciphering of an ancient hieroglyphic or the release of secret documents from World War II is clearly news, though the "event" was long ago. The information is fresh and current to the reader today. There has been a tradition of trying to get *today* into the leads of stories about news a day or even a week old: "It was learned today," or "Washington sources said today." But editors are sensibly coming to accept perfect tense forms as equally newsy: "Ancient secrets have been deciphered." If the information is of fresh interest today, it's news to the reader, regardless of the date of the original event.

It may be objected that the definition, by pointing up reader interest, minimizes the significance factor in news. However, we make the assumption that if an item is truly important to a reader, it will interest the reader too. How could it be otherwise? There is no dull significant *news,* there is only dull significant *newswriting.* If an epidemic threatens a reader's town, or if a change in the federal budget affects taxes or services that concern the reader, the medical or fiscal details should be presented in a way that will interest the reader. If an epidemic is far away or if the budget change really will not affect the reader, it does not deserve much attention. Why should an editor sweat over it? We are, of course, not referring to readers only concerned with themselves or perhaps their immediate families. Typical readers, with some concern about the whole nation and the world, must still focus on what is most significant for them, and the editor should try to help them see and understand that significance.

Editors may fail in taking the easy way out. They know most readers are interested in the rape-murder—or at least tradition says they are interested—so they print it. More significant stories tend to be more difficult to work up. The news staff concludes too quickly that the reader has no interest in or concern about a development in foreign aid or a cabinet change in some remote country. In this age of interpretation, however, the editor's job is often to probe for the relationship of distant or obscure events to the reader, indirect as it may be, and then point that significance up clearly.

This approach to news also helps the editor determine the "size" or importance of a story. Textbooks on newswriting sometimes list qualities which will help the beginning reporter recognize the difference between a big item and a little one. "Proximity" is one, for example; others are "size" and "recency." A flood killing 500 persons is a bigger story than one killing five. Or a wreck killing five persons in our own town means more to us than a wreck killing five outside Cologne. The death of a businessman an hour ago is newsier than the death of a businessman two days ago. All such evaluations are of course made as if all other factors are equal—but usually everything else is not equal in the live news editors handle. They minimize the rules and categories and develop a judgment which relates news to the current needs and interests of readers.

The desires of readers for the superficial as well as the heavy are therefore taken into account. Readers will identify with some stories, and such material—appropriately called "human interest" —will always be used. Reader needs, whether or not the reader recognizes them, are even more important. As pointed out in chapter 1 people have less and less time to keep up with more and more news in a world whose horizons now extend far into space, an intermediary must alert them to the news they need. The editor is the person who decides which messages from Asia and the United Nations and Washington and Main Street are important to the busy readers of his pages. The aim is to alert the reader, and this goal, like the other goals of journalism—to lead, to educate, and so on —would not be valid if the editor ignored the readers' needs.

The evaluation network

Rarely does one person alone decide which stories will reach print. Except with routine local news in small papers, a whole network of writers and editors normally selects stories for the daily press. How vast the problem is can be seen in the fact that the *Chicago Daily News* receives 1.7 million words a day but can print "only" 100,000!

Suppose, for example, that a snowslide in the central mountains of Switzerland injures several tourists. Depending on such factors as the number of deaths and the prominence of the people, the local correspondent or "stringer" will get the news out. For a wire service the copy would most likely go to Berne or Geneva, probably by telephone. The editors there would doubtless send a full story to a central desk in London. If the dead were Latin Americans, the most complete story might go to South America.

Let's assume a prominent businessman from San Francisco is among the dead. London then sends quite a complete story to New York, and this story goes out on a West Coast regional wire. A much abbreviated item will go to most of the other dailies in the country. Lesser wire-service editors become involved in deciding how much of the story can move to papers under them, and finally an individual news editor or telegraph editor decides how much, if any, of it fits his paper. In San Francisco it is obviously a major story, but editors in many other cities will throw it out.

The fate of this story, moreover, depends on the flow of other news. At each point—Berne, London, New York, and on the telegraph desk—editors have to weigh the story with other stories that reach their desks at the same time. This variation in the flood of news means that one day a relatively small story gets a big play, while another day a significant item is buried.

While the telegraph editor is selecting from the wire, a city editor is dispatching reporters to newsworthy events. Writers on beats are deciding which events they find deserve coverage, and how much. The city editor evaluates the overall flow of city news from these local sources while a state editor weighs copy from the state or region, and a sports editor evaluates sports news. Other editors and writers—the business editor, church editor, and women's editor—survey their fields for news significant to their readers.

But who decides whether the accident in Switzerland deserves more or less space than a local court trial? In part this question is solved or evaded by departmentalization. The city editor, for example, will typically have a page or two for display of local news, and the sports editor and women's editor usually have special sections for their copy.

On the front page, however, the biggest stories from all the channels meet in competition. Here the mountain accident faces the local murder, the bill in the state legislature, the statement from the President, and perhaps a World Series game. The newspaper has to have clear staff organization to decide how the stories should be played.

The managing editor, as the title suggests, is the person responsible; but on larger papers "the m.e." rarely makes hour-by-hour decisions on all the major stories from varied sources. These routine decisions are left to a *news editor*. (The telegraph editor may in fact fill this role, or the telegraph editor may, as an assistant to the news editor, make most decisions on wire copy.)

On a typical paper, the news editor weighs the space and position requests of the city editor and telegraph editor. Perhaps the state editor, sports editor or other "editors," such as the writers on science or labor, will bid for front-page space too. There may be discussion, and even loud argument, in which the city editor claims that the new break in a murder case deserves "the line" (banner head), while the science editor contends the new break-through on cancer is the most important story of the year. The news editor has to decide. Obviously, if this person does no makeup, instructions must go to the makeup editor to translate the decisions into type.

On one afternoon paper where the author worked, four or five of the key editors met in the managing editor's office about 8:30 A.M. for a look at the probable flow of each day's news, and decisions were made by the group. Each evening's makeup was sketched out

in committee, as it were. This system lacks the flexibility to accommodate the front page to news that develops around noon. But the
plan has the advantage of greater objectivity about the news, for the
enthusiasms and foibles of a single editor can be contained.

No committee, however, can edit a paper continuously. Individual editors must have the responsibility to make swiftly the decisions
required by the varied flow of news.

The news flow might be roughly compared to a conveyor belt
sending food of all kinds gliding by a person who has to choose the
items to eat quickly, with the need to fit them on a tray hastily, yet
with little opportunity to put something back in exchange.

So telegraph editors have to run eyes quickly down a seemingly
endless roll of stories from the wire services. They tear this one off,
planning to use most of it. They tear off another and spike it; and
another. They draw a long line to show they are trimming off all but
the first two paragraphs of the next lengthy story. The next story
that appears may reverse previous selections. The importance of experience is obvious, for the telegraph editor usually has no time to
ponder relative merits. This person has to make quick decisions,
drawing on an understanding of the world, and suspending prejudices and personal animosities.

The people who open and close the gates on the flow of news, we
have said, are known as gatekeepers. The many decisions constantly
made by writers and editors clearly mean that countless gatekeepers
influence the amount and quality of news in every issue of a newspaper. But for the readers of a daily, that paper's most important
gatekeeper is the news editor, a person virtually unknown to most of
them. How does this editor go about the task of decision? How are
choices made? How do stories rank in importance? How do they get
modified?

Significance of a story is the most important consideration on a
well-edited paper. Closely related to news importance, as has been
argued above, is usefulness to the reader; a story which is not of
world significance may nevertheless be highly significant to an individual reader. Other news is printed for its sheer entertainment
value, because of its human interest. Each story represents a mix of
importance, usefulness, and interest; the biggest stories have the
most of each quality. No formula or rule can guide the news editor
to infallible choices. Only experience sharpens judgment and produces pages which stand critical examination a month or a year
later.

Typically the news editor not only has to choose the news but also
has to make decisions on treatment. If the paper has only one wire
service supplying news, the editor sees only the story filed by that
service. But on larger newspapers a decision must be made on
whether to print the Associated Press story or the United Press
International version. Or should someone on the desk be told to
combine them? Or is copy from a special service better than either
agency story? Or can spot copy from the wire and a backgrounder as

**Weighing
news values**

a sidebar be used? In sum, the editor not only has to decide that a new development in Paris is significant and useful and probably even interesting to his readers, but he also has to decide what treatment they will find most meaningful. As he decides the *which* of events, he must also decide the *how* of display. The chapters on headlines and makeup have shown the several ways the editor quickly directs readers to the major stories and keeps them aware of the minor items.

Gatekeeping

In theory, the news editor coolly and objectively decides on the value and display of news, without fear or favor. In fact, varied pressures squeeze the editor most of the time. News sense may be shaped or even seriously distorted by three general kinds of pressure: economic, traditional, and personal.

Economic pressure

"The advertiser made them use that story," one reader observes. "They'll do anything," says another, "to sell papers." Such frequent comments from newspaper consumers point to the supposed influence of profit on news decisions, and the two sources of newspaper income *are* advertising and circulation.

The threat of the advertiser to full news coverage is exaggerated in the public mind, however. On the well-run newspaper, the advertising and editorial departments are separate and distinct. Good journalists would repulse an advertising representative who approached asking favors. In fact, some editors would make a point of doing the opposite of what an ad person asked. There are doubtless cases where a big advertiser asks and gets favors in the news columns, or where a weak editor gives the advertiser free space or kills a story though the advertiser may not even have asked. But such toadying is the exception.

One journalistic practice which muddies public thinking in this area is the issuing of special supplements. Since advertising of real estate, resorts, or insurance supports these sections, they are filled with news-like puffs about such businesses. The growing tendency on many papers to stuff regular columns with handouts, not only from charities but also from businesses, likewise demonstrates the strength of commercial pressure. Laymen can hardly be blamed if they conclude that plugs can become news if one has money or the right contacts. Objective news editors have to be alert to pressures from advertisers, nevertheless, and they must resist them.

A greater economic threat to objective news coverage is the publishers' role as capitalist or business leader. Decades ago, the famous editor and political leader from Kansas, William Allen White, spoke of the "country club complex" which publishers and editors develop by mixing socially with the wealthy. Every year rising capital costs of newspapers increase this identification of the press leader with the money or power structure. The newspaper's management and top editorial staffers do not think as blue-collar workers or as union men, nor even as teachers and doctors, but as well-to-do business leaders. So a department store owner, for example, may rightly feel he does not even have to mention the ads he buys to get the news treatment he wants. News editors may have to work consciously to play the news straight when they know that those above them assess events in much the same way as the more widely feared advertiser.

If purity toward advertisers is easy to sermonize about, the issues involved in keeping circulation up are more complex and more subtle. Everyone on a paper agrees that it has to sell, whether the aim is to make money, to convey news, or to wield great social influence. A paper that does not sell will die. And if it barely sells, neither the business nor the editorial staff is happy. This pressures every editor to print "what the public wants."

Editors who argue that the public wants serious, solid news coverage find many newsmen who say that the public interest is shallow, as shown by the great popularity of comics and sports. That view may be too cynical. The *Christian Science Monitor,* the *Wall Street Journal,* and the *New York Times* are all serious yet successful. We must recognize, however, that in a sense all three are national newspapers. Of the three, only the *Times* relies heavily on a local market, and that market is the nation's largest and wealthiest.

Papers in small cities might break even imitating the *Times,* but the pressure is to build circulation and profit. Circulation can be built legitimately with stories of human interest. A few news editors will go further, giving in to circulation pressure to print a heavy diet of murder, sex scandals, and other sensations. Successful pandering may win a narrow kind of success.

The emphasis on sensationalism, going back to the "penny press" of the 1830s and the yellow journalism of sixty years later, rests on a low opinion of mankind. Perhaps today the masses are more enlightened than when Barnum profited on the theory of a sucker born every minute. If human nature has not improved, at least education has spread. The idealistic editor can point to the error of radio stations which continually play the latest pop music and win great but impecunious teenage audiences which few solid advertisers want. He can also suggest that more serious and less sensational editing may attract the kind of readers that management and advertiser both want.

One pertinent aspect of this argument is the growing monopolization of the press. In the competitive twenties, sensation was an important weapon for survival. But publishers of monopoly papers with high home delivery now often argue that they can provide higher quality coverage when they have no competition. A monopoly lifts some of the pressure to strive for sensational headlines that boost street sales.

The other side of the monopoly coin, however, reveals the pressure to become lazy, self-satisfied, and careless because regardless of the paper's quality the money keeps rolling in. It is not hard to find this kind of a newspaper.

Traditional pressure

The pressure of "this is the way it has always been done" pushes the editor to evaluate the news traditionally. For example, newspapers for generations have leaned strongly to government news. As history books have long been bound up with the dates of military and political events, newspapers have traditionally blanketed government offices, from the White House down to the town council. Even now, only a few journalists think that a newspaper should have reporters cover science laboratories as closely as they cover police stations.

There are of course good reasons—in terms of reader interest and concern—for keeping an eye on our political machinery. But suppose a news editor reached the objective conclusion that developments in, say, medicine and education deserved more regular front-page space than did a feud between politicians. The mind-set of the whole profession would be upset. City editors habitually have reporters cover government offices, and press services send out daily news budgets heavily weighted with government coverage.

Since a democratic society requires a great deal of government coverage, a still more troublesome tradition is the habit of giving excessive coverage to certain kinds of unimportant and even trivial material. Most papers give sports more space than interest justifies. Heavy coverage, of course, does develop a little more interest in sports news, but there are still frequent complaints that some towns simply will not support this or that sport. All the free publicity fails to spark or to tap deep or widespread interest.

Tradition says also that some kinds of events deserve picture coverage only if the photo can somehow include a pretty girl in shorts and tight sweater. (Needless to say, this particular tradition has come under heavy fire from the various women's liberation movements.) February 2 always has its Ground Hog Day story. Fall and spring bring out a rash of stories about small boys who hate school, apparently because some editor at the time of the Civil War hated school. It is, of course, unthinkable that the authors of such pieces might have enjoyed school writing!

Editors who look at news in these routine ways would have as much difficulty defending their practices as in justifying that newspapers have for years printed astrological predictions—even during this scientific age. Such editors are dated, even though astrology has recently become a fad for some. The modern editor must look at the news in a different way from half a century ago.

Personal pressure

"The boss" is a near and vital concern of the news editor. The superior may be an absentee owner, the top management man locally, the editor-in-chief up on some higher floor, the managing editor in the next office—or a composite of them all. Usually when one or another of these delivers an opinion, the staff transforms this dictum into dogma. Thereafter *this* kind of story *must* be printed, and that type must *not*—and so the newspaper's sacred cows grow up from calves. *That* boss likes cats, and *this* boss has a feud with a particular politician, so the newsmen open the gates to cat stories and close them to mention of the politician.

Worship of a sacred cow is often foolish, as the presumed need for it and even the boss who created it are long dead. Moreover, sometimes the boss's bias is not dictated; it is simply sensed by the staff. If, for example, a Republican paper endorses a Democratic candidate for president, the staff quickly feels the changing wind and is tempted to react in stories, columns, and news play. The same kind of bias is possible wherever a publisher takes a strong position on a candidate or issue. The least conscientious editors can do is check whether their superiors really insist on a certain handling of certain stories. If the bosses really do, editors must decide whether ethics will permit them to go along. If they are professionals, they will resist the personal biases which would distort the news flow—or will look for jobs elsewhere.

Research has shown that publishers do become involved in news direction—"interfere with" may be too strong, though so it may seem to the editor. Significantly, in contrast to popular supposition, publishers interfere less on the big papers than the small. "The closer the geographical proximity of the subject matter, the more active the publisher is in news direction," Professor David R. Bowers of Texas A&M University concluded in his research. Clearly, publishers have constitutional and economic rights to exert such control, but they can cause the newsroom executives both ethical and practical problems if, trying to usurp their professional functions, they pressure journalists to act for the publishers' business interests rather than the public interest.

The narrowness of reader interest can apply severe pressures upon editors to emphasize trivial information rather than news of genuine significance. The staffs of the better newspapers today are made up of sophisticated and educated men and women. Specialists report on education, politics, science, and foreign affairs. Yet many readers dislike or even resent reports about a world they can't quite understand.

In some cases, however, those sophisticated journalists add to the difficulty sometimes by affecting in their writing and editing a condescending attitude toward people of less education and breadth of experience.

A respect for all readers and an understanding of their fears and desires can help a newspaper reduce the pressure to turn out a soothing, innocuous product.

Public pressure—the pressure of his readers—may also tend to distort an editor's judgments. If subscribers cancel when reporters delve into some subjects, the editor may soft-pedal these topics. But the pressure may not be this overt. Merely knowing reader attitudes may tempt editors to compromise. If they know, for example, that most readers are social and political conservatives, they may ignore some news of reform or revolt, or play such stories unsympathetically. Such biasing is unprofessional. To be sure, since we have argued news must interest readers, no wise editor will ignore their wishes.

But the goals of journalism include leading and educating, not giving in to narrow prejudices and preconceptions. Sound, objective news evaluation does not bend, even before the tyranny of the majority.

Guidelines of judgment

To avoid pressures that interfere with good judgment, the editor has several guidelines to aid in evaluating the news.

The most obvious guideline is to avoid the "obvious" story. Events as predictable as the sunrise aren't news. Other obvious stories might be labeled "What-did-you-expect-him-to-say?" The Chamber of Commerce secretary predicts a booming Christmas business. Would anyone expect him to predict bad business? If a President, back from a trip, announces that he had a "valuable discussion" with the prime minister of Outer Nostrum, an editor probably has to print something because the President spoke officially; but his statement is barely newsworthy because no one would expect him to say anything else. And the only newsworthy prediction by a political candidate about the vote, would be "I'm gonna lose."

The editor also should beware of fads. A particular social problem tends to become a national pastime, and the press reflects the current rage by carrying all kinds of stories about it. During one period it may be popular to write at length on juvenile delinquency. It may hold sway for six months or so, then be replaced by drug addiction. Its currency fades after a time and the nation becomes preoccupied with pollution. The next fad might be anything from pre-school education to post-retirement living. All of these subjects are important, but the editor should allow coverage of only major events when the subject has been beaten almost to death.

When editors decide a subject is good enough for detailed coverage, they apply another guideline: story stamina. Will the issue have long-range interest or will it be forgotten in a few days? Subjects that have had staying power are the perils of cigarette smoking and drug addiction. Some subjects of continuing interest have their vitality limited to short bursts of coverage. The ups and downs of the stock market or bank interest may be everyone's concern for a few days, but major daily coverage for weeks on end is too much for the ordinary citizen. A subject with long-term potential may even be killed by too much coverage. Readers can stay interested in stories, such as that of local airport development, if the major decisions are not lost in complex daily stories.

Bias and business

Critics of the press have often charged that many papers underplay consumer stories. They contend that even health stories which discredit a highly advertised product, like cigarettes, usually are given front page play reluctantly, if at all. Yet, they argue, few stories have more long-range importance than those warning millions of cigarette smokers of their odds with lung cancer or heart disease.

One reason for scanty coverage is that old standby, tradition. Editors did not run many stories in the past on consumer news so they don't do it now. But economic pressures play a role, too. Many editors seem reluctant to publish charges made against business groups by the Federal Trade Commission or the Food and Drug Administration. Hence, the press frequently draws criticism for being highly incensed when someone cheats the welfare department out of fifty dollars while saying nothing when a big food manufacturer puts rotten tomatoes in his catsup.

A current example of this tendency to favor business is the coverage of exposes by Ralph Nader. Much of what Nader wrote was first published only in the smaller magazines—those with less than 100,000 circulation. Rarely did a newspaper reprint these articles or create news stories from Nader's facts. The press originally reported his charges on the lack of automobile safety, the filth of some food processing plants, and the perils of pipelines only when they could not avoid doing so. Many of these newspapers were alert, however, to report stories that countered what Nader had charged, though it must be conceded he got wider coverage once he had become a "big name."

This reticence to criticize business was notable a few years ago when several executives of electrical equipment companies went to jail for price fixing. The fixes had cost private firms and the government millions of dollars in excessive prices. A good many papers did not run a line on the story, although most of them manage to report petty thievery in some detail.

Judging at a distance

News judgment is usually easier when the event is close to home. The facts are clearer and they can be obtained more quickly. The news from far away, however, is much more difficult to evaluate. Who can judge the accuracy or completeness of the information filed by wire services from, say, Ethiopia? How informed is the reporter? Does the reporter know the nuances of politics in the country? Are the cited news sources adequate?

Editors who judge the merits of such stories have to rely on their experience, of course, but they can take some conventional precautions. The byline is an obvious clue. They may know that the writer is new in the country and therefore inexperienced. The dateline is another obvious clue. Where the story was filed is a guide as to whether the story is a first-hand report or a synthesis of information from second- and third-rate sources. Names of people quoted in a story can be helpful as editors sniff for authenticity. If it quotes "reliable sources," they should at least be wary. If refugees are quoted, editors should immediately be on guard, for refugees or exiles from any place are hardly objective observers.

When editors are dubious about the reliability of the facts or the sources in a story, they should edit it especially carefully. Their editing serves to warn the reader of their doubt. A thoroughly suspicious story goes into the editor's wastebasket. Even conscientious editors, however, have bitten hard on stories that should have raised suspicions at a half dozen places.

Some of the worst errors have involved reports filed during the height of the Cold War—particularly reports of the death or deposing of a Communist leader. Both wire services and many newspaper editors committed a real blunder in 1960 by printing a story that the incumbent Russian premier had been ousted. The source for the story was a shadowy figure, unknown to the press, yet many papers printed the story. The report was slightly premature: The premier stayed in office another four years.

Stories often cited reports that the Chinese leader Mao Tse-tung was dead when he wasn't. One copyeditor, upon reading such a story, said, "Hmmmm. I think this is the seventh time we have announced his departure."

Such gullibility occurs because some editors can't think of being caught without some kind of a story in case a major event is about to take place. Governmental change in the Soviet Union or China is a big story, but only when it happens, not when a fourth-rate source says it happened.

Wishful editing

This crucial judgment brings into focus another difficulty that faces editors—"wishful editing." Like nearly every other citizen, editors have an element of nationalism in their makeup. They want to report events that they and their government wish would happen. Those wishes can impair their judgment. East-West tensions tempt editors to print stories that are perhaps less than the whole truth, because stories that make the Communists look bad are stories that look good to many Americans.

The danger of wishful editing is that it ultimately betrays the society. American press reports from the Soviet Union for decades demonstrated wishful editing. While some editors got and printed the best information available (and reporters in Russia were always under Soviet restriction), most selected, perhaps unconsciously, "pleasant" news. There were columns of stories that portrayed the Russians as scientific boobs, the state as held together by police threats, and national affairs as hopelessly snarled. It is no wonder that when the Russians lofted the world's first space ship in 1957 the American public came close to panic. Once the hysteria faded, however, coverage of the Soviet Union improved considerably. Yet traces of good guys *vs.* bad guys reporting and editing remain in many U. S. papers.

To make good decisions on news play, the editor must be willing to take a little time to reflect. Unfortunately, some veteran editors tend to think that decisive editing means fast editing. The best editors, however, know when decision requires delay. They read a borderline story two or three times and even discuss it with a colleague. The interests of both the newspaper and the reader are best served by editors who have confidence in their judgment but who take time to let it operate effectively.

Such editors recognize that their own biases form one of the greatest pressures toward slanted coverage. How else can they view the news except through glasses colored by their own opinions and prejudices? Maybe they can see how the staff plays to their views on cats or airpower or pollution controls. Complete objectivity is impossible, but they can strive for it by regularly analyzing their feelings and checking influences on their judgments. They can watch the news play in other papers, including great foreign ones like the *Times* of London. Finally, they can check their perceptions by conferring with other staffers.

But even the way colleagues view the news is not sufficient for really self-critical editors. Colleagues also have their local or national biases. Editors can try sometimes to imagine how a person in Asia or at the United Nations would view the news. Such regular exercise in trying to rise above their own biases, and even those of their profession and nation, would be salutary for the news editor.

Such detachment is possible, and research has shown that editors with strong positions on an issue still can handle a story on that subject fairly. In fact, they might even do a better job simply because they are concerned enough to know whether the story adequately gives the facts.

These varied pressures on every journalist can distort evaluations of the news. Personal integrity, therefore, is the ultimate safeguard of the news stream.

Professional integrity

For many Americans, the Golden Rule is the ethical touchstone. Wouldn't a newspaper be ethical if editors handled the news as they would want news of themselves handled? Not necessarily. The principle is not easily applied to the evaluation of news for a large public. Handling news about an individual the way he or she wants it handled is often not the best from the viewpoint of all the other individuals who make up society. Anyway, the Golden Rule may become very subjective. A managing editor, for example, left out a news item concerning the arrest of a prominent out-of-town newsman. "You wouldn't want it put in about you, would you?" he rationalized to fellow staffers, in a subconscious appeal to a Golden Rule for newspapermen. But such a stand of course opens a paper to all kinds of personal pressure. Whether a story sees print then depends on how much pull a person can develop with the editor, who takes pity on friends. To be an impartial gatekeeper, therefore, the ethical editor in a sense has to be without friends—or enemies.

What news of arrests, suits, bankruptcies, or other unhappy incidents would be printed if the rule were the desire of editors to have such news left out about themselves and their friends? The printing of most spot news items probably makes someone unhappy, and papers would go out of business if they did not seek a higher principle than saving someone's feelings. Sometimes they must print news which hurts individuals. So they apply a standard of fair-dealing to all alike, regardless of the editor's friendships or compassion.

Sound evaluation of news is bound up in professionalism. Professional editors come to look at their tasks not as plumbers contemplating a neat fit, important as that is, but as physicians or educators contemplating their role in the improvement of society. Such editors use as a frame of reference for decisions, not the personal tastes of advertiser, publisher or themselves, but the professional ideals held by the best practitioners of the news profession.

Those ideals can be clarified and firmed up in thought, study and discussion—in talking with colleagues, with professionals at newspaper meetings, with critics of the press, and with teachers and students in good journalism classes.

In chapter 13 we discuss ethical foundations in detail against the background of the book *Four Theories of the Press* by Profs. Frederick S. Siebert, Theodore B. Peterson and Wilbur Schramm. Books like *Four Theories* can be especially useful in thinking through the ethical problems of news evaluation. Another good one for this purpose is *The Press and Its Problems* by Prof. Curtis D. MacDougall of the Medill School of Journalism at Northwestern University (Dubuque, Ia.: William C. Brown Co., 1964); chapters 9 through 12 are particularly helpful with gatekeeping decisions. Professor Schramm, a prominent communications research leader of Stanford University, also examines the bases of professionalism in his *Responsibility in Mass Communication* (New York: Harper and Brothers, 1957). He points out that the newspaper profession can develop "by asking what kind of behavior is necessary in order to carry out the public service obligations of the craft," and adds:

> The greatest step toward professionalizing the mass-communication industry would be simply to emphasize the *individual* sense of responsibility rather than merely the corporate sense—that is, the responsibility of the communicator as a public servant and a professional, as apart from but not fundamentally contrary to his obligations to the business he works for. . . . Let the employers encourage their employees to behave like professionals, and support them when they do so. Let the employees, on their part, take their own responsibility very seriously and cease to hide behind the fact that they *are* employees and that someone else pays their salary and determines policy. . . . We expect [professionals] to operate somewhere above the level of a pitchman, but somewhere below the level of the angels. We want them to try to live up to the peculiar responsibility of informing free citizens in a free country. (p. 347)*

---

*A revised edition of the book, published in 1969 and written with William L. Rivers, says the same thing but with less exactness.

In a free society, few must match the professional responsibility of editors. They must think through their own philosophy of freedom, of objectivity and of responsibility to the community and world. Then, hour by hour, they must apply their standards professionally by passing, trimming, or spiking as they weigh the significant against the trivial and the useful against the dangerous.

7 The telegraph editor

The new technology is bringing vast changes to the job of telegraph editor—just as it is doing in every other newspaper department. In the not-so-old days a copyeditor would move up to the job of "wire editor" and would learn the jargon and technical operations of the Associated Press and United Press International. Once those techniques were learned, the editor seemed secure, for change came slowly. Stories simply arrived by teletypes from all over the world and the editors' main job was to wade through the long strips of paper copy that came clattering off those machines. Those teletypes still clatter but, like the newsroom typewriter, their days are numbered. Some wire service experts think that by around 1985 paper will be used by AP and UPI and telegraph editors only for notes. From a wire service reporter in Tokyo to a wire editor in Oshkosh, nothing will be printed until the story, ready for pasteup, rolls out in the composing room.

The adjustment for editors from copy on teletypes to copy on cathode ray tube screens is moderately difficult. A whole new battery of signals, keys, numbers, and techniques must be learned. But when they are mastered, the editor no longer shuffles paper to find a story or a digest of the day's news. A couple of punches on the CRT console provide the information. No longer will editors stew about getting copy flowing to the composing room, because computers, hooked to those CRTs, will set type in a flash.

It is essential for the wire editor to understand how to handle all those pieces of paper or computer copy if chaos is to be avoided. Yet such knowledge, which can be picked up in a week or two, remains a minor part of the telegraph editor's skill. A good wire editor also needs broad knowledge, careful judgment, an eye for typographical display, and a skeptical attitude.

The knowledge and skepticism are useful in examining the value of hundreds of stories. Judgment helps the editor decide what goes into the paper and what does not. The typographical eye guides the editor in the design and makeup of the paper.

Because of these demands, people who like to deal with national and international news often seek the job of telegraph editor. They relish the task of reading hundreds of stories each day, selecting the ones they consider most significant, and trimming them to fit the available space. Their judgment, if proper, provides readers with a reasonably clear and accurate picture of the world. On small papers telegraph editors may edit the news, write headlines for the stories, and even report some local news or edit other copy. On papers with circulations of 15,000 to 50,000 they probably concentrate on the wire editing and headline writing. On somewhat bigger papers telegraph editors only skim the wire stories, select the ones they want, and direct copyreaders to edit the stories and write the heads.

On the largest metropolitan papers the wire news may be divided, the city editor or state editor getting the stories that originate close to home, and other copy sent to "foreign," "financial," and "national" desks. Sports wires feed directly into the sports department. Copy streams into the newsrooms of the biggest papers from a dozen teletypes or more or, with the new technology, from the equivalent of a dozen machines.

News agencies

The wire services which feed news to the telegraph editor have long traditions.

The first services had extreme difficulties, including low revenues and terrifying transmission problems. Some, more than a century ago, employed carrier pigeons to convey the news, and others used boats or horses in attempts to beat out any competition. While these struggles often were romantic, dozens of little news-gathering services failed. But new ones continued to be formed because editors realized that they had to have some kind of cooperative reporting service. They recognized that each could not afford to have correspondents all over the world and that, if they were to get even minimal coverage of the news outside their own areas, some news association would have to provide it.

After several starts, the first being in 1848 in New York City, the Associated Press formed in 1892. The United Press formed in 1907, and Hearst's International News Service in 1909. INS was sold to UP in 1958, and the merged organizations took the name of United Press International, or UPI.

The AP is a cooperative, with each paper paying for service at a rate determined by a formula that includes its circulation and the population of its circulation area. UPI is a private business and calls its customers "clients," not members. It charges only by circulation.

Because the wires distribute the cost of gathering news, they are a minor expense to newspapers. Their cost will vary from little more than $300 a week for papers with less than 10,000 circulation to several thousand dollars for the metropolitan papers. Even though the total cost for the giants may seem high, no newspaper could afford to duplicate the news coverage of the wire services.

Telegraph editors have the impression that the two major wire services have personalities. AP is known for its reliability, UPI for its bright writing and Latin American coverage. Researchers have documented these impressions in a series of studies. They found, however, that the impressions don't match the facts. Each service appears to be of equal accuracy and "brightness," so far as that can be measured. There is no clear evidence, either, that UPI has superior Latin American coverage.

In the early days of teletype transmission, words came via telephone lines onto teleprinters at 40 words a minute. Later the rate became 66 words a minute. Now, however, special machines deliver 1,050 words a minute, enough to fill a column and a half in a newspaper. Transmission into CRTs is so fast that time is insignificant. This system is so swift that a tremendous number of stories are swimming about inside those computers awaiting selection for publication by telegraph editors.

Supplemental services

While AP and UPI are the only services in the United States that try to cover almost all the news of the nation and world, a dozen or more special organizations provide news by wire.

The *New York Times* has its own service and sells it to more than 200 American and Canadian papers. Each subscriber gets almost all the news the *Times* has, except some from New York City. The stories come over a teletype, just like those used by AP or UPI.

The *Washington Post* and *Los Angeles Times* have teamed up to send special articles from their own Washington and foreign correspondents. The *Chicago Daily News* and *Chicago Sun Times* share a service. The *Chicago Tribune* has a service that includes copy from Knight-Ridder newspapers. The *New York Daily News,* the Scripps-Howard chain, *Washington Star,* and the Newhouse newspapers have wires to lease. The British news agency, Reuters, supplies a modest number of American papers. The North American Newspaper Alliance, NANA, also sends feature stories by wire. Many of these wire services use special delivery mail to provide customers with those news and feature stories that need not be speeded to meet a deadline because they are usually timely for a week or more.

Though none of these services provides complete reports, as AP and UPI do, more and more papers are subscribing to them to supplement AP and UPI. Their cost usually is lower, their news selection broader, and their coverage frequently more penetrating than are those of the two all-purpose wire services. Stories from supplemental services often are slightly editorial, in contrast to the studied objectivity of AP and UPI stories, and some editors think readers find such stories stimulating.

The teletypesetter

Until the early fifties, all wire copy was sent in all-capital letters (fig. 7-1). Editors read the copy, adding a pencil mark under letters that were supposed to remain capitalized. Then the wire services developed the teletypesetter, or TTS, which brought stories to the subscriber's news room in caps and lower case with each line of typed material equal to one line of type (fig. 7-2).

TTS enabled editors to choose stories as before, but they no longer had to send copy to the composing room. The wire service feeds stories directly to the composing room on a special perforated paper tape. This tape can be used to set type. Simultaneously, editors receive these stories on an ordinary teletype, read them to decide which they want to use, and send the numbers of the desired stories to the composing room. The printer snips the tape containing the desired story and inserts it into a specially equipped linecasting machine, which sets stories automatically. Editors send copy directly to the composing room only if they make changes in a wire service story.

The teletypesetter was a big timesaver, for it set type about twice as fast as a human typesetter can. But TTS has some drawbacks. The main one is that its time- and money-saving potential quickly dissipates if the editor really operates as an editor—crossing out a word here or there, eliminating a sentence, or altering the wording slightly. Such alterations have to be set manually and the new lines inserted in place of the automatically set lines. So the editor is tempted to do no more editing than absolutely necessary. Most editors handling TTS only reduce stories, having a printer throw away paragraphs set in type. It is easier and quicker to set the full story automatically and then to throw away some of the type than it is to set manually only the part to be used.

DEFICIT

WASHINGTON (UPI)-THE SENATE BUDGET COMMITTEE WILL BEGIN WORK NEXT WEEK ON A FEDERAL BUDGET FOR THE CURRENT FISCAL YEAR. ITS HOUSE COUNTERPART HAS APPROVED A VERSION THAT INCLUDES A $72 BILLION DEFICIT.

THE VERSION TENTATIVELY APPROVED FRIDAY BY THE HOUSE BUDGET COMMITTEE ESTIMATED EXPENDITURES OF $373.8 BILLION AND REVENUES OF $301.8 BILLION FOR THE FISCAL YEAR WHICH ENDS JUNE 30.

Fig. 7–1. All-cap copy. Before the introduction of the teletypesetter, most wire copy was all-capital and wide-measure. Copyeditors still get some wire copy like this, usually from the paper's own correspondents and local bureaus. Here, the editor has underlined letters that are to remain capitals.

Fig. 7–2. TTS copy. This TTS copy goes to the editor. (An explanation of the wire code is added). The story on punched tape goes to the old-style composing room. A printer snips the tape for stories ordered by an editor and feeds the tape into a linecasting machine. Each line of typed copy equals one line of type.

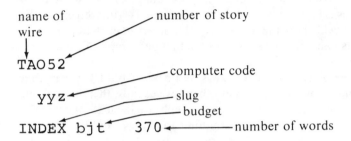

name of
wire ── number of story

TAO52

── computer code

yyz ── slug
── budget

INDEX bjt   370 ── number of words

    BY LOUISE ADAMS

    WASHINGTON AP -- The government's

index designed to anticipate future

economic trends sustained its first

drop in seven months during Sept-

ember, contradicting other signals

showing continued economic growth

into next year, the Commerce Depart-

ment said today.

    The department said its index of

leading economic indicators, a com-

posite of a dozen statistics, drop-

ped nine-tenths of 1 per cent in

September, in contrast to an eight-

tenths of 1 per cent advance in August.

    The decline, however, was not a

sure signal of a halt in economic

recovery. Only 11 of the 12 items

in the index were available for the

September report, and the index is

The real timesaver, however, was the move to the cathode ray tube, for it made use of the computer in setting type. Now telegraph editors can start their work day by pressing a few keys on the CRT or VDT console and "ask" the wire service questions. One question might be, "What are the major stories today?" After what for a computer is a long pause—perhaps five seconds—the screen, in the case of AP, will show the first ninety characters of each major story. UPI, on its "abstract wire," shows the first paragraph of each story. (See fig. 7-3.)

Or an editor can tap a few keys and ask, "Could you run that White House story again?" In another few seconds, there it is, shimmering on the screen. Editors then can rephrase the lead, shorten the story, juggle paragraphs—or anything that they could do with a pencil, scissors, and paste to a story on paper. When the story on the screen suits the editor, a headline can be written, also to appear on the screen, and the whole thing sent to the composing room. In less than a minute both the story and headline roll out of a machine, ready to be pasted onto a dummy as part of a newspaper page.

Fig. 7–3. New York AP. These Associated Press staffers handle copy on CRTs in the New York office. Note in the background, however, the old-style teletypes.

How services operate

The wire services have a worldwide network, and the operation of transmitting the news, called *traffic,* is enormous. Often people work years for a service and still have only a fuzzy idea of how the whole organization works. The basics are not hard to grasp, but understanding is complicated by the fact that wire services are switching from teletypes to cathode ray tubes. That means that there are two systems to learn. The teletype system works this way: The main national and international news appears coast-to-coast on an "A" teletype wire. In messages it is called the "Aye" (rhymes with "hay") wire. Until 1968 the AP and UPI "A" appeared in all-caps on paper eight and a half inches wide but it now is in caps and lower case (fig. 7-4). When reduced to TTS it is called the "TA" wire. The TA wire appears on paper six inches wide. Most large papers and many medium-sized ones get the "A" because it provides a good selection of major news stories; furthermore, it can be thoroughly edited.

Fig. 7-4. "A" wire. Important national and world stories go across the country on the "A" teletype wire. (The "B" wire carries stories of lesser national import.) This example shows copy as it comes over the wire to be edited by pencil. This "teletype copy" will be eliminated in the all-electronic newsroom.

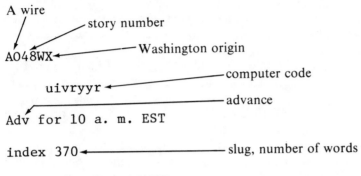

A wire

AO48WX ← story number
         ← Washington origin

uivryyr ← computer code
         ← advance

Adv for 10 a. m. EST

index 370 ← slug, number of words

By LOUISE ADAMS

Associated Press Writer

WASHINGTON AP - The government's index designed to anticipate future economic trends sustained its first drop in seven months during September, contradicting other signals showing continued economic growth into next year, the Commerce Department said today.

The department said its index of leading economic indicators, a composite of a dozen statistics, dropped nine-tenths of 1 per cent in September, in contrast to an eight-tenths of 1 per cent advance in August.

The decline, however, was not a sure signal of a halt in economic recovery. Only 11 of the 12 items in the index were available for the September report, and the index is subject to later revision.

The August increase, for example, was initially reported last month at no change. And, most analysts agree that this is

The "B" wire carries stories of lesser interest or stories useful in certain areas of the country. Such copy is "taken off" the "B" by a wire service editor and put on regional wires, which carry news about one state or a few states. For example, if a story from Washington would interest people in Michigan only, it would go out of Washington on the "B." A wire service editor in Detroit would take it off the "B" and send it over a regional wire, one received by most dailies in the state. This would be done because relatively few papers receive the "B," only a small minority of all "B" stories being of interest to them.

The wire services also provide sports wires, which are all TTS. One provides sports stories; the other, gives sports statistics. The services also have wires for financial news, and AP has a horse race wire. Regional wires have symbols of their own. For example, Pennsylvania's wire is the "P" wire.

Special wires serve as carriers of messages between the main offices of the services. These main offices are called "control points" or "control bureaus." Usually the biggest city in a state is a control point. But one control may cover several states in the sparsely-settled areas of the West, and Boston is the control for all of New England.

The services operate on two cycles a day, the "AMS" for morning papers and the "PMS" for afternoon editions. Each story is numbered, but the numbering starts anew with each cycle. The PMS cycle starts with the first story of the predawn hours. The AMS cycle starts in early afternoon. The first story of each morning cycle appears on the "A" with the number A001. AP starts the afternoon cycle the same way, but UPI starts then with A201.

One office in the nation, of course, has to decide what goes on the "A" wire. The New York bureau has that job for each service. It is guided by a series of messages it receives from "control" bureaus all over the country. Using a separate wire, the controls send little summaries of their stories to New York. The word length of each story is added.

For example, San Francisco may have a story about a new cancer discovery at Stanford. Washington may have six or eight stories. Chicago may have a story about a major speech by a leading governor. Two of the messages filed would look like this:

400--AAA Stanford scientists claim discovery of new

breast cancer detection method.

                  FX July 1 639 APD

600--BBB Minnesota governor calls for nationwide

abolition of property tax as way to finance public

schools.

                  CX July 1 641 ACD

The opening letters and numbers refer to the word length and the wire for which the story is offered. The symbols at the end of each message indicate the control city sending the message. FX means San Francisco and CX means Chicago. The time is added, 639 APD meaning 6:39 A. M. Pacific Daylight Time. Chicago's time is 6:41 A. M. Central Daylight Time.

The New York general desk rates these messages on a priority system. The editor in New York is told when some stories will be ready and whether a story is going to change several times during the day as fresh events occur. With dozens of stories immediately available or scheduled within the next few hours, the editor and aides draw up a "budget" or "news digest." This is a prospectus telling each telegraph editor which fifteen or more key stories to expect. Since perhaps 90 per cent of news is anticipated, telegraph editors have a good idea of what the news day is going to be like as soon as they read the budget. (See figs. 7-5, 7-6.)

Fig. 7–5. News budgets. UPI Report, left, and AP News Digest, right, indicate major stories each service expects to send on a particular Saturday. Only part of the offering is shown.

EDITORS: the UPI report for Saturday includes:

STRIP Washington--New strip mining bill passed by House yesterday tougher than all but two state stripping laws.

OIL London--British oil fields now producing 15 per cent of nation's oil needs.

WHEAT Kansas City--Nation's wheat crop promises to be best in history.

DERAIL Galesburg, Ill.--Amtrak passenger train, with 600 aboard, derails. All 12 cars wrecked, but no one seriously hurt.

AP NEWS DIGEST

for Saturday PMs

NATIONAL

President undecided on signing strip mine bill, which may reach him in week. Interior secretary backs measure.

Wholesale prices climb 0.8 per cent, making 12-month rise 7.9 per cent.

Agriculture secretary lauds U. S. farmers as "lifesavers" for millions in world.

FOREIGN

Italian government shaky and premier may resign in next few days. New left-center coali-

If New York decides that the California water story is a good starter, the computer can be directed to send that story all over the country. New York puts all kinds of stories into the computer and, by giving each a priority code, causes the most important stories to appear in the proper order on the various teletypes: A wire, B wire, sports, regional and financial. Editors then get the kind of paper copy shown in figs. 7-4, 7-5, and 7-7.

Fig. 7–6. The UPI abstract. The first paragraph of stories can be read on a VDT by the editor. When a full story is desired, the correct number is punched and the whole story appears on the screen. In the first example, an editor would punch "0224" and "Grain" would appear. In the next item, punching "0042" brings up "Skiing."

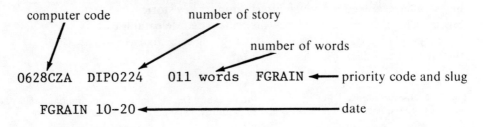

computer code   number of story

                                number of words

0628CZA DIP0224   011 words   FGRAIN ◄── priority code and slug

FGRAIN 10-20 ◄─────────────── date

KANSAS CITY, MO. (UPI)--WHEAT FUTURES CLOSED ¼ to

5½ CENTS HIGHER MONDAY AT THE KANSAS CITY BOARD OF TRADE.

0636CZA DR0042   0295 words SKIING
    D U
SKIING

NIGHT LD

    BY K. C. MASON

DENVER (UPI)--SKI INDUSTRY OFFICIALS EXPECT A RECORD

TURNOUT AT MAJOR AREAS IN THE COLORADO ROCKIES THIS WINTER

DESPITE HIGH PRICES FOR EQUIPMENT AND TICKETS.

Bulletins and flashes   With teletypes, stories of special news value move ahead of other stories, and labels advise editors of their importance. A story labeled "URGENT" moves ahead of more routine stories, but transmission of a story is not stopped to send it. A "BULLETIN" is more important, and a story being sent on the wire will be stopped so the bulletin can be transmitted. The interrupted story usually will have

"BUST IT—BUST IT" inserted to explain that the story will have to be started again later. Generally a bulletin consists of one or two paragraphs, with additional material following as "BULLETIN MATTER." Still more is sent later as "URGENT." Three to a half dozen bulletins interrupt every news cycle, as a rule. Figure 7-7 shows the UPI wire interrupted by the bulletin announcing the shooting of President Kennedy.

Fig. 7–7. Wire bulletin. The word "MORE" in the third line of this UPI transmission marks the start of material leading up to the flash on President Kennedy's assassination. (The symbols used to head these fragments have been supplanted in recent years on all copy except radio wires.)

```
LINKS."  THE DEFENSE HAD IMPLIED IT WILL TAKE THE LINE THAT CAROL'S

DEATH AFTER A SAVAGE BLUDGEONING AND STABBING IN HER HOME WAS THE

RESULT OF AN ATTEMPTED            MOREDA1234PCS

UPI   A7N   DA

           PRECEDE KENNEDY

     DALLAS, NOV. 22 (UPI)--THREE SHOTS WERE FIRED AT PRESIDENT KENNEDY'S

MOTORCADE TODAY IN DOWNTOWN DALLAS.

                          JT1234PCS

UPI   A8N   DA

           URGENT

     1ST ADD SHOTS, DALLAS (A7N) XXXDOWNTOWN DALLAS.

     NO CASUALITIES WERE REPORTEDZ.

     THE INCIDENT OCCURRED NEAR THE COUNTY SHERIFF'S OFFICE ON MAIN

STREET, JUST EAST OF AN UNDERPASS LEADING TOWARD THE TRADE MART WHERE

THE PRESIDENT WAS TO MA

FLASH

   KENNEDY SERIOUSLY WOUNDED

                     PERHAPS SERIOUSLY

PERHAPS FATALLY BY ASSASSINS BULLET

           JT1239PCS
```

Wire jargon   The beginner sees wire copy as a helter-skelter collection of bits and pieces—all kinds of adds, corrections, precedes, subs, etc. The wire services, however, are careful to label everything, so short observation permits anyone to figure out how all the pieces go together. If a "graf" (paragraph) is to be inserted, the copy would say "Insert in A043WX after third graf x x x, President said." The editor merely finds the story labeled A043WX, counts down three paragraphs, notes that the third graf ended with the words "President said," and pastes the insert into the story. The insert will end with "pick up 4th graf, A043WX, x x x he explained." This means that the fourth paragraph will start with the words "he explained." The same system applies to "adds"—portions of copy to be added to a story.

All this labeling disappears in the all-electronic newsroom. The wire service will patch new material into a story and whatever shows up on the screen will be complete. The process is so fast that if an insert and an add are needed, it is simpler to have the whole story reset in the newspaper plant.

Some stories are "undated" because they have no dateline. Usually they pull together information from several different areas, so that the story has no particular place as its focus.

By United Press International

Fighting broke out in four places in the Near East today,

apparently for four different reasons. . .

Occasionally, the dateline of a story will change. If a major unexpected event occurs in Lynn, Massachusetts, the first news may be filed from Boston. An hour or so later reporters may have first-hand reports in Lynn and can dateline stories from there. The wire service, sending on teletypes, will write "Precede Boston" on top of the Lynn stories. This simple instruction tells the editor that this story supplants the one from Boston.

Once in a while the AP or UPI will decide that papers may not like one particular lead. An "optional lead" is then filed and editors may take their pick.

When a wire service discovers it has made a serious error, one that would cause it great embarrassment or possibly produce a libel suit for the service and all papers using the offending story, a "BULLETIN KILL" goes over the wire. This is an order to kill a certain story or part of one. If the errant story should have happened to get into a few papers, the fact that the service filed a bulletin kill might reduce damages in any libel suit. Introduction of the bulletin kill as evidence in court would indicate that the service made a serious and speedy effort to correct the error.

Less serious mistakes are handled with less drama. A simple "CORRECTION" will be filed, and the editor pastes into a story a new paragraph or pencils the corrected material into the copy.

A "SUB" appears perhaps several times a day. This may be a "sub intro" or "top" of a story—the first few paragraphs—to be substituted for the previous top. The original is not in error; the "SUB" material is more complete or better written, or it changes a minor point. More often subs are grafs for the middle of a story to update it. Again, of course, these are techniques that have no bearing in an electronic newsroom.

In a developing story the services keep filing *new leads* as new facts are found or as more events occur. For example, on the night of a presidential election the first lead on the election result story might say that the Democratic candidate has taken a lead in Massachusetts. The second lead may indicate that the Republican has gained strength in New England and may take three states there. The third lead may indicate that while the Republican is doing well in New England he is getting beaten in Pennsylvania. The leads would keep pouring forth every forty-five minutes or so, even after it is clear who the winner is.

Editors are assisted through the news cycle by little wire-service notes, called "advisories," that let them know what else to expect. An advisory sent halfway through the teletype cycle may read like this:

ALL BUDGET STORIES HAVE BEEN FILED. WE ARE TOPPING PRESI-

DENT'S AIR POLLUTION STORY (A043). THERE WILL BE MINOR INSERTS

OR ADDS TO CHICAGO BROWN SPEECH (A022) AND TO CALIFORNIA WATER

STORY (A001). WE HAVE BEEN ALERTED THAT A NEW ITALIAN GOVERN-

MENT MAY BE FORMED TODAY. WE ARE WATCHING AND WILL FILE STORY

IF DEVELOPMENTS WARRANT.

THE AP

1049 AED

As we have said, the electronic system puts all wires onto one line. But in the transitional period, many papers still will buy several different wires and one of them will be the regional wire. Sometimes the regional wire is simply called the "state wire," for it handles news of one populous state. But often it covers several less populous states and has news from all sectors in that region. In this system all

Grassroots organization

bureaus, large and small, funnel stories to the *control* or *hub*, where the computer sorts them and sends them back over the proper regional wire. For example, a story from Madison, Wisconsin, the state capital, would be sent by wire to Chicago, where an editor would decide that only Wisconsin papers would want it. The computer would be directed to send it over the Wisconsin wire.

Madison sends stories to Chicago because Chicago operates as "control" for six states: Illinois, Michigan, Wisconsin, Minnesota, and the Dakotas. Bureaus in cities in these states, such as Detroit or Minneapolis, can put stories into the computer. Chicago can code them so a northern Wisconsin paper will not see a story that is received by southern Wisconsin papers. Or a story written in the Detroit bureau may get coded so southern Illinois papers will get it but Michigan papers will not. Other "controls" in the nation handle news from their areas the way Chicago does.

Small papers needing little copy, and wanting to keep costs low, may buy what is called an *interbureau* wire. This single wire gives them a modest selection of world and national news, state stories, financial and market news, and sports. Wire service computers, with some editorial help, can select the stories for this wire. The small papers need nearly every story on this wire to fill the news hole. When the time comes that wire services no longer send copy on teletypes, the little paper presumably will have to buy the complete service that all other papers get. The little papers then will have the task of sorting through the digests of stories that appear on the screen.

While wire service control bureaus are in the big cities, lesser bureaus are dotted about the country. Some of them may be staffed by one person. University cities, because they generate so much news, often will have a one-person bureau. Most state capitals have a permanent bureau of six or eight employees supplemented by two or three temporary ones when the legislature is in session. The editors and writers in bureaus gather much of the news that appears on regional wires. AP also is free to print stories that appear in members' newspapers but both AP and UPI depend largely on "stringers," or part-time correspondents, for stories outside of their bureau cities. These persons "string" as a sideline, while working on newspapers or at radio-TV stations. They pick up extra money by filing stories from their areas with a wire service. The stringer merely telephones facts to the nearest bureau, where a staffer writes the story and puts it on the wire. Stringers usually work for newspapers also.

With networks of staffers or stringers in nearly every city, the wire services cover the whole country, usually reporting important events minutes after they occur.

Special messages

A newspaper that telephones or teletypes a bureau or control point is usually asking for information. Such a message, called a "query," often questions the accuracy of a statement or seeks clarification of a point. Unfortunately many papers take no real advantage of this opportunity, accepting without question whatever the service sends them. Wire service reporters can make mistakes, and they certainly can be asked for information. The good telegraph editor will query every day or so, to doublecheck on facts or to request coverage of some event.

Messages, in wire service jargon, are mystifying at first glance. Although most of the terms can be figured out, some need a bit of clarification:

Apc—appreciate.

Pox—police.

Scotus—Supreme Court of the United States.

Ohed—overhead. (The story, sent by Western Union because it will interest no other newspaper, costs extra.)

GN—Good night.

A newspaper in South Bend, Indiana might query Washington by way of Chicago. The Chicago office would put a message on the wire like this:

    WX

    South Bend asks story from WX pox on jailing of Ophelia

Glotz of Bean Blossom, Ind., who freed 2 wks ago in another

case by scotus decision.

                    CX Jan. 25 235CST

Special services

The major wire services provide far more than straight news stories. Both AP and UPI offer columnists who deal in humor, foreign affairs, business, Hollywood, TV, finance, agriculture, religion —and even oil!

The services also have departments that provide detailed feature stories that may be timely or may be usable for several weeks. Both services file "advance" stories, many for use in Sunday papers. These often are filed two, three, or four weeks in advance of the publication date. Sunday feature stories are in particular demand because most Sunday papers are bulky, yet little news is made on weekends. By getting such stories early, the newspapers can set them in type during slack periods and "close" some pages a few days early. The services also mail some feature and "filler" copy.

AP or UPI radio wires, with news specifically written to be spoken, submit a group of short news items that would take about four minutes to read aloud on radio or television. With a minute added for a commercial, this becomes the five-minute newscast. A fifteen-minute package also is prepared several times a day. This service has led to the invention of the scornful term "rip and read," as someone unschooled in news can tear off the teletype the latest prepared newscast and go before the microphone to read it. Skilled radio or television journalists, of course, rely heavily on the wire service but add or subtract from the summary as their editorial judgment directs.

Both AP and UPI offer full picture services. The latest machines require only ten seconds to receive and print an eight-by-ten-inch glossy. Papers that cannot afford instant photographs take a slower service or are mailed packets of pictures or mats of pictures. Those who receive the mailings, of course, have to run the pictures a day late.

AP sells *laserphotos,* for the machines use laser beams to print the pictures. (See fig. 7-8.) They have remarkable clarity. UPI gets similar quality with *Unifax II.* Both services use computers to direct photos from one spot to another, and officials say eventually they will be able to code a picture so only a paper in Walla Walla, Washington, for example, would receive it. The services also transmit duplicate color transparencies on many subjects, but their executives complain that many clients do not use them. In one period the UPI experimented by moving a color photo daily but use was disappointing. This service sent out an exclusive picture of a woman leaping from a brightly burning building. Though more than a thousand papers got it, only one tear sheet, indicating use, came in. Except for advertising, newspapers remain almost 100 per cent black and white.

Fig. 7–8. Laserphoto receiver. This machine is used now throughout the AP system. It uses laser beams as a light source and records pictures on dry silver photographic paper.

Special Washington services likewise are available to members or clients. Each wire service has reporters in Washington covering events that are of concern only to regions. If Congress acts on a bill that influences New England, the report probably would appeal only to New Englanders. The New England papers can afford the report because the cost of the services' detailed Washington coverage is shared by all subscribers.

Selecting and compiling

On most newspapers the selection of stories is a major task. Big papers probably use 10 per cent or less of the copy received. The job of sorting and culling takes time, even though the services try to give every possible aid to the editor.

On bigger papers still using teletypes, copy aides take the stories off the wires and sort them by subject. If a war is going on, the "book" of war stories may be an inch thick. Although the editor and assistants cannot possibly read all this material carefully, they do take a quick look at almost everything. Experienced editors make up their minds swiftly, rejecting perhaps half of the material at a glance. They give the rest of the stories a more careful reading, and a few get close attention.

Despite the pressure of time and the flood of news, the better papers encourage reasonably careful reading of wire copy. A nugget of information may be buried in the next to last paragraph of an otherwise worthless story. When an editor discovers such tidbits of important information, they should be slipped into other stories on the same topic or made into separate stories. Local angles to a story may be discovered in close reading.

For example, a newspaper in a university city may note that a former president of the university is mentioned in some detail in the middle of a wire story. The paper probably would want to rewrite the story to emphasize his place in the news.

The following example shows how easily the editor's pencil—or the CRT—recasts a national story to emphasize the local angle for an Oregon newspaper:

```
     WASHINGTON (UPI)-Oregon and two other states have
been granted $11 million by the federal government to
run experimental drug treatment centers.

     The grants also went to New Mexico and New Hampshire.
Each state will set up several centers in key cities to
test "aversion therapy" to addicts who volunteer for the
treatment.

     Oregon will receive $4.9 million, New Hampshire
$.5 million and New Mexico $2.6 million.
```

Sometimes editors combine reports from different wire services to make a balanced story. They might lead with the first two paragraphs of UPI, for example, then insert a couple from AP, and close with a half dozen from the New York Times News Service. The job requires a deft pencil or retyping on a CRT to make sure that the language moves smoothly and that essential information has not been left out. When compiling or interweaving wire stories, the editor should be sure to cross out the various wire-service logotypes and write across the top of the patched-together story something like "From our Wire Services" or "Compiled from Wire Dispatches."

In some instances the editor can insert parenthetically a fact gleaned from another service. If the main story is from AP it may be strengthened with a paragraph from UPI:

(United Press International reported, meanwhile, that the President had decided to stay two more days in Hawaii.)

In this case there is no need to drop the AP logotype.

When editors rewrite wire stories, they omit the logotype but insert early in each story a phrase of acknowledgment like "United Press International reported." This phrase informs the reader that the facts came from UPI but now have a different emphasis.

Criticism of wire services

Though wire services provide most of the news in American newspapers, and often are blessed for it, they do have their critics. The alleged shortcomings of AP and UPI have led many newspapers to buy additional services, like those of the *Washington Post-Los Angeles Times* and the *New York Times.*

Editors often complain that too many stories are weakened by mediocre writing and minor inaccuracies, especially the stories filed from the smaller bureaus of the services. The staffs at these bureaus must crank out dozens of stories a day, often based on information from stringers. There isn't time for polished writing, and some stringers can give incorrect information.

In the late sixties AP in particular developed a policy of adding much more depth to reporting. Most such reporting had been restricted to AP Newsfeatures, a separate division of AP. (UPI has a similar features division.) To increase coverage in depth, AP instituted what it called an "Enterprise" desk. AP reporters working with the Enterprise editor spend weeks or even months digging up information of great value to the reading public. One effort of an Enterprise team resulted in a penetrating article on the plight of the small American farmer. Another examined nursing homes in the nation; the findings were not pleasant. AP even writes series on trends, such as an analysis of a recession or how the stock market, over some months, has gone up or down.

A Special Assignment team for AP in Washington also searches for stories that do not lie on the surface. Staffers there work together or separately, as the task requires. This team was formed because it is too difficult to cover each government department in Washington both steadily and thoroughly.

AP even instituted a department called Modern Living, to cover events and trends of special interest to people younger than thirty-five. The group quickly became known as the "Mod Squad." The idea was that too much coverage concerned older people and that millions of young singles and young married couples had interests and problems that got little press attention.

The wire services came to realize that good reporting and writing took time, so they now spring a few reporters loose for days, weeks, or months to get the kind of story editors want. While AP seems to have taken the lead in more detailed coverage, UPI is not far behind, checking into similar subjects with its *newsfeatures* staff.

A few years back, critics of both services contended that AP and UPI were so fearful of being called partisan that they avoided real investigative reporting. The services quickly admitted that they were extremely careful to skirt charges of partisanship. Some staffers claimed that the services were often actually timid. But such criticism, if proper then, no longer holds up well. AP and UPI have done some careful investigations that have made powerful forces, such as the Pentagon, fume and rage. AP, during the Vietnam war, dug up all kinds of stories on corruption and the penetrating reports of the AP correspondent Peter Arnett riled the military almost daily.

"Vietnam and Watergate changed all the rules," a leading AP official has said privately. He meant that the scandals unearthed in high places by both events were so vast that most of the public no longer expects the press to go easy on admirals, generals, cabinet members, business and labor leaders, or Presidents.

In his closing months as AP General Manager, Wes Gallagher took note of the current enthusiasms for investigative reporting and issued a few warnings.

> What we and the country need today might better be called "accountability reporting" instead of investigative. We have an accountability responsibility to the citizenry on how the nation's institutions are functioning. . . .
>
> Much of this accountability reporting must be *explanatory* instead of *accusatory*. Many times there are no fancy villains, just incompetents and publicity seekers. . . .
> Accountability reporting must be done with *accuracy*, not *innuendo*, and be in an objective, impartial tone.

It would be hard to find an AP or UPI story that was accusatory, but both services have been resourceful in thinking up enterprising stories. When New York first was having financial troubles, AP dug into the money difficulties of all major American cities. When prices go up, both services report how the increases afflict particular areas.

Each New York bureau can simply send a query to "all points" and get information for one main story. As an illustration, if a service wanted to find whether teacher strikes are likely to delay the opening of many schools, a message sent to all bureaus would have facts back to New York in about an hour.

While the wire services have improved sharply in the last decade, "the report" could be improved even more. Part of the problem is that so many subscribing newspapers cling to the old ways and want the wires to give a diet of stories about quarreling politicians, speculative political stories, natural disasters, and the stock market. Stories that do not fall into their stereotypes of news are not wanted by many editors and publishers. So welfare stories that elaborate on "welfare cheaters" are desired, out of habit, and stories that might mention the plight of welfare families are rejected. The fact that children, as well as adults, have rights may be so upsetting to some editors that a story on the subject would go straight to the wastebasket. The same thing happens with stories on the arts, so wire services give almost nothing on painting, music, sculpture, or the theater unless someone steals an expensive painting. The performing arts in New York get a little coverage but are forgotten elsewhere. Yet millions of people go to art galleries, concerts, and plays and read widely about the arts.

Uncritical coverage

Another criticism of wire services springs from their narrow approach to objectivity; they tend to report what various officials say, without qualification or interpretation. This kind of objectivity results, occasionally, in the services' being used by government or business figures to disseminate biased information. The reporters, faithfully reporting what the officials say, may then repeat lies or misleading information. A telegraph editor who suspects reported statements should press a wire service to insert a clarification, such as "Three months ago, the secretary said the opposite was the case. . . . " Or the editor may ask the source for an explanation or request a quote from an opposing source.

The services have matured in recent years by reducing nationalistic bias. During the Cold War, it was common to write international stories as though the reporter was working for the State Department. The general manager of AP finally took pains to remind the organization that reporters should strive to report the facts without cheering for one side or the other. This warning, plus a receding of the Cold War, contributed to a more balanced report.

Reporters, however, still tend to take nationalistic positions, probably unconsciously. It is not unusual to read in a wire service dispatch that a man "was killed by a communist bullet in North Korea." The reporter probably never thought how silly it would be to reverse that sentence and write that a North Korean was killed by a capitalist bullet.

Similar reflex reporting can creep into copy when handling stories about countries with different forms of government. Ideologies rarely are simple and reporters should avoid giving them simple labels, such as pro-American or pro-Chinese. It probably is fair, however, to describe a country's position *on a certain issue* as pro-American. Perhaps it would be more helpful for the reader, however, if reporters abroad did not scurry about with some kind of invisible measuring device to see whether another country's policies are favorable to the United States. A report on *what* happened and *why* it happened would be better. Telegraph editors would be advised to sniff copy carefully for nationalistic bias and eliminate it.

The wire services some years back used to get frequent complaints of bias from members or clients. Some of those complaints were petty or ridiculous. Wire service staffers say that they get few such complaints now. If a charge of bias is filed, however, AP or UPI will try to investigate the charge. If the complainant appears to be correct, the word goes out to be more careful next time. Usually, it is too late to print a correction.

Staffers also report that if they feel aggrieved they are allowed to go over the head of the bureau chief. This chance to plead their cases with higher officials tends to keep bureau chiefs from bowing to any pressure or from being arbitrary and high-handed.

The wire services also have moved to eliminate any hint of payoffs to reporters. Free lunches, a packet of free football tickets, and free trips once were common. Now the wire services accept free entry to a game or a theater to cover a legitimate event but all other "freebies" are banned.

AP and UPI are not totally to blame when significant information does not reach readers. Wire service writers and editors know that sometimes their best stories wind up in newspaper office wastebaskets. When reporters see their quality work tossed aside they tend to write the easy copy that sees print, even if it oversimplifies or distorts the full picture. Fortunately, enough papers these days are printing the best work. This stimulates wire service staffers, for they know that millions of people have access to their stories.

Some guidelines

Individual telegraph editors, however, must struggle to give readers full, accurate, and meaningful news within newspaper space limitations. They may accomplish this by careful use of AP and UPI. They may persuade the publisher to buy a supplemental service. They should broaden their own knowledge by spending an hour a day reading other newspapers. This reading will help them evaluate their own news judgment. Editors in the east should read the *New York Times, The Wall Street Journal,* and *Washington Post,* and the *Christian Science Monitor.* In the Midwest they should read at least a couple of Eastern papers, plus Chicago publications and the *St. Louis Post-Dispatch.* In the South they would check the *St. Petersburg Times,* the Miami papers, and the *Atlanta Constitution.* In the West they would examine the *Los Angeles Times* and the *Denver Post.*

In addition, good telegraph editors need to cultivate these qualities:

Knowledge.   They keep up in the social sciences, particularly the history of the world during the last thirty years.

Wariness.   They test for news content any story on a fad, whether drug addiction, juvenile crime, or high school dropouts. The editor sees the forest as well as the trees.

Awareness of goals.   Their picture of needed coverage should encompass tomorrow's world as well as today's.

Alertness.   They spot the news that will attain maximum readership in their areas.

Organization.   Stories need careful placement in the news pages, rather than being dropped helter-skelter into any hole that fits. Related stories should be kept together.

Balance.   They should mix major and minor stories effectively and be able to leaven the basic seriousness of the paper with humorous items.

Caution.   Planted stories, trial balloons, manipulated press conferences, and calculated leaks should trigger sham-detectors.

A telegraph editor who successfully does all these things accomplishes what Walter Lippmann suggested in the first chapter: brings the hidden facts to light and sets them in relation to one another. These facts, carefully presented and evaluated, will give, as Lippmann said, "a picture of reality on which men can act."

8 The sub-editors

In addition to the telegraph editor, newspapers have four and sometimes five other sub-editors. Each supervises a staff that may range from one to fifty or more persons, and each is responsible for a certain part of the paper.

The best known of these sub-editors is the city editor, the person who directs a staff of reporters covering the city and, often, its environs. A second sub-editor, the state editor, takes care of a broader area but rarely the whole state because few newspapers sell that widely. "Regional editor" or "country editor" might be a more accurate title than "state editor," because such a person supervises the collection of news in the paper's circulation area outside the metropolitan district. As a rule state capital reports and most wire service copy belong to the telegraph editor's province, though technically they are part of the "state" news.

The sports editor cuts across area lines, collecting sport news from everywhere. The sports editor supervises a staff of sports writers, edits their copy, and selects copy from the special sports wires of Associated Press or United Press International.

Like the sports editor, the women's editor collects special news wherever it breaks. That locale used to be exclusive society, but the society page has been democratized. Now most women's pages report more than the social events of the elite. Except on the largest papers, the pages report, at least sketchily, nearly everyone's weddings, engagements, and parties, but these traditional subjects usually are secondary to articles on food preparation, art, hobbies, child care, social problems, and education. Some papers have even quit calling this department the women's section and have named it "the family page." The idea behind this name is that the pages should primarily concern families and their problems and activities. The "women's editor," once called the "society editor," on some papers has become the "family editor."

Some papers have as a fifth sub-editor, the suburban editor. Some newspapers in larger cities without a suburban editor in name usually have one in fact—an assistant city editor assigned to the job.

The task of covering the suburbs has become a difficult one because often there are dozens of little communities, each with its own city government, planning commission, zoning department, and school board. It is almost impossible in a city like Chicago, for example, to print any but the most important news from the suburbs. The *Chicago Tribune,* however, makes a good stab at it by putting out, three times a week, a tabloid filled with suburban news. The "tab," inserted into the regular issue of the paper, has separate editions to cover major sections north, west, and south of the city. Other big city papers include strong sections of suburban news because many people in suburbia, who may work in the city, are more interested in their own towns than in the center city.

The tasks of sub-editors

It would be ideal if every person had a year or more of experience on a desk before moving up to a sub-editor's chair. Preferably, the experience would be as an assistant to a particular sub-editor. But, except on the biggest papers, this kind of background is usually impossible to get. Often a person will be told one day by the managing editor, "You're going to be the sports editor (or suburban editor or state editor)." The person may have had only sketchy editing experience and no steady experience in writing headlines or in makeup. No opportunity has existed to learn how to supervise the work of others. How can anyone make the jump gracefully and safely?

A new editor unfamiliar with the job should cram. Pumping other staffers, including predecessors, for information and tips, and even soliciting criticisms, without indicating a lack of confidence, can help the new editor overcome inexperience. Books, pamphlets, and magazine articles can be checked to broaden knowledge.

The sub-editor, if possible, should delegate a certain amount of responsibility. By doing everything, a person probably will do nothing well. Nor will there be time to do any kind of long-range planning about the job and how it will be affected by changing times. Also, by delegation of duties, the sub-editor becomes available to fill in for the editor during sickness or vacations. Should the editor be promoted or leave the paper, the sub-editor will be prepared to take over.

The sub-editor whose staff can work without constant supervision can set aside a certain time to inspect the territory. Just as it is easy to neglect delegating responsibility, it is easy to neglect this requirement. The rigorous demands of the job can pressure the sub-editor into spending the whole work day bent over a desk, whereas the sub-editor, especially the city editor, should be out checking new developments in the community once in a while and even doing some leg work. Any editor should go occasionally to a meeting on a hot local issue to observe first-hand the changes and debates in the town. Traveling the territory provides a valuable sense of the community, a keen insight into public thinking, and an empathy with the staff.

Empathy is important because each sub-editor has to direct the operations of reporters and, should they exist, assistant editors. The operations need direction to make the section effective, and effectiveness comes with contented, alert, enterprising, cooperative, and professional associates. It is not easy to direct others. Some people cannot give orders without being abrasive. Others swing between joviality and gloom. Some editors demand quality one day and forget it the next.

Supervisors ought to be consistent and reasonable with the staff. When they were reporters or copyeditors they certainly wanted congenial surroundings, a dependable and sympathetic supervisor, and a chance to get an occasional laugh. Sub-editors should at least try to fulfill their own requirements.

But an editor should beware the tangles of doing favors for staffers. A day off given to one person may, because of circumstances, be denied to another. It must be made clear to these people that they couldn't get the holiday because of a scheduling problem, not a personal one. One solution is to give no favors that can't be given to everyone. Yet an editor creates a sense of well-being if occasionally a staffer can go home early, or can slip out during a quiet period to run a personal errand. When the sub-editor is both flexible and impartial staff morale goes up.

Morale improves with other improvements in working conditions. Things like new desks, chairs, and lights are contributions of management that a persuasive sub-editor can obtain.

Praise and criticism

As we have said before, no editor should overlook the value of praise. Most newsmen are immune to ostentatious flattery—they have seen so much that is phony—but they cherish a casual sentence of praise from a colleague. A simple "Good story, Charley," or "Nice headline, Liz!" will do more to spark professionalism than any scroll of merit.

Some papers, as mentioned in chapter 2, get out a little sheet that gives credit for work well done. Others post good examples. Some subtle sub-editors might be able to wangle a personal note from the publisher or editor-in-chief to commend the staffer. Discretion here is essential. The minute that an editor hands out laurels insincerely, the whole staff begins to discount any approval.

One of the best ways sub-editors can improve morale, especially if they take credit modestly, is to get pay increases for deserving staff members. When requested raises come through, they can tell staffers quietly, "Your good work of the last several months means an extra ten dollars a week from now on." Such staffers will not only be pleasantly surprised but also will realize that the superior went to bat for them.

But what happens when a staffer fails to measure up? In the old days, the editor would probably bellow, "You're fired!" Such abrupt dismissal is rare today because editors realize that it is cruel and that it often loses for the paper a potentially good employee. Furthermore, American Newspaper Guild contracts bar dismissal without specific cause.

Instead of muttering deprecations about an inadequate staffer, an editor should aim to be a teacher. A few minutes spent every day helping the new staffer correct shortcomings and speaking favorably about strong points will improve both the newcomer's morale and usefulness to the paper. Sometimes the editor assigns another person to go over a novice reporter's copy, sentence by sentence, to show how it can be improved.

If all efforts fail in getting staffers to improve, it would be better for the newspaper and the employee if they were urged to look elsewhere for work. Staffers who are not fired outright can more easily find another job that they may perform well. Any such conversation with a staffer, of course, should be private. The wise editor, under these circumstances, refrains from suggesting that a person get into another line of work. Many successful journalists have, at one time or another, got such advice and, fortunately, not taken it. But newspeople who recognize they have no journalistic talent should quit. They would be only tolerated on any newspaper and would be better off in another business.

Promising reporters and deskpersons should be encouraged to attend the increasing number of workshops and study sessions being held throughout the country. They should be urged, also, to take formal courses at local colleges or universities. Some newspapers pay the tuition for such courses if the person completes them satisfactorily. The courses need not be on journalism—almost any knowledge can be valuable to a journalist.

Sometimes even a good reporter or copyeditor hits a slump. Then the sub-editor should talk with the individual. Perhaps some personal problem is causing worry, or the job itself has become dull. Talking it out may be just what the staffer needs to regain former verve and skill. Other times the sub-editor can suggest or even provide solutions to the problem. For example, a person who has worked on the desk for a couple of years and basically likes the work may be getting a little tired of sitting all day long. Couldn't a reporting job be arranged? Or a special reporting assignment be made once in a while for a change of pace?

A skillful city editor once noted that young reporters often lapsed when excitement in their personal lives overshadowed their work. A young first homeowner or father sometimes dreams all day of his new acquisitions. Usually, the city editor said, the person came back to earth in a few weeks. If not, a friendly comment, given with a smile, often did the trick. The editor might say, "George, do you believe you could think a little less about that baby and a little more about your job?"

An editor who is critical of a staffer's work should express criticism out of a concern for the person's welfare as well as the paper's.

It probably will only upset a troubled person more if a critic shows no interest in the staffer's problems and only wants to solve the publisher's problems.

A sub-editor soon discovers that the efficiency and morale of the staff depend partly on the flow of work. Everyone around a newsroom knows that news comes in spurts. News may be heavy for a week or more, and then for a few days nothing seems to happen. Some of these quiet periods can be predicted. Summer is the calmest season. Schools and legislatures are on vacation, and most community action slacks off as workers prepare for their holidays. The Christmas season repeats this lull in those civic affairs that produce most of the non-spectacular news in a community paper.

Directing news collection

In some places local news is heavy a couple of days a week and light on others. The city council may meet Mondays and the school board Tuesdays. Both normally provide several stories. The county board of supervisors, another good news source, also may meet on a Tuesday. If the city planning commission meets Monday night, and the zoning board Tuesday, then local government news may well pile up the first of the week. Unless the sub-editor plans ahead for peaks and slumps, many Thursday, Friday, and Saturday pages will be drab and insignificant—not worth reading—and the staff will suffer from being alternately swamped and idled.

During the dull periods the staff should be scratching for feature stories or digging for important information below the surface of events. If it is obvious that the city council will make news early one week about building codes, why not interview the city engineer the week before on new building techniques, or talk to a leading architect on ideas for the city of the future? On the other hand, if the council makes a surprising or especially significant decision on Monday, the rest of the week provides time to follow up on the reasons for the decision and its implications.

The ability to create story ideas is one of an editor's greatest assets; the sub-editor must develop it if the job requires more than a person who gives assignments, edits copy, writes headlines, lays out pages, and pats a reporter's back once in a while. An editor may do all the routine work well, but first-rate status will not come without imagination. And since imagination is always in short supply, an editor should encourage it among colleagues. The willingness to stimulate story ideas and the "play" of stories is a characteristic that develops a spirited staff. People get excited on a newspaper where the editors listen to new ideas and where they are willing to experiment, and reward enterprise. Every sub-editor should have a drawer, box, or basket available for staffers to drop suggestions into. But if suggestions are rejected the contributor ought to know why. An editor who repeatedly ignores ideas quickly freezes staff initiative. Every suggestion needs acknowledgement and at least a word of thanks.

The city editor
Journalists generally concede that the city editor's job is the most difficult of all the sub-editor positions. The person with this task has to supervise the biggest staff of full-time reporters, and must try to fit the talents of these reporters to dozens of jobs. Throughout the work day alterations, suggestions, and specific directions must be given. The city editor gives assignments to reporters and photographers, sees that the copy is edited properly, and checks the fit of local copy to the available space.

On smaller papers the job may seem easier but often is not. While the city editor on a small paper may have only a few reporters to supervise, the task also requires reading all their copy, writing all the headlines, and sometimes producing a few stories on the side. The city editor even must dart into the composing room occasionally to oversee the makeup of pages. Since many reporters on small papers are inexperienced, the city editor must try to make up for their deficiencies with an editing pencil and with some kind of on-the-job training. This training, because of a lack of time, often must consist of an over-the-shoulder comment from time to time or some brief instructions on how to get the information for a certain story.

City editors on medium-sized papers will have an assistant or two. One assistant may handle the assignment chore, with the city editor suggesting a special story, and another may edit local pictures. The editor and assistants all will do some editing of local copy and will mark headline size and story length before sending the copy to the universal desk. The city editor probably will lay out the local news pages.

On the biggest papers the city editor has a half dozen aides, each with a specific job to do. The city editor, acting as chairman, checks the work of others, adding or subtracting copy and accepting or overruling decisions.

This supervisory role gives the city editor the flexibility needed to handle the day's little or big emergencies. The gifted city editor manages to keep most emergencies in the newsroom from becoming severe. This can be done by adequate preparation, which allows the staff to move swiftly in any crisis.

Seeing beyond Now
Preparedness is vital to the smooth operation of a city desk. For a coming election the inept editor fails to prepare for stories that anyone would expect to happen, whereas the well-organized editor plans who will write the story or stories on state legislative races, who will handle city council contests, etc. Someone is chosen to funnel returns from the central counting area to the paper or may even have to plan collection of returns by the paper itself. This work may mean arranging for extra telephones or special lines. All this preparation requires planning, but it means the difference between a confused scramble to get some stories together and the provision of thorough, balanced coverage.

Though an election obviously needs planning if it is to be covered decently, the demands of some events are more subtle. Undoubtedly the *Washington Post* deserves credit for the most comprehensive planning as it mapped coverage of the last episodes of Watergate. The paper announced publicly in February 1974 that it was planning how it would cover the impeachment or resignation of President Nixon! The resignation did not take place for six months, yet when that historic announcement came the *Post* included a 24-page supplement that told in full detail the long story of Watergate corruption that led to the first resignation of an American president. This supplement, with a little additional material, a few days later, appeared as an instant book, *The Fall of the President.*

Almost no newspaper, of course, has the staff, the facilities—or the need—to prepare the way the *Post* did. But every paper should look down the calendar a few months or even years to make sure that they do not muff a good story. For example, a school board issue may be brewing over whether to build a new school and the town seems headed for a full-fledged dispute. The education writer should be on top of it but some help may be required: the city hall reporter might note how the issue spills into city government, a general assignment reporter may visit a neighboring city to see how that town resolved a similar dispute, etc. Or a prominent politician may be getting up in years and just might announce—an hour before deadline—that he or she is going to retire. Good planning would mean that when the announcement comes stories are almost ready on that person's political life, the scramble by a dozen who will battle to take over the retiree's job, and a sidebar on the politician's humble beginnings.

Even when emergencies force city editors to make quick decisions, they should pause and ponder: "Are we getting the whole story? Are we missing anything? Are we over-playing? Have we got the right pictures? What's the best layout for all these stories? What must we cut or drop in order to print this hot news?"

To do the job properly, the city editor must be able to grasp instantaneously the value of news, coach the young reporters, juggle the staff to get the best coverage, and inspire respect, if not admiration.

The city editor soon finds that the clock becomes the main obstacle to good coverage. The newsroom seems to have one paramount question: how much time to deadline, to see whether there is time to print any more than the bare facts of a story and engrave a picture to illustrate it.

The press of time

To keep from being unduly harassed by the clock, the city editor strives to develop top efficiency. Aides are chosen who can move swiftly to solve the problems that develop. Editors learn the strengths and weaknesses of reporters and give the story needing the swiftest work to the fastest writer. City editors avoid answering the telephone, so they won't get tied up listening to some complaint that a copy aide could handle just as well. They work to eliminate inefficient habits. Since paper usually swirls around city editors, they are tempted to set some aside to read later. This is usually a mistake. An excellent city editor once remarked that no one should handle the same piece of paper twice. "Read it and decide what to do with it," was his motto. His desk was never a bottleneck for copy, memos, or letters.

The best city editors today keep tabs on more than the city room. In addition to getting around the city themselves, they read up on its history so they can guide their staffs to write stories that set the social and economic problems of the community in historical context. Tomorrow's newspapers will almost certainly require such emphasis. They will report such things as the changing political power base, local developments in mental health, the deep and often hidden frictions behind violence, or a real critique of the local educational system.

Gone are the days when reporters believed that news consisted of the acts of God and politicians. Stories of crimes, accidents, and fires are essential. A few speculative stories still are important, but they have been bypassed for stories that require careful digging and interviewing to help the reader understand the world at least a little better. Every city editor will have to recognize this change and prepare for the kind of coverage an increasing number of readers demand and all readers need.

The state editor

The work of a state or regional editor often has a direct bearing on a paper's circulation. Many city dwellers will subscribe to a monopoly paper even if its coverage of city news is poor. There is no other place to get local news. But often territory in rural or suburban areas can be contested by papers from other nearby cities. For example, counties of eastern Iowa have traditionally been battled for by the *Chicago Tribune* and the *Des Moines Register,* as well as papers of such smaller cities as Davenport, Dubuque, and Cedar Rapids. The *Register* state desk has the same kind of circulation tussle with Omaha and Council Bluffs to the west. If the state editor slights the news from the outlying areas, the readers there will switch to another paper.

The state editor's chief problem is that most of the staff never is in the newsroom. Communication with reporters is handled by telephone, teletype, or mail. Frequently reporters work only part-time for a little extra money and status. Though they usually have serious journalistic limitations, no one else is available who can do the job as well.

Stringers and correspondents

A sizable number of papers have discovered that part-time rural correspondents are, with a few exceptions, not up to modern coverage. These "stringers" often write poorly, miss good stories under their noses, and find it almost impossible to recognize deadlines. As an alternative, papers have tried to find professionals who are willing to work the smaller towns. These are persons who not only can report well but also have the ability to cover the news of a good-sized region, perhaps a whole county. They can drive over the territory every few days, and, because they get to know the news sources, can do much spot checking by telephone. Some of these correspondents have teletypes in their homes or some little niche that serves as an office. These teletypes communicate directly with the state editor's desk. Stories from these correspondents usually require little editing or rechecking, and the state editor has less frustration keeping tabs on one efficient remote reporter than on half a dozen semi-competent stringers.

Some papers try to solve the problem another way. They use staffers from smaller papers as stringers. A few regular staffers in the "home office" then provide all special coverage. For example, the *Des Moines Tribune* had a strong network of stringers operating under a well-staffed state desk. But to assure stories of interest to readers in smaller communities, the editors pulled a top city-side reporter over to state coverage. His task was to drive around the state looking for features and getting pictures. To city-bound reporters, his job looked like a dream, for in two or three days of driving he could collect his material and do nothing the rest of the week but write the five pieces and play golf. In this fashion, the state desk got daily, illustrated, by-lined feature from obscure portions of its circulation area. Clearly, the system was great, both for the reporter and the newspaper. Later, for various reasons, the system was altered. Now two or three tour the state for a few days each week, then work the rest of the time on the desk.

Professionals willing to be correspondents in smaller communities usually are young and at the beginning of their careers. The state editor should coach these beginners into better writing and reporting by writing them notes about their work and, in particular, by urging them to read their copy in print to see how it has been edited. It is hoped they will pick up tips that will save time for both themselves and the state editor.

Some state editors prefer to send beginners into the field after some specific training. They encourage the managing editor to keep the neophyte in the city for at least a month to work under the discipline of the city desk and to learn to cover events without much direction.

For example, the beginner should tag around with the courthouse reporter for at least a couple of days, soaking up information on the courts and county government. Some assignments could require a little coverage of business, police, labor unions, and city government with its main adjuncts: planning, zoning, sewage disposal, parks, revenue, and traffic.

While most such staff correspondents are young, occasionally a highly qualified older person wants to live in a little town. Though sometimes this person might be able to hold a key position in the city, the rural life is preferred. When a state editor has such a pearl, someone happy in one place and good at the job, everything reasonable should be done to meet the person's needs. A good salary, frequent bylines, and a note of praise once or twice a year from the editor-in-chief or the publisher are the least a good career correspondent deserves.

But in the main reporters work in the field for six months or a year and are ready to move. Sometimes there is an agreement that the person from the far reaches of the circulation district will get the first opening on the city staff. Such promises should not be made casually. A young person told that five or six months hard work in Swampsville will earn a place on the city staff will, as the time drifts on to a year, feel betrayed. If this person becomes bitter and quits, suddenly the editor loses not only good coverage but a valuable staffer. Editors should be honest about future opportunities and keep expectant correspondents informed of any changes in their status.

Of course not all correspondents are in the boondocks. Newspapers in major cities have bureaus in other metropolitan areas, and reporters there can live the city life. Sometimes their lives are easier than the city reporter's because they may have an easier commute.

The *Los Angeles Times,* for one, has a staff in Orange County, south of Los Angeles. The reporters and editors there function much like a city staff, but send their copy into the main plant. The copy is sent back—in type—to be printed in a special Orange County newspaper factory.

Planning state coverage

How thorough should the state coverage be? Obviously, if the state editor covers a sizable area with any kind of depth, many pages will be filled. If only the most important news is skimmed, circulation may dip. The solution is to set guidelines on coverage. They should be worked out in conference with the publisher, managing editor, city editor, and other sub-editors. The circulation manager should be brought in, too, of course, to get the word on the law of diminishing returns. A town of 1,000 with only twenty-two subscribers will not merit much coverage unless the circulation manager believes its circulation can be increased.

Bigger papers usually restrict news from outlying areas. They may have more than a hundred fairly substantial communities in their circulation area; they can't possibly cover each in detail. Smaller papers, of course, will provide quite thorough reports of the few villages under their circulation umbrella, and some papers will print even columns of personal items mailed in by a stringer. The trend, however, is to reduce trivia.

Once policy has been set on breadth and depth of coverage, the state editor has to struggle with personnel. Sometimes there is no alternative to stringers and possibly a few full-timers. To make the best of an inadequate situation, the editor should try to give as much instruction as possible to the "staff." Some papers get out a pamphlet or news sheet that explains how to write news and features. These have to be short if the stringers are to read them, and even then the messages don't always get through.

A pamphlet to guide the stringer should be specific:

> We do *not* want accident stories unless someone is killed or seriously hurt or unless there is an unusual angle.
>
> We do *not* want more than three short paragraphs on weddings, unless the mayor is getting married.
>
> We *do* want stories of some breadth, like the amount of school construction planned in your county for the next three years or the plan to clean up Inky Stinky Creek.
>
> We *do* want stories on politics, government, education, and social change.
>
> We *do* want feature stories on funny or peculiar happenings.

The booklet can be supplemented by a mimeographed monthly sheet that praises good work, naming the author, and that criticizes bad work anonymously. This sheet should be written entertainingly and without malice. It should educate, not persecute. Furthermore, if someone does a first-rate job on a difficult task, the state editor should take a few minutes to dash off a personal note. If the work is not so good, the editor should avoid fulminating. The writer must be called, asked to collect more information, and then told to rewrite the story. If state editors went into a frenzy every time they saw a miserable piece of copy, they would soon be palsied.

The state editor should have the newspaper's librarian maintain a looseleaf booklet of details about the areas that the regular staff as well as stringers report on. Such a booklet would enable reporters to doublecheck all basic information about each town and district, including the spelling of the names of public and business officials.

Editors should make as many calls to get the news or to straighten out inconsistencies as a story warrants. A growing number of newspapers have a contract with the telephone company that provides almost unlimited telephone calls over a large area for a set fee. This arrangement frees editors from having to balance the size of the phone bill against the size of the story.

The women's editor

Over the years the women's pages of the better papers have become a section which is less about the country club set and more about what active women are doing. Consequently, these pages now attract many women besides those fascinated by high society. These women are often more traveled and better educated and have wider interests than women a generation ago. An example of a newspaper's responding to this change was the creation by the *Washington Post* of a "Style" section combining women's news with news of entertainment, culture, and "people."

The cagey editor of the women's pages aims today to attract nearly everyone. The editor should realize that weddings are similar and predictable, so their stories can be told in a few paragraphs. Some weddings have moderately wide interest—at least as wide as some of the other news in the paper—and these stories should cover the essentials of the ceremony and the people involved. Some editors have hit upon the idea of running pictures of the happy couple, in street clothes, instead of only the bride's picture. About twice as many people will recognize one of the two as would recognize only the bride. When non-traditional weddings caught editors' ears a few years ago some found the informality worthy of good picture coverage.

All kinds of social items deluge all papers. Medium and small papers especially find that the publicity chairman of every organization mails in or calls in a story every time the organization serves a cup of coffee—and sometimes when it doesn't. In many cases the item could be of interest only to the organization's members, but the members may already know the information. Since many of these items are really announcements, some papers have used a "Community Calendar" to announce in a line or two what organization is going to hear which speaker, where, and at what time. This device saves a galley or two of type a day.

Other papers have a special column for tidbits that may be interesting but not worth a story:

> Ralph Taylor of 1024 Ackerman has been named to the dean's list at Elmhurst College, where his sister Janice was valedictorian last year . . . Their parents are Mr. and Mrs. Homer Taylor.
>
> Mrs. Roger Smythe has been named by the local PTA Council as an alternate to the state PTA convention in Minneapolis.

Condensation of little news items is used on other pages as well, notably sports and business. It saves space, yet allows many marginal items to be read swiftly.

The sports editor

The sports editor has one advantage over the other sub-editors: Almost all sports news is expected. The editor knows at the start of the work day that several games or sports events are scheduled, so plans for the section can be seriously altered only by such things as the cancellation of an event, the death of a famed athlete, the highly unexpected outcome of a contest, or the setting of some record.

To offset this advantage the sports editor does have some special problems. Some of them stem from the fact that many people find sports and sports stars dramatic and spectacular. Because American sports fans are so intense, sports copy tends to be melodramatic.

The sports editor has to guard against absurdly melodramatic stories. It must be kept in mind that victory for the home team really is not the greatest of glories, and defeat is not the greatest of tragedies. The pages should not treat athletes as supermen either, for sometimes off the field they are far from heroic.

Sports writers, often weak in grammar and strong on clichés, need a watchful editor. Sometimes a writer attempts to be different and brings forth what amounts to an essay on a game. While this may be a fine piece of writing, too often the writer gets so wrapped up in unaccustomed rhetoric that the score is omitted.

Hyperbole, a characteristic of sports writing, should never replace accuracy. Writers tempted to use superlatives to describe the skill of a rookie, the outstanding ability of a sophomore, and the great prospects for this season's team should remember that often the rookie may soon slide back to the minor leagues, the sophomore to the end of the bench, and the team to the league's cellar.

For years, sports writers covering major league baseball teams in spring training exaggerated the facts so greatly that a substantial number of fans became cynical. Today, these early reports are more restrained. A story from a Florida training camp may say, "The White Sox finished fourth last year, and if there is any change this season it will be for the worse."

Editors also must cool copy that heralds a forthcoming contest as the "Game of the Decade." If the game is disappointing, the misled fans will feel doubly cheated. A prediction of the "Game of the Century" is even more dangerous. Since there have been several of these already in the twentieth century, it would be wise not to schedule any more.

Sports publicists, like politicians, constantly push reporters and editors to promote their pet topics. So editors have to be sure they are covering, not promoting, a sport. A generation ago, sports pages ran all kinds of stories on professional wrestling, even though it was generally known that most matches were rigged. Finally, a number of editors, deciding not to promote fraud, quit printing stories and pictures about pro wrestlers. The rapid decline of the "sport" suggested that the wrestling promoters depended on free advertising disguised as news.

Minor league baseball is another sport where almost tearful requests for promotion must be resisted. In dozens of cities around the country sports editors have been asked to boost the home town team. If they decline, team supporters scorn them as disloyal. Yet most of the teams are owned by private businesses, the major league clubs. By excessive coverage, the newspaper actually subsidizes private business. Such baseball teams often get more stories than any other group in town. No other public performance—movie, play, concert, or opera—receives the kind of minute coverage that is given a minor league team that may draw only 500 fans a night.

Sports editors today try to trim coverage of professional and top amateur athletes to make room for unorganized sports. More and more Americans are enjoying sport for its own sake. They sail, ski, surf, hike, camp, fly, shoot, and skin-dive. Because most of these sports, though vigorous, are not competitive, the modern sports editor has to find ways to cover them. Usually this is done with feature stories and pictures.

The good editor always has to be attentive to pictures, not only because photography plays an important part in sports, but because today's readers spend more time watching sports on TV, which means that only exceptional pictures are likely to capture their interest. Consistently good photographs are hard to find anywhere, and sports editors usually have the highest proportion of clichés. This means an abundance of photos showing someone sliding into second base or taking a basketball jump shot. Even the most attentive sports fan is going to ignore them.

The sports editor must demand truly extraordinary pictures, ones which illustrate athletic grace, skill, and intensity. Any editor who demands good pictures, of course, must meet the demands of a good photographer—adequate time, excellent equipment, plenty of film, and the promise of seeing the best pictures in print.

Other sub-editing

Aside from the four or five sub-editors of the typical newspaper are several workers who fall into a middle-range category under the managing editor. Some large papers have a foreign editor who directs, at a sophisticated level, a staff of foreign correspondents much as the state editor directs stringers. Many papers have a "Sunday editor" who may simply put out a weekly magazine section or may be in complete charge of the whole Sunday edition with its magazine and special pages or sections devoted to finance, real estate, books, entertainment, travel, hobbies, television, and so on. Either way, the Sunday editor has a week-long job assembling articles, reviews, and photographs from regular staffers as well as special assistants and part-time writers.

Some "editors" are really specialized reporters. They cover such areas as the arts, education, religion, business, or labor. The term "editor" is perhaps justified for reasons other than status or newspaper promotion, because such a person has more independence than the ordinary writer on general assignment. While the science editor or the music editor usually will direct no staff, each follows the news in his or her areas in the same way as any sub-editor, selects from the flow of ideas and copy and writes specialized stories. Some other editor, probably the city editor, is technically the boss, but one who usually defers to the specialized editor-writer's expert assessment of the news.

Papers for many decades now have divided editing responsibilities into sub-editing areas such as city desk and state desk, but better ways can still be found. For example, the *Des Moines Tribune,* after using the standard plan of having a specialized writer travel the whole state, established an effective sub-editorship which combined the jobs of city and state editor. This person came in very early every morning, surveyed the statewide news situation, and decided on the staff coverage, if any, for points outside the metropolitan area. Writers and photographers could be dispatched 100 or more miles away, sometimes by plane.

The *Wilmington* (Del.) *News-Journal* has a metropolitan desk responsible for coverage in its whole circulation area, which includes the entire state and counties in four additional states. Richard P. Sanger, editor, explained that "maintenance of separate city and state desks is an anachronism in this fast-growing and changing area." Commuting, shopping, and problems go across county and state lines, he pointed out. So the city and state desks were consolidated, and the city editor was boosted into the new spot to channel all area coverage through a single desk.

The Wilmington experience should be noted by all newspapers as they adjust to changing conditions and changing readership. Sub-editors were named in the past to provide specialized editing and staff direction. They generally provided the kind of coverage the publishers desired. But no one should assume that the organization chart of the late 1970s should last forever. State or universal desks, if no longer useful, should be discarded. The growth of suburbs, the shift in public interest, and the increasing specialization of news all force the alert newspaper to examine its operations to see if there is a better way to get the news to its readers.

9 Printing the future is here

Computers dominate the modern newspaper plant. Classified and display advertising, news, columns and editorials all funnel into computers, which send signals to phototypesetting machines. Those machines send forth the ads and news on photopaper that can be pasted onto "camera copy." The camera copy is photographed; a printing plate is made; and the plate is put on a press. Newspapers spin off the press by the thousands.

A visitor to this kind of plant usually is told almost immediately, "All this is obsolete." The statement is true, for every company making printing equipment is preparing to turn out even faster machines or new machines that will abolish one or two steps in the newspaper printing process. As examples, engineers are trying to perfect *plateless printing* in which microscopic jets of ink will be sprayed onto paper to form letters. Printing plates—and presses—would no longer be used. Other engineers aim to develop *pagination,* which would let an editor guide a computer in making up newspaper pages.

Obsolete or not, the new equipment in most newspapers tends to dazzle journalists of any age. The idea of tapping a few keys and having columns of news pop out of a machine startles even people who have seen the process in operation for years.

When the astonishment over the new technology subsides, journalists should take stock of the situation and realize what has happened: *The men and women in the newsroom not only write and edit the news. They also run the typesetting machines.*

It is crucial that beginning journalists grasp this fundamental change. In the electronic newspaper, type is set by machines, not printers. Those machines receive commands from editors. Unless there is some mechanical breakdown, those machines do exactly what they are told. No longer can a printer catch a copyeditor's error. No printer reads copy. No machine falters and gives forth typographical errors. So copyeditors, sending stories to their computers, must be as sure as they can be that they commit zero errors.

Beginnings timid

Newspapers do not shift overnight from the old style printing to the new. Most of them rather timidly buy one piece of electronic equipment, then a few more until much of the paper is tied into computers. Wherever possible newspapers try to keep using existing machinery, so long as it can perform adequately. This means that many papers have hybrid operations, making use of some modern, some old, and some middle-aged equipment. The one piece of machinery that has tended to stand firm is the press, for presses are big, expensive, and durable. New presses are not much faster than old ones. To get a new press requires a place to put it. The paper can't shut down for six months while the old press is removed and the new one installed.

Let's say, however, that a newspaper is using all the latest equipment. Chances are good that it will function this way:

Reporters write their stories on electronic devices, called either Cathode Ray Tubes (CRT) or Video Display Terminals (VDT) as described in chapter two. Much advertising is prepared on those machines, too. Copyeditors read reporters' stories on the CRT/VDT screens and make any corrections or alterations by operating a keyboard. Wire copy comes to the copy desk the same way. Copyeditors write headlines on the screen, too. If a headline is too long or too short, in most cases the computer will reject it.

The copyeditor pushes a key on the CRT and in another room the stories appear on a strip of paper in the desired column width. A dummy, telling printers where to put those stories, headlines, and ads, is sent to the composing room. The printer pastes ads and stories onto a piece of paper the size of the newspaper page. This page is called *camera-ready copy,* a *mechanical,* or a *keyline.* The page is put before a machine, and laser beams scan the page. This process takes two minutes. In another four minutes the laser machine has completed a plate with a raised surface. These plates are put on a *letterpress* press and the paper is printed. The press is called letterpress because paper is squeezed against inked letters—raised surfaces, something like a rubber stamp.

Scanners

Some papers vary the process. Instead of using VDTs or CRTs, they use an Optical Character Reader or a *scanner.* In this system reporters type stories on a special electric typewriter. The words appear on paper, as in ordinary copy, but below each letter is a symbol that the scanner picks up and uses in making a perforated paper tape. The tape, run through a photocomposition machine, puts the proper letters onto camera paper. Other symbols, added by the reporter, will tell the scanner to do such things as indent copy, start a paragraph, or end a paragraph. Editors can use a special pencil to edit this copy or they can type material between the lines.

Fig. 9–1. CRT/VDT keyboard. Reporters and editors may type stories or edit with this keyboard. Note the keys at the top and right that give special instructions to the computer.

reminiscent of the Romantic pianists, weakened the sense of overall

form. Although he shaped individual phrases very well, the dramatic

impact of such a piece is undermined when the smaller units are not

related to the whole.<□

#ϸϸ°The second half of the program was more sϸϸatisfying, ϸϸϸ

notwithstanding my bias to the Sonata in C Major, Op. 103 by

Prokofieff. This piece is indicative of the worst tendencies of the

'ϸϸϸ'neo-classiϸc'' era, superimposing arbitrary dissonances on a

blatant tonal structure, and using all the traditional gestures,

including the most academic sort of rhythm. The performance, luckily

, was just the kind to foster a greater appreciation of the piece,

projecting all the proper moods and highlighting all of its harmonic

pranks.<□

#°The concluding Tarantella by Liszt was ideally suited to Foster's

gifts; he displayed a dazzling technique in this virtuosic tour-de-

force. He ended with the B Major Nocturne of Chopin as an encore.<□

#°-30-

Fig. 9–2. Scanner copy. An Optical Character Reader picks up the symbols below the letters and transfers them into columns for the paper.

After the camera-ready copy is prepared, a majority of American papers make *offset* plates and put them on an *offset* press. The plate is made by photographing the camera-ready copy. The negative from the photograph is put above a page-size piece of thin aluminum which resembles a cookie sheet. The aluminum is specially treated. Light is shined through the negative for a few minutes. A quick chemical treatment makes an image appear on the sheet. This absolutely smooth plate is put onto the offset press. A letterpress press uses only ink. An offset press uses both water and ink. Images of letters and pictures on the smooth plate will attract ink and the part of the surface that is free of images will attract water. Paper does not touch offset plates. The turning press plate sets off—*offsets*—the image onto another cylinder and the paper rolls against that offset roller.

Other methods

Papers with letterpress operations, but without lasers, operate another way. The camera-ready copy is photographed and an old-style *engraving* or *cut* is made of the whole page. This engraving is stereotyped, a process that squeezes papier mache, called a *flong*, against the engraving. The papier mache then becomes a mold, for it contains an impression of the letters. Molten type metal, largely lead, is poured over the papier mache, now called a *mat*, and a concave metal plate is produced. The plate, which weighs about forty pounds, is put on the press, and the newspapers roll forth.

The stereotyping process is slow, cumbersome, and hot. The plates are heavy and awkward. So inventors have sidestepped this method and produced thin, light plastic plates. Instead of stereotyping the page, the printer takes a *proof* on quality paper of the whole page. From this proof the thin plate can be made. The old press which once spun those heavy plates can be altered to accommodate the light ones. The *Los Angeles Times* uses special lightweight plates that can be chopped up and recycled.

Papers that have not adopted the newest technology set type on some kind of photocomposing machine or with a Linotype. Either of these machines can be operated by a human being or adapted to set type by getting directions from a perforated tape. The photocomposition machine turns out a strip of paper, just as a scanner or a VDT does, but the process is much slower. Any type set by any photographic method is called *cold type*. A Linotype drops out lines of type called *slugs*. Each is almost one inch high and the width of the newspaper column. The Linotype method makes these slugs from molten metal and therefore is called *hot type*. The type, a raised surface on one edge of the slug, appears to be upside down and backwards. When ink is applied and paper pressed against the type, the printing is easy to read.

The lines of type, plus headlines and ads, can be put into a metal frame. When the frame is filled with type it is taken to a *mat roller* where the page is stereotyped. As in the other method described, molten metal is poured onto the mat and a page plate is made. The number of papers printing this way is fading fast because it is slow; it requires heavy equipment, and it is labor-intensive.

As mentioned, most papers move toward the new technology one step at a time. So they may have started with classified advertising, a department that once took hundreds of labor hours. By computerizing the operation, tremendous savings were gained. The *New York Times,* for example, once had workers spend three days getting the Sunday classified section organized. A computer now does it in twenty minutes.

Tremendous speed

After classified was automated, display advertising shifted to cold type. With both kinds of ads, most papers made engravings of them while using hot type for news. Papers that had shifted to offset soon used cold type for everything. When video screens became available, papers that had been blending hot and cold type moved with some speed to make the transition to total cold type. Bigger papers continued to use letterpress presses, since so much money was invested in them.

These changes to cold type have meant that the old-style composing rooms with their dirt, heat, noise, and clunking, clattering Linotypes are nearly gone. In their places are machines that look like sleek office equipment, sitting in a cool, clean, carpeted room. It has also meant that where once ten printers worked there now are two or three.

The new technology makes printing processes much easier and quicker, but the changeover has not all been roses. Computers and their allied equipment are sensitive. They break down occasionally, forcing papers to buy an expensive back-up system. Minor variances in heat, humidity, and voltage cause strange things—all bad—to happen. Some companies which produced the equipment did a poor servicing job. Some machines were developed by computer engineers who made little effort to understand the peculiar problems of newspapers. Clumsy equipment resulted. Many of these difficulties have been solved as newspapers demanded better equipment and better service. In addition, some of the misfits quit making newspaper equipment.

Changeover difficult

Most journalists now laugh about the horrible experiences they endured in adjusting to the new technology. Computers ceased to function; copy got set in peculiar widths; stories disappeared somewhere inside the computer; and deadlines were missed by hours. One beginner even pushed the wrong key and a long story got set in letters three-quarters of an inch high! The changeover often was traumatic, and nothing to laugh about at the time. Future changeovers with better equipment and better staff preparation should go much easier.

The new technology was hailed in the beginning as a way for

newspapers to narrow to almost nothing the time gap between news deadline and press time. That hasn't worked out. Some editors report that they have trimmed the time by fifteen minutes, but that the gap still is an hour. Some papers have even moved their deadlines forward. It is clear that so far the new, fast equipment has helped the journalist and the publisher, but the reader is getting no fresher news.

The plus side of the new technology, however, greatly outweighs the minuses. It can reduce typographical errors, speed the whole operation, provide easy additions and inserts to stories, and avoid the flood of paper that afflicts the paper-and-pencil newsroom.

The computer lets an editor dummy the paper exactly, for no longer is story length approximated. The computer measures a story within one-tenth of an inch. Headlines no longer are restricted to six or eight sizes. Almost any size can be made on the computer, and trick heads can be produced easily. As an example, a head can be made with the first line large, the second medium, and the last one small. This can be done with conventional type, too, but the task would take fifteen minutes. The trick head can be done in fifteen seconds on a CRT.

The new technology also saves a great deal of money. While new devices cost thousands of dollars each, labor savings are even greater. One paper went electronic and got its money back in ten months. Others expect full return in two years. The money savings depend on what kind of agreement can be reached with craft unions. Some papers, after long negotiations, have granted lifetime jobs to printers displaced by automation. In these cases, savings will not be so apparent. The question remains in all situations, however, as to how publishers will use their savings. It is hoped by journalists that the profits will be shared with the news staff and that newspapers will hire better reporters and editors and give them time enough to do the thorough job that modern journalism demands.

Some editors, familiar with the new equipment, expect scanners to fade in favor of "the tube"—CRT/VDT. They think scanners are

Fig. 9–3. Paste-up. A printer, under an editor's direction, pastes paper "type" onto camera paper at the Bloomington, Illinois, *Daily Pantagraph*. Note the dummy above the camera paper.

slower and more cumbersome. Then, too, syndicated material that comes ready for the scanner may not be suitable for all scanners. Someone then has to retype it. Perhaps a standard scanner will be adopted so all newspapers can use the same copy.

Other developments help the reporter and editor, even though they have little bearing on printing. A portable CRT is available for reporters covering events far from home. A box holding the CRT, not much bigger than a portable typewriter, can be unfolded, plugged into electricity, and attached to an ordinary telephone. Reporters can write on the CRT and have the signals sent over a telephone line to the computer in their newspaper's plant.

CRTs can be equipped so a paper copy of a story is available. An editor or reporter pushes a button labeled "Print" and out comes a copy. Such copies help editors who want to show the story to someone far from the screen. The great value comes to reporters who are writing a new lead or an insert for a story to appear in the next edition.

Anyone laying hands on a CRT has to know printing measurements. The machine needs to be told how many *picas* wide it should make the column and how many *points* high it should make the headlines.

Printing measures

Points and picas are the two main printing measures. In general, a point refers to vertical measure. One point equals one-seventy-second of an inch. Seventy-two-point type, then, is one inch high. Thirty-six-point is half an inch. Twenty-four-point is one-third of an inch. Most *body type*—the type of news stories—is 8- to 10-point.

The measure for horizontal distance is *pica*. A pica is one-sixth of an inch, so a column two inches wide will have type set 12 picas wide: A half-column cut in such a column width would be 6 picas, or one inch.

A few simple problems and answers will help make these measurements clear.

1. If body type is 9-point, how many lines will there be in three column inches?
2. If a cut is three inches wide, how many picas is it?
3. If the body type of a story is nine inches long and the story has a three-line 36-point type headline, what is the total length of story and headline in inches?
4. How many inches of type will eighteen lines of 8-point make?

The answers: 1. 24; 2. 18; 3. 10-1/2; 4. 2.*

* 1. Three times 72 points gives 216 points for three inches. Divide that by nine to get the number of lines. 2. Since an inch is 6 picas, three times six is the number of picas in three inches. Three lines of 36-point take 108 points. Seventy-two goes into that one-and-a-half times. So add one-and-a-half inches to nine to get the total. 4. Eight times 18 points gives 144 points. Divide by seventy-two to convert to inches.

A pica sometimes is called an *em*. An em technically is the square of the type. Thus, an em of 18-point type is 18 points square—18 points by 18 points. An em of 12-point is 12 points square. A 12-point em, of course, is also a pica wide, because it is one-sixth of an inch. (The em got its name from the letter M, which usually looks as wide as it is high.)

In the hot type process, where printers worked with lines of type called *slugs,* no computer figured out how long stories were. Most newspapers figured out that four typewritten lines would equal one inch of type. This measurement, however, was inexact and often a story was one-half inch too long or too short for the hole. Makeup editors then would throw away a sentence or two so a long story would fit. A too-short story would be lengthened by slipping thin pieces of lead between paragraphs or between lines of the first paragraph. This process is called *leading.* In cold type the same technique is used, except that a printer takes scissors and snips away a bit of a story to shorten it. If the story is too short, it can be cut into several pieces and each piece separated a tiny bit from the piece ahead of it. So instead of pieces of lead, white space is used. Even with cold type, however, this process still is called *leading.*

The well-edited paper does not use so much "lead" that white spaces noticeably fragment the stories. Neither does it stick meaningless little fillers into the bottom of the page to report, say, on the number of miles of paved road in Sumatra. A good staff can produce quality "shorts" which fill space better than remote facts.

Types of type

Quality newspapers usually spend much effort on the appearance of their pages. Part of this job is the selection of type. At the turn of the century body type was small and crowded. Headline faces were squeezed thin, and there was so much of this type that the reader could hardly make out what was printed. Gradually the 7-point body type was replaced by 7-1/2- or 8-point type, and that frequently gave way to 9. Today many papers use 9-1/2- or 10-point; or they may use 9-point on a 10-point slug—meaning that the type is 9-point with a point of leading. Similarly, the old all-capital headlines, with layers of decks, have given way to simple, neatly designed type faces and headline forms in caps and lower case that can be read at a glance. The result has been newspaper pages with white space for "air," body type that can be read without squinting, and heads that have clean beauty. (See figs. 9-8 and 9-9.)

The Linotypes

Even though Linotypes soon will become museum pieces, the beginning journalist ought to have some idea how they work. The Linotype machine has a set of keys much like a typewriter's. When operators tap keys, they release brass *matrices* (molds for letters) which fall into a row where together they become a single mold for a line of type.

1. 𝕿𝖊𝖝𝖙

2. Roman

2a. Oldstyle

2b. Modern

2c. Mixed

2d. Italic

3. Gothic

3a. Sans Serif

3b. Sq. Serif

4. Script, Cursives

5. NOVELTY

Fig. 9–4. Races of type (left). Five major subdivisions, or "races," of type are illustrated. Square serif type, here a subcategory (3b), is sometimes called a race. The fifth race, novelty, sometimes goes by "ornamented" or other names. Most newspaper usage is obviously in categories 2 and 3—roman and gothic. In common backshop parlance "italic" is not a subdivision of roman, as shown, but a slanted, or non-perpendicular, form of roman or gothic faces.

Reading Room Funds Given As Memorial

Tempo bold condensed

Heart, brain ills linked

Vogue

A New Moon View

Century

Pollution crisis in Pittsburgh ended by wind

Bodoni face is used by dozens of American newspapers.

Egyptians Get Town, Oil Field

U. S. SAYS ACCORD ON CURRENCY RIFT WITH PARIS IS SET

Latin style

Antismoking Campaigners See Progress

Century condensed

Fig. 9–5. Headline faces. Races of type (see fig. 9-4) are divided into families. Loosely called simply "faces," they often bear the name of the designer. This illustration shows some of the common headline faces in use. Note that some have serifs and some do not—that, therefore, they are roman or sans serif.

What of spaces? The operator taps keys to insert *space bands* between words and sometimes between letters. The space band is shaped like a wedge, and the thin end goes between the words or letters. When the line of brass "mats" is full, the operator presses a lever. Almost simultaneously, the space bands are pushed upward, making the line snug. This motion *justifies* the line—spaces the letters even both right and left with previous lines. (See fig. 9-6.) The molten metal then squeezes through a slot against the line of matrices and fills the little molds; it solidifies almost instantly into a *slug,* or line of cast type.

The inventor of the Linotype also had to solve the problem of getting the brass mats back in proper order at the top of the machine in their storage place, called a *magazine,* ready to be used again.

The problem was solved by notching each mat much as a door key is notched. The A's have one pattern of notches, the B's another. After each line is cast, the machine takes the used mats to the top and back of the machine where they move into a distributor bar. Hanging by their notches, they automatically ride along the bar, which is grooved in as many different patterns as there are channels to store them. When each reaches the right channel, it drops into the magazine.

Fig. 9–6. Line of matrices (right). A matrix is a small brass mold of a letter. The composing machine assembles these matrices and the longer space-bands (used for spacing between words) in a line, as shown here. It then holds them against a mold into which molten metal is forced and so casts a slug, the metal line of type used in printing. The letters cut into these matrices spell out right to left and upside-down to your eye, "The Linotype's Big Scheme of Simple Operation." The top line is roman; the lower line is italic.

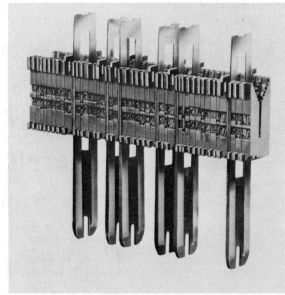

Fig. 9–7. Circulation of matrices. This phantom illustration shows each stage in the movement of the matrix through the Linotype machine. When keys are punched, the matrices drop into line in front of the operator, are cast (at left), and finally are redistributed to magazine (above right).

Pictures, collectively called *art*, are reproduced either by the conventional process of engraved metal or by an electronic method. In the conventional system acid etches hundreds of little grooves into a plate to produce an *engraving* with a pattern of minute raised dots. These print as tiny points on paper and so produce shades from dark to light. The darkest grays of the picture produce bigger black dots and smaller white areas among them; the lightest grays of course make very small dots against relatively large untouched areas. These massed points of black and white are so tiny, however, that the eye mixes them optically to form the illusion of continuous tones of gray. (See fig. 9-8.)

Art by letterpress

Fig. 9–8. Halftone screen. This picture, a corner of a large newspaper, employs a gross halftone screen. The dots are magnified for this illustration. To see how the eye blends the dot patterns used in the screens of ordinary engravings, look at the page from eight or ten feet away.

The dots are made by shooting the picture through a *screen,* which thus becomes a kind of measure in engraving. The best printing requires fine screens, which produce very tiny dots, and high quality paper. But coarser screens, with 55 or 65 lines of holes per square inch, are necessary to make cuts which will not blur ink on coarser paper. Newsprint typically requires engravings of 55-line or 65-line screen. Copyeditors ordinarily need not be concerned about screens, except to know that, should they try to introduce different ones, they will print differently, may cause disharmony, and perhaps may be worse than those habitually used.

An engraving is also called a *cut,* or *zinc,* and most pictures, made up of varying shades of gray, are called *halftones,* because they are neither solid black nor solid white. When no screen is used and when all background material is removed, only certain lines remain, as for cartoons, fashion drawings, or courtroom sketches. They are, of course, no dots. These *line cuts* produce black on white, or gray if the artist has put black lines close together. (See fig. 9-9.)

"I wish they'd let photographers cover these trials -- court artists are sloppy!"

Fig. 9-9. Art work. The artist is useful to the newspaper for humor and variety—and for pictures where photographers are barred. This is a line engraving, to be distinguished from a halftone (cf. fig. 9-8). Reprinted with permission of the **Los Angeles Times.**

Electronic engraving

Electronic engraving uses either a plastic or a metal sheet. The picture fits on a drum and revolves; an electric eye picks up varying light impulses from its varying shades. This eye controls a white-hot stylus above another drum carrying the plastic or metal. Following the shades in the picture, the stylus lightly gouges the plate to convert it to a cut (fig. 9-10). A similar machine with a V-shaped blade literally plows furrows of varying widths into a thin sheet of flexible metal. Parallel lines create the illusion of continuous gray tones.

It is difficult to stereotype the plastic cuts, so many papers simply leave room on the page plate and, with adhesive, stick the plastic to the curved metal just before the presses start to run. Since the metal plates can be stereotyped, they are more popular.

Fig. 9-10. Simple engraving. This Fairchild Scan-a-graver makes quick and inexpensive engravings. Photo or art copy put on the drum at right is engraved on the cylinder at left.

Pictures that appear in offset papers are handled a little different-ly. When the camera-ready copy of a page is being prepared, a piece of red or black paper the size of the picture is pasted onto the cam-era copy. The black or red paper is called a *window*. The camera-ready page is photographed and the window is removed from the page negative. The picture is photographed through a screen and the resulting negative is pasted into the place vacated by the window. The whole page negative then has light shined through it to make a page plate. The little dots for the picture appear on the page, just as they do in letterpress engraving. The quality, however, is better in offset pictures because the paper is smoother and shinier than paper used in letterpress operations.

Laserplates take pictures with no difficulty at all. The picture is simply pasted onto the full-page camera copy, along with the cold type, and the laser beams pick up the lights and darks just as they appear on the copy. The great advantage of laser platemaking is that two steps are eliminated.

The comic pages of newspapers pioneered color reproduction, but magazines long ago passed the dailies in use of color, and color television has contributed to making the newspaper's gray image look old-fashioned. The newspaper magazine of the trade, *Editor & Publisher*, has advised using more color, and it publishes an annual special issue on color to promote its use in dailies.

ROP (run-of-the-paper) color is that printed on the paper's regu-lar newsprint, in ads or editorial. SpectaColor and Hi-Fi are trade names for preprinted color, which can be on higher quality paper. "Preprint" refers to the use of a paper roll already carrying full-color printing by rotogravure, or sometimes by offset, which is fed into the presses and folded into the paper along with regular newsprint. Nine out of ten dailies now offer ROP color. More than half of these provide for *process color*, which uses three colors in ad-dition to black. The eye blends dots of the three primary colors as well as of black to make the different hues and shades of a conven-tional colored photograph or painting. More papers provide black plus only one or two colors, for *flat color*, also called *spot color*. Red alone, for example, will make a vivid headline or rule.

Process color printing requires a separate press plate for every basic color: red, yellow, and blue—with black the fourth color. Other colors are made by overlapping the basic colors. When two color plates are to print overlapping impressions, great care must be taken to get the plates in *register*. This means, for example, that the blue and yellow impressions must coincide exactly to produce a green. Otherwise the printed picture will appear fuzzy. For example, a register only slightly off on the picture of a woman's green dress can give the garment two distinct hemlines, one yellow and one blue.

Register is so difficult that once a color picture or ad is adjusted properly no editor should tinker with it. If, for example, a color pic-

Engraving for offset

Color

ture is running in columns one through four on page one in the first edition, it had better stay there in later editions—unless an editor is willing to argue with an outraged pressman, who probably has a large metal tool in his hand.

Figures show that color advertising has become more popular over the years. The increasing use of color by newspaper advertisers means that editors can add color more easily to news pages. A press prepared to print colored ads is prepared to print other items in color.

It is perhaps surprising that some of the biggest papers in the nation are not the biggest users of color. Neither the *Wall Street Journal* nor the *New York Times* is equipped to use color in regular news pages. The *Daily News* and the *Post* in New York were late in providing even spot color. But the *Miami Herald* and *Nashville Tennesseean,* as well as the *Milwaukee Journal* and *St. Petersburg Times,* each report use of up to two thousand color pictures a year. The number of papers using color photographs, however, has remained small because they are expensive and because many publishers are apathetic about color.

Format

In a William Allen White memorial lecture at the University of Kansas, Gardner Cowles, president of the *Des Moines Register* and *Tribune,* commented:

> On successful magazines, the art director ranks right below the top editor in importance and authority. He has a strong voice in helping decide how a story idea is to be developed. He suggests ways to give it maximum visual impact. He knows how to blend type and photographs so each helps the other. His responsibility is to make each page come alive and intrigue the reader. Newspapers need this kind of talent. Too few have it.

Whether or not it has a regular art director, a newspaper should certainly have expert advice if it plans to change format. The editors then will chip in with their advice, and its usefulness will depend on how much they have kept up on the printing arts. The better papers are ever alert to the possibility of improvement by typographic change. The best designed newspapers these days use the six-column format. Such papers are attractive and easy to read. *Newsday,* a Long Island tabloid, uses a magazine-style front page. The *Minneapolis Star* uses stark makeup, but it is easy to read. Other papers use a large part of the front page for a detailed index. All these papers keep aiming to design their products so they look better and are easier to read.

What of tomorrow?

Some prophets foresee the end of the newspaper itself, with composing rooms, printing, press rooms, and delivery systems gone. Instead, they believe that each home or business might have its own little news box, out of which would come a paper stream of printed news, editorials, feature stories, pictures, and advertisements. This strip would be perforated about every twelve inches so it could be torn into segments and bound to resemble a modern magazine. Operating all day long, and most of the night, the machine could handle both bulletin news and detailed news analyses. This instrument could provide all the speed of radio-television news plus the benefits of depth reporting that the better papers now provide. Like the newspaper, it would be a semi-permanent record; any reader could refer to it a week later or ten years later.

Fig. 9–11. Facsimile. The **Asahi Shimbun** of Tokyo has demonstrated a facsimile receiving set for the home. Like radio and TV, it offers the news rapidly and directly. It has the added feature of producing "hard copy" that the subscriber can mark, cut, save, or recopy.

Facsimile

This device is no dream. It has been possible since 1940, but no one has had both the nerve and the capital to try it commercially. The system, called *facsimile,* transmits the "newspaper" either by wire or radio. Japanese newspapers are now developing facsimile transmission to homes (fig. 9-11) after having used it to transmit a facsimile, or picture, of each page to a remote printing plant, where plates made from the pictures print the actual newspaper. The *Wall Street Journal* does the same thing by transmitting pictures of some of its editions to other printing plants. A half dozen newspapers in Europe have facsimile printing plants. *Correo della Sera* in Milan, for example, transmits pictures of each page to Rome, where a press runs off 30,000 copies or more for the Roman market.

Will facsimile into the home ever replace the conventional newspaper thrown upon millions of porches morning and night? Some think that if facsimile ever comes it will start with the business community. After all, financial needs stimulated the development of telegraphic news services and, indeed, of the newspaper itself. Many offices already have teleprinters bringing them news of the stock market and general business. Dow-Jones, owner of the *Wall Street Journal,* provides this service. But what if Dow-Jones decided to replace the noisy teleprinters, which spew out unattractive type copy, with facsimile? Instead of rolls of wire copy, there could be neat sheets of attractively printed material, including pictures, graphs, and illustrated economic analyses.

If facsimile were accepted in the business community, perhaps some daring newspaper owner would adopt it. Subscribers, given a little box for receiving the news, would pay a monthly bill for service, like a telephone bill. When the box ran out of paper, they could buy a fresh supply at the supermarket. The great capital outlay of starting such a system is, of course, the major factor blocking it. However, problems of delivery trucks in traffic and getting distributors are so severe that they make facsimile attractive.

Cable television

The other main possibility for a shift from the traditional newspaper is cable television. When many communities complained about poor television reception, someone hit on the idea of putting up a high tower to receive signals well and then connecting the tower to individual sets by wire. Some of these cable TV firms have permission from the Federal Communications Commission to make special broadcasts, such as high school football games or a hot city council meeting. These same cable TV companies sometimes show news direct from AP or UPI wires. The TV cameras focus on the copy, and the viewer simply reads the wire report from the screen. Some CATV systems, on a separate channel, have one-paragraph news items appearing on the screen twenty-four hours a day.

This is already a crude sort of "electronic newspaper," of course, but there is no technical reason why it could not become sophisticated. Wire copy could be typed in a neat, appealing form. Pictures could be interspersed with the text. Editorials, advertising, and comics could appear on the screen. This kind of transmission would require that the subscriber be present to "read" the news. But a paper print could be made of the newscast by having some attachment on the television set. Or the telecast could be taped and householders could run the tape through an attachment on their sets whenever they wanted to review the news.

An experiment in England tested this kind of TV news transmission, and it was considered a technical success. It was dubious, however, if it would do as well commercially, for the viewer would have to buy equipment costing at least $100, purchase special paper, and pay a fee for the service.

Around 1970 a few American publishers were paying modest attention to this kind of CATV operation. Interest has waned since, as publishers got wrapped up in the new technology and as CATV failed to live up to its potential.

Big-city publishers may have considered facsimile and CATV because their delivery problems are so severe. In New York it is close to impossible to get trucks through city streets to deliver an afternoon newspaper. That is why the *New York Post* is the only afternoon paper left there. The areas around Manhattan are not so bad for delivery, but acute difficulties exist. Chicago also has terrible distribution problems, accounting in part for the *Chicago Daily News* being the only full-fledged afternoon survivor. The *Chicago Tribune* publishes more or less around the clock, but its traditional publication time is morning.

Satellite printing plants, pioneered by the big Japanese dailies, have reduced distribution problems. The *Los Angeles Times* has a satellite plant, without facsimile, in Orange County, sixty miles south of the city. The *Detroit News* built an all-electronic plant twenty-three miles northwest of its downtown plant. Reporters and editors work downtown and pipe copy via computers to both city and suburban plants. The *New York Times* plans a satellite facsimile plant in New Jersey.

All these changes brought about by the new technology have come to pass because publishers could seize upon inventions, such as the computer and radio transmission, and adapt them to newspaper use. But some firms seek to produce even more startling changes in printing. They may come up with devices that will make what we call the new technology the old technology. The inventions may be so innovative, and the output of the new equipment so inexpensive, that the change will sweep the country, as television did in the late 1940s and the computer did in the last twenty years.

Journalism students of today are bound to be plunged into changes. This does not mean that they will have to learn the complexities of new equipment any more than automobile drivers have to know how to fix the newest car. Journalists, like car drivers, need a basic knowledge of what the machines can do. And they must consider not only how the machines can work for them, but how they can work in the best interests of the public.

The basics of graphic arts will be important to any conceivable graphic presentation of the future. We have known students who saw no practical use for learning about type and layout, but on the job the background has proved useful in unexpected ways—like making up printed blurbs for TV commercials! Without such knowledge and a continuing interest in the effects of technical change, a copyeditor will fall behind in the task of efficiently bringing the news to the community.

10 Picture editing

"The picture magazines, *Life* and *Look,* are dead. Not enough people wanted to look at pictures," the cynic might say. "People can see pictures on television twenty hours a day. Why should a newspaper bother with pictures?"

It's not a frivolous question, for pictures are not the novelty they once were. Television gives us millions of sports images and takes us into committee hearings or even school board meetings. Yet readers still want visual material in their newspapers to help them understand, just as viewers find words on their TV screens help them grasp the news.

TV competition, however, forces newspapers to be fresh and innovative in their visual reports, making sure that photographs complement what is seen on television. It is essential today that pictures add to the readers' understanding of an event or an issue. This means that photographers must have proper equipment and adequate time to get quality pictures. It also means that photographers, reporters, artists, and editors must join to figure how words and pictures can be blended into one layout to inform the reader.

Management

The person who supervises photography on a newspaper, oddly enough, is called the picture editor or the photo editor or the chief photographer. Only a minority of American newspapers have a staff member who spends most of the day editing pictures. The job usually is done on a piecemeal basis by a city editor, a copyeditor, or a photographer. On a small paper the chief photographer takes all the pictures, for no one else on the staff knows how. These staff limitations too often mean that picture editing is treated carelessly or casually. Pictures are not selected thoughtfully, and photographers receive only the sketchiest direction about the purpose of the picture and its possible use. Pictures on such papers tend to be typographical devices to relieve the monotony of a page of print.

Even on papers where there is no picture editor, staffers can learn to reject ordinary pictures, to crop good ones to make them better, and to push photographers to do more than line up a few people and snap the shutter. After some practice and study, almost anyone with a good news sense can sort through a dozen pictures to choose the best two or three, rejecting the routine shots and picking those with originality. Also, the staffer can learn to say, "Not one of these pictures is much good." In such cases photographers must be encouraged to seek different angles, to avoid contrivances like phony props, and to *wait* until a good picture is possible.

While most papers have several staffers dabbling as picture editors, the biggest newspapers may each have a full-time person for the job. These editors may or may not be photographers, but they must have a full understanding of photographic problems and how pictures can best be fitted into a newspaper.

More than any other editor, this person must deal several times a day with all the paper's other editors. Even insiders forget how highly departmentalized the news operation is. The various subeditors hardly confer at all, for there is no need to. The photo editor, however, must talk frequently to the sports, telegraph, city, state and women's editors—even once in a while to the editor of the editorial page. Each of those editors needs pictures and the photo editor must provide them.

At the least pretentious, picture editors are little more than technicians and a liaison between the other editors and the photographers. They pass on assignments, decide a certain amount of policy, select pictures, and crop and size pictures. This may lead to some organizational efficiency, and it is better than having no photo editor, but such a system usually produces routine, uncreative photographs.

Harold Buell, director of photography for the Associated Press, insists that a good photo editor "must have a voice" in how the picture is used if photographers are inspired to do their best work. He means that the photo editor must be able to advise news editors to use one picture, instead of another, to crop in a certain way, and to make the picture five columns, perhaps, rather than three. Obviously, such an editor should be able to explain *why* the pictures need the recommended treatment. Otherwise, Buell says, the photo editor merely runs errands, handling pictures the way a news editor ordered.

The main point of naming a picture editor is to have a person who "thinks pictures" and who has the authority to get the best photographs for the paper. There are various gradations of organization and power to permit this. The papers with the best pictures are likely to have an editor who plans picture coverage, assigns photographers and has authority to hire and fire them, selects pictures or at least has considerable role in selection, makes up a picture page, and directs the artists. The more important the picture editor, the more the job requires managerial skills: maintaining good human relations as well as a workable system for fast production.

Robert Kerns of the Syracuse University School of Journalism recalls that as picture editor for the *Cedar Rapids* (Iowa) *Gazette,* he edited (that is, selected) the wirephotos and distributed them to the various news departments. He worked next to the city desk, assigned photographers, created feature ideas, and made up the picture page, including the writing of heads and cutlines. Kerns, who collaborated on the book *Creative News Photography,* says that as "intermediary between the executives and the photographers" he could appreciate the problems and demands of both groups. "Every editor has the right to order what he wants," says Kerns, who is a photographer, "but he ought to give the photographer the right to interpret the assignment his own way, and then look at whatever he brings back."

Early in his career, Edmund C. Arnold, the typographic expert who wrote *Functional Newspaper Design* and several other books on graphic arts, was hired as picture editor of the *Saginaw* (Mich.) *News* to revamp its photo coverage. The system he devised had Arnold deciding which picture went on every page, except that he consulted with the news editor on front page pictures. Even Arnold says that the method was the wrong way to do it, because it gave the photo editor too much power, but in this case "it worked." The goal on any paper should be to have a person who respects good pictures in charge of photography. Other editors may overrule the choices of the photo editor, of course, but only after a brief and perhaps spirited defense by the photo editor.

Arnold, it should be added, thinks a picture editor should not be a photographer. "The picture editor should have a photographic background but not be a working photographer," he says. "He gets intrigued with the technical victories—whether it was overdeveloped or underdeveloped, and whether he had to hang by his toes to take it—and that sways his judgment."

Many editors would disagree with Arnold, of course, possibly because so many of them are photographers as well as photo editors.

How it's done

One of the biggest users of pictures is the *Chicago Tribune,* one of the most improved papers in the nation. The newspaper runs eight editions, nearly around the clock, and uses dozens of pictures each day. Only a few pictures appear in every edition.

Charles Scott, a veteran photographer who has taught at Ohio University, is the editor in charge of the *Tribune's* fifty-four person staff. Scott has six assistant photo editors, so someone is directing operations at all times. Thirty-five people are photographers and nine people work in the photo lab.

All pictures—wirephotos, staff, or free lance—go to the picture editor. The staff handles the layout of a daily picture page, a fixture at the *Tribune,* although a good many other papers have dropped daily picture pages. Many papers think a full page of pictures does not draw enough readership unless there is a "photographic essay" on a particular social problem.

Scott considers himself a motivator. He praises the work of photographers, and sometimes chides them privately. He encourages them to attend workshops or short courses at company expense. He makes sure they have the best equipment, plenty of film, and time enough to get good pictures. And he tries to tell photographers exactly what he wants, although he admits that a few staffers can simply be told to "get some pictures" and they will come back with beauties.

The task of picking the right photographer for a special assignment also concerns Scott. A woman photographer who was raised on a farm always asks to cover livestock exhibitions and he always grants her wish. She does better work there than anyone else would. When Scott wanted to film a Ku Klux Klan rally in Indiana, he had to select the photographer with care. The wrong person might botch the assignment, wasting a day's work and travel expenses. The person chosen was deliberate, cautious, and patient. He didn't even take a picture until he had been at the rally several hours, getting Klan members relaxed about him and, in a way, unaware that a stranger was among them. The photographer got startling results.

One of Scott's delights with his job is that top editors at the paper like pictures and demand good ones. "They overrule me once in a while," Scott says, "but I always feel they have listened to my arguments—they give me a fair shake." In addition, management lets him give bonuses or pay increases to the best photographers.

When covering a major event, Scott deploys the staff to make sure that the paper has hundreds of pictures to choose from. As an example, when the President of the United States came to town, Scott assigned eighteen photographers. Written directions, given to each, looked like this:

5:35 p. m. President arrives at O'Hare
                    Casper cover,
                    return to office
                    with pix.

5:40 Motorcade heads downtown
                    Hardy, Bona and
                    Leeds cover from
                    Division St. Overpass.

There were lots more, of course, but it shows how meticulously the event was covered.

Every conceivable piece of equipment is provided to help the photographers. Staff cars are equipped with two-way radios. Each photographer carries a telephone paging device and, where necessary, staffers use walkie-talkies.

Scott says that his photographers, first of all, "should be journalists. They have to understand how words and pictures go together." Technical skill comes in second place, he adds, and the merger of journalism and photographic ability make a photojournalist. Such a person is able, with pictures, to communicate—to tell a story dramatically.

The *Tribune* puts a lot of emphasis on cropping pictures, Scott says, to get rid of non-essentials. An artist helps remove some clutter in pictures or makes certain parts more vivid. Once cropped, *Tribune* photos are made reasonably big because, Scott adds, "size gives them impact." He notes quickly, however, that bad pictures are not improved by making them big. "That way you just have big, bad ones," he says.

In nearly all cases the *Tribune* tries to get people in pictures because news usually concerns people. Photos omit people only when it would be ridiculous to put them in. A picture of a chemical plant whose fumes have killed trees, for example, probably would not involve people.

Not many newspapers can afford the *Tribune's* operation. Medium-sized newspapers have fewer people working in the entire newsroom than the *Tribune* has in photo. Any paper, however, can borrow from the best. So even the small paper, with one photographer, can buy good equipment and lots of film and can give that one person time enough to get more than the routine shot. The photographer can be sent to a short course at company expense. Pictures can be chosen with care, cropped with discretion, and made big enough so the reader does not have to squint.

(Cropping can be an art in itself. See fig. 10-1 and discussion of this subject later in chapter 10.)

The art of quality

Good picture editing starts with high quality photos, which means technical excellence of the negative and superior visualization of the content. Every paper has to print many mediocre pictures and a few poor ones. A family brings in a tinted photograph on soft mat paper to go with an obituary; or a reporter persuades the parents of a kidnapped child to let the paper release a badly-lighted little snapshot of the victim. Such pictures fall short of photographic excellence in several respects, yet they will be published, perhaps even in large sizes. Sometimes engraving departments can deliver cuts of fine quality from them, often even better than the original (for example, by improving contrast). Most pictures, however, lose quality by going through the engraving and printing processes. Newsprint is poor paper for photographic reproduction.

Nevertheless, newspaper photographs usually should be big, shiny-surfaced, and sharp. They are printed in large sizes—typically eight by ten inches, though sometimes larger—on glossy paper. They are well-lighted, and they show contrast. The uniform greys of a flat photo make it uninteresting. There must be good definition of tones. (A picture can have too much contrast; in reproductions the

Fig. 10—1. A cropped picture. Normally, crop marks appear only in the margins.

blacks go too black with clots of ink, and the whites lose detail.) Usually the newspaper photo is in sharp focus and freezes motion.

A prime requisite of a quality photograph is a center of interest, the point of the picture. It is like the lead of a news story. The photographer eliminates extraneous details so the viewer's eye goes right to the point of the picture. If the photographer doesn't crop away distracting non-essentials, the picture editor must.

A definite point of view helps the reader understand the picture's significance. The routine photograph is often shot straight on at eye height. For a fresh approach, the photographer may crouch for a low angle—or go up a ladder for a high one—or walk around somewhere to the side to get an unusual viewpoint. "Photo-letters," a booklet published by the newsphoto committee of the Associated Press Managing Editors Association, illustrates this point with the contrast of two pictures on a stock theme: One is the usual shot of a man giving a plaque to another, and the other, with a rather low angle, shows the winner grinning up on his framed certificate, which has been hoisted to his shoulder.

When a President was on the White House lawn signing a bill for more parks, a photographer climbed a tree and shot the scene through the leaves. Both of these examples involve "record" pictures and the photographers had to figure out ways to escape the monotony of the routine record shot.

News photographers sometimes strive for artistic patterns in their pictures. These may be rows of bleachers or bottles, lines of fence posts or windows. But highly-patterned backgrounds that detract from the focal point of interest are avoided. Yet the best photo artist, seeking aesthetic results, sometimes violates tradition. Fuzziness, at least of some parts of a photo, may create a mood. Since stopping the action can mean a dull sports picture, there may be more drama in the blur of a moving arm or leg, and racing cars with lines of motion may at once seem to whiz and be beautiful. It is difficult to do these well. If a blur picture is less than outstanding it is better to use a plain conventional shot.

Nearly all photographers these days find that their equipment and film are so good that they can use existing light for most pictures. Light appears on faces and objects in a way that seems natural. Electronic flash, still useful on occasion, sometimes gives a harsh, flat light that makes some pictures look slightly unnatural.

Fig. 10–2. Unusual framing. The low angle uses the feet of the victim as a frame which, with striking lighting, makes a dramatic photo (taken by Neal Boenzi of the **New York Times**).

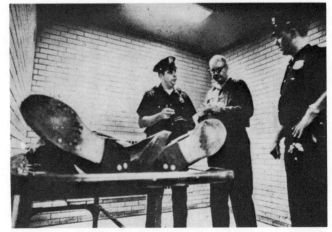

Besides a strong center of interest and a different point of view, good photographers try for appropriate special effects. For example, the illusion of depth comes from using an angle which puts a pertinent subject in the foreground—shooting down a seminar table over the shoulder of a teacher, for example, or including a fireman with hose at the edge of the picture of a building fire. This effort is similar to another useful approach, "framing." Most commonly the frame is produced with a doorway, an arch, or a tree trunk at the edge of the picture (but see fig. 10-2). "Photo-letters" approvingly reproduces two "framed" pictures, one showing a library dedication scene framed by books on the shelves, and the other a church dignitary photographed through a cross-shaped hole in concrete blocks. But once done the gimmick is an instant cliche and should be avoided for a couple of decades.

Essentials of good pictures

Beyond the quality of the technician and the artistry of a creative cameraman, what does the picture editor hope for in the way of content? "The good news picture has two priceless ingredients," writes Dick Strobel, retired AP newsphoto editor at Los Angeles. "It tells a story. It contains action."

That dictum perhaps focuses too much attention on the melodramatic, unless *action* is broadly interpreted to mean something much more than just the halfback leaping to catch a pass. But Strobel's words describe the content of most good newspaper pictures. They show people, people doing something. Their actions tell the story that editors want to put across.

Surprisingly, Strobel includes thinking in his definition of action. A study of many news photographs, he says, will show two things: Almost all are made with available light and almost all show people with minds at work. "The subject must be made to think, to react to stimuli while ignoring the camera," he says. "When this is done, the photographer actually *can* photograph the mind at work, and an eye-arresting picture is the result."

Almost all picture people would agree with *Tribune* picture editor Charles Scott that pictures without people are dead. Of course there are some good ones with no human face or form, ranging from the great natural disaster to the beautiful lake at dawn, but even these have a kind of human interest. They would have no place in the paper if their terror or beauty did not appeal to the emotions of people. At least nine out of ten published newspaper pictures show people or animals or both. Of the eighty-one illustrative pictures in "Photo-letters," seventy-four show people. Three others are of animal-life—a lonely cat, gulls in sea spray, a waiting spider. Thus only four show no person or animal, but three of these stand as art pictures—frosty telephone wires; shining leaves above an old barn; a school bus with a plume of dust. The fourth is a junk yard, on which the editors comment, "Ugh!"

As in the theater, props are important to many news pictures. The photo of a man with a telephone may be hackneyed, but it is somewhat better than the "mug shot" of a person staring into the cameras. Yet best of all would be a photo portrait that seems to tell the reader a bit of the persons' character—as though the reader had a chance to be in the person's presence.

So good photographers take a little time, waiting for their subjects to fiddle, without encouragement, with a pen, a typewriter, or a baseball. Then the props will seem natural.

Some of the worst photographic sins occur when props become too obvious. The use of a catsup bottle, a pointer, a catcher's mask, a Japanese fan could result in a contrived picture that most readers would spot as a semi-fake. Props already in use by the photographic subjects, however, can help produce excellent pictures. The feature shot of a little girl trying on hats before a mirror, for example, or the picture of an old man trudging home from the river, carrying one fish, can have real impact. The devices are not really props, and so their use looks natural.

The photographer, to turn out quality work, avoids gimmickry and corn, such as a politician wearing a cowboy hat or drinking milk from a huge bowl. The routine shot of a routine action, such as the signing of a bill, should be forsaken. So should clichés like handshaking (sometimes called "grin and grab"), award presentations, ribbon-cutting, gavel-passing, and desk-sitting. Worst of all is the line-up, where three or four face the camera and say "cheese." The picture editor must take a pledge never to give assignments that result in corn, routine pictures, or clichés.

A picture editor learns to evaluate photographs as a news editor learns to judge stories—by experience and by observing how other journalists operate. Some pictures are obviously great, others blatantly dull. But the majority of pictures are in between, and only a fraction of them can be used. Those chosen will depend on the day's needs and the editor's personal tastes.

Judging pictures

Broadly speaking, most newspaper pictures fit one of two categories: news or feature. Because papers use a mixture of news stories and feature materials, they usually want both types of photos.

As indicated already, the choice is easy where the picture portrays a great news event dramatically. Perhaps the only difficulty will be in choosing which of several good shots does the job the best. Aside from the size of the event, the other factors of news judgment, such as proximity of the news and timeliness, come into play in picture selection.

In addition to the unusual news photo which can stand alone if necessary because of its significance, many pictures will be used in tandem with stories to supplement the words. They clarify the news account or make it more interesting. Among these are not only the more compelling shots of riot violence and earthquake damage but also photos of the President meeting a delegation, a labor leader speaking, and a demonstrator painting a protest sign.

Even papers much smaller than the *New York Times* will use some pictures of low impact simply because they are a part of the historic record—the chiefs of two European nations conferring, the governor signing a law, the mayoral candidates casting their ballots.

As the news editor does, the picture editor chooses these news photos because, like news, they contribute to portrayal of current information which interests readers. The persons who select pictures are under the same pressures as news evaluators—to choose what will titillate readers and presumably raise circulation; what fits newspaper traditions and fulfills reader expectations (that handshaking picture again), or what suits their own tastes or whims. The good picture editor of course minimizes the effect of these pressures and selects news pictures that communicate the events most effectively. That means few "record" pictures.

Feature pictures are different. From the standpoint of hard news values, they would not be given valuable space. But pictures which are simply interesting as pictures, with minimal news values, primarily have the same purpose as comic strips—entertainment.

Most of them, like the best of feature stories, have human in-terest—the baby in a puddle on a hot day, the beauties getting ready for the contest, the puppy with a bandaged nose. Picture editors should take pains in such photographs to avoid the superficial and the commonplace, unless the commonplace subject has been over-looked by almost everyone.

European newspapers do not use many good news pictures. The better European papers, however, often print a different type of feature picture, the artistic photograph, and some American dailies are tending to use more of these. Art studies are of course familiar in a few Sunday art sections. But in the news pages too the imaginative picture editor may include well-composed pictures of yachts tied at local docks, of nearby cornfields soft with haze, of a skyline at dawn, or of the cow and kitten wending toward a barn north of town. As the popularity of cameras continues to mount, readers are becoming more sophisticated about pictures and more interested in outstanding photographs related to human life.

The good picture editor also tries to develop picture stories. The photographs in these probably combine news and feature elements. The pictures should have individual feature or artistic value and fit together to tell a story.

By reading newspaper studies, the picture editor can determine what kinds of subjects are of greatest interest to readers. However, just as newspapers cannot finally be edited by polls, pictures cannot be selected by surveys. Ultimately, picture editors have to under-stand intuitively what will interest readers. What will interest editors will probably interest subscribers. If they exclaim, "Wow!" about a photo, it probably means that the reader too will feel it has "im-pact." So photo editors must learn to understand themselves. Each editor will naturally have some enthusiasms, but they should not become hobby horses. Or an editor may temper dislike of a certain type of picture because experience has shown that readers react favorably to it. Editors give readers "what they want" if, in good conscience, they can; but they usually select what their judgment says is the best photography.

Ethics of illustration

The tension between what readers want and what they should have suggests the problems in ethics which the picture editor also confronts in making selections. Readers may want the macabre or near-pornographic photo, yet may criticize the paper that uses photographs in bad taste. The picture editor must sometimes walk the hazy, wiggling line between the acceptable and unacceptable.

Pictures of horror have traditionally been prohibited in good newspapers. Any picture of a corpse is normally taboo, but televi-sion films of wars and disasters have softened this rule.

Pictures of a woman and a child falling from a Boston building brought considerable wrath from some readers. Firefighters had worked close to a fire escape and were about to take people down a ladder to safety. Seconds before the rescue, the fire escape collapsed. Stanley Forman, a *Boston Herald-American* photographer, took pictures of the falling people. The woman was killed and the child was hurt. The pictures, distributed by Associated Press, were used widely. Some readers were horrified and said so. Editors rechecked their judgment, decided it was a close decision but that they probably were correct in running such a dramatic picture. Harold Buell, AP's photo editor, said, "You're cursed if you do, and cursed for manipulating the news if you don't."

Nora Ephron, a media critic who wrote on the subject in *Esquire,* noted that no one would have protested if the woman had survived. She maintained the pictures "deserved to be published because they are great pictures, breathtaking pictures, of something that happened. That they disturb readers is exactly as it should be. That's why photojournalism is often more powerful than written journalism."

The pictures contributed to reform, however, for two weeks later the Boston mayor hired 100 more building and fire inspectors. Previously, only seven people routinely checked fire escapes.

The Food and Agriculture Organization of the United Nations had a series of pictures of starving children but held back some because they were "too rough" to go with a newspaper series. When *Editor & Publisher* printed some, editors split, some arguing they could be printed. Especially debated was one of a naked baby, emaciated as a baby bird, which the *Journalists' World* in Brussels used in sponsoring an essay contest under the head "Too Gruesome for Use?" The winner, arguing for use of the picture, asserted: "People must face it—hunger has never had a pretty face."

The sexy shot of a woman in a bikini has a long tradition in American newspapers, but the tradition is coming to an end. Women staffers have led the assault against these pictures, saying something like, "Well, once again you indicate that women are only sex objects—and that a woman without a thirty-six-inch bust is really worthless. Besides, why engrave another one? This picture you have today looks just like the one you ran last week!" Startled male editors may laugh self-consciously or remark that the women in the office don't appreciate true art, but they are now leaving out most of the bikini shots. There is another reason for fewer flesh pictures. Newspapers aiming to raise standards realize that cheesecake cheapens the paper and diverts readers from the serious news.

Devoting a whole page to pictures has long been popular with daily newspapers. The picture page gives the editor a chance to print excellent photographs which can't be squeezed into other pages. Here he puts six to eight photos in varied sizes, the subjects ranging from the gurgling baby to the railroad wreck.

Vincent S. Jones, a Gannett executive, has long pioneered for a

Picture pages and stories

better use of this space. He argues that this variety page or half-page, which just grew, needs planning to be effective. A conglomeration of pictures may stop readers, he says, but will it hold them? Jones says that newspapers used to start all their big stories on page one, but they discovered the jumps to arid inside pages went unread. Using the best pictures all on a single page repeats this error. Usually, he contends, pictures are most effective if they run with, and complement, the news they illustrate.

His suggestion is a picture page made up of related photographs on the same subject, like the series of the picture story. Then the picture page really becomes a display case for the picture story. Limiting the number of photos to four or five also makes a better picture page when one is used.

Individual pictures may tell a story, as we have seen. It may be a feature—the puppy covertly munching hot dogs beside the meat counter. Or it may be a news photo—the hard-jawed policeman as he aims a gun at a fleeing robbery suspect.

However, the term "picture story" usually refers to a series of pictures which together convey the event. The neophyte may mistakenly think that any collection of pictures on the same subject is a picture story. Sometimes such a collection can make a story—all the striking photographs of an Alpine avalanche, for example, put together so that the reader sees it as a unity. But if neither the photographer nor the picture editor strives for unity, the result will probably not be a story but confusion.

Typically, the photographer imposes potential unity on several pictures by selecting a common subject, a person, more often than not. *Time* tells a complicated story in terms of a personality pictured on its cover; newspapers often use the case study approach, as when they explain a new medical plan in terms of how it has worked for one elderly couple. So the photographer may choose one person in telling the story—the actress as she prepares for a new play, or the poverty worker moving among slum tragedies.

The photographer must take pains to see that the person appears in different poses so the pictures will not all look alike. Most readers can recall picture stories which use six or eight monotonous photographs to tell the tale when one or two would do. A greater danger for both photographer and picture editor is the ethical one of distortion. Most stories are bigger than one person; the news of a week-long social workers' convention may be interesting if told partly with pictures of the new president drinking coffee, politicking with one voting bloc, and listening to a dissenter. This is why words are so important. Pictures *and* words can convey facts, moods, attitudes, and impressions to readers.

Photojournalists may tell the story in a simple chronology—a strip of pictures—or they may want to try a magazine format with varied sizes, unusual cropping, and artistic arrangements. Creating a fine picture story can be one of the most creative and exciting parts of the editor's job.

American newspapers get more of their photos from the wire services than any other source. Best known to the ordinary reader is the Wirephoto, a glossy picture which arrives in a flow organized by the Associated Press, sometimes on the new *Laserphoto,* (see chapter 7). Like AP news, scores of these pictures come over the wire from various AP members and bureaus each day. UPI also has Unifax II which rolls a steady stream of quality photographs into the newsroom.

The news services also provide newspapers with mailed packets of glossy photos, and they are not alone. The *Editor & Publisher Yearbook* lists twenty-six specialized agencies where editors can get pictures, as well as many syndicates which handle photos among other materials. Many of these provide pictures in special categories. Religious News Service, for example, has about 900 photo correspondents around the world who channel pictures to the New York photo editor and to 100 daily newspapers as well as to several religious magazines. The pictures may be hard news, as of a clerical protest, but they may be inspirational or seasonal (Easter and Christmas). As with other services, editors may get the entire service for a weekly rate based on circulation, see all RNS pictures and pay for those wanted, or buy individual pictures by request.

A few letterpress papers also can get photos and illustrations in the form of *mats.* Like stereotype mats used in newspaper printing, these are molds made by pressing engravings on a pulpy cardboard, and the purchasing paper simply has to cast them. A shortcoming of both mailed mats and photos is that they lag seriously behind the news, and television already is beating the newspaper pictorially. However, mail is good for feature illustrations. Such mats are useless in offset production.

A close competitor of agency pictures, at least on the bigger papers, is the local photographic staff. Syndicated photographs cost less than ones made by the paper, but of course they can't cover local events. With a single ambitious photographer and a miniature dark room, a paper can have a number of good local pictures for every issue.

In the day of the semi-automatic camera, some newspapers use reporters as photographers. But the idea of the photo-reporter has never really caught on. A major reason is that many editors contend that a person can't report *and* photograph well. Many reporters and photographers will agree. Yet some picture editors feel that a reporter who is out on a story might as well have a camera along and shoot some pictures. The *Beverly* (Mass.) *Times,* for example, has experimented with a fixed-focus, automatic-exposure camera using half a frame of 35 mm. film. Reporters can simply shoot away with fast film, getting pictures which are sharp from six feet to infinity. In a little over a year the paper published about one in four of 3,000 pictures made by reporters. Photographs taken by reporters may be

Sources of photos

Agencies

Local sources

adequate, but they rarely are a substitute for pictures taken by a full-fledged photographer using first-rate equipment. Papers seeking quality pictures and reporting will use specialists for each field.

Free-lance photographers place some pictures with newspapers, especially their magazine sections. Some of the most famous news photographs have been taken by amateurs who just happened to be on the spot. Though there would be headaches of organization, newspapers might buy more pictures from free-lances and amateurs.

Some other local pictures are provided by news sources. Families may supply photographs for the obituaries. Brides bring in their pictures for wedding announcements. Sometimes a reporter wangles a portrait from the family of a victim or a suspect. The picture editor must have a good system to return borrowed pictures. Some of this trouble can be avoided if the news subject comes into the paper's studio for a picture. While there is the ever-present danger of stilted photography, this plan works well for such things as awards and some society pictures.

Public relations sources provide many more newspaper pictures than readers realize or most editors would admit. Most of those glamour pictures come from press agents of screen and television celebrities. Photographs in the women's section that feature new fashions, modern interiors, and luscious foods are usually from publicity sources. Local companies provide varied pictures for the business pages. And as publicity workshops never tire of pointing out, the good photograph from the publicity chairman of even the P.T.A. or hobby group may make the paper. Editors should accept such pictures, however, only if they show quality and genuine news value. Most public relations pictures are distributed for one purpose: advertising. In that case, public relations people should be directed to another newspaper department.

The daily newspaper has one other important source of pictures —its own library, the one-time "morgue." File folders should be established for many subjects and persons that reappear in the news. Many pictures used in the paper, and some which are not used, should be saved, with careful identification. Bigger letterpress newspapers also keep in small envelopes the thin metal cuts of potentially reusable pictures. From its files of glossies and cuts, the newspaper can rush into print photographs of newsworthy people when they speak, win, lose, get into trouble, or die. (Only careless editors use old pictures which are obviously ten or twenty years old; however, there are stories—such as the death of a once-prominent tycoon—when an old picture is better than none, but then the date of the photo should be indicated.)

Picture editors usually have two to twenty times as many photographs as they can use. The task is to pick the best without making some staffers feel unneeded. Photographers are a proud bunch and an editor must try to keep them alert and confident. So editors should ask for picture story ideas and encourage photographers to go out to get the story. From the dozens of prints available, editors then must select, organize, and crop until the pictures tell the story.

Picture editors mark the photos for engravers. They crop pictures to eliminate useless material and *size* a picture to fit a desired page. The sizing problem changes with cropping, obviously, and vice versa.

Cropping and sizing

Many pictures require little or no cropping, because the photographer has focused on the essentials. The experienced editor, however, may wish to crop severely, cutting out anything that seems to detract from the point of the picture. Perhaps only half or even a quarter of the picture will remain.

Cropping

Editors sometimes crop and size in relation to the makeup design, which may require a long one-column cut or a more horizontal picture three columns wide. Usually, the picture is cropped to attain the best photographic result and the makeup is adjusted accordingly. So editors cut out busy backgrounds, superfluous people and objects, and other distractions "to bring the picture out of the photograph." Cropping should accentuate the focus of interest—the part of the picture that catches the eye. See fig. 10-3 and 10-4.

Fig. 10-3. Cropping dramatically close. The high angle in this straight print of the land speed record holder suggests a way to make the picture dynamic.

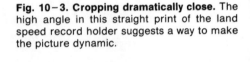

Fig. 10-4. The result. The crop brings the reader face to face with the record setter and suggests the drama of the speed trial.

Advice on cropping may sometimes seem inconsistent, but the wise editor follows the rules that will make the picture most effective. Editors crop ruthlessly, cutting off the backs of heads and bodies from the waist down, and letting imagination supply the missing portions. Yet they should try to retain the essential composition of a good picture. And they should crop only when it is necessary to improve the picture. Bob Kerns suggests cropping to emphasize dominant points of interest (figs. 10-3 and 10-4). Sometimes cropping should be absolutely avoided. Fig. 10-5 tells the story that almost no one showed up at a professional football game when most of the players were on strike. To crop it, as in fig. 10-6, is to destroy it.

Fig. 10–5. No cropping. The lone fan in the stands shows that almost no one showed up for the game.

Fig. 10–6. Cropping out the story. Cropped this way, the picture reveals only a man sitting someplace, possibly watching birds.

As they crop, editors should keep these other pointers in mind:

—Look for other than the "obvious" crop, in order to get results out of the routine.
—In head and shoulder shots, leave a bit of space on the side toward which a person faces.
—Similarly, emphasize the action by leaving space before the thrust of an action, whether a racing car or jumping basketball player.
—Avoid spoiling a hair style or cutting off legs at the ankle.
—Keep vertical lines vertical.
—Retain horizons for perspective, but be sure they are horizontal.
—Avoid fancy and irregular shapes, unless there's a strong reason for them.
—Experiment.

To visualize the picture when cropped, picture editors often frame different portions of the photograph with a rectangle formed between their extended thumbs and forefingers. The same framing can be done with greater precision if they cut *cropping L's* from cardboard—two L-shaped tools which they can place like an adjustable picture frame on the face of the photo. L's calibrated in inches will speed up the estimates for the sizing process.

There is no problem of sizing or scaling if the editor simply crops out of the picture an area exactly the size of the required cut; that is, for example, it is no problem to mark an area a column wide and three inches deep. But rarely does the picture fit engraving needs so exactly.

Sizing

Most newspaper pictures are reduced in the engraving process, although from time to time a picture is enlarged. Both height and width are altered in the change, of course, just as television reduces both dimensions in shifting from a twenty-one inch screen to a twelve-inch screen. The news desk needs to know the dimensions of the cut long before it is made, so the picture and stories can be dummied. It makes a lot of difference in dummying whether the "cut" is three columns by eight inches or two columns by five. Since three of the four dimensions involved are known, it is fairly easy to figure out the fourth.

Assume that a picture is four inches wide and three inches deep. It is to be enlarged into a cut three columns wide, or six inches. The old depth, three inches, is compared to the depth of the cut, which is unknown. A simple equation gives the answer

$$\frac{\text{width of picture}}{\text{depth of picture}} = \frac{\text{width of cut}}{\text{depth of cut}} \qquad \frac{4}{3} = \frac{6}{x}$$

So $4x = 18$, and the cut will be 4-1/2 inches deep.

Or let's assume we have a ten by eight horizontal photo we want to use, cropped full, and that we want to reduce it to a cut five inches wide. How high will the cut be? The mathematically-oriented may see at once that the answer is four inches. But here is the method:

$$\frac{10}{8} = \frac{5}{X}$$

$$10 \times X = 5 \times 8$$

$$X = \frac{40}{10} = 4 \text{ inches}$$

Marking

When editors decide just how they want the photo cropped, they put *crop marks* on its face with a grease pencil. The mark is simply a line a half-inch long or less at the edge of the picture—in the margin, if there is one, so as to mar the photo as little as possible. The grease pencil marks easily, rubs off with rag or finger, and ordinarily does no permanent damage to the surface of the print.

An overlay of tissue paper, folded over the photograph, may be used in the more precise world of advertising and magazines. In the faster processes of the daily newspaper, there is usually less precise instruction. The editor may put two crop marks on the side, to show top and bottom crops for the cut, put two at the bottom, to show the left and right edges, perhaps with an arrow between and a notation "2 col." Engravers then know they are to make a two-column cut, and the height will be worked out mechanically. (If there is only one mark, on the side or bottom, the engraver will simply cut from there to the margin.)

Editors write a slug—like the news story slug—on the back of the photo to identify it in a single word—"crash" or "vote". If the sizing has not been indicated on the face, it will be marked on the back (width first): "2 col. x 4," perhaps, or "7-1/2 x 5-1/2" (for a picture page). It may also be necessary to mark the edition or the section for which the cut is needed. Craftsmen argue that no one should write on the back of a photo, and hard pencil lead can do damage. In fact, many picture editors do put these marks on the back with a grease pencil taking care that the glossy side is on a clean, flat surface. The only alternative for careful work is to paste instructions on a flap, as agencies and free-lances do, or perhaps to use an identification sticker on the back.

At this point, retouch artists may work on the photograph. With tiny paint brush or spray, they can heighten the contrast to get a better cut. Retouching can tone down busy backgrounds or even delete people. Excessive retouching, however, not only gives the final picture a painted look but raises ethical questions of distorting "reality."

The retoucher also puts in arrows, circles, and the X's which "mark the spot." The popularity of these has declined, but they can still be useful on occasion as in showing where cars have skidded or where a halfback has run. Sequence photos are much better.

It is in cropping and sizing that picture editors have the opportunity to employ the real drama of modern newspaper photography. If the routine method is to reduce everything to two or three columns, they will break away to put the best pictures into sizes six and even eight columns wide, where they will leap out at the reader. They will also remember to use white space which, magazine-style, will neatly frame the picture.

Writing cutlines

The picture editor must see that every engraving has cutlines (sometimes called *captions* or just *lines*). Sometimes simply the name suffices for the picture with one person, such as the one-column head shot or the bride's portrait (last name only may be used with the half-column cut.) Necessary explanation for a picture should be in short, clear sentences.

The caption-writer should look at the picture carefully to see what the reader needs to be told. Sometimes the press of deadlines requires the photos be sent to engraving early; then the copyeditors write cutlines from notes without seeing the pictures. This is a sloppy as well as dangerous practice, which will inevitably produce errors. A copying machine usually can adequately duplicate a picture for cutline writing. This way the action or objects to be described can be seen. The writer also can make sure to list every person in the picture.

Like headlines, cutlines are in the present tense: "Crewmen try to check flames ... " or "Joe Doakes of Middle State hurls javelin ..." Of the five *w*'s usually part of the news lead, the cutlines should include at least the *who* and *where*. *When* probably can be skipped, and most of the *what* is told by the picture itself.

Writers tend to worry too much about *what*. If the picture is good, an unmodified, simple verb is enough. It is amateurish to write "smilingly accepts" or "express delight about." If the girl is gorgeous, that adjective need not be included in the cutlines—let the readers form their own opinions. The expressions "is shown" and "is pictured" waste space. However, if the reason for a smile or gesture is not self-evident, the reader deserves an explanation.

Editorializing is as dangerous in cutlines as in news stories. "Club-swinging policeman" may cast an onus on the officer but "eyes blazing defiance, the looter" may shift prejudice in the opposite direction. Let the reader decide from the look of the clubs and eyes. Unless they misrepresent the full story, cutlines should be deadpan.

These other advices should be heeded by cutline writers:

Identify people, places, and things correctly. Identify people "from left," not "left to right."

If a story accompanies the picture, explain the picture, not the story.

Tell the reader what to look for in the picture.

Don't leave the reader baffled. Clear up any ambiguities.

Don't libel anyone.

True *captions*—lines above the picture—have pretty well disappeared from newspapers. But some typographical device can well be used to lure the roving eye to the picture. Often this is two or three words of bold-face caps which kick off the cutlines: **CANDIDATES GATHER**—**Democratic bigwigs of** . . . Or there may be a small headline in a larger type than the cutlines:

Candidates Gather
Democratic bigwigs from upstate counties barbecue . . .

Color photography

Even though amateurs have been shooting color pictures for more than a generation, newspapers have been slow to use color, as we explained in chapter 9. The difficulties of low-grade paper and fast presses are being overcome by printing experts. New developments permit color prints directly from transparencies (slides), which require special equipment to make separations for printing.

Separation, as used here, refers to the process of using color filters to block out certain colors in an image. For example, if engravers use red and yellow filters (or an orange one) in shooting a color picture with blues of sky and sea, they will get an engraving with only those blues. With the appropriate blue ink, that engraving will then reproduce the blues in the original. Similarly they can make separations for the reds and yellows, and the resulting engravings will produce appropriate oranges, browns, lavenders, etc., when printed in combination with the blue plate. The screen is rotated slightly for each separation, so the dots of different colors are close together but not on top of each other. This is *three-color process*. A black-ink plate for grey tones is added for the more realistic *four-color process*.

Other art work

Aside from photographs, line drawings—sketches in black ink on white paper—are the major editorial illustrations used in today's newspapers. Comics and cartoons are the most familiar line drawings, but imaginative editors also use graphs and charts. Line drawings have traditionally headed certain pages and columns, but the modern trend toward clean lines tends to make these look old-fashioned. Editors must take care that they look sharp and open. (See fig. 10-7.)

The picture production person on a large newspaper may have a staff of artists able to create various drawings for different departments. Picture editors on more modest papers, however, handle only maps or charts which come in from picture agencies. These reproduce best if made up as line cuts rather than halftones. The editor can even buy drawings ready-made as mats, which syndicates offer to brighten up the news columns.

The halftone process allows the editor to vary illustration with wash drawings or water colors. Fashion drawings, for example, are sometimes halftoned rather than harshly printed as black-white

Fig. 10−7. Art. The art department can add variety to the mix of type and photos. But trends in illustration change, so the editors should be alert to art that seems old-fashioned if they want a light touch. Compare the styles in these sets of illustrations.

drawings. The artist may get the effect of an unusual halftone by putting lines close, as in cross-hatching, or with *shading sheets.* These sheets are ready-made patterns of dots or lines that can be cut to shade parts of a drawing.

Picture editors may have limited authority to suggest art work other than photographs. On a well-edited paper, however, the staff takes a look at illustration as a whole, so that there is adequate variety and change of pace.

In the future, picture editors will have to keep up with technical developments and with new fads and styles in photography and art. Creative individuals will welcome the stimulation of such change. In it they will see the opportunity to make more attractive and more capable of competing with magazines and TV in an age when news-papers must be more than black and white to be read all over.

11 News crises and edition changes

To many outsiders, the word "newsroom" evokes an image of excited men bellowing at each other, editors screaming at printers and printers screaming at editors, telephones ringing like fire alarms, and copy aides frantically darting from desk to desk. This picture may be great for dramatic presentations, but it would be a horrible way to put out a newspaper. If such turmoil were routine a newspaper could never be printed at all, let alone on time, and the staff would be ready for strait jackets in less than a month.

Newsrooms may not be as serene as libraries, but the noise level is almost always low, shouting seldom occurs, and the staff methodically goes about getting the news into print. The production of a newspaper is a major task, and orderly ways are required to get the job done.

On smaller papers the task is simpler because there is just one edition. Because most papers of less than 30,000 circulation put out only one issue a day, they avoid the emergencies of edition changes. Even so, the staffs of smaller papers are usually kept busy by the problems of a normal news day. In an emergency, they have trouble handling all the extra work. Bigger papers usually can take care of crises more easily because they have a large enough staff to cope with late-breaking stories.

Various emergencies can disrupt a newspaper. The press may break down, illness might send home three or four key people, or telephone and power lines could be knocked out by heavy storms. In 1975 a tornado knocked out electricity and phone service for a small daily in Canton, Illinois. To get the paper out, staffers had to work by candlelight. When a telephone was needed, they had to run across the street to a grocery store to use the only working phone in town. The paper had to be printed twenty miles away. Such emergencies are highly unusual; the "routine emergencies" come from unexpected news breaks.

If the news is spectacular, as many as a dozen reporters and several copyeditors drop what they are doing to concentrate on the big story. Some reporters handle the main part of the story while others get sidebar material. The editors remake page one, directing reporters and photographers at the same time, and struggle to pull together all the copy into a coherent picture for the reader. If the news breaks shortly before deadline, the reporters and editors will be able to print only sketchy details no matter how quickly they act.

One of the biggest stories in the last twenty years was the assassination of President Kennedy. When the wires flashed the news that day in 1963, some Eastern papers already had been printed. But every other afternoon daily paper in the country in one or two hours remade the front page of the paper. All other stories became of third rate importance. Even veteran journalists can hardly believe they got out such good papers in so little time. Morning paper staffs, by working at a furious pace, managed to report the event with amazing thoroughness.

Fortunately, there are few such overwhelming crises. Lesser emergencies, however, are frequent. For example, a major decision by the Supreme Court handed down minutes before deadline suddenly becomes the lead story of the day. Or the governor may take an unexpected step involving the city, and the staff must scramble to report all the ramifications. Editors must adjust quickly. One of the ways they adjust is to expect the unexpected. Each day editors ask themselves the question that they keep in the back of their heads: "What am I going to do if a big story breaks today?" By knowing the available alternatives, they can come up quickly with emergency plans.

Preparation and routines

The well-ordered newspaper, of course, is prepared for all kinds of unexpected news. It has a good library, for one thing, where clippings and pictures of past events can be found in a hurry. Reference books are readily available. One or two reporters can dig out background information from the files while other reporters gather new material and editors juggle stories on page one.

Some papers have material in type ready for a news break involving prominent persons. Using background supplied by wire services, a staff working in slack periods can prepare material and pictures on famous persons who are ill or aged. Some pages may even be made into press plates, ready for the lengthy obituary of a famous person.

To newcomers, writing an obituary before the death may seem grisly. Nevertheless, it enables a paper to cover fully and swiftly the death of someone famous, without taxing the composing room. If two extra pages are necessary, the staff can "jump" the paper's size without difficulty, although few papers increase the number of pages except for a truly monumental event.

In a crisis, staffers should not get so excited that they make the news melodramatic and overplay it. Editors at these times should take pains to double-check their news judgment. The managing editor or news editor might even warn the staff to be certain of the accuracy of information gathered hastily from people whose judgment and powers of observation may be impaired in the excitement.

Editors should consider all the angles that need covering. Should the police be checked? Will comment from the mayor be appropriate or irrelevant? Should the governor be called? Are reporters available to cover not only the main event but also the subsidiary news? While decisions are made on coverage, at least one editor will have to decide what stories to change on page one, and even on an inside page if there is time.

The front page almost always has something expendable: a routine picture, an entertaining but insignificant feature story, a news story that had barely made the front page in the first place. One or all of these pieces could go—or each story could be cut from perhaps ten inches to three. Even two or three good but lengthy stories may be reduced to accommodate the emergency coverage. The news editor can sketch a new layout as soon as it is clear what new stories are being written. A truly big event displaces the lead story, and space may have to be opened up for two or three sidebar stories. In an emergency the newsroom and the composing room have to cooperate more closely than ever, so printers should be alerted to expect new pictures and copy of a big story.

Everyone's productivity picks up astonishingly at these times. The excitement apparently pumps the adrenalin needed for printers to perform more quickly, reporters to write more swiftly, and editors to handle copy at double-time. Everyone relishes the chance to get at least moderately excited, and the experience undoubtedly is a main attraction of newspaper work.

In most lesser crises one reporter quickly writes the story. A single editor edits that story and writes the headline. Another editor will juggle something on page one, so the story—in type—slides neatly toward the presses. The change is almost routine.

Lesser crises

The unexpected often results in the changing of a story already in type. In these instances the editor may put a new "top" on the story, add something to it, or insert some new paragraphs. Often the form is already full, so someone has to make room for the new material. The editor usually first tries to throw out a few paragraphs of the original story to open space for the new parts. If every bit of the original story is important, the editor must decide on cutting or killing an adjoining story of less news value to make room for the fresh information.

When a newspaper is ready for the press room, most papers report late-breaking developments as bulletins. If late news changes only the gist of a story already in type, a one or two paragraph bulletin is set bold face, leaded, and indented. The printer quickly places it between the headline and the body of the story already in type.

For example, a story already set may say that the Senate will vote late in the day on a key issue. Suddenly a wire bulletin reports that the Senate voted three hours ahead of schedule. The editor hasn't time to make over the story, so the copy is marked this way:

⊐ BULLETIN ⊏

BF
9/10

WASHINGTON-(AP)-The Senate today voted 55-43 in favor of a stringent auto safety bill. The vote sends the measure to the President for almost certain signature.

The marks at the side mean that the type is boldface (BF) and leaded (9/10 meaning 9-point type on a 10-point slug). The brackets indicate that the type should be indented one en on each side.

In cold type operations the system works almost the same way. The story comes up on the VDT and the editor, by pushing a couple of keys, can arrange to have the type set in bold face and indented. A new headline is written.

In either hot or cold type systems the copy is hustled to the composing room, where the make-up editor orders an inch and a half cut from some story to make room, and the printer inserts the bulletin. Readers understand that the news broke too late to make over the whole story. Sensing that they are getting last-minute news, they are probably pleased that the newspaper took the trouble to squeeze in the bulletin matter.

Some newspapers, in such situations, would make the press plate, and start the presses rolling, to meet train or bus schedules or to load trucks headed for the suburbs. In perhaps fifteen minutes a new plate with the fresh information would be ready. The presses would be stopped momentarily, the new plate substituted, and the presses started again. This process means that a few thousand subscribers will not get the late development, but many more thousands will have a complete story and headline.

Not all bulletins, of course, mean changes in stories already set. The news of the bulletin, had it been thirty minutes earlier, might have made the lead story of the day, with banner and pictures. But otherwise the editor may only have time to have the printer yank out a three-inch story on page one and slide the bulletin, bold face and indented, into the vacant space. Or the editor may remove a double column picture, set the bulletin matter two columns wide—but indented—and put the type into the hole.

Readers nurtured on old movies may believe that when a spectacular news event occurs, the paper dashes out an extra. Unless they are up in years they probably have never seen a true extra.

A few papers still will have a type block proclaiming "EXTRA" at the top of page one from time to time, but editors are only responding to the old urges to use the word. Such an "extra" is really not an extra edition, only a regular edition with news more dramatic than usual. (When Senator Robert Kennedy was shot, in 1968, the *Philadelphia Inquirer,* in the middle of the night, did get out a genuine extra but it undoubtedly was the last true extra in the nation.)

Genuinely startling news is reported almost instantaneously by radio and television. So, except for the treatments described, newspapers have largely conceded the flash and bulletin to radio and TV. The two- or three-sentence reports on the air, however, create a demand for more details. David Brinkley has said that for news coverage the networks aren't even "in the same ball park" with newspapers.

Emergencies of less importance than news crises require other kinds of handling. If a typographical error produces an obscene word, the letterpress presses can be stopped and the offending material chiseled off the press plate or even smashed flat with a hammer. Similar damage can be done to an offset plate. These crude techniques, however, never appeal to editors who care about the appearance of their papers. After all, a headline looks pretty silly with a word or two gouged away or battered into a black smear. The good editor stretches the circulation schedules five or ten minutes to permit the presses to be stopped and the correction properly made. The good editor also would rather delay the paper a little to get real news breaks than print stories that will be made obsolete within a few minutes by radio or TV. So if a good story breaks at deadline or a really important story already in type gets a shift of emphasis, the competent editor manages to get the latest into the paper one way or another.

Changing the day's editions

All papers deal with changes, and a bigger paper deals with them constantly as every edition rolls on a different deadline. The number of changes, however, has been declining as most newspapers have reduced the number of editions. Changing editions is expensive. Besides, news simply does not shift a dozen times a day. And most papers now deliver 90 percent or more of their circulation to homes. Though street sales are still valuable, they are far less important than they were thirty years ago. And few home subscribers will buy another edition on the street.

The Washington Post

The *Washington Post,* a morning paper with about half a million circulation, is an example of a big paper with only four editions. The first edition, called *the bulldog,* reaching the streets a few minutes after 10 P.M., sells to people who work nights, to those coming out of theatres, to tourists, and to others seeking diversion downtown at night. It also is trucked to the far reaches of the paper's circulation area and mailed to subscribers all over the nation.

The second edition comes out about 11:30 P.M. with some fresh news and with some stories altered to take account of new developments. In the summer the results of some baseball games can be included. This edition circulates in areas a hundred miles or more from Washington.

The third edition, appearing about 1 A.M., is distributed to metropolitan Washington, which includes the District of Columbia and sizable chunks of Maryland and Virginia. This edition has late local and world news, several revamped stories, and final results of baseball games.

The fourth edition, once called a *replate,* makes over page one with the latest information and few, if any, other pages. In the first three editions the *Post* uses either no banner or a restrained one (72-point type or less). The fourth edition usually has a moderately large banner that can be read at a distance, for this edition sells from news stands to people on the way to work in the morning.

Two Syracuse papers

A few papers continue to have many editions because they cover large geographic areas. The morning *Post-Standard* in Syracuse, for example, has seven editions—but Syracuse is uniquely situated to justify them. It is the biggest city by far in a wide section of New York between Canada and Pennsylvania.

Years ago, when newspapers were beginning to expand their territories, the *Post-Standard* built circulation over an area about 250 by 100 miles. Habit is important to all readers, and thousands of people in the small towns of the area got the habit of buying the Syracuse paper. To keep these readers, the newspaper has run editions that include local news for each major region: north, east, the city of Auburn, south, west, and Syracuse itself. The edition changes are kept to a minimum as the paper adapts to readers more than to events.

The *Post-Standard*, except under unusual circumstances, alters page one only once during the evening. Only two inside pages, other than sports, are changed from one edition to another. The first edition has news from the area near Montreal and an area roughly 100 miles north of Syracuse. The next edition scraps those pages for news from another section. The process is repeated until the sixth edition arrives. Local news then is put on those changing pages and alterations are made on page one.

The afternoon *Syracuse Herald-Journal* operates in a similar way with three editions except that page one changes often because during the day news events occur more often than they do in the evening. The reason for this is that customary newsmakers—presidents, prime ministers, cabinet officials, scientists—make most of their pronouncements during the day. Congress and state legislative bodies rarely meet at night.

The trick in handling edition changes anywhere is to make as few alterations as possible while giving the reader late and significant news. Sometimes news may be fresh but not significant. For example, the wire services may give a string of new leads on one event. Each new lead tells the latest development, but the last scrap of information may have little significance for the story as a whole. The editor should look over the various leads and be willing to say firmly, "Forget that latest lead. It doesn't give the whole story as well as the one we've got."

All newspapers strive to get pages moving to the press room every few minutes during the work cycle. Some afternoon papers have two or three editors working through the night, putting wire copy stories on Congress in one pile, for example, and stories on some world hotspot in another. These editors also send to the composing room stories that will not change. This way several pages can be "closed" —ready for the press room—before the rest of the staff arrives.

Other pages, like editorial, opposite editorial (op-ed) and women's, can be sent to the presses early. A sports page, the front page, a key local page can be kept open until the last minute without causing any special rush at deadline.

The developing story

Even if a paper strives to avoid change for the sake of change, there will be much rejuggling on most papers as the editions proceed. Just as some stories have to be lengthened because they have taken on a new importance, others must be shortened because they have lost significance. Some can be cast aside because they have been supplanted by better ones or because readers of this edition would find the information irrelevant.

New headlines often have to be written to highlight new material or to fit a different size space caused by makeup shifts. A story worth a three-column head in the first edition may be dropped to a single-column head in the third, or a local story may require a bigger head in the home edition.

Such changes require a precise written code between editors and printers. One technique is to mark each piece of copy with the edition for which it is to be set. A big "2ND ED" may be rubber-stamped or written atop certain stories. The composing room, then, will not set second edition copy so long as there is any first edition material waiting.

Some papers don't require marking of copy for routine editions. Copy is marked if intended for some future publication, like the Sunday edition, but the editors work on this principle: Everything should be set as soon as possible unless otherwise marked.

Sometimes it is convenient to send copy to the composing room without a headline, marking it "HTK" or "HTC"—in either case meaning "head to come." This system is not necessary, however, if the copy is slugged and a carbon or electrostatic copy kept by the copyeditor. A story, for example, may be slugged "PRESIDENT" and sent to the composing room. A couple of hours later, perhaps, the news editor tells the copyeditor what size head to write for the story. Reading a duplicate story refreshes the memory and the head is written. If the copyeditor normally gets no duplicates, notes on the stories can be used when the time comes to write the head.

Revising dummies

While editing and headline writing are proceeding, someone —usually the news editor or slot person—will be preparing dummies. As editions change, the dummies have to change, obviously, but the new ones indicate only where new or altered stories are to be placed. After the first edition a complete dummy is unnecessary and actually may be confusing to the makeup man. If three stories are to be changed on page one, the dummy would have to refer only to the three places where something is to be altered. The stories to be altered may be dummied "PRESIDENT—NEW LEAD" or "FIRE —NEW HEAD." Such notations show the makeup man exactly what adjustments are to be made in the stories. (See figs. 11-1 and 11-2.)

As soon as one edition has started its press run, the news editor should send a "kill sheet" to the composing room. This sheet is a copy of the news sections of the paper specially marked to indicate which stories should be killed. The printer, before getting the dummies for the next edition, can remove the stories to be discarded and thereby prepare for new material. (It might be noted that while printers are instructed to kill type, they rarely throw it away that minute. They set it aside, remembering the times editors said to kill something and then changed their minds a few minutes after the type was tossed away.)

While great efforts are made to avoid spoken instructions to printers and other staffers, the news editor and the makeup editor may occasionally have brief talks about changes in the dummy. If the paper is small the various editors do makeup as well. To make a last-minute change, they simply walk to the composing room a few feet away and give instructions to the printer about their particular pages. The composing room of bigger papers may be two or three floors removed from the news room, so conversations between a news editor and the makeup editor usually are over inter-office telephone.

Sometimes a story will be dummied in anticipation of getting the facts later, but sometimes the facts don't materialize. An editor has to find a substitute story some place. Many papers have a "bank" of "time copy" for use in emergencies. The staff adds to the bank in slack periods so the editor always will have a variety of stopgap material available.

Once in a while someone in the advertising department makes a real blunder that confuses the whole operation for several minutes. The advertising staff lays out the basic dummy, positioning the various ads throughout the paper. The editorial staff usually has

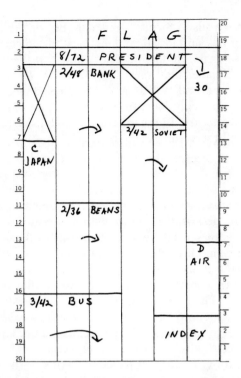

Fig. 11–1. Complete dummy. Most of the front page space of this six column paper has been filled with pictures and stories for the first run of the day.

Fig. 11–2. Revised dummy. The dummy of figure 11–1 has been changed to bring it up to date. A new banner and a new "Bus" lead have been provided, and "China" has been substituted for "Soviet."

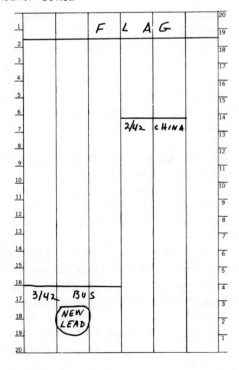

authority to move ads to facilitate makeup, but only rarely are any but the smallest ads shifted. Sometimes, alas, the ad staff will forget to dummy a major ad. Suddenly editors find that the news hole is, say, 110 inches smaller than they had been told. The opposite can happen, too. The ad staff may dummy the same ad twice. In the one case the editors suddenly have to give up six or eight stories that they had planned to use. In the other they have to scrounge to find six or eight to fill the void.

Revising
printed copy

Revising printed copy

While the composing room using hot type prepares for the next edition, the copy desk is working to revise some stories and process new ones. The editors usually work with a copy of the latest edition, which a copy aide has brought to the news room. The system of revision becomes easy to use with a little practice.

Let's assume that the rim person is to revamp that story slugged "PRESIDENT." The story is clipped from the latest edition and pasted on a sheet of copy paper. This sheet then is called a "marker," a "markup," or a "mark." The editor could use a proof of the story, but proofs usually are much harder to find.

On either a proof or a marker the editor writes at the top, preferably with a grease pencil or a crayon, "CX," or "X-correct," or "Krect." The most common is "CX," but all these marks mean *correction*. The printer will know as soon as he sees the marker that he is supposed to correct that particular story.

The editor also crosses out the paragraphs to be killed. If an insert is needed, an arrow goes at the point for the first insert and the insert copy is labeled "Insert A." The second insert point is marked "Insert B," etc. If material is to be added, "TR for add" goes at the bottom. This means "Turn rule for added copy." The printer "turns a rule"—turns over a slug of type at the end of the story—to remind him that one or more adds (additional material) will be coming.

The editor marks the copy to be added or inserted similarly. On the piece to be inserted first comes "Insert A—PRESIDENT." On the other pieces appear "Insert B—PRESIDENT," "First add—PRESIDENT," "Second add—PRESIDENT," etc. Even a "New lead—PRESIDENT" may be necessary. At the bottom of the new lead the editor writes "TR for pickup," which means that the type not killed should pick up with the new lead.

The slug "PRESIDENT" has to be added to all the copy, of course, so the printer will know what story all these new pieces go with. It should be noted, too, that inserts receive *letter* identification but adds are *numbered*.

The editor, after making all these marks on copy, should check everything to be sure each piece is properly labeled. Then the whole packet—marker, adds, inserts, and new leads—goes to the composing room via pneumatic tube. A person called the copy cutter gives the copy to the typesetters and the marker to the person putting the type into forms. The paragraphs to be killed are put aside. In a few

minutes the new type is set and, using the marker as a guide, the
whole story is pieced together as the editor directed. The system can
be observed in the following examples:

Insert A (President)

He said that no tax decision would be made until after

Congress completes action on all appropriations bills and

he sees whether they can be cut.

Insert B (President)

The President urged governors to cooperate in econo-

mizing at the state level along lines he is pursuing at the

federal level to try to subdue the pressures of inflation.

There was no dissent to the idea from any governors.

add one (President)

The President did not mention violence and racial disorders

in outlining to newsmen what was discussed.

add two (President)

On the crime situation, he said he invited each governor to

send a representative to Washington in October to discuss imple-

menting recommendations of a commission on crime. He mentioned

no date.

The cold type operation forces the editor to make most of the changes. No clipping of the newspaper to make markers is needed. The story that needs a change—even if it already appeared in the paper—still floats inside the computer, and the editor can "call it up" anytime. The changes can be made on the video screen and the whole story set again. The system is so fast there is no need to try to avoid resetting two or three paragraphs—or even a dozen. The editor, of course, has to make sure that the old story is peeled off the paste-up dummy and the new one put in its place.

Writing backwards   Some unexpected stories can be written in parts—even the last part first. There is a system for handling this kind of story, too. Assume that a gas main explodes at a busy downtown corner. One or two reporters and a photographer would be sent to the scene, another would check library clippings under "Explosions," and others would be telephoning the gas company, police, fire department headquarters, city morgue, and hospitals. Each reporter might gather bits of news that would be worth a couple of paragraphs. But in the confusion no one can be sure immediately whether anyone was killed, how many were injured, what caused the blast, or how much damage resulted.

While attempts are made to find out all this information, it often is helpful on hot type papers to get as much of the story in type as possible. So the city editor directs reporters to write what material they have and slug each piece "BLAST." Reporters at the scene telephone the rewrite people as soon as they have any information. Rewrite pounds out the facts as they dribble in, using the same slug. The "top" of the story will be written last, giving the fullest account of the who, what, when, where, and why. The lesser details, gathered earlier, can be on the way to the composing room well in advance of the top. This copy is called "A-matter." The "A" stands for add; in effect, these pieces are adds to a story that as yet does not exist.

To help keep these various adds straight, editors mark the first one "10-add," the next one "11-add," etc. The figure 10 is the starter because the lead, which will be written last, may then have as many as nine adds without confusing the numbering system. Ten is safe because a lead almost never has more than nine adds. The adds for the body of the story, then, may look like this:

10- add   (Blast)

One witness, Mrs. Carrie Blasingame, 1013 E. Arlington St., said she had just stepped outside Heller's department store when she heard a terific noise and saw a car flop over less than 75 feet from her. She said that the force of the blast pushed her back against the store front, but that she was not hurt.

11-add (*Blast*) The explosion was the first eruption of a gas main in the city since 1927. That blast killed two persons at Kenwood and Main streets, just three blocks south of today's accident.

When the last add is written, the copy should be marked "add all —BLAST." The last add to the lead must be labeled as an add but with the additional mark at the end "TR—pick up 10-add."

If there have been twenty different pieces of copy on the one story, it is unlikely that everything fits together beautifully. The chances are good that the story needs a bit of reorganization. Someone on the desk should recheck the carbon copies of all the pieces (or work from proof) to make sure that the story "reads"—that everything gets in proper order and that the story doesn't have ludicrous duplications or omissions. If possible a second check should be made from proof after all pieces are put together.

Changes ahead

With cold type the same system prevails except that nothing is sent to the composing room until the whole story is ready. Reporters either have their copy on scanner paper or stored in the computer. When all the pieces have been written the copyeditor assembles them on the video screen and pushes the button. The whole story gets set at 150 lines a minute. The copyeditor must be sure that the various pieces get put into the computer in the proper order. It is possible, of course, for an editor to go to the composing room as the story is pasted into position to make sure each graf naturally follows the one ahead of it. The whole newspaper staff, but the copy desk in particular, must keep searching for ways to squeeze big emergencies into small ones and to eliminate the small ones. Little things are important, such as having names and telephone numbers of key sources close at hand and maintaining a good library. Planning is essential to avoid turmoil and to provide quality coverage.

Journalists at all levels should strive to become "idea people." They should get ideas for exceptional stories, for striking layouts, or for changed makeup. They also should get ideas on how to reduce trivia and to eliminate outmoded work patterns. In the years to come, most importantly, they will need to find ways to make the best use of the new technology so newspaper staffers will not have to break their necks to provide readers with fresh, pertinent—and recent—information.

12 The law and the copyeditor

The slot person assigns a story about a trial to a copyeditor. Down in the ninth paragraph is this sentence: "When Rogers finished his testimony against the sheriff, Judge Wilson launched into a bitter attack upon the sheriff, calling him a scoundrel, a 'woman-chaser' and a 'lewd, lascivious old man.'" The copyeditor has to consider some important questions: Is it libelous? Will the sheriff sue? If it is libelous and the sheriff sued, how much could the newspaper lose?

Or what if a reviewer says this of a play: "Miss Smith did an adequate job of playing Ophelia, but she might have done better if she had laid off the sauce before curtain time." Is this caustic sentence going to get the newspaper into court?

Suppose a story about the mayor starts: "Mayor Hector Adamson was convicted of stealing a horse in 1926 and he served three months in jail for the offense, the Post discovered today." Is it safe to dredge up a story a half century old, even if it is true?

These examples are hardly typical of stories crossing a copy desk, but they show why a copyeditor must be constantly alert to the possibility that, tucked away in an obscure story, is a sentence that will send someone running to a lawyer. That lawyer may decide to call on the newspaper's publisher to see about a tidy out-of-court settlement. He may even reinforce his efforts by stopping off at the courthouse to file a libel suit.

The lawyer may decide to sue the copyeditor, too, since this staffer had a hand in the job. A suit also could be filed against the reporter who wrote the story. The working crew rarely gets sued, however; with only a house partly paid for, a three-year-old car, two children free and clear, and $350 in the newspaper's credit union, the staffer would be too small a target. The newspaper is not. Most newspapers, if they had to, could borrow many thousands. In addition, nearly all newspapers have libel insurance, and lawyers know it.

The costs of libel

Back in 1927 Stanley Walker, in his famous book *City Editor,* advised editors to take an occasional risk on a libel suit, because at the worst the paper would lose only a couple of thousand dollars. That no longer is sound advice, if it ever was. While some libel judgments are for a few thousand, some these days are enormous. Imagine what the future would be for the copy editor whose error let the paper get socked for a million dollar bill. That award is still almost fantasy, but would any copyeditor feel secure about the future if that blunder cost the paper even $5,000?

The cost of losing a libel suit is not only the judgment handed down by the court. The newspaper has to hire trial lawyers, and good ones do not come cheap. Defense attorneys have to be paid even if the newspaper wins the suit.

Two cases decided in the early sixties reveal the potential size of libel judgments these days. In one, John Henry Faulk was awarded $3.5 million after he sued Columbia Broadcasting System and AWARE, a Communist-hunting organization. AWARE had been instrumental in getting Faulk, a newscaster, blacklisted by CBS and all other networks. The judgment was cut on appeal to $550,000, but to most people, including publishers, that still is a lot of money.

The other case involved Wally Butts, athletic director at the University of Georgia. The *Saturday Evening Post* published a statement that a telephone coversation between Butts and Bear Bryant, football coach at the University of Alabama, revealed that Georgia was going to throw the football game with Alabama. The *Post* story quoted only one witness, who said he overheard the conversation by accident. Both Butts and Bryant sued. At the trial in the Butts case, no one else could corroborate the statements of the sole witness. The witness also had changed his story somewhat and, besides, his reputation was attacked. Butts was awarded $3,060,000, although this was cut to $400,000 on appeal. Bryant settled out of court for $300,000. This catastrophe contributed to the death of the *Post.* Obviously libel today is serious, and anyone in the newsroom ought to have a good knowledge of libel law. The copyeditor especially should be as informed about libel law as an average good attorney. If such knowledge tells the rim person that something is libelous, the slot person should be told, "This looks like dynamite to me." If the slot agrees, they can rephrase the offending words, remove the dangerous part of the story, or ask the newspaper's lawyer for advice. In most cases the lawyer is not consulted unless the editors, hoping to run the story pretty much as written, want to be as sure as anyone can be that the story will not cost the paper a suit.

What is libelous?

It would be a relief to all journalists if someone could give them a flat yes or no answer every time something looks libelous, but a lot of cases are borderline. Besides, one never can tell for sure what a jury will decide. When one woman sued a newspaper that reported she had given birth to a litter of pups, almost any libel expert would have said she had a clear case. The jury, however, ruled that everyone knew it was a biological impossibility for a woman to have puppies, so she lost.

Libel is usually defined as *written defamation,* and it applies also to most radio and television programs on the ground that newscasters and performers are reading from a script. But someone is sure to look at the definition of libel and object, "Newspapers and broadcasts defame people all the time." Certainly a story about a man's embezzling $10,000 at the bank ruins his reputation. And a story about a woman's being convicted of running a con game will defame her and keep her from joining the Junior League. Obviously newspapers and newscasters defame people. And they can do it legally because the law provides publishers with defenses which permit printing of certain defamations.

The law offers three main protections for publications printing defamatory information. In general, these legal defenses are the same in each of the fifty states and the District of Columbia. At the heart of the protection is the idea that the public has a right to know many things which are considered defamatory. So papers are given rights, or "defenses," to print such defamation. Theoretically, a person could still sue, but a lawyer would advise against a suit because the paper stands behind one of these three protections for the public interest.

Three defenses

Truth. In some states truthfulness alone is a protection. In others it has to be *truth with good motive.*

Privilege. This often is called *qualified* or *statutory* privilege because states let publications print *accurate* stories about the activities of the courts. Newspapers also may report what takes place in public bodies, like Congress or the state legislatures, and may take facts from various public records. Usually privilege does not cover juvenile courts, activities of grand juries, and lesser public bodies like school boards and village councils.

Fair Comment. A newspaper may criticize the activities of public officials and works or performances open to the public and publicly displayed, such as books, art shows, concerts, plays, athletic contests, and night club acts.

These three defenses need to be examined in some depth.

Truth, under law, is not simply what the newspaper editors believe is the truth or what someone told the newspaper is true. From a legal standpoint truth is what can be proved in court to be true. Occasionally, therefore, a journalist will say, "I know the guy is a crook, but I can't prove it." So a story about him is not printed.

Truth

Sometimes a newspaper running an investigation will get someone's promise to testify to the truth of a charge in case the story ever comes to court. But suppose the trial date approaches and Mr.

Witness is nowhere to be found. Because the truth cannot now be proved, a plaintiff collects a few thousand dollars and the newspaper collects experience. Instead of relying on a witness to appear in a case of libel, many papers take pains to have their sources give them affidavits to be used in case someone sues. The affidavits are sworn statements by the informants that certain assertions made by the paper are true. Newspapers even try to forestall the threat of suit by telling the readers, in effect, that they have the goods: "At least three policemen operate as bookmakers in their spare time, two former policemen *declared in affidavits signed* today." Assuming that the three accused policemen are named later in the story, they and their lawyers are forewarned that the newspaper has sworn statements for court proof.

Something true may still get the newspaper into difficulty. At the beginning of this chapter an illustrative sentence said that the mayor was a horse thief in 1926. Presumably, no reader had known this. If the story is true, one might say that the mayor could do nothing about it. But maybe he could. He could argue that while he had stolen a horse when he was sixteen years old, he had led a respectable life since. The newspaper, he could charge, was being malicious in printing a story that old. (The legal meaning of *malice* is disregard for the rights of others without legal justification.) The newspaper, on the other hand, might argue that the public had a right to know that their mayor had been a horse thief. The case might go either way in court.

Privilege

Since the rights of privilege do not, in all states, apply to *all* courts and *all* deliberations of public bodies and *all* public records, copyeditors should be familiar with the restrictions in their own states or the states in which the newspaper circulates.

They should be aware that accounts of committees of Congress and state legislatures are covered by privilege. The protection does not apply to closed legislative committee hearings. However, any publications issued by such committees are covered by privilege, even though the publications may be filled with material that would be libelous if printed by anyone else.

The question of privilege on the floor of the United States Senate got a workout in the early fifties, during the heyday of Senator Joseph McCarthy. The senator often declared in speeches about the country that the government, particularly the State Department, was honeycombed with Reds. On the lecture circuit he always was careful to speak in generalities and never called any government official a Red by name. If he had, he might have been sued for slander, which is oral defamation.

On the floor of the Senate, where he was protected by law, McCarthy called various people Communists. The press was able to report what McCarthy said on the Senate floor without fear of a libel suit because what was said was privileged. Often the named people dared the senator to step outside the Capitol, where his speech would not be protected, and make the same charges. He never took them up on it.

Another situation involving privilege occurred when McCarthy held a Senate subcommittee hearing in New Jersey. The hearing was closed, but afterward McCarthy held a press conference and mentioned names. The papers printed the names and one man sued. The judge ruled that the press conference was an extension of the subcommittee hearing and therefore was privileged. While this was the decision in this one court, the press should be cautious about concluding that all such press conferences would be considered privileged by all judges.

It is always advisable to remember that application and interpretation make the law flexible. The courts may rule at one time that such-and-such is the law. Within five or ten years, with a different political climate and with different evidence, fresh decisions may result in the opposite interpretation. As an illustration, many of the laws made in the forties and fifties to restrict radical political activity were invalidated by the Supreme Court within a decade or two.

Also, like the protection of privilege in many states on juvenile court proceedings, other laws are not clear. The police blotter, or record book, is a privileged document in some states, but in others either it is not or the law on the subject is fuzzy. It is clear, however, that once a law suit has been filed—is in the hands of the clerk of the courts—the contents of the charges are privileged.

Before filing a lawsuit, an attorney may present *pleadings* to the judge. These are not privileged until they become part of the court record. If the case is dropped or settled in the judge's chambers, they never are opened to the public.

Any part of the trial that is removed from the court record is not privileged. If the judge rules that testimony is "stricken," the protection is taken away. The same applies when the judge "clears the court," for reporters must either leave the courtroom at such times or not print anything that happens in the court after the judge has cleared it.

No story during or preceding a trial should provide any editorial evaluation of the guilt or innocence of the accused. Stories should stick to what has been said for court record. No story should refer to a person as a "killer" or a "burglar" until he has been convicted of such crimes. Obviously, this applies to the headline as well. A person can be an *alleged* burglar, for the word alleged is a synonym for *accused* and should be used accordingly.

Some people have the mistaken idea that if the word alleged is tossed into a story, the newspaper can avoid any libel suit. What if a reporter wrote, "It is alleged that the president of the university, almost immobile from drunkenness, shouted obscenities at the Student Council president yesterday?" There would be no protection unless someone had formally accused the official of this behavior or the newspaper could prove that the report was true.

Reporters often assume that what a policeman tells them is privileged. It is not, although quoting an officer may help prove lack of malice, so any damages assessed may be less. Some papers therefore take chances and tie the phrase "police said" to some defamations.

An arrest, however, is privileged. Nevertheless, it is worth being cautious about. Police may get a little overzealous and arrest people for insufficient cause. So an officer, in the midst of some excitement, may reach out and tell someone he is under arrest. The someone may be the vice president of a university. The newspaper might print a story of the arrest, only to find that while the presses were running the vice president had been taken to the police station and quickly released, with personal and profuse apologies from the desk sergeant, the chief of police, the mayor, and, of course, the arresting officer. The privilege might not hold up now, on the grounds that the vice president was not really considered arrested by the police.

Cautious editors print news of arrests only after an *information,* or preliminary charge, is written out at the police station. This precaution applies especially to mass "arrests" when police sometimes will shove a hundred people into paddy wagons, tell them they are under arrest, take them to a remote police station, and release them. Unless a reporter follows through to see that there is an official record of an arrest, a policeman can deny later, after publication, that a man had been arrested. A denial without a written *information* could leave the paper in a bad spot.

Fair comment

Sarcastic and sardonic play reviews flourished in the thirties and early forties. Reviewers struggled to have something snide or devastating to say about at least one performer, if not the whole cast. That approach to play reviewing spilled over into reviews of books, music, and art. The exaggeration and the strained efforts to be cleverly derogatory, fortunately, is less common today, but editors still must know where to draw the line.

It is legal to pan a play or performance in exaggerated language. The law provides that anything written about the *performance,* including how the person looked while performing, is protected by what is known as "fair comment and criticism." The only qualification is that the writing not be malicious.

One case that has amused law and journalism students for decades concerned a 1901 newspaper review in Odebolt, Iowa. The reviewer covered the stage performance of a singing trio known as the Cherry Sisters. Since horses were common in 1901, the reviewer chose to use equine terms, knowing his audience would appreciate them:

> Effie is an old jade of 50 summers, Jessie a frisky filly of 40 and Addie, the flower of the family, a capering monstrosity of 35. Their long skinny arms, equipped with talons at the extremities, swung mechanically, and anon

waved frantically at the suffering audience. The mouths of their rancid features opened like caverns and sounds like the wailings of damned souls issued therefrom. They pranced around the stage with a motion that suggested a cross between the danse du ventre and fox trot, strange creatures with painted faces and hideous mien. Effie is spavined, Addie is stringhalt, and Jessie, the only one who showed her stockings, has legs with calves as classic in their outlines as the curves of a broom handle.

Effie brought suit and lost. As plaintiff (the one bringing the action), she appealed, but the appellate court ruled against her: "Viewing the evidence in the light of the rules heretofore announced, and remembering that the trial court had the plaintiff before it and saw her repeat some of the performances given by her on stage, we are of the opinion that there was *no* error in directing a verdict for the defendants."

A copyeditor must make sure, however, that a review does not deal derogatorily with the performer's private life, such as drinking habits, sex life, and political views. These are considered by law to be a person's own business—until the performer makes them public business by something like getting arrested for drunkenness.

It is almost taken for granted that the press can criticize public officials with impunity. But newspapers cannot report their private lives under the protection of fair comment, so any report on private activity would have to be defended by proof that the report was true. Some public officials, notably the President, have virtually no private life, so criticism of practically anything they or their families do is allowed by custom, though ethics and taste restrain well-edited papers. Scandal sheets thrive on libel of famous persons and get away with it, for the famous realize a suit would publicize the libel even more—and that more people would believe it.

In recent years the courts have ruled that certain inaccuracies or falsehoods about *public figures* may be printed safely. The landmark decision on this subject was handed down in 1964 by the United States Supreme Court in *New York Times* vs. *Sullivan*. Some three million dollars in judgments had been assessed against the *Times* in behalf of various Alabama figures, including Governor Patterson and four Montgomery city officials. One of the officials was L. B. Sullivan, commissioner of public affairs and thereby head of the police department. The judgments had been obtained because a full page advertisement, placed by a civil rights group, had appeared in the *Times*. The ad said that during a demonstration at Alabama State College police had "ringed" the campus, student leaders been expelled, the "entire" student body had shown their protest by refusing to register for classes, the campus dining hall had been padlocked.

The public
figure doctrine

A substantial number of these statements were not true. For example, nine students were expelled, but for demanding service at a downtown lunch counter. The dining hall never was padlocked, and the police did not "ring" the campus.

The Supreme Court ruling tried the question of malice:

> The constitutional guarantees require, we think, a Federal rule that prohibits a public official from recovering damages for a defamatory falsehood relating to his official conduct unless he proves that the statement was made with "actual malice"—that is, with the knowledge that it was false or with reckless disregard of whether it was false or not.[1]

The *public figure* rule has been decisive in other libel cases. The question that faces editors, however, is what constitutes a public figure. Obviously, the President, a senator, a famous football player, or a noted actor is a public figure. But what about a relatively well-known professor? What about a member of the school board? Are they well enough known to be considered public figures?

There are other tough questions. How incorrect can the news stories be if the public figure defense can be used? How reckless is reckless? Can a newspaper say that Senator Glotzenschlubber beats his wife every other Tuesday? Can a story say that Alderman Leddhedd goes out every Saturday night on a wild binge, when in truth he sticks to sarsaparilla?

No one knows for sure where the borderline is between a public figure and a non-public figure. No one knows how erroneous the stories may be before a newspaper gets in water so hot that the public figure plea won't cool it. Courts define individual, not general, cases.

One court, however, granted Senator Barry Goldwater $75,000 in a libel suit against Ralph Ginzburg and his magazine *Fact*. Ginzburg had published in 1964, when Goldwater ran for President, a story based on the opinion of more than a dozen psychiatrists that Goldwater was not mentally stable. None of the psychiatrists had ever seen Goldwater. The senator was a public figure, all right, but the court ruled that Ginzburg had been guilty of malice and "reckless disregard" for the facts. So at least in that one case journalists learned the outer limits of the public figure doctrine.

If copyeditors set out to find just where the borderline is, they may find their paper in court. Sticking to the provable facts about anyone is the best way to stay out of trouble. The fact that something is legal is no cause for being sloppy with facts or careless with reputations. A loose newspaper is in no position to recommend virtue to anyone else. If a paper sticks to what the editors think is the truth and makes a mistake, it can use the public figure defense with ethical justification.

Libel comes under two main headings: *per se* and *per quod*. Libel *per se* can be translated as "libel on the face of it." To be called a Communist when one is not a Communist has been considered libel *per se* for some years.* The plaintiff would have to bring little into court except the offending newspaper clipping to prove the point. Libel *per quod* is the opposite. One must know the circumstances to determine the defamation. In other words, the plaintiff has to prove that a reputation was damaged. If the court decides that a person was defamed, it has to decide how much money the individual needs to soothe the damaged reputation.

In two historic cases, the plaintiffs did not want money. All they sought was a ruling by the court that they had been libeled. Theodore Roosevelt settled for a one cent judgment. Henry Ford was less restrained. He took six times as much.

Libel is almost always a civil dispute. That is, it is a wrong being argued by two people. (Corporations are treated by law as persons.) No jail or prison terms are involved, unless of course the person adjudged guilty of libel does not pay the judgment.

Criminal libel does exist, but it is rare. To get a criminal libel verdict the court would have to rule that a publication has committed a crime *against society*. In such instances, the newspaper story is held to have been so inflammatory that a segment of society riots, storms city hall, or tries to blow up the newspaper plant itself. In recent decades the idea that a newspaper could produce a riot was remote and the threat of this type of libel academic. Every few years some zealous prosecuting attorney files a criminal libel action, but nothing comes of it.

All journalists should be aware that the newspaper is responsible for *everything* it prints: news stories, headlines, features, comics, advertisements, editorials, letters to the editor, and pictures. Aside from the question of malice, quoting someone else on a defamation —such as the superintendent of schools or a policeman—does not enable a newspaper to avoid a charge of libel. It does not save the newspaper any responsibility if it is someone's signed letter in the paper that contains the defamation. Neither is there any help if the libel is in a paid advertisement. It is no relief, either, to have some letter writer say, "I will stand behind it." Don't bet on it. The paper may be assessed, say, $20,000 damages, and it will run up a $10,000 legal bill defending itself. In addition, it may lose the confidence of its readers. Is the letter writer who says he will be responsible ready to cough up $30,000? Editors might cool off demands from hotheaded readers by saying, only slightly facetiously, "Would you put

Classes of libel

Per se *and* per quod

Civil and criminal

Everything counts

---

* A federal appeals court in 1966 held that a white businessman was libeled when he was called a "bigot."

up a $50,000 bond just in case we get sued for libel?'' At the mere thought of such a sum most letter writers would throw their libelous prose into the waste basket—or at least cross out the offending phrases.

Editors and reporters are often threatened with libel suits. A news source occasionally will shout, "If you print that, I'll sue you for libel!" Actually it is clear that the person doesn't have the slightest idea of what constitutes libel. So the journalist either ignores the threat or gives an ironic rejoinder. If the threats are based on ignorance, as most of them are, the journalist can take a few minutes to explain why the story is either not libelous or not actionable. If this isn't satisfactory, the journalist can suggest that the source consult a lawyer. A substantial number of people assume that they can tell a newspaper what to leave out, or to put in, and successfully sue if the paper disregards their orders.

In any case the journalist is smart to keep calm, although it is tempting to utter some scornful phrase. To maintain good public relations for the newspaper, staffers should be gentle in handling the irate people who dread exposure in print for their real or imagined sins.

Escape routes

While truth, fair comment, privilege, and, to some extent, public figures are defenses against libel, there are several other ways that a libel suit can be voided:

Statute of limitations. The suit must be brought within a specified time after the offending material was printed. In most states this is one year. If the plaintiff brings suit 366 days after the story appeared, no case.

Out-of-court settlement. If a newspaper agrees out of court that it libeled someone, and pays a certain sum of money, that act wipes out any chance of a suit.

Consent. This rarely occurs, but if a reporter showed a news source a story or recited to him the facts or charges that were going to be in the story and the source made no objection, the court assumes that the source "consented" to them.

Once a publication gets embroiled in a libel suit, its publisher, editors, and lawyers have to figure how to get out. In many instances there is no real way out. The publication then tries to show that it tried to mitigate the effects of the defamation as soon as it became aware of its error.

The best evidence of mitigation is a *retraction.* The most effective retractions appear in about as prominent a position in the paper as the libel did. If the libel appeared in a banner headline on page one, the retraction at least would have to be in a prominent position on the front page.

These other proofs of the newspaper's good faith *may* help:

— The offending story was omitted or "cleaned up" in later editions.

— An honest effort was made to retrieve the papers which included the libel. For example, if the libel was noticed ten minutes after the press run was started, the paper would have called back the delivery trucks which had left the building.

— The libelous information had been copied by error.

— The information came from a normally reliable source, such as a police chief or a judge.

— The information was "common knowledge." This claim refers to what "everyone knows." As an illustration, a gangster may never have been convicted of anything, but it is "common knowledge" that he is a gangster.

— The newspaper had used normal precautions. This would require evidence that the paper had double-checked the facts before printing them.

— There were persistent and public rumors about the case.

— The staffers were provoked into the publication, or they printed the statement in a campaign so intense that judgment was swayed.

— The plaintiff can be proved to have a bad reputation.

— There was a "prior article"—that is, the story was printed before and the plaintiff had not complained.

Watchwords

Garrett Redmond, an official of a company selling libel insurance, has said that for years the main cause of suits has been careless crime reporting—of names, addresses, or size of crime. So the copyeditor must particularly watch stories involving crime and the courts. As we said earlier, it is easy for a reporter to refer to "the killer" instead of "alleged killer"—he or she is not a killer, legally, until convicted. Sometimes police catch a person red-handed in a criminal act. To be on the safe side the story had better not say, "Joe Johnson was caught breaking into the McTavish warehouse."

The copyeditor must be especially careful when a story touches a woman's reputation. The courts may not be much concerned by a story hinting that a man was philandering. But even though mores are fast changing, to say the same thing about a woman might still get a newspaper into considerable trouble.

Picture cutlines or even placement of pictures can provide grounds for libel. If a sheriff and an alleged criminal are pictured together. and the cutlines switch identification, one or both might sue. Also, if a cut runs next to a story so readers assume they go together, there may be grounds for action.

Implications and insinuations have to be watched with great care. The plaintiff can establish a good case by bringing only two or three people into court to testify that they inferred something defamatory from something the paper printed.

Not naming individuals in stories may be no protection. It is what readers believe is being said that counts. When a column in a college newspaper denounced a football player, but not by name, several readers, at least, thought the column referred to a certain player who had been accused of a serious crime. Actually, the columnist had meant someone else, but the person who some people thought was mentioned might have collected.

As a rule, a group cannot be libeled. It would be hard to convince a jury that something defamatory about a sizable group really applied to every member of the group. A rule of thumb is that the larger the group, the harder to libel. But this depends to some extent on how emotional the public is about the organization. A magazine once implied that Oklahoma University football players came off the field and squirted dope into their noses. Some of the players sued, claiming that they had shot a peppermint solution into their mouths to relieve dryness. The Oklahoma Supreme Court agreed that the magazine should be relieved of $75,000, which was distributed among some sixty players. The same implications might, perhaps, have been made safely about another large group, say, the Oklahoma marching band. Because band fans are fewer and less excitable than football fans, a court would probably be reluctant to see such an implication as doing an individual harm.

A few other points on libel should be considered:

The dead cannot be libeled, for the simple reason that they can no longer suffer from slights to their reputations. A suit could be filed by the dead person's heirs, but they would have to prove specific injury to themselves, such as loss of income. It is possible, although unlikely, that criminal libel could occur over defamation of the dead.

The newspaper is safe to print charges once they are actually filed at the courthouse, as they have started through the judicial process. But a story had better not report the gist of written charges casually dropped by a lawyer on a desk in the county clerk's office.

A report on what people told a grand jury would not be considered actionable. But since the operations of the grand jury are secret, the presiding judge might decide the newspaper, or its reporters, are in contempt of court. For that, one can go to jail.

Executive acts are considered privileged, but it is safer to get them in writing than to quote them as given verbally. If the mayor tells a reporter that he fired the police chief "for moral turpitude," it would be helpful if the newspaper could get a copy of the letter dismissing the chief. The copy could be saved, in case the chief sues.

Copyeditors should be suspicious of irony. A story that says, "George Zarfoss went to Boston to visit Mrs. Esmerelda Fisher, a 'friend,'" almost asks for a suit by Mr. Zarfoss or Mrs. Fisher, or both.

Once a plaintiff wins a libel suit, the court may award one, two, or three kinds of damages:

Damages

General.   No proof of injury has to be submitted. These are simply presumed, without evidence, to have resulted from injured feelings or humiliation.

Special.   The plaintiff proves specific injury. The actual pecuniary loss is assessed. Some statutes refer, in fact, to "actual damages."

Punitive.   The court grants a cash award as punishment. Such damages may be quite high, to discourage the editors from libelling again. (Punitive awards, by the way, are taxable. The others are not.)

The laws about privacy are fairly new and have not been widely tested in the courts. There has been growing concern, however, about invasions of privacy by the government, particularly with electronic snooping devices. The press has come in for its share of criticism, too, and some of it has been justified. Some newsmen have the idea that anything they want to find or photograph is fair game, never considering if the picture or story could cause unnecessary anguish.

Privacy

At one time it would have been enough for an editor to remind reporters and photographers to avoid the keyhole and the transom. But now a substantial number of people have begun to file privacy suits over photographs taken almost routinely. Someone who stood still for a picture taken by a photographer who explained that it would appear in a certain newspaper may sue, claiming the paper invaded privacy in publishing the picture. Many such suits were filed in Appalachia, which in the late sixties was one of the favorite grounds for "depth reporting of social problems" by reporters and photographers. Some poor people thought that the pictures of themselves or their children were unflattering and charged that the photographs held them up to public scorn.

This development caused some newspapers to get signed permission to publish a picture from almost anyone photographed in the area. It is likely that there will be more such privacy suits. Editors must now take special care about pictures that may hurt the feelings of their subjects. Such care applies especially to the posed photograph or the picture taken casually in a non-public place. The law is quite clear that a picture taken at random in public—on the street, at a football game or political rally—does not invade privacy; the individual has already put himself on public display by appearing in public.

Where privacy may be involved, the newspaper editor is wise to focus on newsworthiness, not sensation. Invading privacy simply to entertain or titillate is dangerous as well as unethical. In court newsworthiness is a defense for invasion of privacy just as truth is for libel. News facts from the public record, for example, would be privileged, as would facts about a public figure. These and five similar guidelines are listed by Don R. Pember in "Privacy and the Press: the Defense of Newsworthiness," a discussion useful to the editor desiring more information about this developing body of law.[2] "The press must remember," concludes Pember, "that when it is called into court in a privacy suit it is the judge or jury who will decide what is and what is not news."

As in several other legal problems involving the press, copyeditors must become reasonably well-acquainted with the privacy laws of their states. The state press association may have the material in booklet form, and a few minutes' reading may save the newspaper thousands of dollars.

Lotteries

Since most papers mail at least a few copies, staffers at least should be aware that postal regulations forbid advertisements and certain stories about lotteries. The regulations mean that any story has to have legitimate news value. The Post Office, however, does not scrutinize each paper in an attempt to find an errant story. It acts only on a complaint, and even so the offender only gets a letter of mild rebuke. Certainly in these days when so many states have lotteries, the regulation has a hard time being enforced. The copyeditor simply should try to cull stories about little bingo games and chicken raffles. A story about a local grandmother winning the Irish Sweepstakes, of course, clearly has news value—and thereby obtains sanctification from the Post Office.

Copyright

Any work published after January 1, 1978 can be copyrighted for fifty years after the author's death. Material copyrighted before that date is protected for twenty-eight years, with a twenty-eight year extension possible. Anything copyrighted, of course, is the property of the author or his heirs and it is a violation of law to reproduce that work without permission of the publisher. The copyeditor should be wary about reprinting such material to avoid getting the newspaper into an expensive and lengthy lawsuit. While nearly all books and magazines are copyrighted, few newspapers take the trouble and expense. The copyeditor's concern with copyright is to avoid reprinting copyrighted material without permission from the publisher. Some newspapers, particularly small ones, often do reprint without permission material from copyrighted magazines, books, and other newspapers. In most cases the owner of the copyrighted material throws up his hands and says, "What can I do? It would cost me a thousand dollars of someone's time to get even an apology from the bum. So I'll let it go." Meanwhile, the unscrupulous editor steals editorials, articles, and cartoons without pushing any one source to legal action—and without having the courtesy to tell readers about the stolen goods.

It should be noted that relatively few papers indulge in this kind of thievery. Those that do usually pick on the small magazines, ones with no legal staff, time, or money to fight copyright violation. Thievery from a big magazine, like *Time* or *McCall's*, is a different matter. Those magazines are able to go to court for copyright violation and get a good-sized judgment, so their articles are rarely filched. Thieves also know that many people would have read the original article—and thus know that the material was stolen.

A newspaper occasionally will copyright a single story, usually something special like the result of some outstanding investigative work by the staff. The copyright also lets the paper print the story before the news is given to AP, if it is a member. AP or UPI may rewrite the story and, though quoting only a little of the original language, mention the source; then the originating newspaper enjoys the national publicity.

A few newspapers have copyrighted every issue to prevent radio stations from "reading the paper" over the air. It should be noted that the offending station would not have to read verbatim from the newspaper to violate the copyright law. A paraphrase of the stories would be a violation, too, although of course it would be harder to prove.

A rule of thumb on reprinting copyrighted material is that 50 words may be quoted directly without getting permission. This is arbitrary to some extent. Obviously, a book publisher would be delighted if a newspaper quoted 300 words—and contributed to the sale of the book. Yet some author may object to the paper's use of twenty-seven words. The best principle is to quote copyrighted material sparingly and always with credit to the author.

13 Ethics for journalists

A rasping voice on the police radio near the city desk announces at 11:38 P.M. that a car has smashed into a utility pole off Hathaway Boulevard. Moments later the sirens of an ambulance from City Hospital scream by below the newsroom. The city editor dispatches a reporter, and within minutes the facts begin to fit into the mosaic of a story. Editors start making decisions, of space, display—and ethics.

The driver, in "critical" condition with a possible concussion, is Oscar Ragsdeal, forty-eight years old, according to the police. His address checks out in the city directory, which lists him as an administrative vice president of First National Bank. Good story. There were two in the car, the second hospitalized in "fair" condition. The police are working on the indentification.

So far there appear to be no serious problems. Straight-forward story: serious accident, prominent man, maybe two—probably front page and no argument. But then the ethical complications begin.

The reporter at the hospital calls again with details on the accident and says he is still trying to get the woman's name.

A woman?—probably Mrs. Ragsdeal. Unlikely, the reporter says, because this woman is in her late twenties and, oh yes, there were a couple of broken whiskey bottles in the wreckage. "Looks like Oscar had something going," says the cynical journalist—but that is a personal, not a professional editorial comment.

The injured woman turns out to be Mrs. Sally Hinslaw, twenty-eight, who has been working in a First National branch since the death of Captain Hinslaw in a Pacific plane crash. Ragsdeal is the brother of the Ragsdeal who is advertising manager of the big department.store at the corner. The women's editor reminds the city editor that Mrs. Hinslaw is the one who is such a close friend of their publisher's second daughter, in the Junior League and all; yes, these are the Hinslaws of the old mining family who are always in the parties reported on the women's page.

Should the editor print the story?

This fiction brings into focus some of the important pressures on an editor's ethics: the chance for a big headline and a "good" front page story. The right of Mr. Ragsdeal and Mrs. Hinslaw to be left alone. The rights of Mrs. Ragsdeal, and of any Ragsdeal and Hinslaw children, to be spared embarrassment. Advertising to be lost from the store and maybe the bank. A segment of the power structure unhappy about the publicizing of social scandal. And not least, the possible displeasure of the publisher.

Maybe the editor should forget the whole thing. But what will television do with it? And how will an editor settle a journalist's conscience, which says to print the news, not suppress it?

The intelligent editor must think out a consistent ethical policy to offer guidance through such thickets. An editor with one policy will see the Ragsdeal piece as a sensational bonanza worth giving the titillating works to the limit of the libel laws. A more moralistic editor might give the story almost as much space and detail, but on an eye-for-an-eye theory that if Mr. Ragsdeal and Mrs. Hinslaw are going to cut capers, they must pay in public. If God made or let the accident happen, who is the editor to interfere with the world's knowing? Still another approach would be to print the news deadpan, fairly and accurately, and let the reader make the moral judgments.

One catch-phrase of ethical coverage is "All the news that's fit to print." That slogan was introduced into a front-page ear (upper corner) of the *New York Times* by Adolph S. Ochs, the publisher who brought the *Times* to greatness. It was 1897, when other New York City newspapers were vying in sensationalism, and Ochs used the phrase to emphasize the thoroughness and sobriety of ethical newspapering.

The cynic may say that the slogan should be "All the news that fits"—or that fits the editor's whims. Everyone knows that *all* the news can't be printed. But "all the news" implies a thoroughness which will not omit stories because of laziness or pressure. "Fit" implies that the editors will avoid sensationalism or pandering to low tastes. Yet they should find it fitting for the public to know what happens, however distasteful or terrifying, and regardless of pressures to leave out some events.

Some such principle would guide most good editors in the Ragsdeal accident. Newsmen of equal integrity might disagree about what to say about those whiskey bottles and how far to dig into the time and cause of Captain Hinslaw's death. But they would print a plain, factual account of the crash, the injuries, and the condition of the victim.

Freedom and responsibility

Some editors might say that what they print is their own business and not the province of philosophers. They would be right, in the sense that a free press is guaranteed by the Constitution, and that professional customs in the United States have evolved for handling these ethical questions. Mores probably control more stories than editorial ethics. Yet there are philosophical and even theological bases for the rights of newspapers to operate as they do, and publishers ignore these at their peril. Society has given journalists wide latitude for their operations and decisions, but what society grants, society can take away. The number of totalitarian countries still flourishing late in this century should be a reminder that press freedom is not automatic.

In the days of medieval kings and queens, there would have been no argument of whether it was right or wrong to publish news of a scandal, even if there had been printing presses and editors. The monarch felt he or she had authority from God to make such decisions. A long trail of Star Chambers and jailed editors led from such dictatorship to a modern democratic system in which editors, within the framework of law, can print without license or censorship. People at first argued, as in the Declaration of Independence, that they had such inalienable rights from God; more recently, they are claimed as essential human rights. The willingness of human beings to suffer and even die for this freedom is still the ultimate test of its survival.

John Milton provided the practical argument for press freedom. In the *Areopagitica* (1644) he argued for the "free marketplace of ideas." If all ideas were freely published, he said, the best ones would win out. It followed that men must have the right to know all the facts and arguments. So he rationalized the editor's freedom as one of the prerequisites for a working democracy. Thomas Jefferson argued for the citizen's right to the truth—being optimistic, like Milton, that a benevolent Providence allowed reasonable and moral people to run their own affairs. His idea of press freedom became one of the guarantees in the Bill of Rights.

But it is a truism that freedom implies responsibility. Those who get liberty must use it responsibly or risk losing it, whether in a developing nation or on a college campus. The grant of freedom to editors to purvey the news necessary to a democratic society carries the implied demand that they will print the news. When the press suppresses or distorts the news, it jeopardizes its claim to freedom. The unwritten expectation of American citizens is that the papers will give "all the news that's fit to print." This is the ethical imperative under which perhaps most editors work.

Recognizing these obligations, publishers sometimes proclaim idealistic platforms or policies. At conventions they are especially prone to make the welkin ring with fine phrases. A major statement of high principle became the "Canons of Journalism," adopted by the American Society of Newspaper Editors when it organized in 1923. This code states that the "opportunities [of journalism] as a

Watchwords
for ethics

chronicler are indissolubly linked [to] its obligations as teacher and interpreter." The canons speak of "sincerity, truthfulness, accuracy," of "clear distinction between news reports and expressions of opinion," of "fair play." But those canons had no teeth and, while mentioned in journalism histories, are now almost forgotten. Few working journalists could quote a single canon.

The difficulty is that, like democracy, freedom, and responsibility, principles of journalism must be stated as abstractions. Pessimists can readily dismiss pledges of *public interest* or *high trust* as pious hypocrisies. The problem is to relate high-sounding dictums to hard cases; and since no paper and no person is perfect, there are inevitably some tarnishes on the best papers, not to mention the corrosions of the worst.

Still, an effort must be made to set standards for the press. If such moral principles as love, compassion, and kindness are given lip service rather than devotion, they serve still as ideals or goals. Journalists need such abstractions to broaden their vision.

Truth is the word that summarizes many journalistic ideals. But what, philosophy has always asked, is truth? Working newspaper people know well enough what truth means on the job and don't worry too much about Truth. They check the truth of small details but also the truth of the big picture, so far as they can discover and portray it.

One important facet of truth therefore is *accuracy*. Newsrooms rightly make a fetish of accuracy about names and addresses. But reporters must be at least as careful about accurate quotation, or about the accuracy of the impression which results from the way facts are put together.

Close to accuracy is *objectivity*. The reporter should keep himself out of the story, and the editors should see that he does. The conventional wisdom of the profession dictates that editorializing will be confined to editorial pages, yet editorializing barbs in stories are always slipping by copydesks. The author knows two or three reporters who produce "stories" that are really editorials, and their editors, with sloppy ethics, by-line them and print them in the news pages. The editor's job is to see that copy is accurate and free of editorial bias, whether it comes from a cub or a Washington or foreign correspondent of a famous press service.

The popular dichotomy of objectivity versus interpretation represents a misunderstanding of the journalist's problem with truth. The short dead-pan news account, the so-called objective story, the feature story, and the interpretive piece are all on one side of objectivity. Opposite them is the subjective story by the reporter who has, knowingly or unknowingly, distorted the news, whether of a minor accident or of international conflict. The sound interpretive story introduces the writer's evaluations (and these are admittedly subjective, with personal coloring), but as fairly and honestly—as objectively—as possible. The corrupt interpretation, by contrast, does not aim at truth but vents the writer's prejudices and slants.

(Editorials and editorial-page interpretations are something else again, differing from news stories).

Intertwined with accuracy and the objective search for it is the concept of *fairness*. Human limitations may prevent a paper's being really accurate and really objective (the words are relative, no matter what grammarians may say), but readers know whether the editors try to be fair. They treat everybody alike. Ideally, they are as gentle with the poor unknown as with the big shot, with the hated political party or enemy nation as with their own faction or country. Perceptive critics of the press see that it is the standard of fairness that is violated when papers blandly print in their news columns accounts which refer to "Huns," "Japs," "Commies," "Birchers," "peaceniks," and so on; the editor may protest that such highly connotative words describe accurately some social moods—but are they ever fair?

Accuracy and fairness are often threatened by pressures on editors. Pressures from government they undersand and can combat. But many critics feel editors are less successful in combatting pressure from advertisers. In an interpretative piece, the *Wall Street Journal* went so far as to say that "many once-principled newsmen have been deeply demoralized by their papers' surrender to advertisers' interest." The paper cited a study by Prof. Timothy Hubbard of the University of Missouri revealing the ideas of 162 business and financial editors who responded to a questionnaire. More than one-fifth of them said that "as a matter of routine they were compelled to puff up or alter and downgrade business stories at the request of the advertisers."

Keeping the watchwords

The threat of unequal or unfair treatment is thus often seen as one of the special favors to advertisers or establishment figures; so publishers and editors may underscore their pledge to print "without fear or favor" by publishing unfavorable news of themselves. The staff of one newspaper long told how a divorce of the publisher's had been printed on the front page. The staff saw that the standard of judgment was not simply the publisher's or editor's personal attitude toward the news but a standard of fair, full coverage. Similarly, the former publisher of the *Pascagoula* (Miss.) *Chronicle* tells how he finally convinced detractors that his was "an honest newspaper printing the news without favor":

> My son Maybin, 14, ran afoul of the law and was hailed into juvenile court. My practice had been to use the names of juveniles in police stories only if the youngsters were repeated offenders or if their crimes were heinous. My son's offense was minor, but his name appeared in a page-one story I wrote myself. He not only was named but was identified as "son of Ira Harkey, *Chronicle* editor-publisher," so there could be no mistake.[1]

The ideals of accuracy, objectivity, and fairness are all contained in the larger ideal of truth. But are these really phony ideals, used to delude, as hypocrites use flag and motherhood? Some hard-bitten cynics among newspaper editors would doubtless say "yes," and their shoddy papers reveal what happens when principle crumbles. Yet even the most ethical editors tend to be pragmatic about high journalistic principle. Pragmatism is an American philosophy that holds that the best way is the way that works best. Americans are idealistic, but they are also practical. So our editors do not usually mount white chargers. They conform.

When the whole American society preaches that killing is wrong but sends its youth abroad to kill and be killed, when it preaches brotherhood but remains calloused about the hurt suffered by many black families, it is not remarkable that this society generates publishers and editors who preach the democratic canons but violate them in practice. They make practical compromises.

The realistic goal for the ethical journalist is to compromise as little as possible, for being pragmatic is not the same as being venal or cowardly. The best editors aim high and therefore hit higher than those who aim low.

Pluralistic foundations

Why is thorough news coverage better than slipshod, or an honest newspaper better than a dishonest one? The answer is self-evident to most of us only because it is woven well into the basic fabric of our philosophical and religious thinking. For there is no more general agreement in America on morals than on political issues. The intellectual problem of ethical journalism is rooted in the pluralistic nature of American society. Some Americans think, at least part of the time, as Christians, others as Jews, a few as Moslems or Hindus, while many eschew religion entirely. Of course some, including certain editors, worship only money or power. What is "right" by one standard is not necessarily right by another.

For example, some church people feel that newspapers should not mention gambling, yet others see nothing wrong if stories promote their bingo parties. One group of Christians wants thorough press discussion on liberalizing divorce or abortion laws; another group deplores it. But the clashes among our pluralistic segments are much more profound than suggested by these so-called moralistic issues. The deep differences among our world views condition the sharp variations in reactions on such questions as America's responsibility to peoples of the world, the proper response to Communism, the sacredness of human life, the relativity of moral values, and the ability of human beings to plan their own destiny. The role of the mass media is not the least of these major issues on which thoughtful Americans can have profoundly different views.

To understand and cope with these differences, we should understand two strands of American thought: first, the religious, or, more specifically, the Judeo-Christian; and second, the philosophical, particularly the pragmatic and utilitarian. We shall then turn to two parts of democratic thought: traditional concern for liberty and individual freedom and this century's growing emphasis on equality and social justice. Throughout, our purpose is to clarify our society's presuppositions so that editors may recognize the assumptions behind their practical decisions.

The Puritan roots of American culture suggest Judeo-Christian ethics as an appropriate beginning in consideration of journalistic ethics. The approach can provide insight, even though there is little agreement on what the Judeo-Christian tradition would require. For example, journalistic morality in an Augustinian City of God would be one thing, in Mao's China another. The colonial New England theocracy did provide an official morality, but that church-led day vanished about 1700. The question is whether this strand in pluralistic thought leads to answers for the U.S. press today.

In this context "Christian" goodness may be considered as referring to kindness, generosity, compassion—in a word, love. It is the virtue extolled in the parable of the Good Samaritan and assumed in the Golden Rule. We saw in chapter 6 that editors cannot print the news with a philosophy of doing unto others as they would have done unto them. Much of the hard news in the paper deals with the wrong-doing or tragedy of people, and editors cannot start leaving it out because they would shrink from seeing their own troubles in print.

Editors sometimes print unpleasant news about someone by reasoning that they would print the item about themselves because society deserves all the significant news. This rationale is close to that of the publishers who print unfavorable news about themselves or their families, in proof of fairness. But with this argument one is moving already from the Golden Rule of Christian love to the toughness of Christian justice.

The Golden Rule has bite because it is highly personal; The philosopher Immanuel Kant extended the Golden Rule to society: act so your actions can become a universal rule. His dictum incorporates both love and justice but diminishes personal involvement. It mediates Christian love to society and therefore helps the decision-making newsman.

Prof. Richard T. Baker of the Graduate School of Journalism, Columbia University, touches on the strand of justice in Christian thought by observing that "even the truth is not enough" for the journalist. Writing in *The Christian As a Journalist,* Professor Baker says:

> You should have extraordinary contributions to bring to your profession as an instrument for a more just society. You should know with precision when and how and where to throw the weight of your journal into the tactical struggles for fairness in human relations. You

should not be cynical and defeated by the tragedies of injustice.[2]

The *Christian Science Monitor* takes this challenge seriously. This paper handles the news in a way consistent with its religiously optimistic point of view.

The utilitarian approach

Aside from Judeo-Christian principles, another widely held ethic promotes "the greatest good for the greatest number." As developed by Jeremy Bentham and John Stuart Mill, utilitarianism argues that good conduct is that which produces the greatest happiness for the most people. By dealing in quantities, utilitarianism appeals to the practical-minded. Another advantage of this concept of greatest-good is its democratic flavor. Milton and Jefferson argued for the freedom of the press as aid to the common reason; utilitarianism applies that freedom to the common good. While religious thought has proclaimed the sacredness of the individual personality, here is philosophy that rationalizes majorities and big circulations.

But for newspaper work this ethic, like the Golden Rule, has its difficulties. There is a practical problem in deciding what really is good for the most people. Can one be sure that the value to the public in printing the name of a rape victim is greater than the hurt to the girl—or vice versa? How, in fact, do you weigh such things? Yet editors can feel "greatest good" does help them weigh.

This suggests a perhaps still greater problem: the tyranny of the majority. Do the masses, just because they possess numbers, have an inalienable right to news whose publication will hurt a smaller group? Or, on the contrary, would a majority "vote" for suppression of news justify keeping the facts from a minority, simply because less good (arithmetically figured) appears to be involved?

Editors who print news of wrongdoing as well as progress, who publish a lot of comics and sports, and who perhaps circulate sensational accounts of sex and violence can rationalize that they are utilitarian. In fact, when they are criticized the reflex of many editors is utilitarian; they say they are giving the public (presumably, the greatest number) what it wants. The very self-righteousness of such contentions, however, underscores the limitation of this philosophy: editors adhering to it too literally may slight the good of the cultured minority with higher taste than the masses, of the politically sophisticated minority jaded by the banalities of mass campaigns, and of the intellectual minority needing the free exchange of ideas and contributing to the real good of society.

To apply utilitarian theory most usefully, therefore, editors must consider the "greatest number of people" not as stupid, faceless masses but as groups of important, reasonable, individuals. Then the editor may justify overruling the restraints of religiously-motivated goodwill and print what he feels serves the greatest social good.

The Golden Rule and the rule of greatest-good do not exhaust the list which could be developed in a pluralistic society. Nor is balancing these two the only way to deal with the ethical problems of newspapering. If we approach the problem now from different theoretical vantage points, we get new slants on the tensions and balances ever present in editorial decisions.

The authors of *Four Theories of the Press* construct a framework important to any modern consideration of journalistic ethics.[3] The two most pertinent concepts for us are the libertarian theory and the social responsibility theory. (The other two theories are the authoritarian and the Communist, which bear only indirectly on our discussion of American journalism.)

Rights and responsibilities

Libertarian theory emphasizes the freedom of the newspaper editor. As we have said, this concept, developed by such men as Milton and Jefferson, opposes the autocrat's power to license and censor. It holds that editors should have liberty to print what they please (restrained only by such necessary laws as discussed in the chapter on press law). The assumption is that one journalist or another will dig out and print what the people ought to have.

The optimism of this theory may seem naive because of the horrible events of the last century and pessimistic intellectual trends since Darwin and Freud. Can men really discover through reason what is best? Many youth today, however, are starry-eyed about man's nature and here, curiously, go along with the assumptions of many of their elders. It is no doubt this tradition of hopefulness about men that most American editors embrace. They oppose government interference and control in the hope that common men will find the truth in what is printed.

This libertarian concept has its aspect of social good, a fact that is often overlooked. Selfishness is not part of the theory, but part of those who work under the theory. Editors—sinful, or at least as limited, as other people—have often abused this freedom; they have printed scurrilous political attacks, exaggerated and faked the news, scandalmongered, and pandered to the cheapest tastes. Before he died Jefferson himself was strongly impelled toward second thoughts about the virtue of editorial freedom. Yet according to the theory, out of the welter of what editors print will emerge the knowledge John and Joan Citizen need for intelligent action. To work today, the theory requires reasonable printing costs and competition unrestricted by press monopolies. Then even those who are most hard-headedly realistic about the difficulties of opening the marketplace to all ideas may still logically contend that the libertarian theory offers the brightest hope of good for society.

Libertarian theory

This social strength of libertarian theory is worthy of consideration because the rival theory of social responsibility, as its name suggests, tends to assume all claim to social good. Its advocates

The theory of social responsibility

accuse newspapers of social irresponsibility and call for social instruments to see that the press fulfills its social responsibilities.

The authors of *Four Theories of the Press* trace the roots of this theory to the 1947 report of the Commission on Freedom of the Press, issued as the book *A Free and Responsible Press.* Known often as the Hutchins Commission—because it was chaired by Robert M. Hutchins, then chancellor of the University of Chicago— this group criticized press performance and listed several demands which society makes on the press. Among its suggestions was "establishment of a new and independent agency to appraise and report annually upon the performance of the press."[4]

Such suggestions and proposals have been increasing since World War II. In Britain royal commissions made blistering comments about the press, and since 1953 the British Press Council has monitored performance. On the ombudsman pattern, Sweden has a "court of honor" *(Pressens opinionsnamnd)* to adjudicate complaints against the papers. Harry S. Ashmore, senior fellow, center for the Study of Democratic Institutions (and former editor of the *Arkansas Gazette*) has urged a similar body for this country. At a meeting of Sigma Delta Chi, Barry Bingham, Louisville publisher, urged that communities have citizens' groups evaluate the efforts of their papers. But almost all American editors have shouted down suggestions like those of the Hutchins Commission as the worthless ideas of eggheads who "don't know anything about newspapers."[5]

Increased pressure to make newspapers more responsive to the needs of the people, however, was almost inevitable from the days of the New Deal, if not from the muckraking period early in the century. In the thirties social control moved from its previous domain of international trade (tariffs) and monopoly (trust laws) to wages and hours, unemployment and old-age benefits, and agricultural supports. Not the least of the intellectual pressures behind these moves were those religious and philosophical concepts of the Golden Rule and utilitarianism.

Conservatives dug in their heels, but greater government regulation has marched into such areas as health and medicine. Many corporation presidents and doctors have repeatedly warned that other businesses and professions would be next. Radio and television had faced regulation from their beginnings, and movement on to other areas of communication was theoretically inexorable. To some, religion or philosophy demand it. So far, the Constitution has protected the press. But basic laws can be modified or ignored. For a generation voters have endorsed numerous steps toward greater control in the name of the public welfare. A social-responsibility theory of the press would naturally garner wide support on similar grounds.

Right to reply

Since 1967 Jerome A. Barron, dean of the law school at Syracuse University, has contended that the First Amendment requires the press to publish minority views. He has argued—unsuccessfully so far—that the courts or Congress should guarantee the public limited access to press columns, such as the opposite editorial page or the letters-to-the-editor section. In a Florida case, a man tried but failed to get the courts to rule that the *Miami Herald must* print his reply to a story which involved him.

In one form the concept of social responsibility is familiar to all working journalists. Chambers of Commerce, city officials, businessmen, and professionals may all argue to leave out, or at least "modify," some stories so they will not hurt the community. One graduate student came back from interning on a Midwest paper, for example, to say that it published *no* news which might be considered harmful to the community.

Advocates of social responsibility theory have several problems in explaining how it would operate. What kind of sanctions will restrict irresponsible newspapers? And if the teeth in controls are real, can the press still be called truly free? What watchdogs will watch the watchdog press? The journalistic battle of the young Ben Franklin against the ruling Mathers in colonial Boston is a bleak memory for the advocates of society's control, however high-minded. Many liberals who are disturbed with press performance would be outraged if society were controlled by the Air Force or one of the intelligence agencies. Venal politicians, perhaps representing the least educated segments of the electorate, could be even worse. Would a cure by social control be worse than the disease of irresponsibility?

Editors nurtured on libertarian ideas tend to see all proposals for outside checks as revival of Star Chambers and censors. What is the practical difference, they argue, between a monarch like King George, a dictator like Hitler, a government agency, and a fancy social-control council? They all want to interfere with printing the truth. Prof. John C. Merrill of the University of Missouri is an authority on the foreign press who has argued that authoritarian regimes use the claim of public interest to censor their press.

> The only way a "theory" of social responsibility could have any significance in any country is for the government power elite to be the definer and enforcer of this type of press. Since in any country the organization of society—its social and political structure—determines to a large extent what responsibilities the press (and the citizen) owe society, every country's press quite naturally considers (or might logically consider) itself as being socially responsible.
>
> Assuming that a nation's socio-political philosophy determines its press system, and undoubtedly it does, then it follows that every nation's press system is socially responsible. For example, the Marxist or Communist press system considers itself socially responsible, and certainly it is responsible to its own social system. . . . The

same thing might be said of the so-called "authoritarian" press system, exemplified in Spain.[5]

Society will want to move slowly in changing a system which has served American democracy for almost two centuries, however badly at times. If editors don't want this change, they relax in the hope that change will be glacially slow. A major part of their ethical and moral responsibility today is to develop instruments of self-control, whether codes or councils within the industry, to obviate the need for outside enforcement of social responsibility.

The libertarian theory is most popular among journalists and publishers, but not all its advocates are within the Fourth Estate. For example, from a perhaps unexpected source, Germany, Karl Jaspers, the famous existentialist philosopher, offers a view of the press quite similar to the views of Milton and Jefferson:

> What we call publicity today is more especially the world of speakers and writers, of newspapers and books, of radio and television. This publicity is not the proclaiming ground for a single truth, but *the battleground for all truth.*
>
> Writers are *the third force between the government and the people,* between the actions of politicians and the inarticulateness of the people. They create the communicating language. But this third force is significant *only if it is independent.* [Emphasis supplied][6]

In this decade libertarian press theory clearly has the edge from tradition, but the concept of social responsibility remains in conflict with it. The authors do not insist on a choice. Nor is America likely soon to make a clear decision between the theories, any more than it has chosen between those other similarly disputed abstractions "free enterprise" and "the welfare state." As the nation appears to be settling for a mix of "capitalism" and "socialism," it may settle too for a mixed theory of the press, with maximum liberty and responsibility for all.

Editorial balance

From the discussion thus far, it becomes apparent that much of the ethical problem for editors is one of balancing. They must weigh the importance of pressures to distort or omit the news against the demands of their own conscience to be thorough and fair. At the same time they must counterbalance the frailty and limitation in their own freedom with the need to be socially responsible. They must put the individual's right of privacy in the balance against the public's right to know, and they must weigh the religious demand for compassion against the utilitarian requirement to do what is best for the most.

Editors, however, are not systematic philosophers who worry much about complete consistency. Pragmatically, and perhaps too hastily, they make a decision, and then another and another. This is journalistic life, and editors have to live with the results. Day to day editorial work focuses on three issues of press ethics. Each of them combines the tensions of different ethical problems, and the editor must develop attitudes on each of the three which harmonize satisfactorily with his or her whole philosophy of newspapering and life.

Good taste

Taste in journalism as elsewhere is a subtle quality that must be learned. In some cultures a hearty belch after a meal is considered a compliment to the cook, but in the United States a child has to learn that "it isn't done in polite society." A boor never learns this lesson; and if such a person gets into an editorial chair, the paper may abound in crudities. But, still reacting against Victorianism, even cultivated editors hesitate to argue for good taste lest they be considered square. Frankness permeates our culture. As a result, the level of taste in newspapers today has doubtless settled much lower than it was during the yellow journalism of the nineties and the jazz journalism of the twenties which today's critics still ridicule.

The popularity of bad taste

The pressures for bad taste in print have increased in the last dozen years. Perhaps it is healthy that readers and writers have been freed from some taboos on coarse words and profanity, when they are heard at every turn. Yet frequent use of these words cheapens language, for obscenities usually shock, instead of communicate. When use of these words becomes news, of course, editors must decide whether to print them. Newspapers today probably would think twice and then use such a phrase as "Get the bastards." In 1968, A. I. Goldberg, editor of the *AP Log,* said, "Thirty years ago the word *bastard* would be represented by a dash or, at the most, a 'b——.' ... Freely quoted in most newspapers recently was the police officer who cried, 'For Christ's sake, stop it!' This was another phrase that before World War II would have been considered blasphemous." Most editors have come to adopt a rule of thumb on this type of language: use it only if essential to tell the story. That means using it rarely.

Community standards

Though the public may revolt against excessively bad taste, looser standards promise to give editors headaches for years to come. Indeed, editors of the next generation may feel socially responsible for cultivating higher standards of public taste if they believe politeness and "breeding" are still essentials of civilization.

Newspapers of course must keep their standards somewhere near the levels of popular taste in their communities, and many factors have been pushing these down. Some put most of the blame on liberalized rulings by the Supreme Court. But the Court too tends to follow popular trends, and the many depressing influences on these include: the debauchery of several wars, the degeneration of plays and novels, the popularity of sexy paperbacks and sensational magazines, proliferation of "adult" motion pictures, and the strains of living in a mass society.

The need to maintain standards in "a family newspaper" sometimes is cited to avoid the worst excesses in the press, but families already find it more and more difficult to prevent the erosion of taste in their children. One of the most important influences on family taste, of course, is television. Even more than the newspaper, TV brings into the family circle a vivid portrayal of what was once scandalous. Motion pictures exhibited with "adults only" signs a few years ago are now available to children in the living room. It takes a quick parent to keep ahead of society in "educating" a child, who may pick up on TV at age five what appropriately might be left until his teens. Many will not blame journalists if, like the tired parent, they give in.

The contexts of bad taste

While they have followed established positions on taste, editors generally have been horrified by foul words in print but blase about foul living conditions in town. The press—and society—have been indignant about an unmannerly act but casual about reports of people slaughtered, maimed, or scorched in a war. Press and society may be outraged by unconventional dress but only mildly distressed when commercial interests desecrate a place of beauty. Yet at this point we are discussing taste, not morals, and even if all the evil that people do were to be abolished, editors would still have problems with the good manners of print.

The problem of taste in newspapers is not, as many suppose, wholly one of restraint about vulgarity, profanity, and sex. There can be bad taste in political writing. In the partisan-press days of the early Republic, editors scurrilously attached political enemies. During the depression of the thirties, newspapers indulged in excessive calumny, and in recent years the issues of Vietnam, civil rights, and Watergate have triggered a barrage of bad taste.

Such issues bring up the difficulty of reporting violence with good taste. Riots and war-time killings must be reported to the public with the graphic aid of pictures where possible. Once newspapers avoided publishing pictures of dead persons. But if for comprehensive coverage present-day editors must use these pictures of the dead from riots and war, why not of the dead from disasters and accidents? Yet a line must be drawn to exclude the macabre and the gory. The grisly photograph and the lurid paragraph must be scratched.

As the chapter on picture-editing indicates, the problem of taste is particularly acute in art work. Restraint must be shown with photographs of cheesecake and gore, and what television may use cannot be the criterion. The fleeting quality of pictures on the screen may lessen the objection to some material on television, but there is a permanence about the printed picture which can make it more titillating or repelling, the factors which come into play in judgments of taste.

So editors must strike balances. They must satisfy the public's need for the facts, but they must also recall the high professional obligations of a free press in the area of taste as elsewhere. They will not let fears of the Nice Nellies keep them from portraying realistic aspects of the cruel and vulgar world as they are. But in an era when public taste has been cheapened and hardened, their greater concern will be to view the press as an instrument to maintain culture and even civilization itself.

The pressure of the age is to make us all faceless fragments of mass society. Names become numbers. We are zip-coded, IBMed, and computerized. College students complain that they are processed like punched data cards, and old people say that they are just Social Security numbers. The press can join the trend by treating people as chaff for the news machines, or it can stand against dehumanization by recognizing and preserving the integrity of individual human personality.

Respect for the individual

The right of privacy is a delicate thing. From the legal side, as we saw in the last chapter, the newspaper can probably get by if its publication of personal matter is closely related to news events, but privacy is more than a question of law. Sometimes press ethics may halt an invasion of privacy which law would permit.

The right of privacy

Since much of their most significant work is always close to invading someone's privacy, newspaperpeople may have to remind themselves not to be too hard-boiled on the question. Ordinary persons, as distinguished from politicians and celebrities, have great sensitivity about "undue publicity." In an actual case a mother was incensed because the media printed and television carried the news that a teenager had shot her passing car with a BB-gun. As a misdemeanor, the shooting became a public record, and an editor could see plenty of reasons for printing the news: The public could judge whether juveniles are delinquent, whether the neighborhood had gangs, whether the police were doing their job, and whether guns should be controlled. The mother could appreciate none of these arguments. She saw no reason why her age should be printed; and she feared that the teenager, knowing her name, would take reprisals against her or her children. Silly? From the editor's point of view, yes. But from the point of view of privacy and her feeling about press invasions, it was her own business whether she was shot at. She wanted to be more than grist for "a couple of grafs." Journalists have to be aware that ordinary citizens have such "unreasonable" feelings.

Another level of respect for individuals is in news about whole masses of people, as in wars and urban violence. Communist newspapers incline to dismiss our millions with the stereotype of

Mass labeling

"imperialistic warmongers." But our press easily slips into such dehumanizing labels too. In World War I we made the enemy an inhuman mass with the word "Huns." Then in World War II it was "Japs." In more recent years those who fight against the United States are often lumped as "Communists," even though it would usually be difficult to prove there was a card-carrying Red among them. It is much the same when reporters write loosely of "black rioters" or "Negro hoodlums," leading white readers to react against a whole black community that may in fact be more than 99 percent non-rioting and non-hoodlum.

With a little care about such issues as privacy and mass labeling, the press can be a good influence in maintaining respect for individuals. This is an area of the newspaper's greatest strength. When focusing on the individual because of honest human interest, journalism can repulse the dehumanizing forces of mass society.

The effects of news

Libertarian editors who say they print "without fear or favor" emphasize their objectivity. They override pressures to print or not to print. And they learn to overlook the consequences of their decisions, for editorial action is paralyzed or biased if an editor worries about how an item is going to affect the co-worker or mother or girl friend of a person in the news.

There is a running debate whether newspapers have much effect anyway. Editorials have been discounted as political factors for decades. Civil libertarians contend that publication of pornography does not increase sex aberrations: "No girl was ever ruined by a book." Communications researchers have been able to demonstrate few clear effects of simple reports and have drawn back from trying to analyze really complex but important problems such as how newspapers influence the vote for President.

Yet if the influence of newspapers cannot be pinpointed, can the effects of home or school or church be proved any more convincingly? Are they any less real for that? Would anyone seriously hypothesize that the media have less effect than parents or teachers? The person involved in the news does not doubt that the paper has an effect. The college football star knows that sports reporting influences his ability to get dates and a pro contract. The embezzler recognizes that at the very least news stories about his deeds can wreck his credit rating.

Editors also know that newspapers have an effect from the actions of publicity seekers asking space and acquaintances phoning to try to suppress news. They hope that the effect is good, and one of the strongest arguments for press freedom is that full reporting has a beneficial effect on the democratic process. They like to point to times coverage has led to ouster of public chiselers and their crusades have brought civic improvements. The development of social responsibility theory urges them to be even more concerned about their paper's effect on society.

As news of one suicide in a mental hospital gets around, other patients sometimes make suicide attempts. From that observation psychiatrists move on to the conviction that news accounts of suicides tend to trigger other suicides. Some of them argue that accounts of a dramatic, "mad" killing, like the Manson murders in the early seventies, stimulate others to attempt such killings. The argument is plausible, since it is obvious that "good" ideas for communities and business catch on because they get press notice. But can an editor start holding back "bad" news lest it stimulate readers to try the same misdeed?

Chain reactions

Suicide is normally played down in papers, since usually the person who kills himself is not of great news importance. If a celebrity commits suicide, that fact can hardly be ignored. Many newspapers have followed the practice of giving few details on the method of suicide. They may omit the name of a poison, for example, on the theory that other depressed persons may want to take the same "out."

Other anti-social incidents are not so difficult to handle. The ordinary burglary hardly attracts others to the craft, nor does a speeding conviction encourage others to speed. In fact, news of frustrated or punished crimes is considered a deterrent.

The problem is touchier where mass emotion is involved. During an economic recession, milk-dumping reported in one agriculture center may set it off in another, and violence in one strike may touch off violence in another. News of violence and rioting seems to create a mass psychology which brings rioting elsewhere.

Newspapers can contribute to widespread panic. If the wire services carried news that an incurable flu had hit several West Coast cities, the whole nation could be panicked overnight. A similar and actual mass phenomenon was the spontaneous flaring up of "hippie" philosophy in many cities at once. While it can be argued that like social causes ignited all of this, it appears that the quick communication of youthful ideas by the media was a major factor, though television was probably more important to this than the press.

Ethical editors, then, have to consider the effects of their papers on the individual and on the society. They must print, without malice or prurience, the necessary news of individuals. The truth will probably hurt less than wild rumors spread by word-of-mouth. One journalism professor advised students to act so that they would not be afraid to have their actions published under headlines on the front page. It is a salutary moral dictum. Yet if they believe that their acts won't make headlines, they should realize that wrongdoing inevitably gets around among those who count. The editor with a sensitive conscience cannot forget that. The problem of the effect of news on society is much stickier. The editor hates to print the news that bad conditions in the community lost it a government

The editor's dilemma

contract or to report news that might spread a riot. But they must be accurate and complete; otherwise they blunt their claim as defender of the public's right to know. Practically, they will find that others disagree about their evaluation of what should be kept from the people and accuse them of venality. Editors weigh and balance personal values and may at times have to compromise a rigid application of personal principles when the public interest is at stake.

Some common problems

Underlying the discussion in this chapter is the assumption that the journalist will live up to the ethical standards of the community. As we assume that cashiers will not dip into the till and that government officials will not take bribes, we assume that editors should be honest. They will not accept gifts which will color their judgment, will not take money to leave news out, and will not promote a pet cause in order to win favors or preferment. But such general principles are more easily stated than practiced. There are puzzling decisions to be made when the newspeople get down to concrete cases.

In instances of obvious pressure from advertisers or the subtle influence of the "country club complex," it is usually assumed that the corrupted figure is the publisher or a top executive. Such convenient goats do not deserve all criticism, however, for pressures to conform afflict the whole newspaper staff. A reporter may say, "I knew the druggists would be sore if I wrote that kind of a story so I put the angle on something else." Or a deskperson may say, "Man, if we printed that we would lose all the car dealers' advertising!"

Personal favor

Reporters, in particular, move among sources who may offer gifts. In most cases the gift is merely a token: a necktie or some handkerchiefs at Christmas, a lunch, or a ball point pen. But sometimes the gift is not a token, but a bribe. For example, reporters covering a professional football team were each given a quality electric portable typewriter at the end of the season. A reporter who accepts a $300 gift can easily slip into softening or eliminating any critical stories about the football team or its management. But wasn't that the purpose of the gift?

As we pointed out in chapter 2, gratuities to journalists are usually far more subtle. An invitation to a special cocktail party, a fancy dinner, or a plush weekend sometimes sways a newsperson into thinking that the merchant in trouble with the Federal Trade Commission is too charming to expose. The reporter's copy reflects this appraisal. Sometimes reporters have been flattered to the point of being obsequious when a President or a governor asks them for advice. Others can succumb to flattery coming from a much lower level.

Journalists, like everyone else, want to be liked and it bothers some journalists to play the role, even occasionally, of the curmudgeon. Perhaps the best advice is that the journalist should at these times ask himself, "What is more important, my ego or the public's right to know the facts?"

Thoughtful reporters in Washington sometimes admit that an invitation to the home of the Secretary of State for a "not for attribution" press conference causes them to crawl at least a little way into the Secretary's pocket. After all, only about fifteen reporters are so honored. What reporters would not be a bit dazzled if they lunched at the White House? For weeks afterward the reporters could drop into all conversations, "When I was lunching with the President . . ."

Other governmental pressures have ethical overtones. A reporter or editor who criticizes the military is apt to be considered disloyal or at least "not on the team." A dissenter from American foreign policy may be reminded sternly that "dissent stops at the water's edge." In one case, a famous columnist critical of a past administration was subjected to a whispering campaign to discredit him as senile. The critic of hometown business operations may be denounced, in public, as a "carping critic who is bringing scorn to our fair city." These pressures, often not expressed so bluntly, are hard to combat because they are subtle. Also, the person who is pressured enjoys being praised by the rich and powerful as a person who "has helped our town a lot." What they probably mean is that the journalist has been a faithful puppet of the elite—a mouthpiece for a few rather than a spokesman for the many.

Public duty

One of the toughest ethical problems facing newsmen is when to be silent. All kinds of responsible people—police, industrialists, city officials—will ask the press to withhold information. The reasons are various, but at the highest levels the customary reason is "the national interest." The best known instance of silence in the national interest was President Kennedy's persuading the *New York Times* to soften a story that the United States was planning to invade Cuba. Later, when Clifton Daniel was managing editor of the *Times,* he said Kennedy had admitted that the paper should have printed the story—it would have saved the nation the humiliation of the Bay of Pigs fiasco.

There are times, of course, when the press is quick to withhold information in the public interest. If the police are about to raid an unlicensed bar or are ready to make an unexpected arrest, the facts are withheld until after the police do their work. But the "interest" had better be clear. Otherwise, the press will not be serving the public, only those who wish to operate in secrecy. Nothing so damages a newspaper's reputation and more encourages rumor than the public's realization that it omits news or favors the police, the mayor, or the manager of the town's biggest industry.

Another practical ethical consideration for an editor is whether to run for public office or to head a special committee. It inflates anyone's ego, of course, to be asked to run; but as a candidate or an elected official, the journalist puts the newspaper in a position either

Political involvement

to be partisan or to be accused of partisanship. The decision becomes acute when the journalist, being objective, believes that he or she is the best qualified person for the office.

One newspaper editor became chairman of a civic committee to investigate new water sources for the city. It was an important job and a position he could fill capably. But the findings of his committee became controversial and the key issue in a mayoral campaign. Much of the public thought that the newspaper was acting as a mouthpiece for the editor's own views on water sources. The newspaper's standing in the community declined even though no bias was ever proved.

It would be unwise to suggest that no journalist ever take public office. Many editors have been good public officials and their papers good public servants as well. But no journalist should take such a position without thorough consideration of the perils and a couple of pledges that the newspaper never will sound like a press agent.

Using freedom responsibly

The ethical newspaperperson, then, must face honestly the basic questions of business integrity and the special moral problems of the news industry. Beyond that, within the ethical considerations of this chapter, the editor must use freedom of the press responsibly. And the best guide to printing a responsible paper is to print the truth.

Accuracy is one facet of truth. The paper gets the facts straight. But accuracy refers to more than the news story. Headlines, photographs, and even editorials have an obligation to be truthful and accurate. The concept of objectivity is a part of accuracy as is the concept of balance. An accurate reflection of the community and world includes good news as well as bad.

Another facet of truth is completeness. Information can be accurate but incomplete, and then facts add up to a half-truth. Thoroughness is an editorial virtue. Good editors are not swayed by political, economic, or other pressure. They are fair to individuals and to movements. Fairness requires that they clearly label editorializing and opinion. As monopoly newspapers take on the coloration of a public utility, the concept of completeness and fairness no doubt means that even on the editorial page editors are obligated to give attention to varying views. They must be fair even to the parties, persons, and ideologies they hate.

Finally, newspaper responsibility means allegiance also to values which make the ethical problem complex. Editors must have compassion and must respect the sacredness of individuals. They must have a proper concern for the effects of their publication in society. And they must print within the limits of good taste. Yet where a balancing of values becomes necessary, even these virtues are in the second order for a free press in a free society. Editors must be careful lest they use "kindness" or "my responsibility to the town" to be weasel-word covers for cowardice. Truth must, ultimately, be the lamp which guides them.

14 Imagination in news editing

An editor must have his own profound vision of things. He cannot seek to fill his newspaper with what the reader wants for the simple reason that no editor *knows* what the reader wants. The editors I have admired have known, however, and quite clearly, what *they* wanted to put in their newspapers, what *they* thought belonged there. And they didn't get their ideas from readership surveys; they got their conception of the *good* newspaper from their own education and interests and understanding and instinct—in short, their own imagination.

—Tom Wicker, *New York Times*

One paper appears tired, listless, routine; another impresses its readers as fresh, dynamic, and challenging. The difference is imagination. An editorial team, given the freedom to use its creative powers, can generate new and improved newspapers in the same way as other professionals discover new methods to save hearts or make homes more livable.

Imagination is needed in many details of headlines, story structures, and display. But this chapter will consider imagination in three major aspects of newspaper operation: excellence of product; the progress and reform of the community; and the people's right to know.

Too often excellence is thought of merely in terms of preserving and imitating what is good. American editors never tire of asserting, somewhat chauvinistically, that they produce the best papers in the world. It may seem to them logical that all they have to do is keep on doing the job they've been doing. The challenge, however, should be to make the newspaper each year at least slightly better than it was the year before.

Imagination
and excellence

True, if there is a better newspaper in a rival community down the freeway or in a city a thousand miles away, the editor can copy its superior features and, using imagination, learn and adapt from other editors. But the real challenge of editing is to create and test new concepts and forms of newspapering.

Imaginative editing, by definition, can't be frozen into a textbook of rules, for it is impossible to anticipate the freshness and creativity that working editors must discover in themselves. Still we can give some hints for applying editorial imagination to problems of modern coverage and the use of specialized writers, editors, and critics.

Creative thinking

The key to creative newspaper work is the editor's ability to generate imaginative story assignments. It is easy to assign a reporter to cover a city council meeting, a school bond referendum, or an explosion at the popcorn factory. Editors can sharpen imagination in assignments by constantly asking about whatever they read, hear, and see, "Is there a story in this for our paper?" In most cases there is not. But perhaps once in twenty or thirty times there is. Articles from magazines like *Harper's, Commonweal,* the *New Republic,* or *Nation's Cities* offer information and insights about problems of general interest, and creative editors should always be thinking how these articles could apply to home base.

A few years ago the big-circulation magazines like *McCall's* and *Esquire* were of little use to the serious newspaper editor, but today they offer solid reporting as well as entertainment. The smaller magazines mentioned previously, however, are better sources of insight about trends in social change. Scholarly magazines, too, are filled with articles that may seem dry, but that contain fresh and even startling ideas. News assignments on politics, foreign policy, economics, sociology, and other topics spring from these articles to the mind of an alert editor.

The same potential lies in current books. An editor need not read them completely to get practical ideas. First chapters, for example, often can be skipped or skimmed. Tables of contents usually give clues to important chapters, allowing an editor to pick and choose the material and thereby digest some books in an hour or two. Obviously, there are volumes that deserve careful attention, but a good editor identifies them quickly and gives them extra time.

Creative assignment

Having found an idea for a story, editors must ask themselves where the staff can obtain necessary information. Will a state official have a few facts? Will someone in city hall be able to add a few details? Is there an expert in the community who could supply more information? Could that expert direct a reporter to other sources? Is there someone who knows the practical difficulties? Do staff reporters have clues about where to find information?

After editors clarify ideas on how to get the facts, they should make assignments to the reporter in detail. A mere "Get a little story on pollution of Hickory Creek" produces "a little story" with few facts. That article will bounce off the reader, and the next day concern for Hickory Creek's foul condition will evaporate. Rather, a note should describe the idea carefully, in such clear detail that the reporter can have no doubt that a thorough story is desired and that certain sources probably are most promising.

It is important, too, that the editor assign the story to a reporter who is interested in the subject. A writer who is unconcerned about an issue—and unable to get concerned—will do a poor job and may even consciously or unconsciously sabotage the whole idea. But the editor should not expect a reporter to signal an interest. Sometimes the quiet person sitting in the corner is itching to dig into a serious and important subject.

Creative encouragement

In a creative newsroom, ideas for stories will come from staff members as well as editors. Some city desks have a suggestion box where reporters, photographers, and copyeditors can drop notes proposing stories. As noted in chapter 8, this source will dry up in a hurry if the editor pays no attention to the suggestions. When editors use a tip, they should thank the person who presented it. When the tip can't be used, the editor should tell the author why. Some papers can even give a small bonus to a staffer for an unusually good idea, and magazines pay well for story tips.

A word of praise for a professional piece of reporting is also helpful. So is posting a good story on the newsroom bulletin board. Mention in a staff publication of outstanding work stimulates more exceptional reporting, and so does a ten-dollar bonus.

If editors take stories as they come, never suggesting changes or seeking more information, the imagination of reporters will wilt. If editors lack enthusiasm, if they are as unconcerned about the discovery of a new cure for cancer as about the Cub Scout cookout, they will drive away good reporters and encourage the mediocre to imitate their dubious success.

Insightful coverage

Good papers today offer depth coverage. The superior ones of the future will search for significance with even more imagination and care. They will seek to discover trends, strive for insight into complex issues, and explore ways to relate their findings to reader concern and interest. Consequently, leading editors will turn more and more to subjects that have not been covered and are not easily accessible. Recognizing the difference between imagination and imitation, they will resist following "new fads." Few editors today are so perceptive. They think they are being imaginative when they run stories about a current social problem that has seized the general attention of the moment. Such subjects come and go, like clothing fashions. For a time, the papers are full of stories on juvenile delinquency, drug addiction, or school dropouts. The subjects are in the spotlight for a year or so—lighted only on their surfaces—and then they fade into the background. A few years later they may again take center stage. The better editors go after subjects, not because everyone else does, but because of their own thoughtful judgment of significance.

Widespread, stereotyped reporting of social and political problems was noted in a criticism of special television news shows. The critic said the networks use and reuse the same material: Space, Race, Reds, and Feds. That harsh criticism may have hit home, for networks now show more imagination. They have explained, for example, how thousands of people lose their lives every year to fire, and how many of those lives could have been saved. They have gone into detail on the Alaska pipeline, and its associated social problems, and the possibilities of new energy sources. Newspapers, in similar ways, have succeeded in broadening coverage of important subjects.

Though little is new under the sun, institutions change and novel events occur. It is the job of the journalist to observe these changes and events, even those that may be barely distinguishable, and to identify them in ways that make sense to the reader.

Not only do the media neglect some changes and events until they explode into spot news; university specialists sometimes fail to grasp what is happening under their noses, and often political leaders badly misread public moods and attitudes. Because of mankind's insensitivity to change, many problems are full-blown before they are recognized. To some extent this is inevitable. Humans seem almost incapable of paying attention to minor problems. Only when they become gigantic—and almost impossible to solve—are they tackled. Even then, it is tempting simply to reduce rather than eliminate them.

Examples are everywhere. Air pollution is dismissed as an irritant until it kills large numbers of people. Nothing serious is done about water pollution until at least one of our Great Lakes becomes a cesspool. Mental health is little more than an unmentionable subject in a family until nearly every member realizes that one of them is in torment. Even when the ills of society are obvious, many people ignore them, apparently assuming that they will go away.

Fusing interest and importance

It is difficult under these circumstances for editors to print the news their readers need if they are to act as responsible citizens. Criticize editors for not printing much of anything about Africa or South America, and they may reply sadly, "We printed stories about Africa, and a readership survey showed that only 6 percent paid any attention. The same thing happened to our South American articles. We can't fill up the paper with stories that only 6 percent will read."

Though the argument sounds irrefutable, there is a flaw in it. The editors are right in implying the paper must print what readers want if it is to survive. But they are wrong in suggesting that everyone has to be interested in everything in the paper. Most items must appeal to large groups of readers, but this principle leaves room for some material that will be read by a minority, even a small one. Of the solid, important story, the editor should say, "The public needs to know this, even though many readers will not read it. So I am going to print it. If the majority of readers skip it, they will still find plenty of other items to interest them."

The editor has to keep in mind *why* people read newspaper stories. Wilbur Schramm, the communications researcher, argues that people read because they expect a reward. They find information satisfying even when it may be "bad news" because it provides a negative reward. College students avidly read about a tuition increase. Motorists read with satisfaction about the elimination of a dangerous stretch of highway, but they also read with concern about the closing of a shortcut. Young people read about the possible bad effects of "The Pill." And older people carefully follow the obituaries. Probably none of these readers, however, will pay much attention to an election in Uruguay or a disease in Tanzania. Such subjects are too remote from their own interests.

The task of the editor, then, is to attempt to link these socially and politically important subjects to the legitimate interests and concerns of readers so that they anticipate—and find—some reward. This is not easy. The editor, working with the reporter, photographer, and artist, must plan with care and imagination, striving for a compelling blend of copy and art. In some ways, the task is easier today than even a decade ago. More readers have attended college; more have travelled, read, and broadened their awareness through television news reports and documentaries. Also the political and economic involvement of the United States with the world has brought a greater public consciousness of that world. So more people are interested in Uruguay and Tanzania than there were a few years ago.

It is easy, however, to exaggerate the increase of interest in peripheral subjects. College does not always educate. Almost everyone knows college graduates who are narrow, ignorant, and scornful of intellect. And many who have traveled extensively are less enlightened about foreign culture than the faithful reader of the *National Geographic.* So the alert editor must search for relevance, attempting to make the readers, through their self-interest, aware and concerned.

Good reporting must be supported by imaginative presentation. To write a story and slap on a two-column head is not enough. Major pieces deserve major treatment. They require striking pictures or art work. They must jolt the reader's interest by presenting the drama of the facts themselves.

Ideas for good visual presentation can be obtained from newspapers that consistently do a good job of combining words and art.

Presenting news imaginatively

Some Sunday magazines published by newspapers manage this effectively. Their small format helps, for if two facing pages offer type and art work, the reader's eyes will have no distractions from the spread. The *Los Angeles Times,* the *Chicago Daily News,* the *Minneapolis Tribune* and *Star,* and the *St. Petersburg Times* are among the papers that cleverly present major stories. Magazines like *Fortune* and *Scientific American* consistently offer dramatic presentations. Editors who actively examine their layouts will discover ideas for exceptional visual presentations that can be adapted to the needs and character of their own paper.

Interpretive pieces need not be lengthy. It has become fashionable in recent years to run "The Depth Story," in which a reporter writes and writes about every facet of one problem in a single report. By itself, the report may be outstanding. But an editor should worry that well-intentioned readers may become overwhelmed and put it aside, saying, "I'll have to read that when I get time." Others may go through the whole thing but forget the single impact after a few days. Because memory must be refreshed, continuing problems need big, medium, and small stories every week or so. They also need display that demands attention.

This kind of presentation is not cheap. It may take capable, well-paid reporters, photographers, and artists days or even weeks to do a short series. This sometimes means an expenditure of several thousand dollars, which only the wealthiest dailies can afford. But smaller papers can do excellent work a little less elaborately. The pictures can be good, if not superb. The writing can be colorful and thorough. The material can be put together in an attractive way, by using devices of makeup mentioned in chapter five, such as boxes, Ben Day borders, white space, little sketches, copy set in wide measure, and a little extra space between columns.

All this takes additional time and money—but it is well worth it if the reader lingers longer with the paper. It may even be financially profitable in the long run: advertisers should prefer a paper on which people spend twenty-five or thirty minutes to one that is skimmed and tossed aside.

Trends to specialization

The specialized writer has come into prominence only since World War II. Specialization probably will continue and spread beyond reporting. In the past, for example, most copyediting "specialization" was done helter-skelter. If a copyeditor had a sailboat, he was given stories about the sea. If she had played a violin in the high school orchestra, she read the music critic's column. This has worked moderately well on some desks, but on better newspapers today it is simply inadequate. Most copyeditors, as an illustration, usually do not try to work over science news because they are afraid to. This means that science stories often are not as lucid as they should be. Increasingly, however, copyeditors who specialize in sciences and medicine, or in urban affairs, education, space technology, the arts, and dozens of other areas, are appearing in major newspaper offices. The American newspaper is generating specialists on the desk as well as in the field.

More and more, perhaps, a copyeditor will work with a team of reporters and photographers on special stories. Suppose that the top editors decide on thorough coverage of the housing needs of the community. The copyeditor will be in charge of the team. The staffers will map out what information they intend to get: the number of substandard houses, the need to mesh housing developments with transportation, the cost of decent housing, and proposals for cuts in building costs. The copyeditor, striving for display that assures maximum readership, will talk to photographers and artists about effective illustrations. All of these journalists—reporters, photographers, an artist, and the copyeditor—may spend several hours or days reading and talking about the problem before anyone leaves the office.

The team of specialists

Reporters will dig up information. Photographers will take pictures to tell part of the story pictorially. An artist may add cartoons, sketches, and graphs. The copyeditor will work and rework the copy into a series, a full page layout, or part of the front page plus some inside material. Thus, the whole issue of housing will be thoroughly covered—yet the writing can be lean and precise, taking up relatively little room. All those who took part in the reporting and editing, meanwhile, have become somewhat expert on the community's housing problems, which will be useful when later specialization is needed.

The future, if this kind of team reporting and editing becomes at all common, will put a premium on planning. The copyeditor in charge of such a team must analyze a problem and set about methodically to investigate it, a task blending imagination and organization.

Though specialization is the trend, the generalist remains immensely valuable. Copyeditors who can do a good job of editing copy about an uprising in Bucharest because they are fairly well-informed about Eastern Europe, and who can also handle a story about heartburn because of considerable knowledge about medicine are good to have around. Besides, some specialists get into the bad habit of writing only for other specialists. They gradually take on the jargon of the specialty and sometimes become part of the speciality's establishment. Well-informed generalists can help the paper minimize such dangers of over-specialization.

The generalist

A generalist, even a new reporter, may be able to spot a story that the expert overlooked because the expert was too close to the scene. The most dramatic example of this problem came when the medical writer of the *Washington Post* went on vacation. His substitute, Morton Mintz, ran across the thalidomide story—which actually had been available to science writers for months. He found that a tranquilizing drug called thalidomide, given to pregnant women, caused deformities in their babies. His story produced world wide alarm and led to closer testing of drugs as well as the elimination of thalidomide in the United States. The story continues to erupt from time to time as papers in Europe reveal the long-term horror of the drug, or report lawsuits against the drug company.

Imaginative coverage of the trends, nevertheless, usually requires specialists. Expert coverage has been long established in two journalistic fields, sports and business. For decades no editor would have dreamed of sending a football writer to cover the stock market or a society writer to cover the World Series. It is perhaps some kind of wry commentary on American culture that experts have been demanded only by our sportsmen and businessmen. More and more, however, the educational level of our culture now demands expertise in the coverage of such areas as science, health, labor, religion, education, and the arts.

It is no longer thinkable, as Scripps believed, that a diplomatic conference can be covered by a police reporter or a church editor— even though both may have expert knowledge of human nature. The foreign affairs expert who writes on international conflicts, the education editor who writes on changes in schools, and other such specialists are positioned to spot the vital trends of war, of student unrest, of cancer breakthroughs, strike threats, aesthetic revolutions, moral upheavals, and the rest. At their best, they are experts strategically placed.*

The critical function

To many, critical writing about music, drama, and other arts is simply a form of news coverage. Some critics, however, see their work as another art, as comment upon a presentation which will guide ticket-buyers and help shape taste. But whether it is art or news, criticism is something that the imaginative editor has to ponder how to improve—or inaugurate.

Again we must consider that newspapers often have done the job inadequately, and realistically ponder how they can improve. Too often, outside of the ten biggest cities, editors have found a music teacher or a reporter who likes movies to review everything from a high school production of *South Pacific* to the local appearance of the Ballet Russe. The practice is not necessarily deplorable. Almost any criticism is better than none, and with guidance the amateur critic may become a fine professional one.

---

*The *Chicago Tribune* once assigned an education specialist, Casey Banas, to work six weeks researching and writing a series "with a fresh perspective" on the Chicago police department. The paper headed a front-cover ad in *Editor & Publisher:* "We assigned the biggest police story of the year to our education writer."

Nevertheless, for some years the bigger and better papers have supported full-time specialists in criticism. Culture has come to "the provinces." Theatrical performances in Houston and symphonic programs in Minneapolis can equal those of Paris or Prague. Our affluent society can support local appearances of artists from New York, London, Tokyo, Bombay, Israel or Mali. These performances deserve more than a public relations handout. By publishing criticism, the newspaper helps readers check their own impressions, guides them to more sensitive appreciation, and stimulates them to awareness of how their tastes differ from others.

The culture boom

The culture boom means also that local presentations are at an all-time high. Appreciative coverage is needed for community drama, local art shows, local museum exhibitions, university dance presentations, community orchestra concerts, church pageants, and photographic shows. In any city of 50,000 or even fewer, one person could be kept busy most of the time covering cultural events, and even if the reviews were only moderately good, the growing number of educated readers would find the local paper more vital because of the coverage.

This observation especially pertains to the motion picture. If attendance is a criterion, the movie houses are the local institutions most deserving critical coverage. Traditionally, papers have printed puffs about movies in return for ads and perhaps "comp" tickets. The system is unfortunate, for the paper gives away valuable space and the film business encounters a generation of people who don't believe what they read about the pictures. We sense a trend toward better cinema criticism in small and middle-sized as well as large communities. While honest and objective reviews may cause some turkeys to lose money, they may contribute to the success of good films. Sound criticism in newspapers around the country might much improve the motion picture industry.

Newspapers hold the same potential for television, though syndicated criticism makes it more difficult for the local TV critic to contribute meaningfully. By the time the television show is over, who cares about critical reactions? Some viewers want to know what others thought, just as they do when they bring the subject up at the coffee break the next morning. Some spot-criticism of bigger shows would be appropriate, just as some local editorializing on global issues is. Where local television shows do something out of the ordinary in documentaries or entertainment, the newspaper ought to take critical note, for other media will. Probably the greater opportunity for TV criticism in most cities, however, is to criticize, from a local perspective, what networks, producers, or certain shows are attempting to do over a period of time. One of the best examples is the work of Sander Vanocur, a veteran TV newsman turned TV critic for the *Washington Post*.

The search for critics

Imaginative criticism in the future probably will be handled either by full-time writer-editors or by groups of part-timers. The full-time writer will have to develop in the same way as any other specialized writer or editor. The part-timer presents the editor with an even bigger challenge. First, recruiting must be careful. The temptation to take just anyone should be resisted; men and women with both aptitude and interest should be sought out with care. The fledgling critic, then, should prepare for professional work by reading a book or two on criticism. Tuition for one or two courses in a nearby school might be supplied. Courses in literature, history, music appreciation, and drama might all be appropriate. The reporter who acted in college plays might take a course in Greek tragedy, and the school music director who wants to try her hand at criticism might take a journalism course.

Finally, the recruit should be assisted to see and hear as much as possible, and not always as an assignment. Here the writer must know the area to be covered. It is as important for the part-time critic to know that the job entails, say, coverage only of music and dance as for any other specialized writer to know what subjects to investigate. Then the beginning critic can read, study, and observe with a focus. Like writing, the way to learn to criticize is to criticize. "The one indispensable requirement for such work is taste," says Walter Kerr, drama critic for the *New York Times,* "and taste is formed, I am convinced, only by maximum exposure to a field."

Book reviewing also deserves the attention of imaginative and creative editors. Today, few papers offer more than token news and criticism of books. There is syndicated criticism, of course, but that puts the newspaper into competition with the more thorough presentation of magazines. More important, the reaction of a local reviewer may be more interesting and useful to many readers than the criticism ground out in Manhattan.

Here the editor may follow the tack of specialization or not. Often local intellectuals who write with grace can review books for general reading. Or the newspaper can find, as do many magazines, an expert to review a book—an engineer at a local plant to comment on the book about scientists in government, and the clothing shop owner to review the volume on fashion history. Admittedly, heavy editing and rewriting may be necessary, but the possibilities are wide if imagination is used to find specialized reviewers. The mayor may review a book on politics, or a school board member may handle a book on education. Publishers provide free copies of the books, and many reviewers are delighted to have the book, a byline, and nothing more.

In all types of criticism, the newspaper has unusual opportunities to develop a role in a field that is free of competition. For more than a generation we have heard how broadcasting pushes newspapers to wider and deeper interpretation. Extrapolating this trend, we are suggesting that editors use imagination also to criticize culture in ways only newspapers can. National media can't localize as the paper can, and local television appears unable or unwilling. The field is free; the gates are wide open.

Imagination should be used both in reforming the paper and in reforming the community. Traditionally the good journalist has served as messenger, watchdog, and crusader. As editorial emphasis moves from deadpan objectivity to depth reporting it also advances leadership and guidance. What values are behind interpretive articles, what standards and goals are being suggested by the very fact of their appearance? The imaginative editor goes beyond the search for internal excellence to visualize, plan, and help build a better community.

Progress and reform

Crusades seem to have gone out of fashion. It is true that many papers, fat and complacent, don't make waves. But the fact remains, as the annual awards of Pulitzer and other prizes testify, that some newspapers still campaign for progress and reform.

Watchdogging power

Crusading often means bucking the powerful people in the community. Wealth means power, and more often than not political leadership is tied with that power. The newspaper publisher and his chief managers are probably close to the Establishment of the community—meeting on committees with them, golfing, dining and drinking with them. It is not easy for a paper to break with and confront this aggregation of power, which provides much of its own economic energy. Picking at the petty politicians may not be difficult, and may even be a pleasant sort of sport; but hitting at the real political, social, and economic power of the city takes more nerve.

Peter B. Clark, president and publisher of the *Detroit News,* views the problem of power structure in a somewhat different way. In a Journalism Day address reported by *Editor & Publisher,* he pointed out that "the writings of most American journalists are informed by explicit or implicit criticism of powerful men and powerful institutions." But:

> In the last two decades, some of the wrong men and institutions have been labeled powerful, while some really powerful ones went unnoticed. We have missed real targets as we flailed away at stereotypes. . . . The professor, the journalist, and the bureaucrat have gained moral influence while the formal church has lost it. Taken as a group, the men of new power establish the fashions in ideas. . . . We are all, to some extent, more likely to criticize strangers than friends. All college-trained journalists (myself included) are far more likely to have professors, government employees, or other newsmen as close personal friends than corporate presidents, labor leaders, generals, or police chiefs.

The new professions are far more like each other than like the old professions. Our backgrounds, educations, experiences, life-styles, tastes, and basic values are more like those of the new men of power than the old. Thus, we write favorably about our friends (or their friends) but we pick away at the men of old power—armed perhaps with tips, leaks, and insights provided by our friends, the new men of power.

Clark's emphasis on finding real power and watchdogging it is appropriate. We doubt, however, that the power shift has been so great. It is true that powerful trustees sometimes have been unable to control students. It is also true that high politicians are routed by the critical power exerted by some professors, some students, television people, and some journalists. These examples seem to us noteworthy precisely because power so rarely operates that way. But whether Clark's vision, or ours, or another is accurate, the task of imaginative newspeople is to seek significant information. Editors, journalism educators, and journalism students should investigate and debate where power lies, watch for its misuse, seek progress and reform, and crusade where necessary.

Clark Mollenhoff, an outstanding veteran reporter of the Cowles newspapers, has argued that a reporter tracking down corruption "should follow the dollar." At times people engage in shady praceices to gain power, to keep power, or to help their friends. But most often money is behind corruption. Editors, without becoming manic about the subject, should routinely check to see whose pocket might be lined as a result of an important proposal, act, or deal.

Editors must, at the same time, realize that there are altruistic people who work hard for changes that offer them no financial rewards whatever. They toil only for what they consider will make a more pleasant or just world. Among these people are those who work for preservation of green space, recreation, family planning, safer highways, improved education, political reform, and dozens of other worthy goals—and even goals the editor may consider mistaken. These people also make news—news of progress. One satisfaction of newspaper work is observing up close a spectrum of the human race, from scoundrel to saint. The editor should not assume, despite confirming evidence on certain days, that everyone is a scoundrel. Imaginative editing includes also the search for "good news" of change.

Challenging prejudice

Impressions, not necessarily accurate ones, are picked up by people from their papers. These impressions are the result of hasty reading, poor memories, and habits of noting only what bolsters their prejudices. A good newspaper should challenge such impressions by printing, from time to time, the cold facts of a situation. For example, every year or so it may be necessary to recap the concrete actions concerning school integration in a community or state.

Not everyone will read such facts, of course, but some will, and perhaps by steady effort the myths, half-truths, and incorrect assumptions can be given a needed burial.

Political figures and others who frequently make public pronouncements often only repeat what is common prejudice. In some instances prejudices are studiously promoted by certain people or groups, and the newspaper must convey the correct information. A sizable proportion of the public, for example, has accepted the idea that everyone on welfare is a loafer. It is commonly said that women on welfare have babies so they can get more money. The editor should check these common impressions. How much more does a woman on welfare get if she has another child? How much does a welfare family get? If a person on welfare got a job for one day, would the income be deducted from the welfare check—and thereby discourage looking for part-time work? The truth would make a story.

Even though the Supreme Court ruled on school prayers in the early sixties, many people assume that the court absolutely banned such prayer. Why not a review story, noting that *compulsory* prayers were abolished?

Or what about the impression that most college football players major in physical education? Why not a story examining the facts?

Dozens of other illustrations could be cited. While these are examples of national impressions, in most towns at least a few local misconceptions are bandied about without correction. Good editors will do their best to get at the truth, even though they may suspect that most subscribers would rather read editorials and stories that reinforce their incorrect impressions.

It is helpful also to consider whether a person making a proposal has a concealed axe to grind. This does not mean that editors must always suspect evil motives. But they should be skeptical. A senator once introduced legislation which would forbid imports of foreign firearms. This sounded like good news to those who supported gun control legislation. But there was a joker in the proposal: The senator came from the state that produced the most firearms in the nation. A ban on foreign weapons presumably would endear him to home industry and the home work force.

Good newspapers pride themselves on giving "both sides"—the pros and cons. William F. Buckley, Jr., is put to bed next to Max Lerner, amid columns that are pro-Democratic as well as pro-Republican. Better papers have their own strong editorial voice, but they open their letters column to replies which rebut and even insult them.

Covering varied viewpoints

Actually, complex issues have more than just pro and con sides. There are various angles which a newspaper has an obligation to cover in both news and editorial pages. A major criticism of newspapers is that they present a narrow range of opinion. As presidential candidates and voters tend to cluster to the middle of the road on issues, so do newspapers. There have always been a few right-wing columnists, from John Chamberlain to Russell Kirk, but columnists much to the left of center have been harder to find. The brilliant I. F. Stone occasionally has his pieces reprinted today but for twenty years he was restricted to writing for his own newsletter. A major challenge to imaginative editors today remains that of finding and developing columnists who can go beyond regurgitating the conventional wisdom and present fresh and stimulating ideas and viewpoints. They may infuriate hidebound readers, but even optimists agree that the country's survival requires creative thought which will jog us out of old ruts. Many papers have found exceptional black columnists who do not limit themselves to comment on difficulties facing black people. Others have hired blue-collar columnists.

Imaginative editors also could turn up local writers who would present strong viewpoints. That happens, but, in a quite human way, editors too often print or reprint "a terrific piece" which is terrific only because it endorses their views. Alert editors should also go after articles from the sociologist who wants a much more basic attack on ghetto problems, the minister who opposes a war (or endorses it), and the teachers' union president who feels a strike may be necessary next fall.

Some dissenting comments will come automatically to the letters column, of course. Editors should take particular care to print those which intelligently present views different from their own. Some editors try to print at least the nub of argument in every letter received. Others pride themselves—wrongly—in throwing away those from their opponents. Every paper receives a certain percentage of "nut letters" which deserve little space, but nothing angers the readership more than knowing that they have no chance to get their arguments into a paper, especially if it enjoys monopoly status through the support of their subscriptions! Publishing the full range of opinion in a community is survival insurance for a paper at the least, but at the most it demonstrates the highest responsibility to the community.

In broadcasting, regulations supporting the right of reply have been formulated, although the networks are contesting them in court. As it has worked out, the equal-time doctrine for political news has hampered the best coverage—yet some important people would like to have such regulations applied also to newspapers. Court cases, as mentioned in Chapter 13, have sought rulings that would require editors to print replies. These cases have failed but they raise important questions of press freedom. Do citizens' rights to present their views outweigh the right of editors to run their papers as they please? And what are society's rights? Taking a tip from this controversy, editors might improve the paper's handling of opinion (and forestall government regulation) by encouraging replies. Too often an editor is content to give a maligned figure a paragraph or two of denial deep in a news story. Some news personalities fear how the reporter may handle their words. Then why not give them some space to state their side? How about a "combat page" where those involved in controversy can slug it out?

In the early 1970s the nation, and the world for that matter, was buffeted with demonstrations, marches, strikes, and riots. That turmoil has ended, possibly because the fury over the Vietnam war ended. But is this feeling of exasperation, anger, and helplessness that apparently triggered those disturbances still with us? Did those demonstrations come about because so many thought only dramatic protests could attract the media's attention? Perhaps editors should examine news definitions to see if they incorrectly give top news priorities to violence and unusual costumes and to bizarre happenings. Also, could editors be alert to the discontent around them and print some columns of dissent? Could they work harder to plumb the feelings of frustration and anger that plague so many ordinary people? The Establishment—white or military or university or labor or corporate—has ways of getting its messages out. The newspaper might provide space for "the little guy" and the powerful. People might stop saying that the newspaper is dull, that "there's nothing in it," if there were more real opportunity for clash of ideas. Editors might, indeed, raise public controversy above the mindless level of recent combats.

Imaginative editing, in short, must challenge every group—the Establishment, the "silent majority," the radicals, conservatives, and so on—and seek new ways to involve ordinary citizens in improving our society. Waiting for a letter to the editor can't be considered an imaginative way to involve such people.

The right to know

In their running battle with government, journalists for some time have emphasized the people's "right to know." Embedded in constitutional law is the idea that citizens must be fully informed to participate intelligently in government. Publishers and top editors like to boast how carefully they watchdog government, but the facts don't bear them out. Reporters dutifully show up at press conferences, ask some obvious questions, and run to the typewriters to report what High Official said. Bob Woodward and Carl Bernstein, the chief journalistic probers of Watergate, have called such reporters "sophisticated stenographers." Some editors, then, deserve the title of "sophisticated chief stenographer," for they print only what the powerful utter. Some readers understandably are curious why, for example, reporters hang on every presidential word but can't seem to walk two blocks to cover a hearing on why insurance rates differ so greatly. Instead of nit-picking with critics, good journalists should listen to the criticism and correct their own flaws. Editors even could hope that more readers *demanded* better journalism. Their demands might make it easier to get a better budget, hire more and better staffers, and put out an improved paper.

Emphasis on the reader's right to know brings us back to the subject of attaining excellence considered at the beginning of this chapter. There discussion was on internal organization and planning for improvement. The subject is further illuminated by considering excellence in light of what the reader needs to know.

The reader's needs

In some ways the flaws of the newspaper are the flaws of the modern university. Students pick courses in history, political science, economics, and literature. Unless they are unusually sharp, they may not see how economics affects politics and how history affects literature. Some educators and some students would like to figure out how to mesh these subjects, in order to provide an understanding of the world we live in, the world we used to live in, and the world we may live in.

The newspaper provides a similar smorgasbord. There are stories about politics, economics, social movements, education, and conservation, but there is little effort to interrelate them. Editors, if they think of it at all, apparently assume that the reader will put all these subjects into some loose order. It is quite an assumption, for most of the nation's editorial pages reveal that editors themselves are not gifted in catching the ties among all the subjects they cover.

Many editors, of course, are concerned about this fragmentation and try to relate one piece of news to another, so perhaps it is a safe prediction that more and more newspapers will try to help readers understand the interlinking of events that pass before them. Today, we are limited to grouping of associated news events, an occasional news analysis, and a boldface insert directing the news reader to check an editorial on the subject on page 22. Good as this is, it is not good enough. Part of the solution may be in the blend of the visual and the written word, as already discussed.

How can the editor meet the demands of the better-educated and more skeptical reader? Many press observers think modern editors should function with these goals in mind:

—to discover what the readers want to know, and to sense what they need to know. The need can be obtained by careful reading, listening to intelligent critics, and diligent observation of the community.

—to keep alert to developing events, even though those events may not be worth a story for several days or weeks.

—to report government and education in the community with thoroughness and care.

—to explain how the reader can make a successful living, which would include money, job satisfaction, and the simple pleasures of life.

—to assist consumers so they avoid buying, for example, shoddy merchandise and poor quality food. This would include information on how they can reduce the ravages of inflation.

—to report the truth on economic conditions.

—to examine events to see whether the traditions of news reporting should be altered to reflect changes in society and in the reading public's needs.

—to be alert to assaults on human liberty, and to educate the public about democratic principles.

—to be as fair and honest as possible, for a newspaper's most precious asset is credibility.

Perhaps the ideal editor would be one who is pushing constantly to get readers to attend to the serious events and trends of their time.* Without such an editor, the newspaper is little more than an entertainment sheet. The job of prodding and luring the reader requires subtlety—and patience. A reader will not get interested in Africa or even air pollution by reading one story. William Rockhill Nelson, founder of the *Kansas City Star,* talked about the need for patience by citing his paper's campaign for a new bridge across the Missouri River. For years, he said, his paper ran news stories, feature stories, editorials, pictures, and cartoons about how the bridge was needed, how it would be needed even more in the future, how commerce would be assisted with a new bridge. The effort paid off. The bridge was built—but only after an editorial campaign that lasted ten years.

The reader's nature

Such hammering at the public consciousness must be done if the citizen is to grasp the significance of what is all around him. To accomplish this hammering, without boring or irritating the reader, requires imagination. The editor must be able to present this information in dozens of different ways and, in most instances, in ways that the reader will think give him reward.

The most obvious play of imagination comes in the selection of stories. Problems never will be acute to the reader unless they are brought close to home. Even a newspaper in Phoenix should report that Lake Erie is so polluted that it has little marine life left. The public needs to know that. But a reader in Arizona is not going to be as concerned about Lake Erie as a resident of Ohio. The editor must take the shocking story of Lake Erie's pollution and tie it to conditions at home.

It takes no great imagination to do this. Water pollution in one's own area can be checked. How pure are the streams nearby? How

---

* During the Depression, a neophyte pollster, George Gallup, told Columbia journalism students that the newspapers were missing a real bet in failing to give news about where job opportunities were. Papers are still missing that bet.

about the lakes? Is the supply of pure water in any danger? What would happen to the water supply if the area's population doubled within twenty years? How can the present pollution be shown graphically, with words and pictures? What is the state water control board doing about polluters? Scolding them? Fining them only $500? Who is on that pollution board? Is anyone there a polluter?

Stories that result from investigation should not be pelted at the reader. A story today may be followed up in a couple of weeks. An editorial or a cartoon could be run from time to time. More ideas might be produced. Is there a conservation group? What does it propose? What is being suggested in other areas? Would those suggestions apply here? These local stories can be reinforced with national stories about water pollution. In so selecting and highlighting vital issues, the editor meets the real needs of readers.

The paper's teaching role

The newspaper of tomorrow may set aside certain sections for unabashed teaching. A generation or more ago newspapers ran serialized novels each day. Some even published a short novel in the Sunday supplement. To this day, papers run crossword puzzles and bridge columns. Why not a learning column?

With the superior color printing available there could be a series on the history of art, with a text of perhaps 1,000 words under a four-column cut of a famous painting. A little quiz could be printed, for self-grading, every few days. Readers probably would not immerse themselves in the subject the way they would if they were taking a formal course in art history. But perhaps they would learn something about art and so appreciate it more.

The art course might run a month and then there could be a shift to economics, or a study of the short story, or geography, or transport. Perhaps even serious non-fiction could be serialized. Rachel Carson's *The Sea Around Us,* for example, would be an excellent book to serialize for a month. It would be possible that the "learning column" could always appear in a corner so the reader could clip each piece and put all of them into a folder.

Other instructional stories could be presented. The workings of the court system baffle many people, and yet news stories about the courts rattle off such words as appellate, mandamus, stay, and tort, as if anyone past the sixth grade were familiar with them. The series could tell the process of arrest, arraignment, the setting of bail, indictment, and trial. Another series could report on the history of the Bill of Rights, explaining in detail why the grand jury system was implanted there or why a person could not be accused of the same crime twice.

Already newspapers sometimes republish a series of articles or special layouts, such as housing stories, in a booklet. Such booklets are sold or given away as newspaper promotion. This practice will probably spread even to medium-sized papers. The booklet preserves the reporting beyond the admittedly short-lived newspaper story, helps promote the paper, and, best of all, serves as a reference work on the topic.

It is even possible that a newspaper might use the pictures and stories for a documentary film. This could be done inexpensively, with a stream of pictures (more than were used in the newspaper) serving as a backdrop to the words being spoken by a narrator. The film could be loaned or rented to interested schools and organizations. Again, the material would be excellent promotion for the paper.

The *Los Angeles Times* frequently publishes reprints of long articles or a series. One on prisons is used extensively in journalism classes as an example of careful and complete writing and research.

A few American newspapers have published books. Many of these have been "instant books," in which several reporters each swiftly wrote three or four thousand words on some part of a big story. Copyeditors quickly read copy and a printing firm does the rest at breakneck speed.

The *Wall Street Journal* has put out a half dozen books, and the Associated Press published books soon after the murders of President John Kennedy in 1963 and Senator Robert Kennedy in 1968. The *Los Angeles Times* even owns a book publishing firm. Only a few big newspapers, however, have the staff and money to attempt book publishing, but probably more will make the effort in the remaining years of the century. Perhaps eventually the books will be filmed and the reader, instead of holding a book in his hand, will project the words, in 72-point type, onto the wall. Books, or filmed books, will require the services of good editors, some of whom will be pulled off the copydesk to do the job.

There are schools with classrooms. There are schools of the air. As imaginative editors fulfill the challenge of meeting the readers' right to knowledge, they can create a school where the newspaper is the textbook.

15 The editor and journalistic writing

Editors on newspapers deal with writers and their writing in a number of ways, the most obvious being copyediting. The first three chapters covered problems of correcting and improving news stories; now we focus on more theoretical or philosophical problems. Copyeditors and other influential editorial employees must develop a philosophy of newswriting style, inculcate their ideas in their writers, and help them write better.

The relationship of editor and writer may be on a one-to-one basis. Traditionally, the city editor assigns a reporter to a story and then sees that the job is done well. But as newspaper journalism becomes more thorough, an editor plays the role of a good athletic coach or committee chairman. A sub-editor, perhaps in consultation with the managing editor, decides whether to put two or three reporters on a series covering an important subject, or to organize a team for a complete investigation. The sub-editor then provides the leadership for the creation of the copy until it is finally edited and published.

Team leadership

As chapter 14 pointed out, an editor should recognize and develop good ideas for major stories. Sometimes a subject is a natural because an alert reporter brings in a tip from some contact, and the appropriate editor simply has to allocate time to dig into the question. The assistant city editor may hatch the idea for a great series while driving to work. Some of the best ideas may develop as a few editors and reporters are lunching, or perhaps talking shop at a picnic.

But as newspapers move to develop more and better interpretive and specialized pieces, editors have to set aside time to be creative and work out ideas. The newspaper office traditionally has been too hectic for other than the obvious ideas to be recognized. While some newspapers show initiative, in the last decade or two it often has been the magazine editor or the producer of an occasional TV documentary who has launched the really penetrating studies on subjects like violence or poverty. To be similarly effective, newspaper editors must seek quiet to ruminate about the community and trends and the problems they and their neighbors face, and so discover what readers need to know more about. The idea for an investigation of teen-age use of a new drug probably will hit any editor in the eye. But some knowledge of social developments and some pondering are necessary to recognize the need for a series on abortions among the community's women, changing rates of illegitimacy, or the fate of adoptable babies.

Perspective reporting

It can be argued that interpretive reporting is just good reporting. It is true that "in-depth" or "enterprise reporting" or "backgrounder" may simply be a fancy title for the old-fashioned digging which was a part of good newswriting any time. Yet the complexity of modern issues and the social need to understand them require more resources, more reporters, more thought, and more leadership. Wes Gallagher, general manager of the Associated Press, has pointed to the shift toward investigative reporting and what he calls "perspective reporting."

"Today's problems are much more complex and investigation of them takes a lot more time and effort," he said in a William Allen White Memorial Lecture. "It is a rare case when one reporter can gather enough facts in a short time and come up with a story that will be authentic enough to convince and hold the attention of our new readers. . . . We can convince only by the most detailed presentation of facts, for facts alone have the ring of truth." He continued:

> The other great weapon that we have is perspective reporting that can and must be used on the daily flow of news. . . . Perspective reporting is presenting news in its proper relationship to the whole and in relation to other news in its own time. Perspective reporting dissects the situation today and compares it with the past. . . . Perspective reporting requires a cold, logical approach to the news. It requires dogged pursuit of facts until the writer is convinced that he has everything he can possibly dig out. The facts must then be sorted and logically presented.

A sample investigation

Gallagher complained, for example, that the federal government was simply too big to be covered. There were 1,222,000 employees in the Department of Defense, he said, 80,000 in Agriculture, and so on. To deal with that coverage problem, the AP established a Washington-based group of reporters, called the Special Assignment Team. Its reporters ignore deadlines and look for "the submerged dimension" of the federal government. Team stories have made nationwide headlines as reporters probed waste in the Pentagon and theft of American fuel in Thailand. Team members get leads to stories by reading government reports or from tips. Sometimes these tips come from people high in the government. Then, like police investigators, they conduct lengthy interviews and check records. In one instance, two members spent five months digging, which included line-by-line reading of fifteen volumes of hearing transcripts.

This kind of digging netted the Sun Newspapers, a group of weeklies in the Omaha area, a Pulitzer Prize. Their investigation examined the famous Father Flanagan Boys' Town—known simply as Boys Town—in Nebraska. The story became known as the "exposé without bad guys," for no real scandal was uncovered, but the inquiry opened the Boys Town books and brought a dozen other reforms.

The Sun group had been curious for some time about where Boys Town spent all the money it raised in mail appeals. It was obvious at the start of the investigation that officials at the home would give no information. So, in the best investigative technique, reporters began nibbling around the story's edges. The best edges turned out to be reports filed by Boys Town with governments or governmental agencies. Boys Town is an incorporated village, so it had to file a budget and an operations report. It had its own post office, and it had to file a few reports with the postmaster general. Since Boys Town is a school, certain state reports were required. Because it is a non-profit corporation, various other information had to be filed with the state. It is a child care operation, so other reports were given to the state welfare department. Since the home had bought land, records of deeds, purchase prices, and tax records were available.

Reporters in their twenties started gathering material for a "general historical piece" on Boys Town. They quickly found that the home received some $200,000 each year in federal and state subsidies, although the home claimed that it "got no funds from church, state, or federal government." The school also said it trained 1,000 boys, when the real figure was 665. Boys Town property was valued at $8,400,000, nearly all tax-exempt.

A few staff members at the home talked guardedly to reporters about low pay, rejection of innovative suggestions, and discouragement to boys who wanted to go to college.

It was learned that Boys Town sent out 34,000,000 fund appeal letters in one year. Professional fund raisers estimated that perhaps $15,000,000 would be attained by such voluminous mailings. It became obvious to the staffers, who were checking various figures, that Boys Town spent no more than $5,000,000 annually altogether. Without counting bequests, the staffers decided it appeared that the school had accumulated $100,000,000 over the years.

Suddenly the investigators found that Boys Town had filed a ninety-four page form with the Internal Revenue Service. The form was public information. When the form's figures were digested it was clear that Boys Town's net worth was not $100,000,000 at all, but $191,401,421—and that it was rising at the rate of $17,000,000 a year!

By this time the papers had a big story, but it was only fair to seek comment from Boys Town officials. So reporters questioned the archbishop of the diocese, the director of the home, and, finally, members of the board of directors. No one contradicted the facts gathered by reporters. But the reporters did not get any extra information either.

In a few days the papers carried a front page special report. The headline read:

BOYS TOWN
America's Wealthiest
City?

On page two was a copy of a fund-raising letter, "There will be no joyous Christmas season this year . . .". Page three had a reproduction of the IRS form's first page, showing both the net worth and $25,900,000 annual income. The story, plus sidebars and art, covered eight full-size pages

Within days, wheels started to turn at Boys Town and in a few months the board canceled fund raising for the year, announced a $30,000,000 endowment of an institute to treat speech and hearing defects in children, promised $40,000,000 more for a national center to study child development, and hired a management firm to re-examine the home's whole program. Other reforms followed.

The investigation showed that a small staff, working together, could marshal facts for a story that the public needed to know.

Investigative
leadership

Editors supervising investigations function as any good team leader does: goading, persuading, inspiring, and pushing. They guide the collection of information because they usually have more experience and can be more dispassionate than the reporter on the hunt. Furthermore, two or more editorial heads generally are better than a single reporter's. Editors work over story drafts to make sure there are no holes—and no libel. They question the investigators, and they suggest lines of inquiry that reporters may have missed. They tap their own experience as reporters and editors to make sure the best job is done. Most importantly, perhaps, they keep telling themselves and the special reporters that there must be no mistakes. They realize that one error in a story may cause the whole investigation to collapse. The people being investigated will shout, "See? The paper's making up the whole thing!"

As mentioned in the Boys Town story, editors advise investigators to start by asking seemingly innocuous questions at low levels. Underlings, unaccustomed to dealing with the press, often spill facts that higher level people would keep to themselves. As the story forms a pattern, reporters move to quiz more informed people and to seek more crucial documents. The best human sources are the disgruntled, the idealists, or those who relish a kind of conspiratorial role. The disgruntled often seek revenge. The idealists seek justice. The "conspirators" hope to be anonymous sources of information. Each type may be overly zealous, and may give false or distorted details. This is why investigators often insist on corroboration of a fact before it is printed. If reporters cannot sift their information for fact, the editor should.

In the search, it is not enough to get oral accusations on reports. Documents are essential—letters, memos, canceled checks. All may be crucial. Editors and reporters should realize that their greatest ally here is the copying machine, for it will duplicate evidence in seconds. That evidence often makes previously silent people decide to tell reporters their whole story.

In the enthusiasm of cracking a big story, journalists may forget a sense of ethical conduct. Theft, lies, fakery, or threats may be precisely what is being investigated. A journalist either should not use these shabby practices or should use them only after full soul-searching. Too often reporters and editors have wrapped themselves in the flag of "public interest" and dashed off to pull shady or even criminal acts.

Editors should realize, too, that most investigations do not look for scandalous or illegal conduct. What may be sought is evidence of ineptitude or incompetence. Or, as in the Boys Town story, evidence of money-seeking, improper power, and hoarding. This is why editors and reporters should take care to avoid accusations and strident language in their stories.

Sometimes editors must use a firm hand to get the news the community deserves. In one middle-sized city the social welfare reporter got the go-ahead to do a series on black employment in local business and industry. He was so thorough that he conducted scores of interviews over several weeks. As time passed, the information in the early interviews began to get stale. The paper's interest flagged, perhaps in part because the lengthy investigation brought worried inquiries from industrial leaders. When the brief series finally appeared, it was weak—much weaker than if it had been done with more dispatch. Perhaps the city editor should have assigned a second reporter to help collect information. Perhaps the editor should have told the reporter at a certain point, "You've got enough material. Write it!" In any event, firm editorial leadership was missing.

Editors also have leadership roles with various non-staffers. As indicated in chapter 8, the state editor may have to teach the country correspondent the basics of straight writing. Steady, clear communication is essential to lead a team of part-time stringers. Similarly, a good foreign desk provides leadership for its foreign correspondents—staff and stringer. A major complaint of reporters who write

Aides of the team

abroad is that the home office does not communicate but leaves them too much on their own.

Free-lance writers and photographers also can be valuable. They should be treated courteously even if the paper can use only a little free-lance work, and they should be encouraged and guided if the quality of work is poor but promising.

Amateurs should be given pointers about producing the articles or pictures the paper can use. The magazine of the *Houston Chronicle* has a form that explains its needs in subjects, pictures, manuscript preparation, and deadlines, and its method of payment. Queries on ideas should be answered, not ignored. Rejected material should be sent back promptly, even if the editor is busy and overburdened, and checks for accepted material ought to be mailed quickly. Smart editors supplement their regular staff operations when they provide effective leadership for part-timers and free-lances.

The editor as teacher

More advanced editors in various slots must serve as instructors in English and journalism, especially with greener reporters. At worst this teaching is hit or miss; at best it must be sandwiched into the few moments that editors and writers can find together in their busy schedules.

Editors first of all have to be clear on their goals for good writing. Do they want thoroughness, brightness, or both? Then, in countless observations, corrections, criticisms, and sermonettes, they show writers how they are, and are not, measuring up.

Outlines and structures

Every journalistic neophyte soon learns that news stories are constructed on the pattern of the "inverted pyramid." The most important facts go into the first paragraph, or lead, and other information follows in short paragraphs of less and less importance so the pattern can be diagrammed as a triangle standing on its point, a two-dimensional inverted pyramid. Perceptive editors discover soon enough, if they have not already learned it as reporters, that this pattern applies only to the simplest news items, unless "inverted pyramid" is understood in the most general terms, as different stories require different forms.

Traditionally, the feature story has always been an exception. Writers can start features with a question or an anecdote or a quote, among other devices, and may write chronologically or according to some other non-triangular logic. Sometimes features are diagrammed as pyramids sitting on their bases, but this pattern is no more applicable universally than the triangle is to news stories. An editor who started to revise a feature to fit any such preconceived pattern would soon stop, frustrated and foolish.

What, then, *can* editors discover about the structure of complicated stories, and what can they hope to teach advanced reporters?

In his popular English textbook, *The Practical Stylist*, Prof.

Sheridan Baker of the University of Michigan argues that the writer should find a *thesis* to begin a piece. A thesis can be stated as a debate resolution, "Resolved that . . ." When writers thus clarify their aim, they find that the supportive information falls into logical order, into an outline.

This approach has some validity for most news stories, since the beginning states the point of each piece (though not argumentatively as the word *thesis* implies). The concept is most applicable to the work of the editorial writers when they attempt persuasive editorials, but in the newsroom Baker's thesis on theses is generally valuable. It reminds editors to look for clear exposition of the main point close to the top of a story.

Another rhetorical tradition classifies writing forms, such as the essay, into a natural (and obvious) pattern of three parts—beginning, middle, and the end, standing like three rectangular blocks piled one on another. The middle block might be subdivided into several flat rectangles (or paragraphs) of development. The bottom block is conclusion. This plan fits nicely with Baker's, if the top block contains the statement of thesis.

This tripartite form again may seem more suited to essays for the editorial page than for front-page news accounts. The shift toward more and more interpretation, however, makes this observation less and less certain. What is a series of articles but a number of blocks? And as background, depth, and perspective become writers' watchwords, they are less concerned with the first-paragraph punch of the inverted-pyramid and more concerned with the clarity emphasized in the beginning-middle-end structure.

Analysis of news stories over many decades shows that actually they are not simple triangles. Usually they are a number of triangles on a string, like fish. The story unfolds in two or three paragraphs, then recaps with more detail, explains at length in a third triangle, and perhaps adds minor detail and color in still another. Consider the story of a major fire in three or four buildings. The first section quickly recounts the deaths and damage. The next section reveals how it started and spread and how fire-fighting forces were marshaled. The next triangles tell who discovered it, of the efforts to confine it to the first building, and of a call for outside help. There may be a snippet about two suburbs that sent equipment and men. A block of type may inquire into insurance. Then in more leisurely fashion the writer may present the whole chronology again, quoting the passerby who thought he saw smoke, the watchman who opened the inner doors and discovered the blaze, or the woman who threw her baby into the fire net.

The story may form a more complicated pattern than even a series of triangles, as figure 15-1 suggests. A triangle that tapers off to the inconsequential point would bore a reader. Rather, each triangle becomes blunt-bottomed. Some are hardly triangles at all. Can a

Complex patterns

chronological account be called a triangle, since start, middle and finish are equally essential to the tale? Is a list of injured a triangle? Blocks and wedges are more appropriate to clear portrayal of the way a long story is put together.

The copyeditor who sees news articles in some such schematic fashion will understand better how they can be rearranged and tightened. Perhaps the inner logic requires that a paragraph or two near the end be moved up to a higher position, even though these sentences are in themselves quite trivial. Or perhaps cutting a minor detail in the heart of the story will strengthen the whole.

An editor able to analyze advanced writing can quickly show reporters where their work is solid and where it is loose or rambling. This analytic skill is especially useful in working with an investigative team. Structuring the long series becomes like outlining a lengthy magazine article or a book. Formal logic has to be related to the likelihood that a reader's interest will wane, and to the technical

Fig. 15–1. Story patterns. These patterns are a more realistic picture of complex news stories than the traditional inverted pyramid. The more complex the story, the more likely it is a combination of triangles, wedges, and rectangles. Copyeditors who recognize these variations will be able to reshape a story effectively.

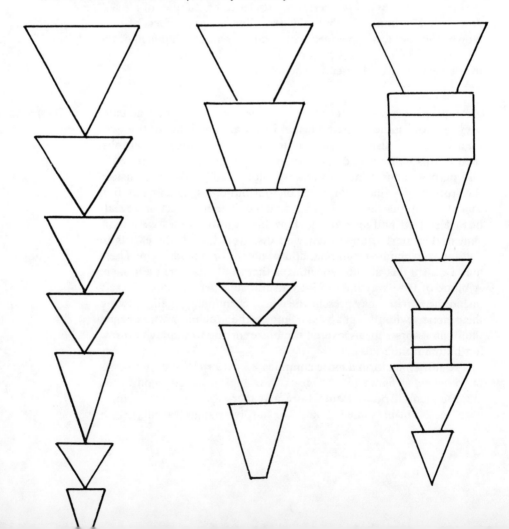

demand that the individual pieces be a certain length. "Can we shift this block into the first article in the series, and can we give the third piece some punch by building up this anecdote?" Sometimes these deceptively simple questions lead a writing team into a type of outline they hoped to have left in Freshman English.

It may be useful to think of the modern news story not as a triangle but as a freight train: The diesel supplies the power and the pace, and a series of boxes follow with the information. More than other types of writing, news stories have minimal transitions and internal references. With little concern, a copyeditor can shift paragraphs around. The building blocks of many stories seem almost interchangeable. To the extent that the news fits this train pattern, writer and editor both can shunt the box cars in and out of the line, pushing those with less important freight to the end, where an editor or printer can uncouple the last few.

Whatever the pattern, the story must be logical. That logic need not be of the I, II, III type. It can be chronological or it can be psychological, in the sense that the reporter moves the reader from one point of interest to another. The chief sin is rambling. It is "circling and droning, reminiscent of buzzards hovering, swooping over a victim until he drops," in the words of a prominent magazine editor and gifted writer himself, Norman Cousins, of the *Saturday Review*. Good organization of thoughts is the key to good written or oral communication, says Cousins, adding: "The prime element in this process is sequence. Ideas have to be fitted together. The movement of a concept or an image from the mind of the speaker to the mind of the listener is retarded when words become random chunks rather than sequential parts of an ordered whole."

Both reporters and editors rarely think of the most effective ways to structure their accounts. They play by ear and do the job as journalists have for decades. Therefore, the editor-teacher must jog both writers and copyeditors to strive for patterns that will communicate best in today's paper.

More should be done on newspapers to discover fresh, new ways to present material related to a central story. Instead of one long story, why not five short stories which are sidebars to each other? Why not play three or four related stories, perhaps with a box or editorial to explain their common theme?

Magazine editors appear to be more ambitious in developing new patterns of presentation. They have tried boldface summaries, called precedes, at the top of articles in trade magazines. They have boldfaced the first paragraph of new sections. Some have tried narrative, near-fiction techniques; others have paired two pieces, one light and illustrated, the other serious and editorial. Newspaperpeople may find stimulating ideas of writing patterns and related graphic displays in the best edited magazines.

The meanings
of style

"Style" is used by newspaper editors in at least two senses. The uniform system of spelling and capitalization is called style, as we discussed in chapter 2 on copyediting, but the form and presentation of newspaper prose are also style.

Good journalistic style is not florid, not ornate, not rhetorical. The late journalism dean Frank Luther Mott used to say the best journalism is also good literature, as clearly demonstrated in the reporting of Ben Franklin, Stephen Crane, and Ernest Hemingway. English professors have long contended that good prose is usually plain and straightforward and therefore clear. "The approach to style is by way of plainness, simplicity, orderliness, sincerity," says William Strunk, Jr., and E. B. White's *The Elements of Style*. And so it is to good newspaper style too.

Effective prose communicates ideas and information. It might be argued that some English is used to convey an ambiance or feeling without presenting much fact. But such usage in news reports is rare. Journalistic style has to be functional. The need to convey ideas quickly from one mind to other minds underlies the need for simple, clear writing.

What language scholars call "standard English" is appropriate to newspapers. Neither the formal English of the academic book nor the "non-standard" or colloquial dialect of folksy talk has much place in newspaper pages. For most purposes, reporters and editors should choose their words from the broad range of language understood by most moderately educated people.

Standard English is threatened on the one side by jargon and gobbledegook. Reporters close to many professions may fall into legalese, academic pudder, or bureaucratic gibberish. On the other side is a threat from what has traditionally been known as slang —faddish talk. Noting the likenesses between the academicians and the hip talkers, the editing authority on the *New York Times*, Theodore Bernstein, has pointed out that both groups substitute their own redundant words for normal English. Both have some intent to be secret and so obscure to those not of the in-group. Newspapers must abjure both kinds of fringe English if they are to communicate with a diverse readership.

Advocates of plain, simple style sometimes face the objection that this kind of writing is dull and lifeless. It need not be. Concrete nouns and strong verbs close to human experience can make a simple sentence vivid and lively. Yet sometimes even a good writer will fill a story with the stereotyped and obvious until it shrivels and dies.

"Over the years, wire service reporting had gotten flat, had leveled off to an efficient but uninspired pattern," said Roger Tatarian, former UPI editor, to explain why UPI stressed readability. To help make its style more human UPI introduced a category, "Personal Report," to personalize stories traditionally done impersonally. Reporters were instructed to write first-hand pieces and even use "I." In a staff memo Tatarian said: "The use of the *I* can be effective only if it is not overdone, and if it is done logically and naturally. There should be enough of it to give the flavor of a letter to the folks at home, but not so much as to make the writer hog the center of the stage."

Other editors might adopt this view as they try to develop reporting styles which are at once simple, lively, clear, readable, and communicative.

An examination of style by editors comes down to their analysis of the grammatical ingredients of the story. As the physicist probes molecules, atoms, and electrons to try to understand matter, the editor digs into paragraphs, sentences, and words. Admittedly, there is a mystic quality in the overall effect of writing, for the whole somehow turns out to be greater than the sum of the parts. Still, some of the mystery can be penetrated by looking at the individual blocks and the ways they fit one another.

The sources of style

In most writing the paragraph is an obvious fundamental block. The formal outline of an essay or a book divides into topics, subtopics, and sub-sub-topics; each sub-sub-topic may be treated as a paragraph. Such a unit will have a topic sentence (actually a sub-sub-topic sentence) supported by five or a dozen or more sentences. With proper transitions, such paragraphs clearly reveal the structure and movement of the work.

Paragraphs

Such paragraphs set in column widths, even for six-column pages, might each run four or five or even ten inches. Even set in the wider measure used for editorials, they would look forbidding. So journalists, including editorial writers, use shorter paragraphs, often only one or two sentences long.

Copy is not effectively formed into short paragraphs by haphazard chopping, as some reporters and copyreaders apparently suppose. Nor is simply breaking most stories into one-sentence paragraphs enough, as it once was in more sensational papers. The best procedure is to search the "normal" paragraph of the topic-sentence variety for the clusters of ideas within it. Thus a twelve-sentence unit may prove to be made up of four to six smaller pieces. Each piece then may become a newspaper-type paragraph, and each may run one or two, perhaps three, sentences, but rarely more. In type the paragraph will be a horizontal rectangle or a square rather than a formidable, vertical rectangle. At the same time, if writers see the relation of these shorter paragraphs to the overall pattern, they are able to write in a more logical style.

A paragraph should rarely run over fifty words. In typescript, a paragraph of four or five lines is beginning to run too long. If such a paragraph has even two or three sentences, they must obviously be short—perhaps an average of fifteen words, though no such figure should be taken arbitrarily. Length is thus one criterion of the good

Sentences

sentence, and newspaper sentences are usually short compared to those in books or scholarly magazines.

Sentences also should be straight—that is, clear and to the point. "English is going to pot, and one of the reasons it's going to pot is the way it's taught," complained Dr. Don Cameron Allen, professor of English at Johns Hopkins University. "I teach students to write a straight sentence. That's what English is all about. You will find excellent examples of good straight sentences in good American newspapers."

Though grammatically most straight sentences are simple, few compound, and even fewer complex, newsmen might pay more attention to what is known in English classes as the periodic sentence. The elements in American sentences are somewhat loosely tied, but not quite haphazard. By contrast, the periodic sentence builds from beginning to end, so the last element is the climax. That gives writing punch, like this: Mayor Jones paused over the document, frowned, and then, as his face and neck reddened, shouted, "Never!" Of course, putting an idea at the start of a sentence also can have impact: "Cut taxes" was the cry of most of those testifying.

Three common faults of newspaper sentences easily identified by the editor-teacher are the *clogged*, the *overburdened* and the *too-complex*.

The clogged sentence simply packs too much information between the capital letter and the period. Writing dense sentences used to be considered good style but is now old-fashioned. For example, no desk today should pass a sentence with this beginning:

> Jonathan Doakes, 41, of 6357 Harmondale Drive, a carpenter and part-time plumber, who told reporters he had never been in trouble before, and a companion, who gave his name as Samuel Smithson, 53, of 6359 Harmondale Drive, also a carpenter, were arrested today after what was, according to witnesses, a scuffle over the way another neighbor, Clyde Hendricks, 32, of 6358 Harmondale Drive, should build his fences.

The modern way is to rewrite, "Two carpenters were arrested today after a scuffle over the way a neighbor should build his fences." The specifics can wait.

The overburdened sentence, although like the clogged, is not so much packed with facts as overstuffed with ideas. The writer loads too much freight onto the sentence before hitting the period key.

> Like the legislature's redistricting plan of 1976, the proposed new constitutional amendment now before the Senate Judiciary Committee, and soon to go before the House Rules Committee, not only deals with the congressional district problem but also the issue of one-voter-one-vote, according to regulations set by a previous ruling of the Supreme Court.

Break it up; simplify.

The too-complex sentence resembles both the clogged and the overburdened. Its writer is following the dictum to get away from the simple Dick-saw-Jane sentence. It is good advice, expecially for essays and editorials, but the newswriter can overdo by throwing in too many clauses and phrases.

> Since the recent outbreak of warfare and because of popular reaction to the news, especially in view of the fact that it came on the heels of revulsion about the pact of Vienna, the Communists and their satellites, not only in Eastern Europe but in much of Asia, have restricted travel by foreign newsmen who will now have to obtain stories from an official press bureau.

Again, break it up.

Writers of these three faulty types of sentences have in common the laudable attempt to pack a lot of information into a short space. But an overconcentration of facts or ideas or grammatical style makes a story opaque. The antidote in each case is to lighten the load of each sentence. Even the most intelligent readers need frequent periods to "catch their breath."

A fruitful suggestion for writing better sentences is summarized in the slogan, "One idea, one sentence." Elements in the preceding stories such as the carpenters' addresses, the old redistricting plan, or that Vienna pact should be cut away from the verbose illustrative sentences above. The main idea of each sentence then will stand out so the reader can grasp it quickly.

Editors of the *New York Times* have pushed the one-idea-to-a-sentence theme for several years. Their second-guessing bulletin, *Winners & Sinners*, has occasionally pointed up the value of the concept with illustrations from the paper. Here, for example, is one sentence which would be much easier to follow if divided:

> The proxy fight—latest in a series that erupted this year, including such other big concerns as GAF corporation and Midas International Corporation—that will be climaxed at the annual meeting in Wilmington, Del., may also be the last hurrah for Darryl F. Zanuck, the 69-year-old producer and tycoon of Hollywood's golden years, who is likely to retire as chairman and from the entire Fox scene soon regardless of which side wins.

Here is another sinner from the *Times:*

> In Montreal, leaders of the American Bar Association killed Wednesday a resolution denouncing a key provision of the civil rights bill aimed at preventing discrimination in the selection of Federal jurors.

Of the second example the *W&S* editor commented: "The facts are all there, but the reader has to go to work on them. He has to take it from the bottom: The bill is against discrimination. Fine. But the resolution denounces this provision. Uh-uh. But wait a minute—the bar leaders have killed the resolution. So it's fine again, eh? In other words, the bar leaders took a stand in favor of preventing discrimination in the selection of Federal juries. Why not say it in some form similar to that?"

Words   The strength of sentences depends ultimately on the choice and arrangement of their words. Good editors become expert on these basic blocks. Instead of the vague, the abstract, and the unusual, they seek words which are *direct, concrete,* and *familiar*—words which build vivid and accurate pictures for most readers.

Some editors prefer words of Anglo-Saxon background to those with Latin roots. Generally, pithy words are from Old English, flowery ones from the Romance languages (i.e., those descended from Latin, the language of the Romans). Actually, a combination of words from both streams often most effectively provides variation and texture. Accuracy and strength, as well as commonness, should guide word choice, and vitality in verbs is especially important. Forms of "to be" are generally static—as in that clause—so editors prefer verbs which act, which suggest movement. One-syllable words often generate the most power. Reducing the sentence usually adds strength. Pare away weak or unnecessary adjectives and adverbs. (If this paragraph demonstrates its own preachments, it is because of vivid words like *roots, pithy, flowery, works, texture, static, guide,* and *pare.*)

Choice of the right word nowadays is complicated by rapid changes in language. Again, a number of guides are available. The third edition of *Webster's New International Dictionary* embodies mid-twentieth century language and so is available in most newsrooms today. But the third edition gives few value judgments on words. For a more regular, though more conservative evaluation of words, some editors prefer the second edition, compiled in the thirties. A good guide to modern American usage is the *Dictionary of Comtemporary Usage* by Bergen and Cornelia Evans. Also valuable is the revision by Sir Ernest Gowers of the famous *Dictionary of Modern English Usage* of H. W. Fowler, a classic in England. Theodore Bernstein of the *Times*, quoted earlier, has four helpful books, the first based on *Winners & Sinners: Watch Your Language, More Language That Needs Watching, The Careful Writer: A Modern Guide to English Usage,* and, most recently, *Miss Thistlebottom's Hobgoblins.*

Commenting on the third book, literary critic Granville Hicks said that of the six guidelines Bernstein suggests for judging good usage, he preferred this one: *Observation of what makes for clarity, precision, and logical presentation.* Hicks points out that this rule prohibits some newer usages that obscure rather than clarity. While

Hicks admits that the misuse of "like" for "as" will not greatly damage the language, he believes that the growing confusion of "infer" for "imply" does debase common English. Such distinctions may seem picky. But effective writing depends upon careful and correct choices precisely at this level of language.

A final word on jargon

As we said before, jargon confuses more than clarifies. In medicine or law, to be sure, a specialized word may add precision. In education, argues Dr. James S. LeSure of the Connecticut Department of Education, jargon actually can confuse even educators. But teachers use phrases like "peer acceptance" and "group practice" because these seem to give them professional status, even though parents don't know what they are talking about. So Dr. LeSure wrote *Guide to Pedaguese*, "a handbook for puzzled parents" that may also help education writers.*

"When you get your degree you can't wear it around your neck to prove you're educated," the late urban reformer Saul Alinsky wrote in *Harper's* magazine, "so instead you use a lot of three and four-syllable words. Of course , they aren't any use at all if you really want to communicate with people. You have to talk straight English, using a small word every time you can instead of a big one." Such advice is good not only for educators and sociologists but also for reporters and editors. They communicate best when they use simple words in straight sentences in brief but well-organized paragraphs.

Theories of readability

In a computer age when so much of life is quantified, it is tempting to analyze and measure language in the search for better communication. Can English be approached scientifically? Can the clarity or interest of a piece of writing be weighed or measured? Yes and no. No calipers or scales exist to indicate accurately whether sentences convey their message well. But quantification of newspaper copy may help a writer analyze style.

What can be measured? The stylists and critics we have examined indicate the qualities we might hope to quantify: difficulty of words, complexity and density of sentences, use of cliches or jargon, strength of verbs, and so on. The problem with measurement is that many of these stylistic qualities defy objective judgment.

Readability theorists who search for objective measurements have centered on judging the difficulty of words and sentences, which is certainly a key consideration. This factor is measured in the "fog index" developed by Robert Gunning (explained in *The Technique of Clear Writing*) and in the "Flesch formula" described by Rudolf Flesch (in *The Art of Readable Writing* and other books). After

---

*The U. S. Government Printing Office issues an inexpensive booklet with similar aims, *Gobbledygook Has Gotta Go* (1966).

study of these and other practical applications of readability theory, Dr. Jeanne S. Chall of Ohio State University identified four significant reliable measurements: vocabulary load, sentence structure, idea density, and human interest. The first two relate to the Gunning-Flesch work, and the third is associated with clogging and overburdening. We shall look at the fourth below.

The Flesch formula

In the late forties, AP hired Flesch to advise on improving writing. So practical journalistic use was made of a "readability formula" he had devised. His scheme rests on two assumptions. First, the number of syllables in samples of 100 words each increases as the writing becomes more difficult. Second, the more short sentences in the samples the easier the reading. Actually, short words in short sentences can be hard going, but since the opposite is more often the case, the assumptions seem justified.

Starting with them, one can randomly choose a few samples from news stories, interpretive stories, or editorials. The writer counts the syllables and the number of sentences (to find average sentence length) and works out the Flesch score according to the mathematics or charts in Flesch's books. If the sentences average fifteen to eighteen words each and if there are 145 to 155 syllables in each sample, the writing scores as "standard" and is suitable for much newspaper writing. Such sentences are not very long, obviously, and such a vocabulary includes a great many one-syllable words. However, using more long words or making the sentences more complex (and therefore longer) will almost certainly make the writing more difficult.

Paring sentences to an average of twelve words each and vocabulary to 130 or 140 syllables per hundred words results in what Flesch rates as "easy." If news stories were written at this level—and few are—less-educated readers would doubtless grasp them more readily.

The chart in figure 15-2 gives a quick check of readability, according to the ideas of Flesch and Gunning. If the editor selects a random sample of 100 words of copy, he or she can count syllables and number of sentences and plot the coordinates, perhaps with help of an L-shaped cardboard. An editor should check several samples before making any generalizations about the paper, and should consider hundreds of samples from different pages over a considerable period of time before determining that the readability of the paper needs special attention.

Applying the test

Using the Flesch method, two researchers compared news stories to editorials in several West Coast dailies. They found both forms difficult, but the news was actually less readable than the editorials! "The median readability level of news stories analyzed in this study indicates that most of them can be readily comprehended by only those people with a high school diploma or a college education."

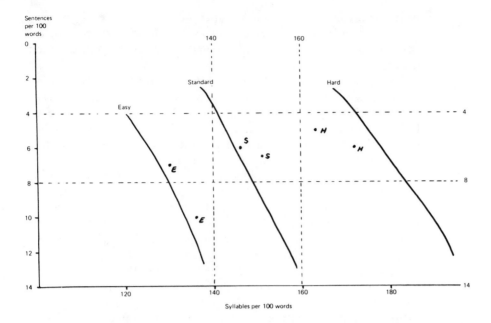

Sentences per 100 words

Syllables per 100 words

Fig. 15–2. Readability chart. Count the syllables in a 100-word sample of news copy and find that number on the horizontal line. Then count the sentences (to nearest quarter) in the same sample; find that number on the vertical line. The intersection of the coordinates (a cardboard cut in the shape of "L," as for picture editing, will help) identifies the simplicity or difficulty of the sample. The graph shows samples with the following counts plotted to indicate three major categories: Easy, Standard, and Hard (marked with E, S, and H, respectively).

Editors want copy which will, as these researchers say, reach "audiences from a wider range than that."[1]

Recognizing that some writing passes muster as "readable" but is still dull, Flesch later developed a "human interest" formula. The most important factor in these measurements is the use of what he calls "personal words"—he, she, Mr. Brown, Susan, etc. He also counts, but gives less weight to, "personal sentences," which include quotations and direct address to the reader. Fortunately, news stories deal with people, so a degree of human interest "comes naturally." However, some writers tend to abstractions, especially in writing of such subjects as government finance or sociology. To counteract this, editors can remind reporters that they must bring human beings into their copy.

Being concerned to make news writing easier and more interesting does not mean editors must seek the lowest common denominator of readership. True, they should provide some material, aside from sports and comics, which is clear even to poorly educated readers. And they should try to reach a broad readership. But some papers that have directed all content toward the "average" person have declined in circulation and general economic health. The successful papers of today continue to improve the quality of content a notch

Assessing the audience

or two every few years. If a newspaper did choose stories for only a ninth grade audience, it would omit much information on science, the arts, serious economics, the inner workings of politics, and dozens of other subjects.

To argue that because the average *formal* educational level of a community is only 10.3 years the paper must be written for high school sophomores assumes that people learn nothing after they leave school. It also assumes that those with little schooling and little experience are newspaper readers. It is more realistic to assume that those above average in education and intelligence are the most avid readers. While still including news of interest for those who are not so lucky or concerned, the mix of content should emphasize news for them. Nonetheless, editors should insist that stories always are lively and clear, as well as fact-filled. Even the most intelligent readers who are able to cope with scholarly journals, may be pestered with distractions while reading the newspaper. Like everyone else, they must sometimes get the facts from the paper without much concentration. This means that the writing must be appealing and easy.

But Tom Wicker of the *New York Times* is right when he says, "Nobody yet ever made a writer out of a hack by setting up rules. . . . And to the man who tells me that every story can be written in 600 words, or 750, or whatever, I say that that is merely a rule; and I take my stand with Joseph Pulitzer, who said with a writer's exactness and a lawyer's flexibility that the prescription was 'terseness—intelligent, not stupid, condensation.'"

Neither readability nor human interest concepts should be viewed as magic cure-alls. They can help journalists check on their talent for good copy, and no more. The good editor, as team captain, must above all continue to study overall story organization and the effective use of style.

16 Editorial management

Time and space are major problems for newspaper editors—the time of staff and the white space of newsprint. Money, a great deal of it, is needed to manage both of these, so the higher echelons of editors must also tackle budget questions. The managing editor's basic job is budget—budgeting of staff time, of news hole, and of money allotted to editorial. To administer this budget management relies on communications. Except for a few hours of reading and thinking, managing editors spend most of their work-week communicating so they can be in harmony with their organizations and communities. One of the ironies of newspapering is that, although the editor's business is communication, few of them are better with internal communications than are executives in any other business.

Internal communication

Newspapers use virtually every means of communication employed in modern social organizations. Staff members meet and confer in formal groups, then break up to meet and talk informally. Each editor talks individually with other staffers, chatting across desks or over the telephone with a police reporter at the jail, the stringer in the state, or the cub in trouble. Top editors drop in on sub-editors or look over a reporter's shoulder. They casually chew over ideas with colleagues at lunch. Grouping desks by department in the newsroom facilitates communication. The grouping often leads to conversation that stimulates editorial effort and creativity.

Editors also communicate in writing. They send memos and notes. The smart chiefs post material on a bulletin board, teletype messages to outlying staffers, and distribute work plans, news budgets, and assignment sheets.

These are obvious ways editors communicate, but they might use them more effectively by taking time to ask themselves apropos each message: What is the best way to communicate this? A general meeting? A quiet talk? A private memo? A note for the bulletin board?

Internal communication problems generate bureaucratic weaknesses. Any newspaper with more than three or four staffers, like any college with more than three or four professors, tends to become a little bureaucracy. Staffers complain about "too many meetings" or "so many memos I don't have time to read 'em all," as if humans somewhere managed organizations without memos and meetings. Still, good editors avoid the bureaucratic dangers of confusion, excessive complexity, and impersonal coldness. In the language of communications theory, they do not clog the channels with messages until the output is only noise. Editors who keep their communications brief, clear, warm, personal, and human will have a staff—and a newspaper—that reflects their effort.

Management style

Every editor inevitably develops a style of administration and so puts a personal stamp on procedure. Some editors are authoritarian, barking orders and pulling rank. Others are more democratic, discussing rather than dictating.

In college one used to hear much of developing a "winning" personality. The emphasis indicates that the successful leader likes and understands people—and knows how to persuade them for a purpose. As in other lines of work, however, a fair number of martinets and neurotics get into high editorial positions. For a while, at least, the wheels turn despite the friction and resentments. A few editors have used callousness to build a successful paper, but more have failed.

A newspaper manager ought to keep in mind that proud and talented reporters, editors, and photographers will resent being treated like drones. To bring them into the mainstream of decision-making usually means a better paper and a more satisfied staff. The paper then becomes "our paper," not merely "the paper."

Editors should make an extra effort to fit young men and women and their ideas into the operation, because they often have fresh ideas and can write or edit for a young audience. Young staffers probably have always complained that the management, usually middle-aged or above, is behind the times. Some of their criticism springs from youthful impatience, yet there is often a real lag as newspapers—and other institutions—cling to the old.

To put it another way, newspaper executives must themselves try to be open, flexible. They should take pains to review their policies frequently. Some rules perhaps never were wise or workable; now they hamstring and stultify. It is not unusual for a new staffer, hearing of a newsroom taboo, to mutter, "Who thought up that stupid rule?" If there is a good reason for the policy, it ought to be explained. But editors must avoid defending outmoded standards with the cliché, "We've always done it that way."

Some flexibility and imagination are helpful also in the editorial managing of money. It is one thing to be economical and another to be parsimonious. Few things annoy a reporter or sub-editor more than to have the management pinch pennies on taxi fares or ordinary newsroom supplies. One small newspaper chain even makes the staff furnish pencils. Such nickel-chasing damages staff morale and raises questions about the capabilities of management to manage anything.

The number of moss-backed manager types fortunately is declining. Increasingly, newspaper plants are clean, attractive, and comfortable. Coffee, soft drinks, and sandwiches are available in a lunch room. Lighting is adequate. The noise is muffled and the work space is uncrowded. Some newsrooms nowadays even have carpets.

Budget problems

Top officials on the editorial side—executive editors or managing editors—have a certain number of dollars under control each month or year. How much control they wield can vary considerably. The publisher himself may hold the strings of the purse tightly. Or an executive editor, given virtually complete power over editorial budget, may choose to decentralize responsibility, sharing it with department heads such as the sports editor or the metropolitan editor.

In newsrooms across the country money questions generate most of the headaches among managing editors. They are not trained as accountants, and their rise through the news ranks probably indicates that figuring budgets is one of their least favorite tasks. On one hand, good managing editors must get the most work for the salary dollar. On the other, they have to demand from the publisher or business manager a budget big enough for editorial excellence. Like a union official, they always seek more money for the staff. To the extent they succeed in getting a fair share of net income and wisely spending it, managing editors produce the quality which creates a newspaper's reputation. Failure brings deterioration and decay so severe that even the casual reader notices.

If chief editors represent all the editorial underlings—as university deans may represent school faculties and students in parleying with top administrators—they also serve as the representative of management. Reporters and department editors may feel such editors front for the publisher just as deans are accused of fronting for administrations to hold down faculty salaries or throttle students. They have a delicate role to play. They have to interpret the realities of publishing to staffs no more enthusiastic about budgeting than the top editors are. At the same time, the chief editors must convince everyone, above and below, that they are honest and fair.

Salaries and the Guild

The wicket is especially sticky in bargaining with the journalists' union, the American Newspaper Guild. The Guild's job is to convince all levels of management to give editors and reporters a better break in pay and working conditions. Steps to organize this union were taken in 1933, in the depths of the Great Depression, by newspaper columnist Heywood Broun. Since it is organized on industrial trade union principles, the Guild includes not only those employees in editorial but those in advertising, business, circulation, maintenance, and promotion. Membership hovers around 33,000.

Union locals for papers in more than a hundred cities in the United States, Canada, and Puerto Rico now have agreements with publishers. Major magazines and both wire services also have Guild contracts. The Guild estimates its contracts cover more than half the newspaper circulation in the United States. Even though managing editors may have been members on their way up—and many top American editors have been in the Guild—they often have to take part in union negotiations on the side of management.

The Guild is continuing pressure to raise the minimum pay for experienced reporters photographers and copyeditors, called journeymen. The so-called "top minimum" of $200 a week was first adopted by the *Washington Post* in 1964. It jumped to $300 in 1970 and to $475 in 1976. Though beginning reporters still start at about $150 a week on many papers, the Guild has locals in sixty-five cities where journeyman minimums of more than $300 are in contracts. Associated Press and United Press International paid $349 minimums in 1976. These figures indicate that reporters and copyeditors on the larger newspapers are making between $15,000 and $25,000 a year. Compared to salaries in teaching, nursing, social work, etc. the unionized journalists' income is quite good.

The Guild, of course, also toils for cost-of-living increases, medical insurance payments, more vacations and holidays, and a shorter work week. Most Guild members now work a 37-1/2-hour week, with overtime payment for any hours worked beyond that amount.

In the dickering—and sometimes bickering—with the Guild, managing editors can be crushed between the stones of management and staff. But if they are strong, and if they maintain good humor, they can often mediate differences. The man or woman of integrity will be trusted when the staff is told frankly about how far the publisher can go on wages and fringe benefits. At the same time he or she can press management to remember that not only the newspaper's reputation but also its financial strength rests on quality, which in turn depends upon competitive salaries.

Managing editors may not fret if they cannot get the money they want for stenographers and copy aides. But they can bleed if they see their best staffers leave for higher pay at other papers. If they need two new reporters, and they persuade the publisher to give them $20,000 for salaries, they know they can pay each $10,000. They also know they can't buy much experience or brains for that. But if they can get $32,000 they may seek one staffer in the $18,000 range and another at around $14,000. Such salaries might attract seasoned reporters even from a bigger paper, if the editor has the imagination to offer a degree of reportorial freedom, dynamic newspapering, and simple appreciation for work well done. The editor with clear goals and drive can attract writers who admire sharp leadership; but in the end even that editor needs dollars in the budget.

The Guild also has tried in recent years to gain minor control over what once were thought to be the sole prerogatives of management. Some Guild contracts, for example, allow removal of a byline when the reporter requests. This may appear to be a minor point in the abstract but in a concrete situation it can be extremely important. Sometimes reporters contend that their patched-up and altered stories are either unprofessional or erroneous—and they don't want their names connected with them. Tentative moves are being made to give the staff a chance to veto management's choice, say, of managing editor. Guild members argue in such cases that they know better than the publisher the kind of person they can work with and who meets professional standards. Many European newspaper staffs have such power. So far in the United States, however, only one contract says that the Guild shall be "consulted" when certain top editors will be hired.

The budgeting of news space, like the budgeting of money, is a source of cooperation—and friction—between business management and editorial chiefs. As indicated in earlier discussions about news, the news hole (the amount of space devoted to other than advertising) varies from day to day. The reading public may have little appreciation of the need to expand or contract the amount of editorial material as advertising sales go up or down, but all managing editors recognize this fact of publishing life. One of their tasks is to plan and establish routines that can handle a quick change which may result from the unexpected sale—or loss—of one or two big ads.

Budgeting the space

At the same time, to be fair to readers, the managing editor wants some stability in the size of the news hole. The publisher has cause to scream if the percentage of advertising drops to, say, 50 percent. He will go bankrupt if the news hole widens. But it is the managing editor who should scream if advertising goes up to 70 or 80 percent. There is no set proportion suitable for all papers, but the managing editor should get nervous about quality when the news hole drops much below a third. It takes planning and discussion day in and day out to maintain a satisfactory balance. One of the advantages of the new technology, however, is the low cost of setting type. Now editors may not have to concern themselves so much about throwing away stories that reach the composing room.

Even when it does not cost much to set type electronically, it still is wasteful to have many stories that never see the light of print. Managing editors can control space, and thereby newspaper income, by careful planning. They accomplish this usually by adjusting the news hole to the amount of advertising each day. For example, on Monday and Tuesday, when advertising is light, the news hole may be 110 columns. The space for news may jump to 140 on Wednesday and Thursday and drop to 120 on Friday. The new technology plays a role here, too, for it takes little time with modern typesetting to get 20 more columns into type. The extra columns require, of course, more local reports and more wire copy. Both of these take time to produce and process.

Proper use of the news hole demands consultation with sub-editors to see whether a few columns in one department can be shifted on certain days to another section. For example, sports demand a lot of space on most weekends, while the women's department might be able to give up a little space—if it can be returned early in the week. Such consultations eventually must bring in the advertising manager so the ad dummy can reflect these planned adjustments each day. The good editor, naturally, will aim to fill the paper with quality news and features even when the space jumps twenty percent. Readers can become irritated if much of what is called news only fills space around all those ads.

A good example of this kind of filler appears in many papers on Wednesday or Thursday when the big grocery ads appear. A "food section," in elaborate color, goes on for twenty pages sometimes with the news hole filled with pictures of gorgeous dishes, stories containing complicated recipes, and tales of how the well-to-do serve their food. Much of this material is filler to nearly all readers and in some cases is an advertising payoff. Some papers mix into those pages consumer information on how to get the best food buys that week and how to prepare those products into tasty and nutritious meals.

Food, of course, is a part of the editorial smorgasbord that includes national, state, and foreign news, local stories, and all kinds of features. The managing editor usually has the last word on those syndicated features that may range from the humor of Erma Bombeck to Jack Anderson's political column on the editorial page. Most papers buy more of those features than they need so they can take their pick of the lot each day.

Budgeting the people

More important for editors than allotment of dollars and white space is the budgeting of time, for both their staffs and themselves. It is best if, from the start, editors consider this budget question not in terms of hours and minutes, but of people who work for them. What are their wants and needs? What will satisfy and stimulate them as employees and as human beings working with other men and women?

Journalists work on something more important than the manufacture of pickles or shirts, and wise editors run their shops so that the employees keep sight of this. Their feelings of significance ultimately give them their job satisfaction; and though good feelings cannot replace good pay they do contribute to a quality paper. Editors find ways to help staffers express themselves as individuals, to be creative: the photographer to get that special art shot, the reporter to dig into his or her exposé without fear of losing editorial support.

So the good editor operates as democratically as possible, turning decisions over to groups or committees. Such procedure introduces all the well-known shortcomings of democracy—delays, circumlocutions, slowness. But it also sparks spirit and creativity. One newspaper editor, reminded that the newsroom was shabby, let the Guild unit form a committee to recommend plans for redecoration. The committee members, excited about the task, suggested inexpensive changes that made the place attractive and convenient. Reporters and sub-editors alike felt that they had done well on a job normally considered management's baby.

An editor needs patience and wisdom to use this kind of cooperative approach. People are people, and committee operations are not always so sweet and sunshiny as some theorists suggest. Reporters and desk editors are sometimes selfish or ignorant; they can make mistakes and overlook the obvious. A majority vote guarantees neither genius nor saintliness, and one bonafide neurotic can derail the best-intentioned editorial team. Still, the neurotic and the selfish and the ignorant have to be dealt with, for staffs are built on earth rather than in heaven. If editors retain their humor, they will be able to guide the fit, misfit, and the semi-fit of their newsrooms with a helping hand rather than a threatening fist.

Of course key editors must eventually promote the fit staffers, overlook the semi-fit, and fire the misfit. In these and other ways, they may undertake basic reorganization of their staff structure. But most of the time each editor has to learn to get the job done with the motley assortment already drawing paychecks.

Supervising the team

Since managing editors are usually the major figures in the newsroom, it is necessary to look at supervision from their point of view. On small papers managing editors do much of the copyediting themselves, lay out the pages, check makeup, and write an occasional editorial. There rarely is enough time—or staff quality—to do anything first-rate, although a surprising number of little papers do good work.

On big papers the managing editor may have a half dozen assistant managing editors, each supervising a special department, such as foreign news or metro coverage. The managing editor then becomes something of a chairman of the board, examining the whole product critically and prodding top editors to keep looking for ways to improve writing and reporting. At critical times, of course, that "chairman" may move into the middle of the news room to direct key editors and reporters.

Managing editors easily can be saddled with all kinds of pesky details, such as time cards, overtime slips, and expense accounts. Unless they are careful they will spend hours each day handling clerical duties. A competent secretary can handle most of these chores, plus writing most letters, and give the M.E. time to manage. The good manager looks for efficiencies, tackles personnel problems too big for a sub-editor to handle, and studies how the staff can be juggled or strengthened to produce a somewhat better paper today than was printed six months ago.

The managing editor might find, for example, that hiring a clerk or a copy aide could relieve several staffers of routine work. The newsroom may be clumsily arranged so each staffer wastes several minutes each day dodging equipment. A minor shift of the furniture may smooth operations.

Perhaps the woman writing features in the women's department would be just the person to bolster the city feature staff—or be ready to come onto the copydesk. Maybe a sports writer has tired of the job and would like a crack at general assignment under the city editor. The managing editor must ponder such changes if the staff is kept alert and stimulated.

Many changes will result from conferences with sub-editors. But not any kind of conference will do. A weekly meeting where no one has prepared criticisms or suggestions ends up in a long, tedious bull session, filled with gripes and half-baked ideas. A one-hour session, however, where each sub-editor reports on plans for the next month or offers concrete suggestions for change, can yield all kinds of ideas and a sense of cooperative management.

The managing editor will also have to confer with the advertising manager so they may gain an appreciation of each other's problems and perhaps solve at least some minor production problems. A talk with the circulation manager may result in a slightly earlier deadline for the first edition or a decision to trim coverage in Bogtown because there is no hope of increasing circulation there.

The managing editor must be wary of associating almost exclusively with six or eight sub-editors and executives in the business department. Reporters are important, too, and a few chats with them can strengthen relationships and give the M.E. ideas from other staffers. The managing editor can contribute to staff enthusiasm in little ways, too, such as taking a reporter to lunch, financing a news room picnic, or having sandwiches and coffee brought in when much of the staff is on overtime to handle some major event.

Most of all, perhaps, the managing editor needs to sense when to do nothing and when to keep still. Sometimes the best change is no change. Certainly an arrogant, all-knowing editor who constantly juggles and shifts will irritate and even enrage a staff, particularly those members who have spent months learning a part of the craft.

Commenting from the writer's viewpoint, Tom Wicker of the *New York Times* has said that the editor must rely on the eyes and ears of the reporters.

> He may point [reporters] where he thinks they should
> go. He may send them back if they miss the target. He
> may see, with the sharp eye of his own knowledge and
> understanding, room for improvement and demand it.
> But he may not, in the long run, override or ignore the
> reporter's primacy of knowledge, intimacy of contact,

vital instinct of truth, and considered expression of meaning. . . .

[The] editor often can be blind to significance, overcome by the limitations and conditions the newspaper process so copiously imposes on him, and callous of his prime asset—the reporter.

The managing editor should continually review the editorial operation for improvement. What new spot would excite and hold one of the better staffers? Which weak links need replacement? Is a basic reorganization needed?

Improvement and reorganization

Editorial hiring is still one of the soft spots of newspaper management. Too often it is hit-or-miss. An opening goes to a person who happens to drop into the office, or to one who persists, rather than to the best journalist available for the salary. As the good university dean watches promising instructors around the country and keeps files on the careers of men and women who may not be given an offer for five to ten years, well-organized managing editors watch bylines on papers they can raid. They get acquainted with reporters at newspaper and professional meetings and on university campuses. When they lose a specialist in urban affairs or religion, they are able to pick knowledgeably from the best.

Newspapers recruit in journalism schools, of course, but often they are not searching for someone to hire upon graduation. Rather they seek a list of people who might be considered for jobs in a couple of years, when the young reporters have gathered a little experience elsewhere.

The editor may promote from within, of course. Morale rises when staffers see that the editor look around the newsroom to pick someone when a job opens. It may be that the would-be expert on urban affairs or religion is now writing obituaries or society notes. If managing editors take the time to chat with their men and women, they will know what their interests and talents are—and perhaps encourage the city editor to let some promising writer try out on a different subject.

The *Dover State News*, a small Delaware paper, encourages staffers to follow their special interests. Each person has an "enterprise" beat in addition to the regular tasks. So one covers night life, another special sports, and someone else the "little people"—those who quietly do valuable and interesting things.

Editors with tight budgets can rarely go scouting about the country to snap up one of the four or five best in a particular field. They need to develop their own. This can be done outright by asking staffers what they would like to cover if they had the chance. Then the staffer could be given a little time to read in that field, to attend a workshop, or to study at newspaper expense at a local college.

Home-grown specialists

Almost no specialist starts out in a specialized field. Young people get out of college, take a general assignment reporting job or a desk spot, and sometimes by luck stumble into a specialty that fascinates them. They learn on and off the job until they are genuine experts. Young staffers, of course, can prepare for the break when it comes. They can study and observe—and tell the managing editor, for example, "If the courthouse beat is ever open, I'd like a crack at it."

In improving their editorial staffs, imaginative editors may want to emphasize particularly this development of specialists. Here they might take a tip from competing media in shaping goals and the staff to reach them. Recently, magazines devoted to specialized topics—travel, electronics, or boating, for example—have made the most spectacular circulation gains. "Public television," going beyond educational TV, tries to put on programs to attract not a mass audience, but big segments of the population interested in special topics. Similarly, editors need not feel that every story must interest everyone. Some writers could well devote at least part of their time to cover medicine or psychology or other specialized topics of great interest to a segment of readers.

Fundamental changes

Sometimes more than shifting and upgrading of staffers is necessary. Fundamental reorganization may be required after careful study. To grow in a changing environment, a newspaper has to change. If suburbs are growing and circulation broadening, the staff must be reshaped to provide different or wider coverage. Are the slums festering and threatening the city's life? Then a reporting team, not just a police reporter, must cover the problem. Are staff leaders so busy or so unimaginative or so locked into routines that coverage is bland and uninspired? Then basic changes have to be made to release new blood and imagination.

If encouraged, good reporters and editors can pinpoint organizational flaws and suggest remedies. Dean I. William Cole, director of Northwestern's Urban Journalism Training Center, reports that scores of reporters taking this advanced program are impatient with the way newspapers are managed. Among their criticisms:

— The old beat system does not work on many urban stories, which involve a number of beats. This calls for some sort of team reporting approach.

— The city desk is a bottleneck because the city editors are expected to do the impossible. They do not have time to coordinate the local staff. They need more assistants.

— City desks too often frustrate top management and the reporters. Management knows that reporters are not doing a first rate job of anticipating stories and that too many stories are superficial and miss the point. When key editors try to change this, the city desk types just won't give an inch. They say, in effect, "This is the way I always did it and it worked for me, didn't it?"

Other basic managerial problems have been noted by Norman E. Isaacs, publisher of the *Wilmington News* and former editor of the *Louisville Courier-Journal*. He told a convention of the Associated Press Managing Editors' Association that managing editors take on too much work, crowding out time for imaginative thought or even for evaluating the day's paper. He continued:

> This leads to another serious failing. The chief task of a managing editor should be in training his key people. Yet if he doesn't even have time to himself, how can he train others? This lack of training down the line shows up in stereotyped thinking—with the overburdened managing editor the chief of the stereotyped clan.

The editor's attitude

To supervise and reorganize effectively, top editors must have the standards or goals of the paper clearly in mind, for they are not merely managing but managing *to a purpose*. If perfection is impossible, then their target can be at least improvement. At the retirement of Lester Markel, long-time Sunday editor of the *New York Times*, a colleague recalled: "His mental set when approaching any job was not 'Is it good?' but 'What can I do to make it better?'" Editors must know where they want the paper to go, and have the courage to drive it there.

Gardner (Mike) Cowles, former president of the Des Moines newspapers and editor-in-chief of Cowles Communications, Inc., complains that too many editors are "too careful, too cautious, too fearful of being controversial. To be a great editor, a man must be meaningfully involved in the important issues of his world; he needs *to care passionately.*" Cowles advises young journalists:

> Dare to be unpopular. If you win a popularity contest, you probably aren't doing your job. You can and should be respected—but not necessarily popular. Always edit just a notch over the heads of your readers. They want to read a publication they can look up to and one which stimulates them to think—even if they are occasionally annoyed.

We need not further define goals here. They are analyzed and advocated in the chapters dealing with ethics, editorial imagination, policy, and the future of newspapers. Managing editors are—or should be—always working with standards in mind, always reconsidering them, always checking whether the paper measures up.

Establishing priorities

So these editors must establish priorities. No paper can be all they would like, or even a very high proportion of it. Something has to give way; something has to be advanced. Editors must have the courage to focus on unpopular social issues but also to decide that no money or energy is available to ride out on this or that hobby horse, though important and influential and even highly moral forces press for it. Wicker has compared the editor's task to the reporter's:

> If the reporter is supposed to get into his story the right things in the right order, no more and no less, to make you hear, to make you feel, to make you see, what he has understood—then the editor has the equally sensitive job of getting the right things in the right order, no more and no less, in the newspaper.

How well editors succeed depends first, then, on how clearly they see and enforce the priorities that will take the paper to its goal.

As they clarify those priorities, editors communicate, not only facts or instructions, but also the *feel* of policies and standards. Then they check how well the communications are heeded. At the end of the work day, many an editor sighs at simply seeing the miracle of getting the paper out again. That sigh is both a confession and a profound self-criticism. Executive editors or managing editors somehow have to organize themselves and their staffs so that they have the time to evaluate as well as marvel at the daily miracle. They must not merely glance but also read slowly—they must reflect and contemplate. What values are coming across? Only as they seriously ask such questions, day after day, week after week, and strive to get them answered right, are editors really dealing effectively with goals and standards. Perhaps the best title for top editorial administrators would not be executive or managing editors but evaluation editors.

Broadening leadership   High position and high standards combine to push editors into leadership. They must lead the staff, but they also sought to lead in the community and the profession. Precisely because their activities relate to the way editors do their jobs in the office, editors have to decide whether they will take on leadership roles in politics or community service. A few decades ago, editors ran for office and took party posts. Today only the unusual editor does. Hodding Carter, editor of the *Greenville* (Miss.) *Delta Democrat-Times*, is one who has become involved in many facets of his city's civic life, arguing that he is "first of all a citizen." Because his paper has a monopoly and locks into the city's economic life, he says, "I have no right to be the town scold without taking part in the town's life."

The argument against involvement is that editors involved in controversy as citizens have trouble maintaining the newspaper's objectivity on vital issues. On the other side, however, editors who stand above community involvement may isolate themselves from a penetrating understanding of the forces and yeasty ideas which are at work all around the paper.

However editors resolve the dilemma of participation in the community, they have the duty to help provide leadership for the profession. They may attend the American Press Institute at Reston, Virginia. They may send staffers to a professional seminar at a nearby school of journalism, may accept election as secretary of a managing editor's association, or may work on a special journalistic committee. Irving Dilliard, a great editorial page editor of the *St. Louis Post-Dispatch*, has argued that a major characteristic of the good editor is "devotion to the improvement of the professional group." Remembering such heroes of press freedom as John Peter Zenger and Elijah Lovejoy, ideal editors "work year after year to protect it and to improve it." They speak up against government interference and each day ask themselves what have they done to help the republic and its press. Practicing his preachments, Dilliard served as national president of Sigma Delta Chi in the forties.

In professional service, editors develop "contacts" who can help the paper in one way or another. But they also help produce the professionalism and climate which make all newspapering better. No newspaper of quality can remain as an island washed all around by mediocrity and repression. At its best, professional leadership helps guarantee the survival of good newspapers in future generations.

Sharp editors, however, also establish firm priorities for their own time. They don't spread themselves too thinly over community and professional needs. Finally, back at the paper, they have leadership jobs. Gardner Cowles links that leadership to the newspapers' peculiar role of public responsibility, unique in the media—a responsibility which includes serving as "the monitor and conscience of their communities and the nation."

Apathetic editors fail in that responsibility. They rely on the wire services and do no more than hope that reporters will bring in good stories from their beats to fill the columns. As a result, many issues are dull, news-thin, and weak in social responsibility. To counter that, Cowles suggests:

> Any real newspaper needs several good reporters and photographers who are not tied down covering spot news in the conventional sense, or covering a set beat, but who are free to dig out and work up material that is topical, but can be held for a week or a month until desperately needed on an otherwise dull news day. But this takes advance planning. It takes ideas. It takes imaginative leadership from the top editor running the news room.

17 Problems of policy

The *St. Louis Post-Dispatch* carries this statement of policy by its founder each day in its masthead:

THE POST-DISPATCH PLATFORM

I know that my retirement will make no difference in its cardinal principles, that it will always fight for progress and reform, never tolerate injustice or corruption, always fight demagogues of all parties, never belong to any party, always oppose privileged classes and public plunderers, never lack sympathy with the poor, always remain devoted to the public welfare, never be satisfied with merely printing news, always be drastically independent, never be afraid to attack wrong, whether by predatory plutocracy or predatory poverty.

Joseph Pulitzer

April 10, 1907

Every newspaper should work out a clear and consistent concept of its aims and operations. The set of principles or guidelines for its procedures—the chart which sets its course—is called its policy. A newspaper policy may be Republican or Democratic, independent or non-partisan. It may range from liberal to conservative on social questions. And policy has a good many other facets, including the paper's attitude toward news, toward the community, toward reform.

Much of the policy is unwritten, carried in the heads of editors. Some points may be vague, some may be inconsistent. But it does offer a kind of "common law" which governs the way future decisions will be made.

The official policy of a newspaper is the publisher's responsibility. That is elementary, but there is so much obfuscation on the subject that the blunt statement of the object is necessary. Policy is not set by reporters, by the clerks in classified advertising, by advertisers, by the unions in the composing room, by the professors at the local college, or by the subscribers in the well-to-do part of town. All of them may influence the publisher,* but ultimately he or she decides debatable policy issues.

In the American economy the publisher's power over policy rests on ownership. Our system does not give control of the press to the state or co-operatives, much less to any interest group. As the person paying the piper calls the tune, the person or corporation that puts up the capital for a paper decides what it will say—and what it will not say.

One indication of confusion on this point is the perennial tendency of some college editors to claim greater power of policy than the colleges are willing to give them. In a private college, individuals put up the capital on which the student paper ultimately rests, and in a state institution, the taxpayers provide most of the funds. The locus of real power is obscured by talk of campus democracy, by the fact that students may subsidize the paper, and by the efforts of wise administrators to give editors maximum freedom. But if there is a libel suit, the institution, not the editor, pays. When student journalists don't like it that way, they quit, perhaps to start their own paper off campus. Then they meet the bills and pay for any libel suits, and they have a publisher's freedom to print and not to print, within the bounds of law and ethics. (Nor would they then, having put energy and money into their paper, probably be inclined to hand it over to others to run as they pleased, without strings! It's not the nature of publishing—or ownership.) Though it would be nice to get "something for nothing," there is no way to get the freedom to print as one pleases without paying in energy, money, and risk.

Because modern newspapers require substantial capital, only the prosperous or rich can own one that appeals to more than a small segment of the public, as "alternative" papers do. It is possible, of course, to rent rooms and a couple of typewriters and to turn out a cheap offset newspaper. Such papers were common in the late sixties, when they were called "underground" papers. Only a few survived. Costs were too high, income was too low, and human strength had limits.

Lest the press picture appear bleak, it should be added that most publishers are more interested in checking balance sheets than in advancing policies. They hand down word on policy. More often, they turn day-to-day policy over to men and women who will formulate policies they approve. When Col. "Bertie" McCormick was chief of the *Chicago Tribune*, a Northwestern University professor often asked *Tribune* editors whether memos instructed them to be anti-British or anti-labor. The teacher never found that the colonel gave

---

*Some papers are co-operatively owned and veteran staffers own stock in others. Some staffs benefit handsomely from profit-sharing plans. Many newspaper corporations sell stock on the open market. In all these instances, the views of more than a single publisher obviously count.

such orders—the staff simply edited the paper on those lines because they thought he wanted it that way. Sometimes, indeed, the true policy-maker of a paper is not so much the real-life publisher as a kind of newsroom phantom the editors visualize to represent the publisher's wishes.

Though the publisher ultimately is responsible for policy and can change it, the top editors may have considerable influence in shaping it. Their first duty is to examine the phantoms for realities. They may find that the staff still worships sacred cows that the publisher slaughtered long ago. Changing conditions naturally demand new policies, which editors can either make or suggest in hope of approval from the top. At minimum, they can try to influence the publisher to adopt the best policy. As policies prove unworkable or unwise, editors can also encourage the publisher to change them. The editor has special professional competence, after all, and a smart publisher will consider any reasoned arguments. As an example, the managing editor of a paper in Rochester, New York, asked a copyeditor how he thought their paper could be improved. He replied that the paper printed almost no news about neighboring Canada, just across Lake Ontario. The editor agreed, and it became policy to give more attention to Canadian events.

The editor's role in policy

It is possible that a strong and somewhat brash sub-editor will, in effect, change policy by switching content. The publishers may not notice it, or may even approve the change. They could grumble a little but not take the effort to order a reversal. They might be annoyed, of course, to the point of transferring the editor to a different job.

One troubling complication in this owner-policy situation is the ambiguity of absentee ownership, which today is widespread. At its worst, the absentee system means that the owners are interested only in the money a paper makes; management pinches pennies, lets editorial quality deteriorate, and adopts policies designed to save dollars rather than to better a community. At its best, however, absentee ownership may give dedicated professionals the authority to run a good paper.

William Randolph Hearst, Sr., personally sent editorials and orders through his whole chain of papers, and his editors everywhere reacted like bright puppets. But that is old-fashioned. Hearst papers under William Randolph, Jr., now have a much looser system. Gannett papers make such a point of autonomy that only recently has the term "chain" been used to describe them. They called themselves a "group" before. Looking back over his long career, the president of the Knight-Ridder Newspapers, John S. Knight, said: "We don't believe in having a central headquarters with teletype machines sending out editorials and instructions. Our papers are all run by the men in these respective cities. . . . Other than within the bounds of prudent management, we don't exercise any control over their discussions or policy." Local editors can learn readily to live with policy questions when they are decided by people with local roots, including themselves.

In looking at the publisher's role, it is also wise not to get too exalted a concept of what policy formation is. The publisher does not send down a code to some Moses. Such a code could no more cover all cases than do the Ten Commandments, and, in any event, it would have to be interpreted by busy copy editors. The newspaper business is a pragmatic one. Let's say the publisher decrees the paper should be fair. Fine, but is it fairer to put in this news fact or leave it out? By repeatedly answering this question writers and editors form policy.

Or suppose a publisher orders that the paper support such-and-such a candidate. Professionalism decides how far the editors can go with such a policy, and if it is pushed too crassly, the paper—and the publisher's bank account—will suffer. In short, policy is not like a statue, which is formed once and for all; it is more like a hedge, which editors can prune and nurture.

Goals and policy

Policies stem from a newspaper's objectives. Where the goal is full and fair coverage, editors can develop specific policies to reach it. But if the aim is simply to make as much money as possible, other policies are required. In his book *Responsibility in Mass Communications*, Wilbur Schramm lists six facets of the "emerging code of new responsiblity." These are separation of editorials from news, accuracy, objectivity, balance, fairness, and reliability. Already, as ethical goals are envisioned, the outlines of a newspaper policy begin to emerge.[1]

In research on readers' ideals it has been found that "accurate" and "fair" rank first and second. "Ethical" and "adequate" come next. These match those attributes listed by Schramm. Evaluative terms like "interesting," "prompt," "profitable," and "conservative" scored poorly. One might be cautious on such findings, however, for almost anyone would guess before such a survey was taken that most people would vote for "accurate" and "fair." They sound so respectable. One might suspect that a reader may say he or she would put top priority on "accurate," but in reality would choose "interesting" when it comes to pick a story to read. Nevertheless, professional journalists should establish accuracy and fairness as the leading demands they put upon themselves.

The editorial mix

Magazines operate with what editors, borrowing from chemistry, call a formula. The term refers to the combination of ingredients —articles, photos, stories, cartoons, and so on—which regularly go into the publication. The shifting nature of the news makes it more difficult to stabilize a newspaper's formula or "recipe." A heavy admixture of foreign news may be best on one day; several local stories may demand treatment on the next. Nevertheless, the concept of a formula helps show how editors develop practices which reach policy goals. The serious paper has one editorial mix, the frivolous another. Descending from the heights of press ideals, we get to the practicalities of policy by considering three major ingredients—opinion, news, and entertainment.

Opinion

It is a truism that the American newspaper separates news and opinion, with the editors' views confined to the editorial page. Though the ideal may be violated, the policy remains sound. If editorial writers stay within the bounds of law and good taste, few questions are raised about their right to support or oppose candidates or programs. Whether the publisher sets editorial policy or hands the task to the editors of the page, decisions about the stands to be taken in these opinion columns are a keystone of the paper's overall policy.

Policy also has to be made for syndicated columns. Some editorial pages carry only columns which support the paper's own positions. A more common policy is to select columns which give "both sides." A vigorous, aggressive paper might, however, adopt a policy of selecting—even of finding and cultivating—columnists who will argue a wide variety of stimulating and nonconformist opinions. Vigorous leadership on the editorial page was advocated by Robert S. McCord, editor and publisher of the *North Little Rock* (Ark.) *Times,* in an article which won a Sigma Delta Chi writing award. Deploring that editors of many weeklies and small dailies include "no opinion, no interpretation, no comment," McCord declared such an editor "not only is cheating himself out of the fun of being a newspaperman but he is cheating his readers."

Guidelines also must be established for letters to the editor. One prominent editor threw away letters he disagreed with, but only after phoning or writing their authors to tell them off. This bizarre policy obviously angered many subscribers. A more sensible and common policy is to print as many letters as possible. Writers are thus encouraged to contribute. If at least a little of every literate contribution is used, the policy wins wider reader support.

Whether to insist on the writers' names on all letters is another policy matter. In a survey by the Pennsylvania Newspaper Publishers Association, 96 out of 128 publishers and editors said they had a policy of publishing letters without the name when anonymity was requested. But 32 said they were against such practice, arguing that anonymity encourages crank letters and lets writers vent spleen at the expense of others, including the newspaper.

News

If accuracy and fairness are desirable goals, independence is a leading virtue in policy on news. Selection of the news, as indicated already in discussions of news evaluation and journalism ethics, must be free from influence by editorial page policy, advertising pressures, or the biases of publisher or staffers.

Completeness and breadth of coverage are also important in news policy. Editors and publishers of papers outside the largest metropolitan centers sometimes complain when press critics hold up the thoroughness of the *New York Times* as an example. Though papers with smaller resources cannot offer such a wealth of news, the goal for even a paper of 50,000 should be coverage in breadth and depth of "all the news that's fit to print." By carefully selecting and editing news from local staffers and from the wires, editors can cover world news with at least moderate thoroughness and local news with completeness and enterprise.

As we discussed in chapter 6, newspapers should aim to cover constructive as well as destructive events and trends. We indicated in the discussion on ethics that there might be more emphasis on the constructive. The outstanding ethical example of one religious body's journalistic effort, the *Christian Science Monitor,* is enlightening on this point. The *Monitor* does not ordinarily print unpleasant items; because Christian Science emphasizes the basic goodness in the universe, the paper developed from this faith plays up the wholesome and plays down the bad. Christian Science views evil and sin, disease and suffering, as unreal. It follows that a newspaper founded on this view would print only news rooted in the real or true. So the *Monitor* usually does not print news of crimes or deaths or disasters. Evil is thwarted by its editors, and many newspaper readers wish that other journalists would follow the example.

No newspaper worthy of the name can ignore the popular concern with wars and urban violence; so, although trying to deal positively with such events, the *Monitor* makes the pragmatic compromise and does print news of these man-made disasters. This paper's general bias toward "good news," however, is wholly satisfactory only to members of this church and perhaps a few others, since most Americans probably want newspapers which give accounts of evil.

Newspapers, of course, print a great deal of "good news." Stories on medical advances, tax cuts, the arrest of a dangerous criminal are all examples of "good news." But what is good news to one person may be bad news to another. Democrats rejoice when papers print the "good news" of their party's victory. To Republicans the news is bad. A boost in the price of XYZ stock is good news to the stockholder but bad news to the person who sold the same stock yesterday.

A sizable number of people wish the press would play down the bad news. Businessmen often want journalists to keep pretending that the economic picture blooms with roses when in fact business is down eight per cent over the previous year. Sports fans go into rages if their heroes are described as anything less than magnificent. But faking, slanting, or distorting the news can be dangerous. People can be badly misled and take steps that cause considerable anguish. As an example, if a paper kept trumpeting how a city was growing, the people might approve a big school-building program, and then find later that so many buildings were not needed. The paper loses credibility when it smothers "bad news" and keeps the public from having the facts necessary to correct flaws.

To examine good news and bad news, David Jacobs, when he was assistant managing editor of the *Long Island Press* in Jamaica, New York, checked a random, thirty-six page issue. The front page held three "particularly violent stories." But the tally of hard news showed 11 columns of "happy" or "good" news; 27 columns of "benign" or neutral news, and 10 columns of "bad" or violent news. Counting in women's and sports pages as largely good, he figured that only 10 of 278 columns were "bad." There is probably much less "bad" news in papers than most people think.

A few papers for a time tried to promote the "positive side" of the community by printing lots of stories about civic accomplishments and saying little about crime, accidents, job layoffs etc. Most of them gave it up after a few months. The efforts usually were strained; editors were forsaking normal news judgment; and the whole attempt smelled of Boosterism, not journalism.

Entertainment

It would be foolish for a newspaper to have a policy of "no entertainment," though some observers apparently feel that should be the goal. It is true that certain papers strive for mostly entertainment. On the other hand, in response to the disillusioning development of television largely as entertainment, some editors have felt that seriousness is the best competing policy. The policy of a paper on this score must, of course, be tailored to its readership. But, along with opinion and news, entertainment has a legitimate place; it has traditionally been a part of newspapers almost since they emerged from flysheets, and it should continue in any editorial formula. The question is, how much of this leavening ingredient should be included?

Sometimes editors beg the question by contending that everything they print should be interesting—i.e., entertaining. That is neither possible nor desirable. Some important developments, such as crises in the gold market, are by their nature dull to ordinary readers. They can be explained clearly, and even interestingly. But it would be fatuous to twist these stories into entertainment.

Sometimes human fallibility dismisses as entertainment only that which does not fit its own tastes. Thus, male-oriented papers pontificate about eliminating women's-page frivolity, such as fashions, but never question the inclusion of endless features about professional football—for sports interest men and are therefore "important."

An honest, objective look at newspaper policy would include an analysis and categorization of what is proper to the editorial page, what is real news, and all the rest. "The rest" tends to be entertainment—comics, advice columns, sports, feature photographs, society items, and much of so-called "women's news." (Editors might differ as to whether cultural coverage—book reviews and music criticism, for example—are entertainment or a part of the news/opinion spectrum, but such features are part of a good mix.)

Sound policy would prescribe a balanced admixture of entertainment to keep the paper from dead seriousness or hopeless frivolity. (Since the *New York Times* is so often cited as quality journalism, it might be noted that its editors have consciously tried—and succeeded—in the last decade to brighten its pages with material that must be categorized as entertainment, such as personality features and the humorous columns by Russell Baker. And while the *Times* carries no comic strips, the "serious" *Monitor* does.)

One guide to whether entertainment succeeds is to check if a sizable part of the readership actually reads it. One sometimes senses, as eyes wander over the two or three pages of cartoons in an out-of-town paper, that half of them might be omitted with little loss of circulation. From time to time editors do drop a comic and remark on how few complaints they get. Their policy might often be more ruthless toward rejecting the conventional if they really want to project a serious image. One editor of a paper with 13,000 circulation gave up *Little Orphan Annie* as she was descending to earth in a parachute—and only four readers complained.

Comic strips which are witty or satiric came close to disappearance a few years back. One of the great ones, Walt Kelly's *Pogo,* dropped out about a year after Kelly's death. His widow said she could not continue to draw the strip in the smaller panels now used by newspapers. Charles Schultz' *Peanuts* survived, of course, and Garry Trudeau's irreverent *Doonesbury* has captured large readership, particularly among the young. Some new strips, *Frank & Earnest* and *Born Loser,* have revived humor in the comics. These fit properly into the budget as entertainment. Some strips, however, dip heavily into politics or superpatriotism to the extent that some critics think they belong on the editorial page.

Political cartoons have a hallowed place in world journalism, and editors both express opinion and win entertainment points by using good cartoons. These belong on the editorial page, although a few papers put them on page one, where readers sense that they really are editorials. The *Los Angeles Times,* however, shifted the brilliant work of Paul Conrad onto the opposite-editorial page, saying that Conrad was free to express his own opinions, which did not necessarily always match those of the editorial page.

The newspaper as public utility

In the somewhat mixed economy of the United States, the newspaper today fits somewhere between the old libertarian theory of maximum editorial freedom and the emerging theory of social responsibility. Editors do not make policy as do the puppet editors of *Pravda* in the Soviet Union. And no matter how ardently Jeffersonians might wish it, they do not today have the freedom to be irascible and irresponsible, as did the editors when Jefferson was President. The role of the newspaper in the last years of the twentieth century must be thought out in new terms.

The image most appropriate for the American newspaper in the next couple of decades is probably that of public utility. The metaphor is imperfect but instructive. A telephone company or an electric corporation enjoys a monopoly that even free-enterprise enthusiasts rarely question. Though public commissions may control some aspects of the business, such as determining whether its rates are fair, the utility is relatively free to plan, purchase, and expand. Yet utility executives recognize that they must serve the whole community and cannot arbitrarily ignore any citizen, providing bills are paid. Similarly, the newspaper enjoys many protections under the Constitution and by informal tradition. It holds responsibilities both to the community and to individuals, no matter how odd their ideas may appear.

The public-utility concept may help publishers and editors form policies which are realistic for this day. The newspaper, as public utility, is a business but not just any business. It has a trust, which might even be called sacred, to convey the information of a democratic society. Citizens have as much right to criticize how well it does this job as they have to criticize long-distance telephone service.

The newspaper is also a humanitarian enterprise, but not like the Red Cross. Rather, it is a business like the gas company, which serves people as it earns. The American Telephone and Telegraph Company may advertise as if its only goal in life were to bring cheery families together by wire, but ultimately it exists to produce profits for AT&T stockholders. The legitimate money needs of a newspaper should not be forgotten in fogs of humanistic rhetoric.

Businessmen publishers often sound hard-headed when they speak of their properties and profit and insincere when they carry on about their ideals. For their part, intellectual critics are inclined to be cynical about the business aspects of publishing and naive about the humanistic potential of our present newspaper system. Businessmen and intellectuals might find a common realistic ground if they recognize the modern newspaper as a public utility, requiring policies that produce profits and at the same time serve society well.

Consumers of newspapers, too, should examine their views with more care. Often lay critics of the press demand fuller coverage, more courageous reporting, and less advertising, yet they might be the first to complain if their demands were met. They most likely would not read the wider coverage, would howl if a courageous reporter raked a little muck in their own back yards, and would object to paying a nickel more to help the paper reduce advertising.

Any editor, then, should not rush to accept the standards offered by critics. Human beings like to make lofty statements, but they often fail to match those statements with performance.

Let us, finally, consider how the concept of the public utility relates to policy aims. We have written about such goals as accuracy and fairness, which define the newspaper's stance toward informa-

Three aims of policy

tion. But related aims emerge from its dynamic role as public utility, and these have three overlapping phases or levels.

Community betterment

It would be difficult to find a publisher who would not say that his policy is to improve the community. That goal is minimal, but it is also a major challenge.

It will illustrate a paper's potential for community betterment if, in a seeming digression, we focus on an issue where most papers have failed and where many are still failing: their coverage of minority groups, and specifically of the Negro, Puerto Rican, and Mexican-American communities. During the sixties, editors met thorny problems in covering the so-called Black Revolution and the growing discontent of Chicanos. Those problems eased somewhat in the seventies, but no informed journalist would expect the task ever to be easy.

Basic to the problem is the fact that until about 1970 almost all newspapers were edited by whites for whites. Communities with "white schools" and "white churches" also have had "white newspapers," and blacks quite properly were bitter about a "white press." The black has been "the invisible man" to white society, including white editors and reporters. They still simply don't see the world as a black reader does, and some continue to be blind to their blindness.

In the last several years, however, black brides have had their pictures in nearly all women's sections; classified ads no longer mention race; and stories almost always use racial descriptions only when they are pertinent. So things have changed, although blacks will say quickly that they have a long, long way to go.

A traditional source of criticism has involved labeling: Mexican, Puerto Rican, Negro, colored, women. Part of the trouble is the general problem of identification. How can you make clear, sometimes, who people are without some label, such as student, Moslem leader, Bircher, women's liberationist, veteran? Editors can reduce the problem if they do not use labels which reinforce stereotypes. If a black person gets in the paper only when a crime is committed, a stereotype is bolstered. If a woman is called "attractive blonde, mother of three" we reinforce the stereotype that a woman's main purpose is to look good and have babies.

Other labels change

Just as most papers now will not use racial labels unless they are essential to the story, increasingly they are alert to labels that irritate many women. Progressive papers have warned staffs not to use descriptive phrases for women that would not be used for men and that stories should be scratched if the tone is "pretty good for a woman." So such terms as "a 5-feet, 4-inch, 123-pound graduate of Wellesley" no longer need appear, unless perhaps the woman is playing on a football team.

Similar stereotyping can be found in other areas. Students, for example, are often irritated when their elders ask "what students think about" a certain issue. Students rarely can be so neatly catalogued——and neither can racial, religious, or even political groups.

Old people also dislike being lumped into one category. Some stories indicate that all old people are poor, sick, feeble, and crotchety. Almost everyone must know several elderly people who would not fit such classification, so editors should aim to eliminate the feeble stereotype, too.

Certainly almost all Americans, journalists or not, have become more sensitive to people's feelings—and pride—about race, ancestry, occupation, and age.

Snickers or sneers against all kinds of minorities seem less common than they were twenty years ago. Yet out of ignorance some reporters still drop into a story a phrase that may cause a group of citizens to boil over. Gross examples of this problem could be seen in stories about American Indians that say they are going to have a *pow-wow* and possibly *smoke the peace pipe*. A more common error would be the story that says Bill Smith, the fullback, is majoring in economics and has an A-minus average. The implication is that he is an oddity, since the stereotype says that most football players are dumb.

Fixations on roles can become more rigid with photography. Pictures of a whittling mountaineer, a co-ed studying in a swim suit, or a black man idling outside a pool hall contribute to a sort of myth about certain kinds of people. In almost no case would a photographer or a journalist knowingly aim for such clichés.

The difficulty is that in the past many newspaper people had no idea that their stories, headlines, and pictures irritated certain people. Fortunately, when their insensitivity or ignorance was pointed out to them, they generally corrected the problem. Many of these blunders would have been avoided, of course, if journalists had read with care some of the stories that appeared in their own papers. Feminism, for example, has been around a long time. So have the anguished cries of oppressed black people. Stories on these subjects have appeared hundreds of times in the American press. People could hardly claim to be journalists if they were not aware of the prejudice, insensitivity, and chauvinism that crept into so much newspaper copy.

The turmoil of the last twenty years has produced all kinds of marches, demonstrations, and even riots as some people have sought their rights and others have battled to conserve power and positions, however humble. Journalists often have been harried in covering these events, and sometimes they were unprepared to report the charges, claims, violence, and anger that these eruptions produced. With some justification, the press was criticized for printing the statements of the most militant and neglecting the advices of the thoughtful. As journalists gained experience with clashes, particularly those that involved school busing, they were able to give sober and accurate accounts of what was going on. In some cases, those who were shouting the loudest were ignored and attention was given to those quiet people who suggested ways to reduce or resolve the tensions. Great care was taken to avoid inflammatory, hyper-emotional statements that distorted reality.

The lessons here could be carried into all parts of journalism. Surely too many journalists have responded eagerly to the scathing statement, the exaggerated claim or the spectacular event without bothering to seek reasoned and restrained comments. Many politicians have complained bitterly that their meticulous, cautious, and studious proposals get ignored by the press while a dramatic but shallow plan by someone else appears on page one.

Some bad habits

American newspaper staffs often have been wedded to habit in coverage and sometimes have been inept in recognizing the sensitivities of all kinds of people. Yet the evidence shows that reporting is more careful and thorough than it was even ten years ago. Certainly the press is far more aware of how people have been stereotyped by the public and newspapers. Reporters, editors, and photographers have listened to the complaints and, over the years, corrected at least the most glaring flaws.

The most recent rise of feminism has contributed immensely to the change. Women long have been valuable members of news staffs, as reporters, critics, women's page staffers, and, occasionally, copyeditors. But almost none of them advanced to top positions. By now, however, women everywhere have modified the mind-set of male editors, and they frequently have become managing editors, city editors, and even editors-in-chief.

Blacks, Chicanos, and other minorities have scrapped and argued for staff positions and for a fair break on coverage of their events. Unlike women, there usually was not one of their own in the newsroom to make a squawk. But they fought their way inside until now nearly every newspaper of size has a few black or brown faces in the newsroom. As mentioned before, the big papers have black columnists who frequently educate the whites and give large numbers of black readers the feeling that, at last, they are getting their side of the story told.

Crusades

It may be the policy of the publisher and editor to pick evils to fight and to conduct what has long been called a "crusade." In news stories, pictures, cartoons, and editorials they hammer away to clean out gamblers, build a civic center, get the city manager plan adopted, or "run the crooks out of city hall."

Crusading easily slips into imbalance and unfairness, but it is exciting journalism. If crusading seems not so general or potent as it was a generation or two ago, the annual recognitions in the Pulitzer Prizes and the Polk and Sigma Delta Chi awards suggest that many papers still have crusading policies. To the crusader, merely giving the news is too slow a road to community betterment. Even when a paper is not seeking a crusade, important events are thrust upon it in such ways that honest journalists are forced to look for the hidden facts if the paper is to meet its responsibilities. Recent Pulitzer Prizes indicate that several papers have plunged into what often would be unpopular frays to correct abuses which involve people's lives or fortunes.

Pulitzer Prizes have been given in recent years to these papers or reporters:

The *Riverside* (Calif.) *Press-Enterprise* for reporting corruption in handling property and estates of the Agua Caliente Indians. One judge, in a former capacity, had been granted $250,000 in fees for representing thirty-three Indians as their guardian.

Wall Street Journal reporters Stanley Penn and Monroe Karmin reported links between American criminals and gambling interests in the Bahamas.

Newsday conducted a three-year inquiry into crooked politicians in eastern Long Island.

Ronald Linscott of the *Berkshire Eagle* won an editorial-writing prize for opposing an unnecessary highway.

The *Louisville Courier-Journal* ran a long campaign to control strip mining in Kentucky. The mining had caused stream pollution and terrible erosion.

Articles by Gene Miller in the *Miami Herald* brought the release of two persons wrongfully convicted of murder.

In these cases the newspapers probably did not make an extra nickel from circulation or advertising. It is also probable that the papers spent thousands of dollars to get the information. The Louisville case would have brought powerful and angry opposition from mine companies and some miners.

Leadership

Policy may also concern the newspaper's role in community leadership. This leadership is continuing, perhaps less intensely than the crusading burst, but in a more vigorous and directed fashion than that necessary for general community betterment. For example, take the perennial issue of schools: A paper may work for community betterment simply by giving thorough coverage of what is happening in local education. A crusading paper may go after the hide of the superintendent or try to get its candidates elected to the school board. But a paper oriented toward leadership might search out the opinions of teachers and parents, discuss alternate possibilities on its editorial page, and develop interpretive stories showing how similar communities have tackled similar problems.

A paper may operate on all three levels at different times, or even at the same time. Most of its effort may go to straight coverage and editorials which help the citizens themselves better their community. The paper may crusade on the high-school drug problem, while, simultaneously, its editors may move in and out of leadership efforts on pollution or street violence or international combats. A newspaper will be most effective, however, if the publisher and editors plan a coordinated policy small enough for the staff to handle yet big enough to make an impact. Too often the crusade starts out dramatically and then, like so many heralded grand jury or congressional investigations, it fizzles because of inadequate planning.

The community agenda

In one vital aspect of policy, a newspaper cannot avoid contributing to the community's betterment or, perhaps, to its decline. The paper's policies influence what the citizens think about. Television and radio, ministers, professors, and clubs all have some part in picking out the big issues for local discussion, but the influence of the newspaper probably outweighs all of them. The paper establishes the agenda of concerns, as if it were chairman of a giant town meeting. If the paper prints a lot about muggings, the people worry about muggings. If it gives complete coverage to meetings that deal with construction of new schools, the readers will be talking about new schools. Riots or pornography or peace activities or drugs become public concerns or not as the paper covers or ignores them.

Especially through interpretive stories, the newspaper sets up the agenda of public discussion and action. If it does not cover, say, the desires or demands of the black community, it is difficult for community leaders to stir up public concern. If it does print such material, however, the public becomes aware. Editorial endorsement of a candidate or policy may be the kiss of death. But, unobtrusively, the policies of the paper work to change the community for better or worse; the staff simply establishes the agenda.

18 Newspaper editorial research

A Washington reporter, made editor of a West Coast newspaper, pondered his first move. After some deliberation he hired a research firm to tell him what kind of community his paper served. The results showed that everything about the town was medium: education, income, job possibilities, cultural interests. So the editor aimed the paper slightly above the level of the readers and attained moderate success.

The *Chicago Tribune* polled its readers and found that the average age was fifty-four. It did not take much deduction to realize that next year the average age would be fifty-five. So the *Tribune*, long a dry, fusty newspaper, changed its format, hired some young staffers, and directed much of its content toward younger readers. The paper's circulation, which had been skidding, leveled off.

A medium-sized midwestern newspaper wondered how readers liked its columns. A survey astonished the editors. The column they thought appealed to young swingers captivated only one group: old women.

In all these cases the newspapers conducted fairly elaborate and moderately expensive research. Many newspapers these days are willing to spend a lot of money for facts on which they can base decisions. It is possible that this research may be inaccurate or even misleading. But in the main, careful and methodical research gives editors accurate, timely information they could not get by themselves through observation, calculated guesses, or unsystematic interviews.

Newspapers need not spend a lot of money, however, to help reporters, copyeditors, and sub-editors get quick information. Simple polls can be taken by high school boys and girls, under proper supervision. A few adults may question several hundred people on the telephone. Questionnaires can be dropped in the mail to subscribers.

Before any newspaper dashes off to sign a contract for several thousand dollars with a research firm, the editors might look about to see what kind of research aids can be provided within their own plant.

The library

The obvious place to start is the newspaper's library. If it is inadequate, staff members probably spend hours hunting for information. What they do find is probably sketchy or even wrong. A good library, staffed by a competent librarian, can save a newspaper money by saving staff time, and it can greatly improve the paper's content.

Libraries can concentrate on collecting local information if the paper ties in with super-libraries on computer lines. The *Milwaukee Journal,* for example, has its vast collection of city and Wisconsin material on computer tapes. A paper elsewhere in the state, for a fee, can tap into the *Journal* computer to get information, say, on how the state legislature voted on prohibition a half century ago. The *Journal* buys service from the *New York Times,* which has taped national and international facts. If a newspaper in Madison, for example, was tied to both services, a reporter could type questions on a keyboard, perhaps to find the record temperatures in Wisconsin and the nation. The *Journal* computer would give the Wisconsin figures in a flash and the *Times* library would provide the temperatures for the rest of the country. This kind of linkage may be expensive but the savings on space and librarians would be substantial.

All editors and reporters should have a few files of their own. Clips, magazine articles, book titles, pamphlets, and notes can be slipped into a big folder and pulled forth from time to time to get facts to bolster a story. If these can't be kept in a newsroom drawer they can be stored in some filing cabinet in the library.

One mine of information that editors can tap is the Census Bureau. Almost all data from this source are free, and editors can find dozens of facts there to help them in their work. The Census Bureau provides information on the average family income of a community; the proportion of people over the age of sixty; the number of people who are college graduates; the number who did not finish high school; the proportion who work in factories, the percentage of the population that is black; and other similar information.

With no more than what they find in five minutes' reading of a Census Bureau pamphlet, editors may decide to trim sports a little, add a few more stories of concern to old people, select a wider range of foreign stories, and drop a couple of features.

But editors might make grave mistakes if they add and subtract with only demographic information in mind. They may make assumptions that would be so wrong that readership and circulation would drop.

Newspapers with genuine research departments can offer more reliable help. The *St. Petersburg Times* has its research department give the editorial staff exact information on which stories are read.

As an illustration, researchers examined readership of a story head-lined:

U.S. Autos Said Safer Than Foreign Compacts

A picture of colliding cars accompanied the story. The results looked like this:

	Noted	Read
Total	71%	60%
Men	83	63
Women	78	58
18–39 (age)	75	55
40–64	77	59
65 & over	83	64

It is noteworthy that the picture readership was four to ten percentage points *less* than story readership.

These percentages may seem low, but of ten stories or pictures on page one, the auto safety story was the second-most read.

This kind of readership polling can offer surprises. One might think, as an illustration, that almost all readers in Florida, where so many readers come from other parts of the country, would read listings of temperatures in cities all over the country and Canada. The information was placed conspicuously on page two of the *Times,* yet only forty-seven per cent read it. The figures give other clues, however, for sixty-eight per cent of those over sixty-five read the temperatures. Presumably, older people were most concerned with weather far away, possibly because they did not live in Florida all year.

With readership facts, editors can make good decisions on news content. They *know* that certain features are read well or poorly. They *know* if letters to the editor are the best-read part of the paper. With this information they can decide, perhaps, to have more of one kind of a story and less of another. Editors may decide, however, that if editorials are poorly read it is the fault of the editorials—so the editors make them better. If world news gets light readership, perhaps it needs better display or improved editing.

The *Chicago Tribune* handles editorial research differently. The paper had done almost no such research until 1970, when it set up a reader panel. Some 2,000 adult readers from 1,100 households, upon invitation, became members of the panel. Some of these read-ers were subscribers and others got their papers on newsstands. These panel members received questionnaires every six to eight weeks. In the continuing program, the questionnaire may ask how often the paper is read, what other papers are read, how much time each day is spent with the paper, whether election campaign cover-age is fair to all parties, and similar questions.

The panel is not quite representative of the population, for it tilts slightly in favor of the well-educated, affluent, and older people. The *Tribune* finds that it gets better responses from such a group. All panel members are sent a modest gift—a drinking glass coated with a picture of a historic Tribune front page. Panel members seem pleased with the gift and with being asked. Response to the questionnaire usually is close to 100 per cent.

When the *Tribune* sought information on comics readership part of the questionnaire looked like this:

7. How often do you read each of the following comics appearing in the Sunday Tribune, Today comic section? The second color comic section?

		Regularly	Occasionally	Seldom	Never
	ARCHIE	1	2	3	4
	BARNEY GOOGLE & SNUFFY SMITH .	1	2	3	4
	BEETLE BAILEY	1	2	3	4
	BLONDIE	1	2	3	4
	BONER'S ARK	1	2	3	4
	DONALD DUCK...........................	1	2	3	4

Sometimes the *Tribune* wants to look at a section in depth. Then it interviews subscribers. As John Timberlake, the research manager, says, "We probe for the more subtle nuances of attitudes and reactions which a self-administered questionnaire would miss. We have used this approach to uncover attitudes among young readers toward the newspaper, among women to evaluate the women's pages, and among all readers to evaluate the Sunday magazine." Timberlake adds significantly, "We have found that the group research *works best when the editor concerned is involved from study inception to presentation.* In one case, an editor attended all group sessions and participated in the presentation of results to editorial management. Through this involvement, we feel that the editorial people see the research as theirs in a sense and are much more likely to feel comfortable with the results and, most importantly, *to act on the results.*"

Both the *Chicago Tribune* and *St. Petersburg Times* research departments also provide information for stories. The *Times* calls this kind of research the Pinellas Poll, since St. Petersburg is in Pinellas County. The researchers, for example, tabulated all kinds of information on the area's condominium housing. So prices, number of units, number of empty units, sales, etc. were tallied. The facts were given to a reporter who put them into a concise story that interested a sizable bloc of readers. Another Pinellas Poll disclosed that automobile sales were sagging. Full information on that story was tabulated, too. Reporters could gather such information, of course, but researchers usually are better at tallying and analyzing data.

The Tribune Poll sticks closer to opinion polling and is careful to avoid non-scientific methods. For too long newspapers used man-in-the-street interviews or helter-skelter telephoning and tried to pass these off as opinion polling. Fortunately, these kinds of "research" bring so many derisive letters from readers nowadays that editors have cut out most of them.

The computer can be of great help in sorting facts for stories. The human brain simply cannot absorb or pull together hundreds of scraps of information the way a computer can. A few papers, as a result, have been willing to let a reporter or a team of reporters meticulously gather facts and feed them into a computer. As an example, a reporter may want to find exactly what prison sentences have been given by area judges. Facts would be tallied on every case of robbery, burglary, assault, theft, and so on that had gone through the local courts for the last five years. The reporter then could give this kind of report: Judge A gave harsher sentences than Judge B. The average sentence for larceny was two years but terms ranged from six months to eight years. White collar crime brought modest sentences. Criminals represented by public defenders most often got severe sentences.

Such comprehensive fact-gathering serves the public well, for it gets the full story, and it takes the wind out of those who spout generalities based on impressions or fragments of information.

The editor without specialized training in communications research may do some simple but useful investigations. Serious opinion research should be left in the hands of professional pollsters, but there are some simple internal investigations where common sense suffices.

Ideally, editors would discuss research ideas with the research staff, but usually there is no such department. If a research department exists, it is often too busy to undertake all the questions an alert editor might raise. Most of the time, then, editors are on their own. As a first step they might, during office hours, take a course or two in research techniques of communications, psychology, or sociology at a nearby university. Certainly they would at least want to read a few books that provide elementary insights. (See Bibliography.) One does not have to be a statistician to know that 56 percent of the vote wins an election or that 95 percent foreign news on a front page is too high. Minimal self-education may save an editor from a serious error, such as assuming that valid conclusions on

Elementary behavioral research

readability can be drawn from calculating Flesch scores on two or three stories. Just as important, such research training will help editors interpret the media research findings which come to their attention, including the countless "studies" now reported on news flow.*

What kind of rudimentary research, then, can editors undertake? Front-page news is a good place to start. Editors may want to check hunches—that there are not enough humorous stories on page one, for example, or that there are too many stories from the state capital. It is no trick to set up a simple method to find out. The editors can establish categories such as local, area, state—or humorous, human interest, serious—depending on the focus. Then they can categorize, count, and record the stories on page one of every issue for a week or two, or every other front page for a month. When they strike a total, find an average, and discover trends and patterns, they have a reasonably accurate picture of the choices editors have been making for the front page. Perhaps emotions about the legislative correspondent, for example, pushed legislative stories to the front. Many questions remain, but at least they have some data, rather than mere impressions, to inform them about future handling of front page news.

Clearly, editors would be foolish to make blanket accusations that there is too much capital news if their count is made only during a period when the legislature is in session. Editors should check pages throughout the year before generalizing. Common sense should keep them from making unwarranted conclusions—if they remember to apply the common sense.

Use of the news hole is also relatively easy to assess. What hunch —or hypothesis—does the editor want to check? Is too much or too little space going to pictures? Is the sports editor right to gripe that fewer columns are given to sports? Again categories can be set up, and this time the column inches of stories put into each slot are measured and added, perhaps by a copy aide or an eager young reporter. The editor finds, say, that the average daily use of photographs in the paper last month was 130 column inches, or about 10 percent of the paper's average news hole. Is that too much or too little? Did papers with 15 to 20 percent of the news hole given to pictures really look better? A ruler points the way for evaluations and decisions.

Or perhaps measurement shows that, because of an unnoticed shift in advertising, the women's editor is actually getting a full column a day more than allowed by the budget set up three years ago, and the sports editor averages 16 fewer column inches a day. The editor now has data for action.

---

*A useful 11-page booklet, *How to Conduct a Readership Survey of Features,* is available from the News Research Center, American Newspaper Publishers Association, P. O. Box 17407, Reston, Virginia 20041.

Reading ease and human interest levels of writing can also be checked, according to the theories discussed in chapter 15 on writing. Here again it is wise to establish categories first. Perhaps it is useful to know the average score for 500 samples drawn at random from the paper during the last month. It is more useful, however, if 100 samples each are calculated from wire copy, local news, editorials, sports copy, and business writing. Then editors can make comparisons and suggest improvements. They may not be too bothered to discover that a college education is prerequisite to understanding the editorials. But they should be upset if readability testing shows that an eighth grade graduate would find the sports coverage too difficult.

Some basic studies

While editors probably will want professional researchers to undertake their audience studies, a staff can and should learn about its region through its own digging techniques. At the Columbia Graduate School of Journalism, Prof. Walter B. Pitkin, a popular and sharp writer *(Life Begins at Forty)*, required students to research thoroughly the circulation area of some small daily. Students wrote Chambers of Commerce, dug through Agriculture Department reports, and in other ways learned everything possible about their areas—the industries, employment levels, cultural activities, income, and so on. An editor might undertake this kind of research from time to time, to check guesses and impressions about shifts in jobs, decline of dairying, rise in incomes, and the like. Such inquiry yields not only story ideas but also an understanding of the community.

Academic research

It is unfortunate that antipathy exists between professional journalists and academic communications researchers. The practicing journalists often sneer at the researchers as "the chi-squares" and the researchers snap back that the writers and editors can't see past their "green-eye shades." Some of the sniping is deserved, even if it is juvenile. Too many journalists are content to keep doing things the way they have been done for thirty years. And too many researchers laboriously hunt the obvious or produce research of slight merit. Surely an editor reading *Journalism Quarterly,* where much of this research is published, would sigh and ask, "Who cares?"

Yet once past the practical research done by newspaper staffs and a few others, how else but through academic research will editors find how human beings react or act? How else will they discover how messages are received or ignored? How else but through research will editors grasp at least some understanding of psychological and societal pressures on readers—and staffers?

Journalists need concrete information to help them understand people and how those people can be served better by newspapers. To reach this goal, researchers need to abstain from trite and inconsequential findings and concentrate on shining a little light onto human conditions and journalistic problems.

Actually a number of academic researchers have produced work of value to journalists. The late Chilton Bush, who taught at Stanford, Jack Haskins, of Tennessee, Walter Geiber of San Francisco State, and Galen Rarick of Ohio State are among those who have turned out research directly helpful to editors. Rarick handles research for the American Newspaper Publishers Association. Because of the type of research done by these men, papers moved to the six-column format and 10-point body type. They concentrated on newsier pictures. They tightened writing and dumped outmoded features. Wise editors scan such findings in their quest for ways to make work easier or to help make reading easier. The "impractical" research should not be ignored either, despite frequent temptations, for among perhaps fifty pieces of pure research there may be one that will seriously alter an editor's conception of the world.

It should be noted that journalistic research is not limited to newspaper staffs or academics. The ANPA farms out content research from headquarters in Reston, Virginia, and runs a research operation in Easton, Pennsylvania. The Easton facility limits its work to technical equipment, seeking ways to reduce printing costs. Some firms handle research on a contract. The famous ones are George Gallup, Lou Harris, Carl J. Nelson Research, Opinion Research, and Market Opinion Research. The Gannett newspapers bought the Harris firm in 1975.

Mass communications research

All these various researchers, using scientific investigation, seek to discover how people act or behave. They try to find why people read one kind of story and not another, why they dislike or like certain papers, why one story is soothing or irritating. Mass communications theory and research are concerned with behavior that affects buying, reading, rejection, anger, pleasure, disgust, and dozens of other human reactions. As a subdivision of the behavioral sciences, such as sociology and psychology, mass communications research focuses on people's attitudes and responses to newspapers and other media.

Typically, it is quantitative—it measures and counts, in pursuit of objective knowledge. Statistics help determine the significance of the calculations. If research generally is the careful investigation of a subject, then the researcher in mass communications scientifically studies the way humans act and react with the media—as journalists, decision-makers, readers, and so on. Even a study of news display or story content may be viewed as an effort to get at the way such communicators as editors act.

Several kinds of professional research are useful to newspaper editors, though many lack both the money and the time to use such help. Television executives, who depend on rating systems, are much more research-oriented, and magazine editors have shown more concern than newspaper people for scientific studies. Still, many editors can find useful information in six areas of research: content, effects and influence, reader interest, audience, graphics, and gate-keepers.

Research on content is similar to the rudimentary studies of front page and news hole. Content analyses can determine accurately the percentages of material on various topics, the balance of news on politicians, the number of times certain concepts are repeated in the news columns, even the number of prejudicial color words in so-called objective accounts. Such analyses help editors ponder the quality of what is published.

Content analysis

Attitude research is one of the most difficult and, unfortunately, one of the kinds least attempted. People are concerned about the influence of TV and comic book violence on listeners and readers, especially young ones. But the little solid research on the subject must compete with the many guesses by psychiatrists, concerned parents, disciples of Marshall McLuhan, and others. Newspapers seldom use such research, and yet from the point of view of editors this facet would probably interest them most. Do their editorials persuade? Do the news photos rouse? Do interpretive stories stimulate? An editor can ask family members, friends at lunch, and acquaintances at a party what they think, but such queries cannot carry the weight of thorough, objective research.

Effects and influence

One vital question is whether the readers' perceptions of a story match the communicator's. One doctoral candidate discovered that a high proportion of readers took political cartoons to mean something different from what the cartoonist said he intended. Editors should know not only whether readers read but also whether they get the messages correctly!

Finding out what people actually read and what interests them is obviously important, so newspapers frequently judge readership by "reader traffic" surveys. Researchers ask "did you happen" to read this, or that, and they can come up with percentages of those who "began" or "read most" of a particular story or ad. This gives a rough indication of whether readers were interested. Getting at the degree of interest is a subtle problem. Readers asked whether they were interested may misrepresent—or simply not remember clearly. And even if they do remember and are honest, past interest is not a sure guide to what will interest tomorrow.

Reader interest

Because advertisers want to know about readers and listeners, most corporate research dollars for communications research go into surveys of the audience. Countless studies tell how many readers are college graduates, own two cars, or buy a major appliance

Audience

once a year. Apart from commercial value, if a paper makes a good study of this kind for its advertising department, editors should use it to understand their circulation area. It is important for them to know, for example, how readership is split among men, women, and teen-agers.

Graphics

Studies have been made of which type face and what column widths are optimum for easy or rapid reading. Graphic arts research overlaps with studies of effects and interest as researchers look into what head type pleases most or what ink colors demand attention. Unfortunately, a great deal of typographic expertise is traditional rather than based in sound research. One of the greatest editorial needs is for more studies of graphic arts.

Gatekeepers

In focusing on the people involved in communication, research looks not only at the receivers but also the communicators, the senders of messages. Reporters, copyeditors, and sub-editors all control gates which regulate what part of the news flow gets into the paper, and where. So their perceptions, goals, and prejudices are important. Editors will be wary of testing colleagues psychologically, but studies of gatekeepers in the media generally can give them clues to the strengths and weaknesses in their own organization.

The research attitude

As research spreads among newspapers, it should influence editorial thinking at every level. The good researcher's emphasis on precision and thoroughness in fact-finding matches the journalist's traditional emphasis on care and accuracy. The editor who applies the attitudes of research to the editorial job will think in fresh ways, whether in a story involving statistics or in planning for revolutionary change in the whole operation.

Newspapers deserve many of the criticisms aimed at their handling of scientific data, for few editors and writers have adequate knowledge or concern about the methods of science. Economists and experts in finance often are appalled by newspaper interpretation of monetary statistics. Too many editors are so short of confidence in their scientific knowledge that they throw away science stories or run them exactly as written.

Great care must be used by editors in handling public opinion polls. Scientific polling by Gallup and others has replaced the pseudo-scientific "straw ballots" by individual papers, though some worthless newspaper polls survive as an anachronism. But when a politician or a party commissions scientific polls and releases only such results as they wish—and when they feel they will help most— newspapers have to be alert. Unfortunately, they are sometimes fooled.

Editors play close poll figures as if they revealed a difference, when in fact they do not; the margin of error which wipes out their relevance is ignored too often. In some campaigns candidates are often only one or two percentage points apart. Since margins of error are always three to four points in such polls, these are meaningless spreads. That is, if Candidate X has 39 percent and Candidate Y has 37 or 38, Candidate Y may actually be ahead. Yet newspapers headline the "fact" that X is ahead.

In other ways, polls have embarrassed editors, yet flimsy, contrived polls still get big news play. For example, at least a full year before presidential nominating conventions, pollsters are tallying support for potential candidates. So a headline proclaims:

McGillicuddy Out Front in Presidential Race

The story then lists the candidates and the percentage of support they have among the populace. It may run like this:

McGillicuddy	18
Gates	16
Fry	14
Carlson	12
Knight	10
Undecided	30

Such stories are ludicrous. Voters have rarely made up their minds on candidates a year ahead of the conventions. Experience shows that the person on top one month may be at the bottom next month. Often the best-known name goes to the top in early polling. Wouldn't it be much better to use the space to examine the voting record of just one potential candidate?

Or consider the question, "Do you favor the governor's proposed income tax? The chances are good that only a bare majority is aware of the proposal and that no more than ten per cent really understand the issue. So all that is really found, if respondents are honest, is that people don't know much about public affairs.

Editors should also make it a point to move outside their own professional and social circles and their own neighborhoods to talk with a cross-section of readers. "One of our top editors," says the research director of one large newspaper, "makes it a practice to make the rounds of the many neighborhood pubs to get the feel of the type of person who is a fairly large segment of his audience." Such down-to-earth "research" can usefully supplement the best computerized study of audience profile.

An editor's starting point for research is a need for more information. There is little point in measuring, questioning, and analyzing just for fun. Research is a problem-solving tool. So what is the problem? Does the editor want to know what cartoons are read or what kind of story dominates the Metro Page? Perhaps the problem demands research beyond the capacity of anyone on the staff—but often a simple method will give a relatively accurate answer.

For example, one managing editor wanted to remodel the editorial page to increase readership. He wrote to some thirty editors in surrounding states for editorial-page tearsheets. All but two responded. He checked the topics, the width of the columns, and the size of type. He then incorporated on his own page the best of what he found. It is an example of elementary research which any other editor could profitably follow.

Editors whose papers have research departments should check doubtful stories with their own experts, just as they check possible libel with their attorneys. Sometimes they can consult communications researchers, sociologists, psychologists, or statisticians at a near-by university. But for the best handling of scientific research there is no substitute for skill on the editorial staff itself. Future editors will be interested and educated in research and young staffers already are aware of its value.

Editors must rule

It should be made clear that the good editor will not let the research department run the newspaper. The researchers may offer readership studies and analyze other data. They may advise dropping some stories and adding others. They may suggest an editorial policy change to draw more readers. But the editors must have the final word on news selection and display. They must be able to say, "We know research says money stories are read by only twenty per cent. But money stories are important, so we are going to make them as sprightly and interesting as we can—and run them."

Good editors will use research as one of many tools in their kits. Research can give them facts to guide their judgment. Other tools will be experience, education, professionalism, and an ethical sense. Proper use of all these tools will produce an alert, timely, pertinent, and interesting newspaper. Such a paper is needed if people are to work their way through the stream of major and minor issues that confront them.

19 The future of newspaper editing

Newspapers almost certainly will concentrate in the next several years on adjusting to the new technology. Key editors will spend hours every week checking the new equipment, deciding whether to buy other devices, and seeing that staffers know how to function efficiently in the electronic newsroom.

As papers shift to the new methods, the whole news staff will have to be trained well. If they are not, as many have already learned, the transition becomes chaotic. Proper planning and training can make the adjustments at least tolerable. Papers that already have gone electronic must be alert to further changes and plan for new alterations.

Intensive planning will be required in coming years. Most papers, shifting to the new technology, form committees to guide the publisher in making the right equipment purchase. Top editors sit on these committees, obviously, but occasionally a reporter and a copyeditor are included. It seems likely that lower-level staffers eventually will share in long range planning. Wise executives realize that participation in decisions by the working staff reduces fears and anxieties among the journalists on the paper.

Planning should not be limited, of course, to preparation for new machinery. It should include news coverage, staff expansion, the rejection of dated practices, altered makeup, and the direction of research.

Planners will spend considerable time studying trends in the local economy, society itself, and the paper's circulation area. Managing editors will be alert to any expansion of the economy to see if the news staff can be expanded. Alert journalists at all levels will watch for subtle changes in tastes and interests. Newspapers will pay more attention to the young. Until recently most stories about those under twenty only snickered at youthful whims and rapidly changing lifestyles. The main reason for this attitude was that editors were no

Identifying trends

longer young themselves. They took a condescending approach to news about youth that seemed to say, "Look what these kids are up to now!" Many papers now realize that they ought to cover the music, theater, writing, and style of young people seriously. More papers probably will shift in this direction because their sense of professionalism demands it and because the circulation department would like to corral these young readers.

Any journalist, of course, would be wary of getting over-excited about any particular trend. Every student is aware of how campus attitudes often change in one semester. The national mood can change almost as quickly, moving from confidence to gloom within a few months. Excitement about drugs, for example, may change swiftly to deep concern about abortion. The good editor in coming years will be aware of these shifts but will not follow them slavishly, pumping out stories that satisfy temporary interest in a subject.

Looking ahead

Prophecy often can be made most accurate by examining the developments of recent years. With this in mind, it appears probable that the best papers will be moving in these directions:

Front pages will have five or six stories and a picture or two. Few stories will be jumped.

Each inside page will contain at least one strong story. Readers will be directed to most of those good stories by front-page references.

Stories of little consequence, like minor crime and accidents, will be either ignored or limited to a couple of paragraphs.

Crime itself will be treated as a social problem and given much attention.

Editors will be skeptical of stories that offer easy solutions to such problems as poverty, crime, pollution, and economic stagnation.

Slowly, perhaps, less emphasis will be given to news of the last few hours and more attention will be placed on summations of events of the last several weeks.

More space will be devoted to arts, books, and travel.

A wider range of opinion will appear on editorial pages. The number of opposite-editorial pages will increase.

The popularity of Washington political columnists will decline in favor of home-based writers.

Speculative political stories will continue to be condemned by editors, but their use will continue. (Journalists can't break the habit of anticipating what will happen politically *if* certain things occur.)

All but the small papers will have staffers who spend much of their work day covering the arts, business, youth culture, education, labor, etc. Big papers will continue to have specialists, but the medium-sized papers will have semi-specialists.

Papers will give up the "depth report" when such reports are only long, not deep.

The use of color will increase, but only slightly.

The quality of pictures will get better steadily.

Investigative stories will continue to get strong play but their popularity will decline somewhat.

Few journalists will be in awe of presidents, university officials, labor leaders, governors, or big-corporation executives.

More attention will be given to news of changing women's lifestyles, old people, medicine, nutrition, and recreation.

More newspapers will belong to large chains. The home-owned newspaper will be considered an oddity, or even quaint. Big newspaper chains will continue to expand into other fields—or be bought up by expanding conglomerates.

These prophecies require a reasonably stable world to come true, of course. Wars or other catastrophes could upset everything. So could an economic crash, or a large increase, say, in energy prices. Widespread feelings of exasperation or frustration might send the country into quarreling factions that would strain the economy and disrupt society. The press itself may be considered the cause of dissidence and recession, producing newspaper boycotts. The recent past, however, seems to indicate that the world will be buffeted in the tail-end of the twentieth century, but no more so than it has in all the years to date.

The Gannett Company, a chain owning more than seventy newspapers, has formed a planning committee to guide its corporate development. John C. Quinn, vice president for news, heads the committee. He has made these predictions:

Readers are going to becoming more involved with their newspapers, and they will demand higher qulaity.

Newspaper editors will harness the production revolution to give themselves more time and ability to serve their readers.

Newspaper management in all departments must become more responsive and responsible in serving the wants and needs of their communities—on the business side for the economic health of the community and on the news side for the community's intellectual and informational well-being.

Readers will become more aware of the value of their freedoms and the fact that freedom of the press belongs not to newspaper publishers and editors, but to newspaper readers. These readers demand that their local papers tell them not only what they want to know, but also what they may not like to hear.

Newspapers and readers will reduce the hostility that sometimes exists between them. Both will try to understand and serve each other.

Examining trends

Better educated readers

It is tempting to rub the crystal ball gently and predict a public ravenously devouring newspapers filled with meaty information on politics, economics, science, and the arts. Instead of being tied to concern over who won the Cub Scout citizenship award or whose fender was crumpled at Mulberry and Vine, the publisher then could "give them what they want"—quality.

A strong statistical case can be made for this kind of fantasy. Millions are going to college. A record number are working for advanced degrees. Millions have graduated in recent years. People seem to be more alert to change and to their society. More quality newspapers should result from the current willingness of the general public, not merely the young, to buy serious books and subscribe to more and better magazines. And it is no longer unusual for people of modest means to have traveled extensively outside the United States.

But before we see Utopia in the crystal ball, we ought to look at the reality that surrounds us. Although large numbers attend college we must realize that many reject the education offered there. They resist knowledge and retain their prejudices through four years of college. With their degrees they only settle somewhat comfortably, subscribe to the *Reader's Digest*, and spend hours each night watching whatever pops up on the television screen.

Despite educational advances and increased knowledge about the human personality, people seem no more able to be rational today than they were fifty years ago. We sometimes think human beings are rational, forgetting that they are often a crucible of emotions. We easily switch from rational tolerance to irrational envy. We can even rationally build passion into hatred. Our reading can reduce our emotional prejudices, but it can also reinforce them. Formally-educated people, then, often are as full of fury, as narrow, and as ignorant on many subjects as the uneducated. Many persons with advanced degrees are uninterested in politics, government, and law, even though these subjects greatly influence their lives. Some do not even vote. Many who travel extensively gain little from it. They go abroad on American airplanes, stay at American hotels, go to

American-style restaurants, and, with a few exceptions, speak only to fellow Americans or, showing their tolerance or insecurity, to the British.

But if journalistic prophets cannot hope for a nation of highly intelligent people thirsting for information, they should not underestimate the public's interest and tastes. The papers that today underestimate change are sterile and listless, with declining or static circulations.

In general, the most financially successful publications have emphasized thoroughness in reporting the news. As we noted previously, papers like the *Washington Post, Boston Globe, Los Angeles Times, Wall Street Journal,* and *New York Times* have enjoyed steady circulation gains. Smaller papers have enlarged their coverage by subscribing to the wire service provided by the *New York Times* or to such supplementary information as provided in the service offered by the *Washington Post* and the *Los Angeles Times.* These facts indicate that a growing public prefers to buy papers of breadth and depth. When the public supports such papers, advertisers are eager to buy space. The resulting victory is both journalistic and financial.

More thorough coverage

This kind of development almost certainly is going to spread. Success has many imitators, and as other publishers see how prosperous the quality papers have become, they too will improve their coverage. The public also can be expected gradually to increase its interest in public affairs. The better papers will de-emphasize spot news—the events of the day—in favor of long-range, detailed reporting. There will be less attention to the very latest utterance of a presidential candidate, for example, and more detailed reporting of what the candidate has done in the past and how his position has changed.

For years Americans were accustomed to a higher birth rate, which meant a youthful population. Drops in the rate are changing age ratios and shifting the focus of news to the old, a previously neglected minority growing in size due to medical advances.

Decreasing birth rate

Will the lower birth rate continue? If births increase again, will more young people get liberal educations which lead to newspaper reading? Will the demands of a technological culture push more students into technical secondary education? Will such students give less emphasis to the social sciences and humanities than before? Newspaper planning committees will have to remain alert to these questions if reporting is to examine society's changes.

The half-century debate between liberal-arts education and journalism school education for journalism careers promises to go on indefinitely. Without attempting to resolve that dispute, we can sug-

Educational background

gest that there will be a role for both kinds of education, as well as for a third type which has been emerging and which we will discuss below.

Editors need a liberal education in history, philosophy, art and other humanities. Though critics of journalism schools are sometimes unaware of it, students in such a school get general education. They receive training in skills, plus an opportunity to apply their liberal training to practical problems involving ethics, creativity, reform, and integrity. Edward W. Barrett, former dean of the Graduate School of Journalism at Columbia University, outlined succinctly, in his presidential address to the Association for Education in Journalism, the ideal education for journalists of the future.

> The primary aim of education for journalism is the development of disciplines, arts, and attitudes of mind.
>
> The discipline of giving attention to the distasteful as well as the appealing; the discipline of learning to guage one's best effort to fit an allotted time span; the discipline of continuing self-education.
>
> The art of expression that is lean, direct, precise, and deft; the art of grappling with a complex new subject, extracting information from inarticulate specialists, and synthesizing the findings faithfully and coherently; the art of recognizing fine points of accuracy and subtle gradations of meaning.
>
> The attitude of profiting from criticism; and the attitude of approaching new problems with the open-mindedness and imagination that make solutions possible.
>
> Above all, one seeks the attitude of ruthless fairness, of reporting what he dislikes as honestly as what he likes —in short, true intellectual integrity.

We have discussed the third form of emerging education, the importance for journalism of communications research and of automation. In addition to having both liberal education and professional knowledge of techniques and traditions, the future editor needs to understand the new technology and what it can do for newspapers. The undergraduate journalism student must at least be aware of the new trends, but many serious students will want the specialized knowledge which comes from a master's degree or even a doctorate.

Practical research

This suggestion touches another live controversy of recent years between communications theorist-researchers and the newsroom oriented educators. Here again, as journalists need both skills training and liberal arts, they require behavioral science as well. Some communications experts talk esoterically and impractically of computers, quantification, encoding, and information retrieval. And some have so little solid journalism experience that they are more sociologists or psychologists than they will ever be media experts. Nevertheless, some develop real knowledge, as distinguished from common sense guesses and prognostications the unwary sometimes mistake for "research," which will be invaluable to the future of journalists and journalism.

One important area has been little touched by any researcher. That is the problem of news comprehension and retention. The journalistic researcher of the future ought to study seriously how people learn and why they forget. The most upsetting part of news work is that even superior reporting and editing draw only a few careful readers. Most skim the basics and then forget them within a few days. Perhaps educational psychologists could help a paper better serve its readers.

One way to help the reader remember is to repeat. Repetition has to be subtle, however, so the reader who does remember will not skip the story complaining, "I read this last week." The newspaper might use review techniques instead. For example, the "box score" reporting so common on the sports pages could be used more in the regular news pages.

A sizable number of papers already use this presentation for major votes in Congress. A boxed story may report that the Senate passed a measure forty-eight to forty-four, then list the votes of senators from the paper's circulation area. Other papers, before elections, list the voting record of home-based legislators. The wire services, during a big event, sometimes file an "at-a-glance" summary of the main facts. Much more of this kind of summation is needed. It is easy for readers to skim innumerable stories about a peace conference, a trial, or a strike without ever having a chance for a quick review. The box score approach offers this by reporting, on the peace conference, that Country A has made certain demands, Country B has made others, and they have agreed on Points 1, 3, and 4 but still disagree on Points 2 and 5. If one is wary of oversimplification, this technique can serve as the kind of review that every student knows is so valuable before an examination.

Some prophets have predicted the use of drugs as a way to improve learning and remembering capacities. The budding editor, however, should expect human beings in the future to be like readers today: ordinary persons who have to be lured into reading by good writing, pertinent material, and good typographical display.

Mid-career training

Because professionals can always learn more about these elements of journalism, the newspapers of the future must provide more training for people who have been on the job five years—or twenty years. Other professions now have in-service or mid-career training, and it should be a regular part of the professional press. It is possible that most good young journalists in the next two decades will have a thorough formal education, and some will have advanced degrees. Yet they will eventually need refresher courses and classes in new techniques and ideas.

The Nieman fellowships at Harvard provide a year of study for some thirty journalists each year. No degree is given; students go to classes of their choice and take no examinations. More recently, special periods of study, less than a year, have been set up at Northwestern and Stanford for experienced journalists. The Washington Journalism Center was founded to give more training to young, relatively inexperienced men and women. Other opportunities exist for studies lasting a few weeks or a month. The American Press Institute at Reston, Virginia offers several seminars a year for specialized groups of working journalists. Some grants allow a journalist simply to read at a major library for several weeks. Many papers expect their top reporters to read for a few hours a day on company time to keep their minds attuned—and perhaps to dig up information for stories.

A few newspapers give staff members leaves of absence for study or travel. The academic sabbatical—a leave with pay—may be adopted by newspapers. Perhaps union contracts some day will give journalists two or three months off every five years. Union contracts in some other fields have been granting such leaves for a decade.

If this sort of vacation comes to newspapering, journalists would be wise to use the time to improve their knowledge by reading, discussion, and travel—plus the refreshment of mind and body that a change can provide.

True professionalism for the newspaper of tomorrow, in short, rests in part on the encouragement of learning and fresh thought among professional journalists as well as journalism students.

Problems of pay

Economic stagnation has made entry difficult into almost all occupations in recent years. Newspapers have restricted their hiring, sometimes shrinking staffs slightly. Veteran journalists have not been lured into government, public relations, or business, as they were in prosperous times. Those veterans have remained on newspapers, leaving few openings for young, inexperienced reporters and copyeditors. This condition seems likely to continue so long as the nation's economy sputters. Journalism school graduates, as a result, will have to be content to start their careers on small or medium-sized dailies. Metropolitan newspapers hire almost no one these days straight out of college.

This situation disappoints young journalists, who a few years ago would have been snapped up by the better papers. The young should not succumb to dejection, however, for they may get their most valuable and varied experience on smaller papers. Their chances still are good that within six months to a year they will be able to move to a paper that suits them better.

Some young people may find that smaller papers provide interesting and satisfying work. Some of these newspapers give heavy responsibilities to people only a few months out of college. Sometimes these young staffers can see reforms brought about by their stories, pictures, or editorials. Few beginners in big city newsrooms have such opportunities. Young journalists, by themselves, sometimes can change a fair paper in a smallish town into a good one.

Publishers have long complained that the newspaper business is less profitable than other businesses. This means, they often say, that they cannot pay journalists decent salaries. But is this the truth? Certainly publishers never release their profit statements unless they have to. The big chains which sell stock publicly must announce their profits quarterly and their profit trends, even during recessions, have been up. Many papers already could pay better salaries. As the new technology allows great labor savings in mechanical departments wage scales could go up even more.

Professional prospect:

Salaries for experienced journalists have been rising sharply but in many places they still lag behind those of other professions. The sagging economy in the mid-seventies kept beginning salaries, except on papers with American Newspaper Guild contracts, at about the same level they had been for years. Cost-of-living increases have not been granted beginners. It has been difficult for beginning journalists, therefore, to get as much salary as beginning public school teachers.

Generally, reporters, copyeditors, and photographers on Guild papers or papers threatened by Guild organizing have been paying exceptional salaries. The *Washington Post* in 1977 paid experienced reporters and photographers at least $529 for a 37-1/2 hour week. Copyeditors got a minimum of five per cent more, making their annual income $29,000. The average Guild member in newsrooms around the country was making slightly more than $335 a week, or more than $16,000. Ninety-four papers in 1977 paid more than $300 weekly, and about half of them were above $350. Many papers pay extra for assistant. city editors, Sunday editors, state editors, and others in supervisory positions. Fringe benefits usually are as good as they are in other businesses.

Hundreds of smaller papers lag far behind. Some pay news editors or managing editors less than the Guild reporter average. Others take advantage of any economic downturn and offer beginners as little as $125 a week. A few have the nerve to ask a journalism school graduate to start at $100! Anyone starting at such salaries can hardly expect to get raises of more than five dollars at a time. No trained persons would take such a salary unless any kind of job was necessary to tide them over for a few months.

Low salaries in many medium and small newspapers cause bright young men and women to leave as soon as possible for bigger papers, TV, or public relations. This situation is disheartening, especially when young people find the smaller community appealing and would like to stay if they could make a moderately good income.

To be better, newspapers, both large and small, will have to gain more revenue and invest it in more editorial talent. They will have to meet the competition. In public relations, salaries often top newspaper pay, $14,000 to $20,000 being common for men and women with limited experience. Some public relations people say they like news work better but feel working standards are higher in the PR positions! Newspapers will attract and keep such individuals for responsible editorial posts in part by paying better and by embodying the integrity, the zeal for coverage, and the creative crusading which we advocate throughout this book.

Establishing trends

A leading newspaper does not merely reflect the polls and follow the trends. It establishes trends. The best newspapers of the future will not only report what happens in society but will also consider what should happen and what will help to make it happen.

Newspapers could better their communities and their own relationships with them by spearheading improvement. This would involve responding to sound forces in the community and at the same time encouraging community members to press for advance. Communication between editors and readers may be most helpful if it is somewhat formalized; this requires new ventures, which range from "press councils" to revamped approaches toward the letters-to-the-editor tradition.

The press council idea has been debated for a generation, but publishers usually have opposed it. They contend that they know best how to run their newspapers or that such a council interferes with the First Amendment. Some publishers declare that they have enough to do without having to confront a council every week or so.

It is tempting to pick press council members from the prosperous, well-educated people in town. These are the people whom editors and publishers tend to associate with anyway. They can complain to newspaper executives over lunch. If a council aims to educate an editor, it ought to include trade unionists, blacks, Chicanos, teachers, a police officer, a small business owner, a lawyer, and a person from some big corporation. This way nearly every group will be able to get across a point of view and editors will get suggestions from people it has been easy to ignore.

A National News Council was set up in the mid-seventies to hear complaints of bias against the press. The NNC received fifty-nine complaints in its first two years. Five of these—less than ten per cent—were upheld, thirty-three were found unwarranted, and twenty-one were dismissed.

Despite the fact that few examples of bias were found some newspapers still have refused to deal with the National News Council. It is too early to tell if this Council has caused writers and editors to be more cautious or careful with what gets into their papers. Reporters and editors undoubtedly are not saying to one another,

"This is a hot story. We'd better watch it or the National News Council will be after us." The Council, however, gets journalists to think more about fairness; this should result in less bias creeping into news columns and news broadcasts. The Council also may give some individuals who feel aggrieved by journalistic treatment a feeling of redress. The result may contribute to better journalism and to a public less hostile to the press and its power.

Most press councils act as watchdogs of the press in one city, but the Minnesota Press Council listens to charges of inaccurate reporting in all news media for the whole state.

A few papers have decided to hear public complaints by themselves, so they have set up an ombudsman. This person, to function well, must have real autonomy so there is freedom to criticize the editor, publisher, chief stockholders, or anyone else. Few publishers, perhaps, would be able to pay an ombudsman and then have that person accuse the publisher, for example, of greed, ineptitude, or gross prejudice.

Ombudsmen, however, have been able to chide fellow staffers and management.

The results are something like this: "I have examined the complaint of the mayor, who contends that a shortage of $125 in the city clerk's office was grossly overplayed by our paper. We printed fourteen news stories on this shortage, all of them with multi-column headlines. The total of these stories was 212 column inches. In addition we ran four pictures and wrote one editorial. It seems clear that the staff exaggerated the news value of this relatively minor disclosure and I would advise cooler analysis of news value in the future."

This sort of self-flagellation may cause veteran journalists to scream, "We already put most of our mistakes on page one for everyone to read! Why do we have to pay for our own staffer to embarrass us?" Having an ombudsman, however, says to the public, "We know we aren't perfect. So we are going to pay a good salary to an experienced journalist to listen to your complaints. If those complaints are not valid, they will be rejected. If they are valid, the ombudsman will say so and we will print his findings so everyone in town can read them. It is not pleasant to call attention to our flaws, but we can take it." As in the case of press councils, aggrieved persons may feel that they have recourse. A little piece of research is valuable in assessing the worth of an ombudsman. It was found that a staff with an ombudsman likes the idea. A staff without one doesn't want one. *

A growing number of papers is using similar methods to mollify readers and correct staff errors. For example, The *Chicago Daily News* has a Bureau of Fairness and Accuracy. Complaints and comments are investigated and, if printable, appear in a special column.

---

* David R. Nelsen and Kenneth Starck, "The Newspaper Ombudsman as Viewed by the Rest of the Staff." Journalism Quarterly, Autumn, 1974, p. 453.

One complaint objected to a story which told about two teen-agers killed in a crash. The story said they were high school dropouts. The complaint said that the story thereby implied that the people were "only" dropouts and not important to society.

There also may be new approaches to public discussion. Newspapers have long had letters-to-the-editor, interviews with the prominent, and statements by experts. With better educated readers could a more advanced and meaningful kind of open forum be developed? Aside from the "combat page" previously discussed, a newspaper might, for example, pose important questions and then publish written contributions a certain day on a discussion page. The queries might range all the way from "Should the U.S. withdraw its troops from Korea?" to "What is the most pressing educational problem in Ourtown today?" Perhaps the paper could first print essays by knowledgeable citizens to start the readers writing. Bonuses would perhaps help. One corner might be given to teen-age replies. Editors should use their imaginations to stimulate fresher kinds of public discussion than have already been used a generation or more.

As we have pointed out in the chapters, what the newspaper prints becomes the subject of community argument, and what it ignores may be ignored by the public. To help establish trends instead of always bending with them, alert editors must provide news that focuses the citizens' attention. Do they make readers talk about TV stars? Or do they help them argue about new health hazards?

Newspapers already are giving more serious attention to social issues, so editors who choose to push on in that direction are only furthering what appears to be a solid trend. Editors are squeezing the minor news to make room for detailed reports on pollution, education, poverty, military affairs, federal budgeting, economics, welfare, medicine, and urban problems. Women's pages have stories that also appeal to men and children. The arts and culture are being covered better than before.

These are healthy trends, and they should continue through the seventies. Sharp editors with social consciences will find and print the important news in the future. Better means and better men and women for communicating important information to and from readers will enable a newspaper to provide better leadership for community and nation than ever before.

Appendix a: tips for copyeditors

Most editors-in-chief tell their copyeditors to "use words correctly." Good advice, of course, but hard to follow. What is correct? Who said so? What about new words not yet in dictionaries? Which dictionary is correct? Not only are there new words, but new meanings of old words, as with *hip, cool,* and *pot.*

Newspapers use a standard for the meanings of words. If they did not, the reader would be confused frequently by jargon, slang, and malapropism. Usually the standard is the big dictionary in the middle of the newsroom, even if the edition is twenty years old. Some supplement is needed, however, to cover words newly accepted into the written language. On the other hand, an editor should take care to avoid words or meanings that he thinks will appear for a short time and then pass into obscurity even as they are being listed in a new dictionary. Perhaps a good guide to word usage in a newspaper would be to cling to the old, so the meaning of language does not change every generation, but adapt to the new if it brings freshness and vividness to the language.

Editors should not only be alert to changing usage, they should spot redundancies, grammatical errors, and misleading language. To this end we offer the following tips on usage, grammar, and spelling.

The following words and phrases are often mistakenly used.

Actual fact or *true fact.* A fact is by definition true.
Advise, for *inform.* "He was *informed* [not *advised*] of his wife's illness and *advised* to call her doctor immediately."
Alternative, for *alternate.* "He had an *alternate* [not *alternative*] plan. It gave the voter a choice of *alternatives.*"
Alumna. One female graduate; the plural is *alumnae. Alumnus* means one male graduate; the plural is *alumni,* which also is the plural for a group including both men and women.

Amateur, for *novice.* A novice is a beginner; an amateur is one who works or plays for fun, not money; a *professional* works or plays for money. Because the professional is usually highly skilled, an amateur is sometimes complimented by being called "professional."

Amused, See *bemused.*

And etc. Etc. stands for *et cetera,* which means "and the rest" in Latin, so the "and" is redundant.

Anxious, for *eager.* "He was *eager* [not *anxious*] to try, but his mother was *anxious* for his safety."

Ask. In its varied forms it can often be dropped. "*Asked* what he thought about the game, he said he thought it was good" can be simply "He said he thought the game was good."

Author, as a verb. "He *authored* a text" should be "He wrote a text."

Baby girl (or boy) *is born.* Redundant, as no one is born fully grown.

Badly injured. No injury is good; say "severely injured."

Beautiful. The word involves a value judgment, and some crank is bound to disagree, especially over a "beautiful woman."

Bemused, for *amused.* Bemused means dazed, preoccupied, or confused.

Boat, for *ship.* Technically, boats are carried on ships; generally, a boat is a small vessel.

Bridegroom. See *groom.*

Broadcasted, as the past tense of *broadcast.* "The program was *broadcast* daily."

Brutal beating. No beating is gentle.

Collide. This verb refers to a bumping of two moving objects. "The car hit [not *collided with*] a telephone pole and then *collided* with another car."

Complected or *complexioned.* The noun *complexion* has no adjective form. "She is fair *complected* [or *complexioned*]" should be "She has a fair *complexion.*"

Completely destroyed. The "completely" is redundant.

Comprise means contain, embrace, or include. The whole *comprises* the parts.

Consensus of opinion. "of opinion" is redundant, as a consensus is a collective opinion.

Controversial usually is a waste word. "The crowd shouted down the controversial proposal" can be simply "The crowd shouted down the proposal."

Contusion. See *laceration.*

Critical, for *critical condition.* A sick person in *critical condition* is seldom *critical.*

Currently. Usually redundant if the sentence is in the present tense. "He is *currently* appearing in *Macbeth*" can be simply "He is appearing in *Macbeth.*"

Devout, for *religious. Devout* is an exceptionally high degree of devotion—too high for the layman to measure.

Different than, for *different from.* "Each house is *different from* [not *different than*] the one next to it."

Dove, for *dived. Dove* is the colloquial, not the written, past tense of *dive.* "He *dived* [not *dove*] from the side of the boat."

Due to, for *because.* "He was late *because* [not *due to*] the battery went dead. He had been *due to* meet us at noon."

Eager. See *anxious.*

Elderly. Be cautious about this word, as even persons of seventy-five may be sensitive about being called *elderly.*

Esquire, the honorable, and other undefinable titles should be omitted.

Etc. See *and etc.*

Fewer. See *less.*

Foreseeable future. Who can see into the future?

Forgotten. See *gotten.*

For the purposes of can be simply *for.*

Freak accident is a cliché. Let the facts show that it is peculiar.

Gauntlet, for *gantlet.* A *gauntlet* is a glove and can be thrown down; a *gantlet* is a form of punishment and can be run.

Gotten, for *got. Gotten* is the colloquial past participle of *get,* but *forgotten* is the regular past participle of *forget.* "He had *got* the man's address but had *forgotten* to get his age."

Groom, for *bridegroom.* "The *bridegroom* had recently been employed as a *groom* with Smith Stables."

Ground rules. Except in reference to baseball games, skip the "ground."

Half mast, for *half staff.* Flags may fly at half mast on a ship but at *half staff* ashore.

Hung, for *hanged.* "Spectators *hung* over the wall to see the murderer *hanged.*"

Inform. See *advise.*

Jewish rabbis. Rabbi is Jewish by definition.

Laceration, for *contusion.* A *laceration* is a cut; a *contusion* is a bruise.

Ladies, for *women.* All *ladies* are women, but not all *women* are ladies. So call all women *women.*

Less, for *fewer. Less* refers to a general quantity; *fewer* refers to the specific items that make it up. "*Fewer* dollars earned means *less* money to spend."

Located, for *situated. Located* means "found," and *situated* means "placed at." "He *located* the school, which was *situated* five miles from town." As in this example, even "situated" can often be dropped without loss of meaning.

Majority, for *plurality.* In an election, a *majority* is more than half the votes, and the *plurality* is the margin of victory. "Jones was elected by a clear *majority* (64%), rolling up a *plurality* of 115,000 votes."

Media, for *medium. Media* is the plural of *medium.* "Television is an important *medium* for a political candidate today."

Militant, for mere *protestor* or for *rowdy.* A militant is a fighter for a cause; a rowdy fights for selfish reasons. A *protestor* may be against violence entirely.

Monies, for *money. Money* is collective, so the plural is unnecessary.

More unique or *most unique. Unique* is an absolute, so cannot be modified.

Novice. See *amateur.*

Orientated, for *oriented. Oriented* is the proper past tense of *orient.*

Panic, riot, disaster, etc. should not be used unless the facts clearly indicate the need for strong words.

Per (in *per year, per day,* etc.). Skip the Latin; use *a* year, *a* day. *Per annum* is doubly unfortunate.

Plurality. See *majority.*

Presently, for *now. Presently* is a long word meaning *soon.*

Prior to should be simply *before.*

Professional. See *amateur.*

Protestor. See *militant.*

Raised, for *reared.* Children are *reared;* animals are *raised.*

Reason why is redundant.

Red-headed, for *red-haired.* Be accurate. Do you mean the scalp or the hair?

Religious. See *devout.*

Resides is a fancy way of saying *lives.*

Revert back is redundant.

Rowdy. See *militant.*

Ship. See *boat.*

Situated. See *located.*

Sudden explosion is redundant.

Superlatives (like eldest, fastest, biggest) should be handled with care. Often someone will be challenged to find something that surpasses your example.

The before a plural noun is usually unnecessary. "The voters filled the polling booths" could be simply "Voters filled the polling booths." Let your ear be your guide.

These kind should be *these kinds.*

Thusly should be *thus.*

To death is often redundant, as in "strangled to death" or "drowned to death."

Unaware of the fact that should be simply "unaware that."

Utterly, flatly, sheer, categorically, definitely, and many other such adverbs only pad most sentences.

Very should be used very seldom.

Whether or not, for *whether.* Because it implies an alternative, *whether* rarely needs to be followed by *or not.*

Wise is a bad general suffix. Other*wise* is fine, but health*wise,* automobile*wise,* tax*wise,* etc. smack too much of advertising shoptalk.

Journalists often need review of these grammatical points.*

About may indicate approximation; *around* implies motion. "He weighs *about* 150 pounds and runs two miles *around* the track each day."

Adjective phrases should be hyphenated. "The *2-year-old* boy ran to the *sad-looking* man.

Adjectives referring to health or emotion. See *feel.*

Affect is a verb and means *to have influence. Effect,* as a noun, refers to a result. "His speech *affected* the audience deeply; the *effect* was a silence so profound one could hear the crickets outside the tent." As a verb, *effect* means *to bring about* or *accomplish.* "His work *effected* a cure." Note that as a verb *effect* is usually unnecessary. "His work cured her."

Agreement. A subject and its predicate, and a noun and its pronoun, should agree in number. "The *group* of boys *was* trying to break down the door. The *girls* inside *were* screaming in panic. The *group* lost *its* steam when the dean appeared and told the *boys* he had called *their* parents."

Among. See *between.*

Apostrophe (to indicate possession). See *possessives.*

Around. See *about.*

As. See *like.*

Beside refers to nearness; *besides* means *in addition to.* "*Besides* being sheriff he was dog catcher, so he built the dog pound *beside* the jail."

Between refers to two persons or things; *among* refers to three or more. "The power of government is divided *among* the legislative, judicial, and executive branches. The legislative power is divided *between* the Senate and the House."

Capitalization (in quotations). See *quotations.*

Commas setting off appositives or interrupters come in pairs. "John Smith, senator from Vermont will speak today" should be "John

---

* Adapted from a section in *High School Journalism Today,* Gene Gilmore, ed. (Danville, Ill.: Interstate Publishers), 1967.

Smith, senator from Vermont, will speak today." And "The meeting, surprisingly enough went off on schedule" needs a comma after "enough."

Contrary-to-fact statements. See *subjunctive mood.*

Doubt, statements of. See *subjunctive mood.*

Effect. See *affect.*

Either pairs with *or; neither* pairs with *nor.* "*Either* he *or* I is at fault, but *neither* he *nor* I admits guilt." Note that both *either* and *neither* require singular verbs.

Farther refers to distance; *further* refers to thoroughness. "He wanted to check *further* on the flood damage, so he walked *farther* out onto the bridge."

Feel, when it refers to health or emotion, requires an adjective, not an adverb. "I feel bad about not calling him back." "I feel badly" would imply an impaired sense of touch. The same rule applies to *look, sound, smell,* and *taste.*

Gerunds coupled with a pronoun require that pronoun to be possessive. "I could watch *his dancing* for hours."

Hyphenation, of adjective phrases. See *adjective phrases.*

It's and *its. It's* is a contraction of *it is; its* is a possessive pronoun. "*It's* too bad the store lost *its* lease."

Lay and *lie. To lay* is a transitive verb and thereby takes an object; *to lie* is intransitive and thus takes no object.

Transitive:	He *lays* bricks for a living.
	He is *laying* the box on the counter.
	Lay the box on the counter.
	He *laid* the box down.
Intransitive:	He *lies* in bed till noon.
	He is *lying* in the sun.
	Lie down for an hour or so.
	He *lay* down to rest.
	His head *lay* on the pillow.
	He has *lain* there long enough.

Like is a preposition and requires an object; *as* is a conjunction and requires a following clause. "She looks *like* her mother, just *as* [not *like*] we thought." *Like* may be used as a conjunction in a simile. "He performed *like* Artur Rubinstein."

Look, when referring to health. See *feel.*

Neither. See *either.*

Nor. See *either.*

Or. See *either.*

Possessives. To form the singular possessive, in most cases, add an apostrophe and an "s." "The dog's coat is glossy." To form a plural possessive, in most cases, add the apostrophe. "The dogs' coats are wet." If a word ends with an "s" sound, add only the apostrophe if it has more than one syllable. "Rabinowitz' book is well-written; Ross's book is dull."

Prepositional object. When a pronoun is the object of a preposition, it should be in the objective case. "The decision was between *him* and *me.*"

Quotations.

A quoted sentence needs only one capital:

"It is a difficult problem," Smith said, "but we can solve it."

Two quoted sentences require two capitals:

"The well is dry," she said. "We must get water elsewhere."

A quote within a quote takes single quotation marks:

"New devices let people 'hear' atomic explosions thousands of miles away," he said.

When quoted material continues for more than one paragraph, save the *ending* quotation marks for the end of the quoted material:

"The well is dry," she said; "we must get it elsewhere (no quotation marks).

"Maybe we can get it at the next farm."

Set and *sit.* *To set* is a transitive verb and thereby takes an object; *to sit* is intransitive and thus takes no object.

Transitive: He *sets* tile for a living.

He is *setting* plants in the garden.

Set the box on the table.

He *set* the box down.

Intransitive: He *sits* here regularly.

She was *sitting* in the chair.

Sit down, please.

He *sat* in front.

Have you *sat* there before?

Smell. See *feel.*

Sound. See *feel.*

Subjunctive mood. The subjunctive mood expresses wishes, doubts, or things contrary to fact. It requires a plural verb. "If he *were* seven feet tall, he would be on the basketball team for sure" (contrary to fact). "I wish I *were* old enough to be President" (wish). "He acts as if he *were* unable to speak" (doubt).

Taste. See *feel.*

Touch. See *feel.*

Were. See *subjunctive mood.*

Reporters often misspell or confuse these words:

accommodate
advice, advise
allege
amateur
arctic
bridal, bridle
calendar
canceled
canvas, canvass
capital, capitol
category
cellar
cemetery
chauffeur
cite, site, sight
compliment,
  complement
conscious
coroner
corps, corpse
council, counsel
defendant
desert, dessert
emigrate, immigrate

flew, flu, flue
floe, flow
guerrilla
hemorrhage
judgment
knowledgeable
lessen, lesson
libel, liable
lose, loose
mantel, mantle
mileage
missile
Niagara
nickel
ordinance, ordnance
peaceable
penitentiary
personal, personnel
Philippines
plaque
prairie
precede, proceed
preventive
principal, principle

privilege
rhythm
separate
sergeant
sizable
soccer
sophomore
stationary,
  stationery
there, their
weird

Appendix b: glossary

ABC. Audit Bureau of Circulations, which compiles statistics on *circulations.*

Ad alley. A section of the *composing room* for *makeup* of ads.

Add. The copy added to a story; also, one *take* or page of a story, such as "Add 1."

Ad side. The section of the business office where advertising is prepared; sometimes a synonym for *ad alley.*

Advance. The story written in advance of an event and held for *release;* also, a story written on a forthcoming event.

Agate. Five-and-a-half-*point* type, usually found only in classified advertising or lists.

Agate line. A measurement of advertising depth. Fourteen make one inch.

Air. See *white space.*

Alive. Usable copy or type.

Alley. A section of the *composing room.* See *ad alley.*

All in hand. The situation when all the copy has been sent to the *composing room.* All pages for the *edition* are *closed* and "ready to roll."

All up. The situation when the *copyeditor* or reporter has finished assigned work.

AM. A morning newspaper. AMs is the cycle sent by a wire service to morning newspapers.

A-matter. Copy set in advance of the *top* of a story, sometimes called *10-add* material because it is added to *lead* paragraphs of a story.

Angle. The emphasis of a story.

ANPA. American Newspaper Publishers Association.

AP. Associated Press, a cooperative newsgathering organization.

APC. Wire service jargon for "appreciate."

APME. Associated Press Managing Editors association. The editors represent AP member newspapers.

Art. Any illustrative material, such as pictures, graphs, and sketches.

Ascender. The portion of a *lower case* letter rising above average letter height; contrast to *descender.*

ASNE. American Society of Newspaper Editors.

Astonisher. An exclamation point.

Audience research. The study of newspaper readers—their education, wealth, etc.

Back room. The *composing room;* usually on smaller papers where it adjoins the news room. Also called back shop.

Back shop. See *back room.*

Bad break. An unattractive or confusing division of type in a story of more than one column. A column may end with a period, giving the impression that the story has ended, or there may be a prominent *widow.*

Balloon. A device used in comic strips to make words appear to come from a character.

Bank. A part of a headline, sometimes called a deck or, if the lower part a drop. It also means a storage place for stories or ads set in type.

Banner. A headline running across, or nearly across, the top of a page; also called streamer, line, ribbon.

Bastard type. Type that differs from the standard *point* system.

Beat. The area assigned to a reporter for regular coverage; also, an exclusive story, or scoop.

Ben Day. An *engraving* process that provides shading effects in line engravings. Editors use Ben Day mostly for borders on key stories.

BF. The abbreviation for *boldface.*

Binder. A small *banner* across an inside page. It sometimes shelters several related stories.

Bite. To cut a story so it fits the space allotted to it. The part cut is called a biteoff or a bite.

Biteoff. See *bite.*

Blanket. See *offset.*

Blanket head. A headline covering several stories, each with lesser headlines. See *binder.*

Bleed. To run a *cut* right off the edge of a page; also, the cut so run. Sometimes a cut run to the edge of the outside column is erroneously called a bleed.

Blind ad. A classified ad which gives a box number instead of the advertiser's name.

Blind interview. An interview story which does not reveal the name of the source, referring to him as "an informed official," "an unimpeachable source," etc.

Blotter. A police department's record book.

Blow up. To enlarge printed or pictorial matter; the enlargement so made.

Body. The story itself, as distinguished from the headline and the illustration.

Body type. The type normally used for news stories. The size is usually 8-, 9-, or 10-*point.*

Boil or *boil down.* A *copyeditor's* direction to reduce a story substantially.

Boiler plate. Editorial matter, usually *features* and pictures, mailed to small papers in *matrix* or metallic form; a derisive term for poor, inconsequential stories.

Boldface. Dark or heavy type, as distinguished from *lightface;* sometimes called fullface. **This is boldface.**

Book. A group of several stories on the same general subject, usually from a wire service. See also *take.*

Border. The strips of type metal surrounding an ad, story, or headline.

Box. To enclose a story or headline with four *rules* to give it more prominence; also, such an enclosure.

Box-all. The instruction to put the headline, *body,* and, possibly, picture of a story in a single *box.*

Break. The division of a story continued from one page to another or from one column to another. Compare *jump, bad break, break-over, wrap, carryover.* Also, a story breaks when the event occurs or when the news becomes available to reporters.

Break-over. The part of a story continued to another page. The page where break-overs are placed is called the break-over page, carryover, or jump page.

Brite. A short, amusing feature story; short for page brightener.

Budget. The listing of stories expected by a wire service or by another news gathering group; also called news digest.

Bug. Any fancy typographic device used to break up areas of type, especially in headlines. Compare *dingbat.* Bugs are used with restraint by today's editors. The word also refers to the telegrapher's key and to the label of the International Typographical Union.

Bulldog. The newspaper's first *edition* of the day.

Bullet. A large black dot used for decoration, to separate sections of a story, or, at the left edge of a column, to mark each item in a series.

Bulletin. Important and often unexpected news. In wire service parlance only a *flash* is more important.

Bulletin-form. A wire service term for filing a story in short installments, or *takes.*

Bulletin precede. The latest facts of a story already set in type when the bulletin arrived. The precede is stuck in at the top of the story.

Bureau. A subsidiary newsgathering force placed in a smaller community, a state capital, or the national capital by a newspaper or wire service.

Business-office must. A story labeled "must" by the business office, which means the story cannot be omitted. Usually it is a page-one *box* promoting the paper itself.

Byline. The reporter's name atop the story.

C and lc. The abbreviation for *caps and lower case,* used to specify the conventional capitalizing used in ordinary writing; contrast to material marked "caps," which means the compositor should set every letter as a capital.

C and sc. The abbreviation for *caps and small caps,* used to set material all in capitals but with the pattern of *C and lc.*

Cablese. See *skeletonize.*

California case. A drawer with compartments for pieces of type.

Cathode Ray Tube. An electronic device with a keyboard on which stories may be written and edited. The story appears on a screen. The devices, connected to computers, are used in setting cold type.

Canned copy. Prepared news or editorials sent by a *syndicate* or publicity organization.

Caps. The abbreviation for capitals; also, upper case. Every letter or a word so marked is capitalized. Compare *C and lc* and *C and sc.*

Caption. A headline appearing above a picture; now, through misuse, commonly a synonym for *cutline,* the words under a picture.

Carryover. See *break-over.*

Casting. A *plate,* usually an ad or picture, made by pouring molten type metal over a papier mâché *matrix.*

Casting box. The equipment used to cast a printing *plate* from a papier mâché *matrix.*

Catchline. See *guideline.*

Center. To place type in the center of a line.

CGO. Short for *can go over.* Copy that could be held for another day.

Chapel. A union local for printers, stereotypers, or pressmen.

Chase. A frame in which type is placed to make a page *form.*

Chi square. A test of statistical validity; used in communications research.

Circulation. The number of copies a paper sells in a particular *edition;* the department in charge of distributing the paper.

Circus makeup. A now rare *makeup* system which uses many large headlines scattered seemingly as random on a page.

City desk. The place where the city editor and his assistants, if any, work.

City editor. The editor in charge of the reporters covering news within a city and its environs. On smaller papers he also edits his reporters' copy.

City room. The news room, where reporters and editors work.

Clean copy. A story needing little editing.

Clean proof. A *proof* needing few corrections.

Clipsheet. A sheet of publicity material which its backers hope will be clipped and reprinted. AP and UPI, however, send filler material on a clipsheet.

Closed. A page *locked up,* ready for *stereotyping* and therefore not to be altered except in an emergency.

Col. The abbreviation for column.

Cold type. Print produced photographically or by a machine resembling a typewriter. Strips of paper so "printed" are pasted on a *dummy* and photographed, and a *plate* for an *offset* press is made from the negative.

Color. A story with human interest, often describing places and people in detail. But a "colored" story is a biased, or slanted, report.

Column inch. One inch of type one column wide; a standard measure of advertising space for smaller papers.

Column rule. A thin line separating columns.

Communicologist. A communications researcher; often used in derision.

Compose. To set type. See *compositor.*

Composing room. The mechanical department; in particular the place where type is *composed* and put into *forms.*

Composing stick. The small metal tray in which a *compositor* arranges type he is setting by hand.

Compositor. Someone who sets type professionally, either by hand or by machine.

Condensed type. Type narrower than the standard width of a particular type *face,* giving a squeezed appearance; contrast *extended type.*

Content analysis. A research method to analyze published material.

Copy boy. An errand boy in the news room. "Copy girls" perform the same duties.

Copy cutter. A *composing room* worker who cuts copy into various *takes* to facilitate quick typesetting. He also distributes copy to various *Linotype* operators.

Copydesk. A desk, frequently horseshoe-shaped, around which *copyeditors* sit to edit copy. The *slot,* inside the horseshoe, is in charge.

Copyeditor. A person who edits copy; a copyreader.

Copyreader. See *copyeditor.*

Copy writer. A person who writes advertising copy.

Correspondent. A reporter who files stories from places outside the newspaper's city area. The person may be on salary or may receive a flat fee or a per-inch rate See also *stringer.*

Country copy. News from rural areas, often written by a part-time *correspondent,* or *stringer.*

CQ. An abbreviation for "correct"; used in copy but not as a symbol on *proof* or on a *mark.* See also *CX.*

Credit line. A line acknowledging the source for a story or picture.

Crop. To cut away parts of a picture to eliminate unwanted material or to make it a particular size.

CRT. A cathode ray tube.

Cub. A beginning journalist.

Cut. To reduce a story's length; compare *bite.* As a noun, an *engraving* and therefore any *art.*

Cutline. Any explanatory material under a piece of *art.* Compare *caption.*

Cutoff rule. A horizontal line, the width of a column, used to separate material.

CX. An abbreviation for "correct." The editor puts this symbol on *proof* corrected in the newsroom, or on a *mark*. The symbols "X-correct" and "Krect" are also used for this purpose. All three abbreviations are used on edited copy to show the typesetter that something that might seem wrong is right. See also *CQ*.

Dateline. The words that give the story's origin and, often, the date on which the story was written, e.g., CHICAGO, Oct. 1 (UPI)—.

Dayside. The shift of day workers in the news room.

Dead. Copy or type that will not be used.

Dead bank. A storage area for *dead* type.

Dead stone. See *dead bank*.

Deck. See *bank*.

Descender. The portion of a *lower case* letter going below the baseline; contrast *ascender*.

Desk chief. The head of a particular desk.

Dingbat. Any typographical device used for decoration. Compare *bug*.

Dinky dash. A short dash used to separate items in a series.

Dirty copy. Matter for publication which is sloppy, full of corrections, and badly marked up; contrast to *clean copy*.

Display ad. All advertising except classified and legal.

District man. A reporter covering a particular district of a city or rural area.

Dog watch. See *lobster trick*.

Dope story. An interpretative story often based on background plus speculation.

Doublet. The repetition of some fact; also called doubleton.

Doubleton. See *doublet*.

Double-truck. A two-page layout, either news or advertising, which eliminates the margin, or *gutter,* between the pages.

Downstyle. A style with a minimum of capitalization. Contrast *upstyle*.

DPR. The telegraph symbol for Day Press Rate.

Drop. See *bank*.

Drop head. A headline with each line stepped (and so also called a step head):

President Says
Budget Deficit
Above Estimate

Drop line. See *drop head*.

Dummy. A diagram of a newspaper page used to show printers where stories, pictures, and ads are to be placed; occasionally called a map.

Dupe. A duplicate, usually a carbon copy; also, a story that appears twice in the same *edition*.

Ear. Either upper corner of the front page, often containing a slogan or a weather report.

Edition. Each *run* of a newspaper *issue.* There may be market editions, early editions, final editions, etc.

Editorial. Generally all the non-advertising and non-business material or operations of a newspaper; also, one of the opinion essays of the editorial page.

Editorialize. Putting opinion in a story or headline.

Electrotype. A copper-plated reproduction of type or *art;* usually used in advertising or book publishing.

Em. The square of the type size. An em in 12-*point* type is twelve points high and twelve points wide. Sometimes erroneously used to mean one-sixth of an inch; see *pica.*

En. Half an *em.*

End dash. A dash at the end of a story; usually about six *picas.* It is sometimes called a thirty-dash.

Engraving. A *plate* from which pictures and drawings may be printed; see *cut.*

Etaoin Shrdlu. A *Linotype* operator sets these "words" to fill out a line he plans to throw away. The letters make up the first two vertical rows on a *Linotype.*

Exchange. A copy of a newspaper sent to another newspaper publisher as part of an agreement to exchange subscriptions.

Extended type. Type wider than the standard for a particular *face;* contrast *condensed type.*

Extra. A special, or extra, *edition* published because of spectacular news; now rare.

Eye camera. A camera specially arranged to record a reader's eye movements; used in research on *makeup.*

Face. A particular design of type; also, the printing surface of type.

Fake. A false story.

Feature. A story emphasizing the human interest or entertainment aspects of a situation; usually in narrative form. Also, material such as columns and comics brought from a *syndicate.* As a verb, it means to give prominence to a story; to emphasize a part of a story.

FF or *ff.* The abbreviation for fullface. See *boldface.*

File. To transmit a story by telephone, telegraph, or cable. As a noun, it refers collectively to the back issues of a paper; also, one day's production by a wire service.

Filler. Short stories, usually *time copy,* used to fill small spaces in the paper.

Fingernails. Parentheses; sometimes called toenails.

First-day story. The first published account of an event.

Flag. The newspaper's *nameplate* or *logotype,* often erroneously called the *masthead;* also, a *slug* or piece of paper inserted into printing *forms* to remind printers that a correction, *add,* or *insert* is required at that point.

Flash. The highest priority of news sent by a wire service; used rarely.

Flat-bed press. A press which prints from a flat surface.

Flimsy. Thin paper used for carbon copies; sometimes the carbon copy itself.

Flong. A cardboard-like sheet used for making the *matrix* in *stereo-typing.*

Fluff. Inconsequential material.

Flush. The instructions to set type even, or flush, with a margin; "flush left" means flush with the left margin, "flush right" with the right margin.

Flush head. A headline whose lines are even on the left:

President Says
Budget Plan
'Unrealistic'

Fold. The area where a full-sized newspaper is folded.

Folio. The line at the top of the page giving the page number, the name of the newspaper, the city of publication, and the date; also, a measure for legal advertising.

Follow. A story that *follows up* a *first-day* story; also, a *second-day* story; also, a story *shirt-tailed* to a similar, but more important, story.

Follow up. A story that gives the latest news of an event reported earlier.

Folo. An abbreviation for *follow.* Also see *folo copy.*

Folo copy. The order to set copy in type exactly as written.

Font. A set of particular size and style of type.

Form. A *chase* filled with type.

Format. The physical appearance of a page, section, or book.

Four-color process. A printing process using four different engraving *plates,* each printing one color—black, red, blue, or yellow—to make natural-looking color.

Fourth estate. The public press.

Front office. The business office.

Fudge. A part of a press *plate* that may be removed or chiseled away so last-minute news, usually sports scores, can be inserted; also called a fudge box.

Fullface. See *boldface.*

Full line. Type that fills the line, making it both *flush* left and flush right; a line that has no room for spacing.

Future. A reminder of a forthcoming event. Such notes are put in a "future book" to be used in making reporting assignments. "Futures" are stories to be used within a few days or weeks.

FYI. The wire service abbreviation for "for your information."

Galley. A metal tray to hold type; also, about twenty inches of type.

Galley proof. A *proof* of a *galley* of type; used to check the copy for errors before it goes to press.

General assignment. A reporter without a beat; available for widely-varied stories.

Ghost. A ghost writer; a person who writes stories or books for others' signatures.

Glossy. A shiny-surfaced photograph, best suited for *photoengraving.*

Goodnight. A wire service may end its *AMs* cycle with this word; an editor may call it out to a staffer, thereby indicating the staffer may leave for the day.

Graf. Short for paragraph.

Graveyard shift. The work period that covers the early morning hours; also called *lobster trick* or *dog watch.* Staffers on this shift may write and edit, but they are there primarily to cover emergencies.

Gravure. A process for printing from an intended surface. See also *intaglio* and *rotogravure.*

Gray out. A section of a page that has no typographical contrast, giving a gray appearance.

Green eyeshade. A somewhat sentimental term for an old-time newspaper staffer; refers to a former custom among deskmen of wearing green eyeshades.

Guideline. The first word or two of a headline, written at the top of the copy to identify it; also called *catchline.* It is sometimes confused with *slugline.*

Gutter. The margin between facing pages.

Hairline. An extra-thin *rule.*

Halftone. An engraving using small dots of varying depth to produce shaded effects, as in photos; contrast to *line cut.*

Handout. A press release.

Handset. Type set by hand.

Hanging indent. A headline with first line set flush left and others lines slightly and equally indented:

President Says
Budget Plan
'Unrealistic'

Hard news. Stories based on specific, recent, important events.

Head. Short for headline.

Head schedule. A sheet that displays headline types used by the newspaper; it includes the unit count for each type face so the editor can quickly figure how much space a word will take up in the headline. Popularly called the "hed sked."

Head slug. A *slug* which does not print, separating the headline from the story with blank space.

Head to come. The notice to the composing room that the headline will be sent after the story; abbreviated HTK or HTC.

Headwriter. A writer of headlines; usually a *copyeditor,* who writes the headlines for the story he edits.

Hed sked. Short for *head schedule.*

Hellbox. A container in the *composing room* for unwanted type.

Holdover. See *overset.*

Hole. See *news hole.*

Hot type. Type made from molten metal; usually from a Linotype.

House organ. A publication issued by a company primarily for its employees.

HTC or *HTK.* Abbreviations for *head to come.*

Human interest. The quality giving a story wide appeal. It often contains information on human foibles or oddities or heartwarming and sentimental matter.

Indent. To leave extra space on either side of a column.

Index. The summary of the contents or highlights of a paper; usually on page one.

Initial. A large capital letter at the beginning of an article or paragraph, common in magazines but sometimes used for magazine-style matter in newspapers.

Input. Material put into a computer.

Insert. Copy or type to be inserted into a story.

Intaglio printing. The *gravure* process that prints ink from a depressed surface.

Interface. An electronic connection.

Inverted pyramid. A headline form with each line centered and shorter than the preceding one:

President Reports
Deficit Plan
Today

Also, a news story with facts arranged in descending order of importance.

Issue. One day's newspaper, which may have several *editions.*

Ital. or *itals.* Abbreviations for *italics.*

Italics. Type with letters slanted to the right; used for cross references in this glossary. Contrast *roman* and *oblique.*

ITU. International Typographical Union, to which most printers (but not stereotypers or pressmen) belong.

Jim dash. A dash about three *picas* long, often used to separate a regular story and a *shirttail.*

Job. A commercial printing order.

Job press. A press used only for commercial printing.

Jump. See *break-over;* also, to continue a story. Compare *break.*

Jump head. The headline over the part of the story that was continued, or *jumped,* to another page.

Jump line. A line noting a story is continued (e.g., *Continued on Page 6*).

Jump page. See *break-over.*

Justify. To space out a column to make the type snug, or to space out a line of type so it is *flush* left and right.

Justowriter. A machine, basically like a typewriter, which sets *cold type.*

Kicker. A few words usually to the left and above a headline, to give it emphasis; sometimes it serves the same purpose as a *deck.*

Kill. To eliminate all or part of a story. Compare *mandatory kill.*

Label head. A headline, usually without a verb, that only labels the news and thus is listless (e.g., *List of Graduates*).

Laser. Beams used in newspaper platemaking or in photographic preparations.

Laserphoto. AP's picture machine, which uses laser beams.

Late watch. See *lobster trick.*

Layout. A planned arrangement of stories and pictures on one subject; also, the whole typographical arrangement of a newspaper.

LC or *lc.* Abbreviations for *lower case.*

Lead (pronounced "led"). A strip of metal used to separate *slugs* of type. Strips are placed between paragraphs to justify a column.

Lead (pronounced "leed"). The first paragraph or two of a story; also, the story given number one position as the best of the day. Also, a *tip.*

Lead ("leed") *editorial.* The first, and most important, editorial.

Lead ("leed") *to come.* A device, used rarely, to indicate that the story's *lead* will come later. Compare *ten-add.*

Leaders ("leeders"). Dots or dashes to take the eye across a column; often used in tables.

Leftover. See *overset.*

Leg man. A reporter who gathers information and telephones it to a *rewrite person.*

Legibility. The quality of a type style which makes it easily and quickly comprehended or perceived; contrast *readability.*

Letterpress printing. The process by which ink is transferred to paper from a raised surface; the traditional method of printing.

Letter space. The insertion of thin spaces between letters to *justify* the line.

Library. A collection of clippings, newspaper files, and reference books; formerly called the morgue.

Ligature. One character of type that includes more than one letter (e.g., *fl* and *œ*). The initials of the wire services, such as AP and UPI, are also known as ligatures.

Linage. A measure of printed material based on the number of lines; also, the total amount of advertising over a given period of time.

Line. See *banner;* also, *agate line.*

Linecasting machine. A machine that casts line of type. Compare *Linotype.*

Line cut. An engraving which prints only black and white; also called line engraving. Contrast *halftone.*

Line gauge. A printer's ruler.

Lino. Short for *Linotype.*

Linotype. The brand name of a machine which sets hot type one line at a time; also a loose term for all similar machines.

Lithography. The process of printing from ink impressed on a sheet; also called photolithography. See also *offset.*

Live. Designation for type that will be used in the paper going to press.

Lobster trick. The shift on duty after the last *edition* of a morning paper has gone to press; the night shift of an afternoon paper. Sometimes called lobster shift, late watch, and dog watch. See also *graveyard shift* and *nightside.*

Local. A local news item; usually a *personal.*

Localize. To emphasize a local angle in a story.

Locked up. See *closed.*

Log or *logo.* Short for *logotype.*

Logotype. A one-piece line of type or a *plate* bearing a trademark, name, or frequently used phrase. A newspaper's *nameplate,* or *flag,* is a logotype.

Lower case. The small letters of type. The term originated with early type cases, which had the small letters near the bottom. Contrast *upper case.* See also *downstyle.*

Ludlow. A typecasting machine used for headlines or advertising. It casts *slugs* from *matrices* that are *handset.*

Magazine. An attachment on a *linecasting machine* for the storing of *matrices.*

Magazine style. See *upstyle;* also see *initial.*

Mail edition. An *edition* sent primarily to mail subscribers.

Makeover. To make a new page *plate* to correct an error or to include late news; also called replate.

Makeready. The series of *composing room* processes that prepare material for printing.

Makeup. To arrange type and pictures to produce a desired effect. The noun refers to the resulting design.

Makeup editor. An editorial employee stationed in the *composing room* to supervise the *makeup* of the paper.

Makeup rule. A thin piece of steel, shaped something like a protractor, used by printers in page *makeup.*

Mandatory kill. An order from a wire service to eliminate (*kill*) a story, probably because it has a serious error or is libelous.

Map. See *dummy.*

Mark. A story from one *edition* clipped and pasted on a sheet of paper to be marked for changes in the next edition—corrections, indications of inserts, adds, or new leads. Also called a markup or marker.

Marker. See *mark.*

Markets. A section of the paper that includes news of livestock, commodity, and stock markets.

Markup. See *mark.*

Masthead. A statement of the paper's name, ownership, subscription rate, etc., which often appears on the editorial page; often confused with *nameplate* or *flag.*

Mat. Short for *matrix.*

Matrix (plural: matrices). A die or mold from which type is cast. It can be papier mâché, from which the page *plate* is cast, or a brass die, from which lines of type are cast. Commonly referred to as mat.

Mat roller. The machine which squeezes the papier mâché matrix against the *form,* preparatory to making a page *plate.*

Measure. The length of a line of type, or the width of a column.

Media Records, Inc. A company that records data on newspaper advertising.

Milline rate. A method of measuring advertising rates in relation to *circulation.*

Monotype. A typecasting machine that sets each letter in a separate piece of metal.

More. A word placed at the end of a sheet of copy to indicate that the story has not ended.

Morgue. See *library.*

Mortice. An opening, usually rectangular, for the insertion of material, such as an opening in an *engraving* for a heading.

Must. An order from a superior that a certain story must run in the paper that day. See also *business office must.*

Nameplate. The *logotype* that carries the newspaper's name at the top of page one; also called *flag* and, wrongly, *masthead.*

NANA. North American Newspaper Alliance, a news *syndicate* specializing in feature stories.

National advertising. Advertising placed by an advertising agency, usually for a product sold nationally.

NEA. National Editorial Association, a group of weekly and small-daily editors; also, Newspaper Enterprise Association, a *feature* service.

New lead (pronounced "leed"). Also called new top. A fresh opening paragraph or two for a story. An editor may think the reporter's story basically sound but in need of a new *lead* to catch the reader's interest. Or the story may have been published earlier and need a new beginning; see also *second-day story.*

News digest. See *budget.*

News hole. The space in a paper allotted to news reports and illustration, the rest being given to advertisements, comic strips, etc.

New top. See *new lead.*

Nightside. The night shift of a newspaper. See also *lobster trick.*

Nonpareil. Six-*point* type.

NPR. The telegraph symbol for Night Press Rate.

Nutted. Type indented one *en.*

Obit. Short for *obituary.*

Obituary. A story reporting a person's death. For a well-known person, it is often written before he dies; the facts of his death are simply incorporated into the pre-written story of his life.

Oblique type. Slanted type, but without the handwritten appearance of *italics.* Contrast *roman.*

OCR. Optical Character Reader.

Off its feet. Type that does not quite stand vertically and therefore makes a poor impression on the paper.

Offset. A photographic method of printing. Copy is photographed and a *plate* made by "burning" light through the negative onto a sensitized sheet of thin metal. The part exposed to light, or "burned," absorbs ink while the rest of the plate rejects it. The plate, wrapped around a roller, transfers, or offsets, the ink to a rubber roller called a blanket, which actually imprints the paper.

Op ed or *opp page.* Abbreviations for "the page opposite"; usually the page devoted to columns and *features* and placed opposite the editorial page.

Optical Character Reader. An electronic device that scans copy to start cold type production. See *scanner.*

Overset. Set type that cannot be used because space is filled; called holdover or leftover if it can be used in the next issue.

Pad. To add useless words to stories or headlines.

Page proof. A *proof* (test printing) of a full page. Such proofs often are taken of the front page before it is made into a *plate.*

Pasteup. Pasting cold type onto camera-copy preparatory to making a printing plate.

Patent or *patent insides.* Pre-printed material, usually on one side of a sheet so local news can be printed on the blank side; used rarely now, even on the smallest weeklies. Also see *readyprint.*

Perforator. A machine used to perforate a paper tape from which type can be set mechanically; also, a person who runs a perforator.

Personal. A one-paragraph item about minor family news; a kind of *local.*

Photocomposition. A photographic process to "set type." Actually, letters are formed on film which is photographically printed; then that print is photographed in the *offset* process to make a *plate* or scanned to make a *laser plate.*

Photoengraving. See *engraving.*

Photolithography. See *lithography.*

Pi. Jumbled type, or, as a verb, to jumble type; past tense or adjective form is "pied."

Pica. Twelve-*point* type; also, a printer's measure—one-sixth of an inch. It is also called *pica em* or, wrongly, *em.*

Pica em. See *pica.*

Pick up. The instruction at the bottom of copy to tell the printer to pick up other type and add it to the story. In wire copy, it tells the editor where *adds, inserts,* etc. "pick up" into the story.

Pix. Short for pictures.

Planer. A wooden block pounded against type in *form* to make it level.

Plate. A *stereotype* page or an *offset* metal sheet from which newspapers are printed.

Platen press. A small *job press.*

Play. The typographical emphasis given a story, or the emphasis on a certain fact in a story. Facts or stories can be "played up" or "played down."

PM. An afternoon newspaper.

Point. A type measurement—one seventy-second of an inch. Hence, 72-point type is one inch high, 36-point one-half inch, etc.

Policy. The newspaper's position on how it handles news.

Policy story. A story that supports the newspaper *policy.*

Poll. A field study of opinion on an issue. It may be a scientific *public opinion survey* or merely unscientific guesswork.

PR. Public relations.

Precede. A new lead or story, taking precedence over a previous wire service transmission and usually intended to precede it. A *bulletin precede* could be set in type and placed ahead of the earlier story.

Pre-date. An issue printed before its announced date of publication. (Metropolitan morning papers put out an *edition* in the evening with the next day's date on it.)

Preferred position. An advertising term that refers to an advertiser's receiving a special place in the paper for his ads. Usually the advertiser pays extra for this preference.

Press agent. A person hired to get favorable publicity for an individual or organization.

Process color. A printing method that mixes primary colors optically to produce a full range of colors.

Proof. A test impression taken from type set and ready for printing. It allows errors to be spotted and corrections made before the paper goes to press. See also *galley proof.*

Proof press. A simple press used to make *proof.*

Proofreader. An employee in the *composing room* who reads and marks *proof* to make sure it conforms to copy.

Public opinion survey. A scientific study of the expressed attitudes of a representative sample of a population; often used before elections.

Public relations. The craft of issuing news of and creating a good image for an individual, agency, or firm; more professional and comprehensive than the work of a *press agent.* Often shortened to PR.

Puff, puffery. A publicity story or a story that contains unwarranted superlatives.

Pullout. A newspaper section, often a tabloid, easily pulled from the rest of the paper.

Puncher. A *teletype* operator.

Put to bed. See *all in hand.*

Q. and A. Copy including question-and-answer material, as in court testimony or a long interview.

Quad. A blank character used in spacing type. An *em quad* is square; an *en quad* is half the width of an em quad.

Query. A question raised in a message to a wire service; also, a request by a freelance writer to see if a newspaper or magazine would be interested in a particular article.

Railroad. To send copy to the *composing room* with little or no editing; to put type into *forms* without *proofreading.*

Readability. The quality of copy which makes it easy to grasp; contrast *legibility.*

Reader interest. A type of research to determine the degree of appeal different materials have for the reader.

Readership. Research on the amount of newspaper copy which readers notice or read; also, the people actually reached by a publication, as distinguished from *circulation.*

Readout. A subsidiary headline that "reads out" (explains in more detail) from a *banner.*

Readyprint. Paper already partly printed with ads and *features,* so the rest of the space can be filled with local news and ads. See also *patent.*

Register. The correct placement or matching of *plates* in color printing so colors are exactly where they should be.

Release. The date and time at which a news source says information may be released to the public; also, a publicity handout; also, authorization for the use of a photograph.

Replate. See *makeover.*

Reprint. Published material that came from a previous issue or from some other source, such as a magazine.

Reproduction proof or repro proof. A fine *proof* on quality paper for use in preparing a *plate,* as in *offset.*

Retail advertising. Advertising placed by local merchants.

Retouch. To change a photograph, usually to improve it for *engraving,* by painting sections out (or in) with a small brush.

Revamp. To alter a story by shifting some of the paragraphs, but not by rewriting it. See also *rewrite.*

Reverse. Letters or *engravings* printed the opposite of normal, as white letters on a black background.

Reverse-6. The eye tends to scan the news page in a line resembling a reversed number 6.

Revise. A second, and presumably correct, *proof*—made after errors were noted on the first proof.

Rewrite. To write a story again, or to *revamp* a story from a wire service or from another newspaper; also, to write a story telephoned to the news room by another reporter. See also *rewrite man.*

Rewrite man or *rewrite woman.* The reporter who takes facts from one or more reporters, usually by telephone, and writes the story; also, a reporter who revises stories written by other reporters.

Ribbon. See *banner.*

Rim. The outside edge of the *copydesk,* which is traditionally horse-shoe-shaped.

Rim man. A *copyeditor,* so named because he sits on the *rim.*

Roman type. The common vertical type which is popularly contrasted to *italic* and technically to *oblique.*

ROP. Short for *run of paper.*

Roto. Short for *rotogravure.*

Rotogravure. An *intaglio* printing process using etching on copper and a rotary press; also, a section of a newspaper featuring photographs so printed.

Routing. Gouging metal from a *cut, casting,* or a page *plate* so only part of the surface will print.

Rule. A metal strip which prints a line dividing columns, stories, or sections of advertising; usually one or two *points* thick, but see also *hairline.*

Ruled insert. A story that accompanies another but is set off from it by *rules.*

Run. An *edition,* in the sense that the edition is "run"; also, a *beat.*

Run in. The instruction on copy to have material in tables or paragraphs run together without paragraphing.

Running story. A story—actually many stories—continued for several days or more.

Run of paper. An order meaning that an ad, picture, or story could go almost anyplace in the paper. Also, color printed by regular newspaper presses.

Sacred cow. A person or institution unethically deferred to by being given special news treatment.

Sans serif. See *serif.*

SAP. Occasionally used in messages to mean "soon as possible." The superlative SAPPEST is used humorously.

Scanner. See *Optical Character Reader.*

Schedule. A record of stories assigned or already processed.

Scoop. See *beat.*

Screen. A mesh through which pictures are rephotographed in making *engravings* or *cuts.* A fairly coarse screen is used in making newspaper cuts.

Second-day story. A story previously published but now carrying a *new lead* or some other revision to make it news. Also see *follow.*

Second front page. Usually the front page of a second section; also called split page. Sometimes page two or page three gets the name because it carries important news with little or no advertising.

Sectional story. A story received in pieces or sent to the *composing room* in sections; also, a story that would be of interest only to readers in a certain area.

See copy. The direction to *proofreaders* to check the *proof* against the copy.

Send down or *send out.* The direction to send copy to the *composing room.*

Separate. A story related to another and displayed separately, but usually nearby.

Series. Related stories, usually run on consecutive days.

Serif. A tiny finishing stroke or squiggle at the ends of letters in most type faces. A face with simple, square corners is called sans serif.

Set. To arrange type, either by hand or by machine, for printing.

Shirttail. Material added to a major story; also, a short *follow.*

Sidebar. A story that emphasizes one part of a main story and appears alongside it on the page.

Sidelight. A kind of *sidebar,* often dealing with a personality or one aspect of an event.

Side story. See *sidebar.*

Signature. An advertiser's name, often in distinctive type, in his ad; often printed from a *logotype.*

Sizing. Determining the size of an engraving, or cut.

Skeletonize. To reduce copy by eliminating articles, some conjunctions, etc. in order to minimize cable tolls; now rarely done. The skeletonized language is called cablese.

Skyline. A line running above the *nameplate,* at the top of the page.

Slant. To emphasize a certain part or angle of a story; also, to distort the news. Compare *color.*

Slot. The inside of the horseshoe-shaped *copydesk;* occupied by the slot person, who directs the *copyeditors* sitting around the *rim.*

Slot man. See *slot.*

Slug or *slugline.* A mark on a story, usually one word like "blast" or "money," for identification as it passes through the news room and *composing room.*

Small caps. Capital letters smaller than the regular capitals of a particular type face; used almost exclusively in magazines and books, and rarely there. See also *C and sc.*

Soc. Short for society; sometimes "sox."

Solid. Lines of type set without space, or *lead,* between them.

Sox. See *soc.*

Space grabber. A publicity seeker.

Spike. A spindle, usually for unwanted copy; also, to eliminate, or *kill,* a story.

Split page. See *second front page.*

Split run. The dividing of a publication run into two or more slightly different versions, sometimes for research. For example, to check the effectiveness of a new ad, one version would have the new ad and one would have the old.

Spot news. Information about a specific, recent occurrence, as contrasted to a story about a trend or continually developing situation.

Spread. A prominent display, usually with *art.* Sometimes the large, multi-column head over the material is called a "spread head."

Squib. A short news item.

Standing. Material kept in type because often needed, such as a column heading or the *nameplate.* A headline used repeatedly, such as the head over baseball standings, is called a standing head or stet head.

State editor. The person who edits the news from the newspaper's *circulation* area outside the metropolitan region.

Step head. See *drop head.*

Stereotype. A cylindrical or semi-cylindrical *plate* of a page. A papier mâché *matrix* is squeezed against the original type to make a mold. Molten metal is poured over the mold to make the stereotype.

Stet. The abbreviation for "let it stand," written above crossed-out words to indicate that they should be set in type after all.

Stet head. See *standing.*

Stick. A rough measurement meaning about two inches of type. See also *composing stick.*

Stone. A metal- or marble-topped table for page *makeup.* See also *turtle.*

Straight matter. Regular editorial material set in *body type* without variations from convention.

Straight news. A story with only the bare facts, without *color* interpretation.

Streamer. See *banner.*

String. Newspaper clippings to be added up by or for *stringer* to see how much they should be paid. The term comes from saving the clips on a string; as a verb it means to work as a stringer.

Stringer. A part-time reporter living outside the newspaper's central area. See also *correspondent.*

Style book or *style sheet.* A specific list of the conventions of spelling, abbreviation, punctuation, capitalization, etc. used by a particular newspaper or wire service.

Sub. A piece of copy that substitutes for something in a previous story.

Subhead. A headline, usually one line of *body type* in *boldface,* that appears every few paragraphs. It should describe the news in the paragraph or two following.

Symmetry. A style of page *makeup* that balances elements on the page so neither the top nor the bottom, the left nor the right, dominates.

Syndicate. A firm which sells and distributes columns, comics, *features,* and pictures. A wire service technically is a syndicate, but is rarely called by that name.

Tabloid. A newspaper half the size of a regular eight-column, twenty-one-inch newspaper. The dimensions usually are five columns by sixteen inches. Though some "tabs" are sensational, the term is not a synonym for *yellow journalism.*

Take. A section of copy, usually a page long, sent to the *copydesk* or to the *composing room.* See also *book.*

Tear Sheet. A newspaper page sent to an advertiser as evidence that his ad was printed.

Telegraph editor. The person who supervises the editing of news from wire services; thus often called the wire editor.

Teleprinter. See *teletype.*

Teletype. A machine that automatically types out news coming from a wire service; also called teleprinter and ticker. It can be used to transmit, as well as receive, news.

Teletypesetter. An attachment to a *Linotype* so it can set type from a perforated tape; commonly referred to as TTS.

Ten-add. A method for sending details of a story to the *composing room* before sending the *lead.* The initial piece of copy (*take*) is labeled 10-add, the next 11-add, etc.

Think piece. An interpretive article.

Thirty. The end of a story; written "30."

Thirty-dash. See *end dash.*

Thumbnail. A *cut* half a column wide.

Ticker. See *teletype.*

Tie-back. A reference in a story to some previous event—to help the reader's memory.

Tie-in. A story or part of a story linked to some other event.

Tight. A situation of little or no room in the whole paper, in a particular story, or in a line. See also *tight line.*

Tight line. A line too crowded for proper spacing between words.

Time copy. Material always current and therefore timeless; can be run whenever convenient.

Tip. Information that may lead to a story.

Toenails. See *fingernails.*

Tombstone. To place similar headlines side by side so the reader tends to read from head to head rather than from head to story.

Top. The first few paragraphs of a story.

Top deck. The main part of a headline.

TR. The abbreviation of *turn rule;* in proofreading, to transpose.

Trim. To reduce a story carefully.

Truck. See *turtle.*

Trunk. The main wire of a wire service.

TTS. The abbreviation for teletypesetter.

Turn column. A few papers continue column eight, page one, to column one, page two, and eliminate a *jump head.*

Turn rule. A direction to the printer to turn over a *slug* because an addition, *insert,* or correction will be made at that point. The slug then becomes a reminder, which must be removed before printing.

Turtle. A metal cart, often called a truck, used to transport page *forms* to the *mat roller;* often used as a *stone.*

Type high. Any material high enough to print. The standard height of type is .918 of an inch.

Typo. Short for typographical error.

Undated story. A story with no specific geographical focus, such as a war in the Near East, and therefore no specific dateline. The source of the story is printed at the top, such as "United Press International."

Under-dash material. Prepared stories, principally *obituaries,* ready for publication. When an event makes the story timely, first come a few paragraphs about the event, then a *jim dash* or *dinky dash,* and then the prepared material (under, or following, a dash).

Underline. See *cutline;* also *caption.*

Unifax. UPI wirephoto machine.

Universal desk. A desk that handles copy from several departments of the paper, usually city, wire, and state.

Upper case. See *caps.*

Upstyle. A style that capitalizes more words than most papers do; also called magazine style. Contrast *downstyle.*

Urgent. A wire service designation for an important story, but less important than a *bulletin.*

Video Display Terminal. The same as a Cathode Ray Tube.

VRT. Video Display Terminal.

WF. The *proofreader's* mark for *wrong font.*

White space. The blank space, also called air, around heads, ad copy, and stories; left blank to make the printed material stand out.

Widow. A one- or two-word line at the end of a paragraph; usually unsightly if the last line of *cutlines* or the first line in a column. See also *bad break.*

Wild. Copy that may run on nearly any inside page. See also *run of paper.*

Wire editor. See *telegraph editor.*

Wirephoto. A system owned by Associated Press for transmitting pictures over wire.

With story. A story or picture running with a bigger story.

Wrap. To place type in two or more columns under a multi-column headline. See also *break.*

Wrapped up. See *all in hand.*

Wrong font. The designation for a letter of type different from the style used in the story.

X-correct. Same as *CX.*

Xerography. A new process for printing with static electricity and without ink.

Yellow journalism. Sensational and often deliberately inaccurate reporting.

Citations

Chapter 1

1. Willbur Schramm, *Mass Media and National Development* (Stanford: Stanford University Press, 1964), pp. 42-43.
2. W. H. Ferry and Harry S. Ashmore, *Mass Communications* (Santa Barbara, Calif.: Center for the Study of Democratic Institutions, 1966), p. 10.
3. Walter Gieber, "News Is What Newspapermen Make It," in *People, Society, and Mass Communications,* ed. Lewis Dexter and David White (Glencoe, Ill.: The Free Press, 1964), pp. 173-82.

Chapter 12

1. The quote from a Supreme Court ruling on "actual malice" is from Robert M. Bliss, "Development of Fair Comment as a Defense to Libel," *Journalism Quarterly* (Winter, 1967), 627-37.
2. Don R. Pember, "Privacy and the Press: the Defense of Newsworthiness," *Journalism Quarterly* (Spring, 1968), 14-24.

Chapter 13

1. Ira B. Harkey, Jr., *The Smell of Burning Crosses* (Jacksonville, Ill.: Harris-Wolfe, 1967), p. 45.
2. Richard T. Baker, *The Christian As a Journalist* (New York: Association Press, 1961), pp. 117-18.
3. Fred S. Siebert, et al., *Four Theories of the Press* (Urbana: University of Illinois Press, 1963), chapters 2 and 3.
4. For useful discussions of the report of the Commission on Freedom of the Press "twenty years after," see Edward Engbert's discussion in *The Center Magazine* (October-November, 1967), 22f., as well as the entire issue of the *Columbia Journalism Review* for Summer, 1967.
5. For details on successful operations of press councils in Redwood City, California, and Bend, Oregon, see William B. Blankenburg, "Local Press Councils: an Informal Accounting," *Columbia Journalism Review* (Spring, 1969), 14-18.
6. John C. Merrill, *The Press and Social Responsibility* (Freedom of Information Center Publication No. 001, University of Missouri, 1965), p. 2.

Chapter 17

1. See the chapter on "Truth and Fairness" in *Responsibility in Mass Communications* (New York: Harper & Bros., 1957; rev. ed. by William L. Rivers and Wilbur Schramm, Harper and Row, 1969), pp. 217ff.

Bibliography

Baskett, Floyd K. and Jack Z. Sissors. *The Art of Editing*. New York: Macmillan, 1971.

Crowell, Alfred A. *Creative News Editing*. Dubuque: William C. Brown, second edition, 1974.

Evans, Harold. *Handling Newspaper Text*. New York: Holt, Rinehart, and Winston, 1973.

Garst, Robert F., and Theodore M. Bernstein. *Headlines and Deadlines*. New York: Columbia University Press, Third Edition, 1961.

Riblet, Carl, Jr. *The Sold Gold Copy Editor*. Chicago: Aldine, 1972.

Root, Robert. *Modern Magazine Editing*. Dubuque: William C. Brown, 1966.

Westley, Bruce. *News Editing*. Boston: Houghton Mifflin, second edition, 1972.

Editing, general

Arnold, Edmund C. *Ink on Paper²*. New York: Harper & Row, 1972.

Arnold, Edmund C. *Modern Newspaper Design*. New York: Harper & Row, 1969.

Burt, Sir Cyril. *A Psychological Study of Typography*. Cambridge, England: Cambridge University Press, 1959.

Butler, Kenneth B., and George Likeness. *A Practical Handbook on Borders, Ornamentation and Boxes in Publication Layout*. Mendota, Illinois: Butler Type-Design Research Center, 1960.

Cogoli, John E., *Photo-Offset Fundamentals*. Bloomington, Illinois: McKnight & McKnight, 1960.

Dair, Carl. *Design with Type*. Toronto: University of Toronto Press, 1967.

Lewis, John. *Typrography: Basic Principles*. New York: Reinhold, 1964.

Liberman, J. Ben. *Printing as a Hobby*. New York: Sterling, 1963.

Tinker, Miles A. *Legibility of Print*. Ames: Iowa State University Press, 1963.

Typography

Photography and picture editing

Feininger, Andreas. *The Complete Photographer*. Englewood Cliffs, N.J.: Prentice-Hall, 1965.

Feininger, Andreas. *Roots of Art*. New York: Viking, 1975.

Fox, Rodney, and Robert Kerns. *Creative News Photography*. Ames: Iowa State University Press, 1961.

Hurley, Gerald D. and Angus MacDougall. *Visual Impact in Print*. Chicago: American Publishers Press, 1971.

Rhode, Robert B., and Floyd H. McCall. *Press Photography*. New York: Macmillan, 1961.

Rothstein, Arthur. *Photojournalism*. Philadelphia: Chilton, 1965.

Writing and style

Baker, Sheridan. *The Practical Stylist*. New York: Thomas Y. Crowell, 1962.

Bernstein, Theodore M. *The Careful Writer*. New York: Atheneum, 1965.

Bernstein, Theodore M. *Watch Your Language*. New York: Atheneum, 1965.

Bernstein, Theodore. *Miss Thistlebottom's Hobgoblins*. New York: Straus and Giroux, 1971.

Bryant, Margaret M., ed. *Current American Usage*. New York: Funk & Wagnalls, 1962.

Callihan, E. L. *Grammar for Journalists*. New York: Ronald, 1957.

Chall, Jeanne S. *Readability: An Appraisal of Research and Application*. Columbus: Ohio State University, 1958.

Copperud, Roy H. *A Dictionary of Usage and Style*. New York: Hawthorn, 1964.

Copperud, Roy H. *American Usage*. New York: Van Nostrand Reinhold, 1970.

Estrin, Herman A. and Donald V. Mehus. *The American Language in the 1970s*. San Francisco: Boyd & Fraser, 1974.

Flesch, Rudolph. *The ABC of Style*. New York: Harper & Row, 1964.

Flesch, Rudolph. *The Art of Readable Writing*. New York: Harper & Bros., 1949.

Follett, Wilson. *Modern American Usage* (edited and completed by Jacques Barzun). New York: Hill & Wang, 1966.

Gowers, Sir Ernest. *Plain Words: Their ABC*. New York: Knopf, 1955.

Hayakawa, S. I. *Language in Thought and Action*. New York: Harcourt, Brace & World, 1964.

Klare, George R. *The Measurement of Readability*. Ames: Iowa State University Press, 1963.

Perrin, Porter G. *An Index to English* (Revised by Karl W. Dykema and Wilma R. Ebbitt). Glenview, Ill.: Scott, Foresman, Fourth Edition, 1968.

Newman, Edwin. *Strictly Speaking: Will America Be the Death of English?* Indianapolis: Bobbs-Merrill, 1974.

Rank, Hugh, *Language and Public Policy.* Urbana, Illinois, National Council of Teachers of English, 1974.

Strunk, William S., Jr., and E. B. White. *The Elements of Style.* New York: Macmillan, 1959.

Byerly, Kenneth R. *Community Journalism.* Philadelphia: Chilton, 1961.

Cranford, Robert J. *The State Editor and His Problems.* Lincoln: University of Nebraska Press, 1961.

Rucker, Frank W., and Herbert Lee Williams. *Newspaper Organization and Management.* Ames: Iowa State University Press, Revised Edition, 1969.

Sim, John Cameron. *The Grass Roots Press.* Ames: Iowa State University Press, 1969.

Tebbel, John. *Open Letter to Newspaper Readers.* New York: James H. Heineman, 1968.

Organization and management

Ashley, Paul P. *Say it Safely.* Seattle: University of Washington Press, Third Edition, 1966.

Associated Press. *The Dangers of Libel.* New York: 1968.

Fisher, Paul L., and Ralph L. Lowenstein, eds. *Race and the News Media.* New York: Frederick A. Praeger, 1967.

Gerald, J. Edward. *The Social Responsibility of the Press.* Minneapolis: University of Minnesota Press, 1963.

Gross, Gerald, ed. *The Responsibility of the Press.* New York: Fleet, 1966.

Hale, William G. *Law and the Press.* St. Paul: West, Third Edition, 1948.

Haselden, Kyle. *Morality and the Mass Media.* Nashville: Broadman, 1968.

Hulteng, John L. *The Messenger's Motives.* Englewood Cliffs, N. J.: Prentice-Hall, 1975.

Lofton, John. *Justice and the Press.* Boston: Beacon, 1966.

Lyle, Jack, ed. *The Black American and the Press.* Los Angeles: Ward Ritchie, 1968.

MacDougall, Curtis D. *The Press and Its Problems.* Dubuque: Wm. C. Brown, 1964.

Ethics and law

Communication theory and research

Phelps, Robert H., and E. Douglas Hamilton. *Libel and Slander.* New York: Macmillan, 1966.

Rivers, William L., and Wilbur Schramm. *Responsibility in Mass Communication.* New York: Harper and Row, Revised Edition, 1969.

Siebert, Fred S., Theodore Peterson, and Wilbur Schramm. *Four Theories of the Press.* Urbana: University of Illinois Press, 1963.

Wittenberg, Philip. *Dangerous Words.* New York: Columbia University Press, 1947.

Backstrom, Charles H., and Gerald D. Hursh. *Survey Research.* Evanston: Northwestern University Press, 1963.

Berlo, David K. *The Process of Communication.* New York: Holt, Rinehart and Winston, 1963.

Budd, Richard W., Robert K. Thorp, and Lewis Donohew. *Content Analysis of Communications.* New York: Macmillan, 1967.

Budd, Richard W. *An Introduction to Content Analysis.* New York: Macmillan, 1967.

DeFleur, Melvin L. *Theories of Mass Communication.* New York: David McKay, 1966.

Dexter, Lewis A., and David Manning White, eds. *People, Society, and Mass Communications.* New York: The Free Press, 1964.

Franzblau, Abraham N. *A Primer of Statistics for Non-Statisticians.* New York: Harcourt, Brace & World, 1958.

Haskins, Jack B., and Barry M. Feinberg. *Newspaper Publishers Look at Research.* Syracuse: Syracuse University School of Journalism, 1968.

Klapper, Joseph T. *The Effects of Mass Communication.* Glencoe, Ill.: The Free Press, 1960.

Lin, Nan. *The Study of Human Communication.* New York: Bobbs-Merrill, 1973.

Nafziger, Ralph O., and David Manning White, eds. *Introduction to Mass Communications Research.* Baton Rouge: Louisiana State University Press, Second Edition, 1963.

Osgood, Charles. *Measurement of Meaning.* Urbana: University of Illinois Press, 1957.

Wright, Charles R. *Mass Communication.* New York: Random House, 1959.

Miscellaneous

Aronson, James. *Deadline for the Media.* Indianapolis: Bobbs-Merrill, 1972.

Aronson, James. *The Press and the Cold War.* Indianapolis: Bobbs-Merrill, 1970.

Bagdikian, Ben. *The Information Machines*. New York: Harper & Row, 1971.

Emery, Edwin. *The Press and America*. Englewood Cliffs, N.J.: Prentice-Hall, Second Edition, 1962.

Hohenberg, John. *The News Media: A Journalist Looks at His Profession*. New York: Holt, Rinehart and Winston, 1968.

Krieghbaum, Hillier. *Facts in Perspective*. Englewood Cliffs, N.J.: Prentice-Hall, 1956.

Liebling, A. J. *The Press*. New York: Ballantine Books, 1961.

Peterson, Theodore, Jay Jensen, and William O. Rivers. *The Mass Media and Modern Society*. Second edition, Rinehart, 1970.

Rucker, Bryce W. *The First Freedom*. Carbondale: Southern Illinois University Press, 1968.

Schiller, Herbert. *Mass Communications and the American Empire*. New York: A. M. Kelley, 1969.

Smith, Ralph Lee. *The Wired Nation*. New York: Harper & Row, 1972.

About the authors

Gene Gilmore has worked as an editor on papers ranging from the *Alma* (Mich.) *Record* (circulation 3,600) to the *Washington Post* (circulation 550,000) and the *Philadelphia Bulletin* (circulation 625,000). For seven years in between he was telegraph editor of the prize-winning *Gazette & Daily* in York, Pennsylvania. He started teaching in 1957 at Syracuse University and has been on the journalism faculty at the Urbana campus of the University of Illinois since 1963. His degrees are from the University of Michigan and Syracuse.

From 1968 until his death in June 1970, **Robert Root** taught comparative literature at Eisenhower College. He came to Eisenhower as a member of the charter faculty after sixteen years as a professor of journalism at Syracuse University. Before he began teaching, he had been a practicing journalist for twelve years. His experience included such positions as editorial writer for the *Des Moines Tribune*, special correspondent for the *Christian Science Monitor*, managing editor of *Leader's Magazine*, and part-time writer for the *Syracuse Post-Standard*, the *Rochester Times-Union*, the Associated Press, and the *New York Times*. His degrees were in humanities (PhD, Syracuse) and journalism (MA, Columbia).

Index